CW01045397

ONE HUNDRED YEARS OF SERVITUDE

Political Economy of Tea Plantations in Colonial Assam

ONE HUNDRED YEARS OF SERVITUDE

Political Economy of Tea Plantations in Colonial Assam

RANA P. BEHAL

Tulika Books

Published by
Tulika Books
35 A/1 Shahpur Jat, New Delhi 110 049

First published in 2014

© Rana P. Behal 2014

ISBN: 978-93-82381-43-3

Printed at Chaman Offset, Delhi 110 002

For
Amalendu Da
who inspired a generation of young historians

Contents

Tables and Charts

Charts

Acknowledgements

Over the period of researching and writing this book, I have incurred huge debts to many individuals and institutions. Their unwavering support and warmth has been the main source of inspiration for me to go on working '*lahe lahe*', as they say in Assam, towards its completion. I wish to acknowledge my gratitude to all of them. I owe a special intellectual debt to Sabyasachi Bhattacharya for his long years of support, advice, friendship, and his critical comments and valuable suggestions on the draft of this monograph. I have benefited immensely from the moral support of and discussions, at different stages of writing, with Prabhu Mohapatra, Basudev Chatterji, Chitra Joshi, Sumit Guha, Indrani Chatterji, Marcel van der Linden, Jan Lucassen, Hermann Kreutzmann, Chris Bayly and Nitin Varma, who helped me overcome many shortcomings. I remain, however, solely responsible for any shortcomings the readers might detect in the book.

The incentive to work on this subject stemmed from two important sources: my engagement with labour history in the 1970s at the Centre for Historical Studies, Jawaharlal Nehru University (JNU), and my travels to Assam to pursue love. While I successfully achieved the latter within a few years by getting married, it was a long haul to keep up with the former – and the final outcome is this book. Both survived because of Ben (my bride of 37 years), and my affiliation to the Association of Indian Labour Historians (AILH) since its inception in 1996. Interactions with a wide range of historical, anthropological and sociological scholars who participated in several AILH international conferences on labour history kept my interest alive in the subject.

Over the years, collective and individual interactions with Amalendu Guha, Tanika and Sumit Sarkar, Neeladri Bhattacharya, Dilip Simeon, Madhavan Palat, Indu Agnihotri, Nitin Sinha, Sashi Upadhyay, Sasikumar, Aditya Sarkar, Indivar Kamtekar, Michael Mann, Ravi Ahuja, Harald Ficher-Tine, Gadi Algazi, Ralf Hoffrogge, James and Nancy Duncan, Eric Mcyer, Marcelo Badaro, Henrique Espada, Sidney Chalhoub, Ravi Vasudevan, Radhika

Singha, Francesco Melfi, Rukun Advani, Anuradha Roy, Philip Oldenberg, Andrew Liu, Bikram Barua, Monju Barua, Ron and Rukmini Barua, Hiren Gohain, Arupjyoti Saikia, and Maan Barua helped clear ideas and perceptions about my work.

My colleagues at Deshbandhu College, University of Delhi, T. Thomas and Iqbal Singh, provided valuable and critical suggestions. Anand, Subhash, Baljit, Bikram, Biswajit, Vishu, Kuljit, Sanjeev, Bajrangi, Vibhas, Lalit, Manoj, Shareena, Sabita, Neelam, PK, Unni, Elizabeth, Sunita, Preeti, Shashi, Chandrika and Veena were encouraging with their support and camaraderie.

At the International Research Center, Berlin, where the final journey of putting together this book began in 2009–10, my colleagues Jurgen Kocka, Andreas Eckert, Babacar Fall, Alice Mau, Jacob Eyferth, Therese Garstenauer, Jurgen Schimdt, Patrick Harris, Richard Rottenberg and Gerd Spittler were generous with their suggestions and critical comments on my presentations. I am eternally grateful to Felicitas Hentsche, Maite Kersaint, Constanze Roberstein, Sebastian Marggraff, Stephanie Lammert, Jutta Haegele, Norman Leymann and Tom Vogelgesang for their warmth, cooperation and support, which contributed hugely to my everyday work and towards the completion of this book. For all the help and support in providing finishing touches to the final chapters, I wish to thank Hermann Kreutzmann, Stefan Schuette, other colleagues and students at ZELF, Freie Universitaet, Berlin, during my stay there in the summer of 2013.

Over the years I have been a beneficiary of financial and academic support from various organizations for the research work involved in making this book possible. For that, I acknowledge the award of fellowships from the Trustee of the British Indian Golden Jubilee Banquet Fund and Centre of South Asian Studies, Cambridge University in 2005. The writing of the book commenced with a fellowship in 2009–10 at Re:Work, the International Research Centre, Work and Human Lifecycle in Global History, Humboldt University, Berlin. The work on the book continued during my short stay, during the summer of 2011, at the Centre for Development Studies (ZELF), Freie Universitaet, Berlin; and my extended stay there during the summer of 2013. I thank Deshbandhu College, University of Delhi, for granting me academic leave to do research for this book.

I would like to extend my gratitude and thanks to the staff and librarians of the National Archives, Nehru Memorial and Museum Library, Central Secretariat Library and Ministry of Labour Library in New Delhi; Ratan Tata Library, Delhi School of Economics, and the University of Delhi Library; National Library, Kolkata; Assam State Archives and Department of Historical and Antiquarian Studies, Guwahati; District Record Room in Deputy Commissioner's Office, Tezpur; Tocklai Tea Research Centre, Jorhat, Assam; British Library and Guildhall Library, London; Cambridge University Library and Centre for South Asian Studies Library, Cambridge; Glasgow University Archives; Clwyd Record Office, Howarden, UK; Berlin State Library, Humboldt University Library and Free University Library, Berlin. My thanks to Mr. Jayraj Mahanta for allowing me to access his father, R.C. Mahanta's papers at their home in Jorhat. I am grateful to the editors of *Economic and Political Weekly*, *Calcutta Historical Journal*, *Journal of Peasant Studies*, *Modern Asian Studies* and *International Review of Social History* for allowing me to use part of the material previously published by them.

My family and friends have been a constant source of love and affection, tirelessly pushing me towards the finish line. Suvritta, Sikha, Prita, Sudipto, Prasenjit and Julliet, Shahid, Prita Singh, Sadia Bajwa, Nicole Ahuja, Malini Thadani, Shalini Advani, Pankaj and Nellofer, Ajay and Shiromani, Malini Mundle, Madhu, Raghunathan and Harriet, Neera, Moromi, Utpala, Lata Palat, Mala Bhattacharya, Michael Fisher, Paula Richmond, Geraldine Forbes, Shelley Feldman, Susan Wadley, Sabine Asfelm, Maria Framke, Thamas Kummerow and Luise Rurp, Angela Haard, Simran Gell, DP and Dingi, Shalini Randheria, Toni Huber and Mona Schrempf, Markus and Krittka, Mukul Manglik, Brij and Kamini, Pradip, Piya and Mithuva Krishen, Sasikumar, Supriya and Jayram, Veena Oldenburg, Ruchira and Ajit, Jayati and Manik, Bharat and Roshmi, Sanjoy Hazarika, Anne and Mukul, Sanjoy and Sangeeta Bhattacharya, Amar and Vrinda, Mukul Manglik, and Falguni provided warm bonds of friendship and an intellectually stimulating and vibrant social life. I thank K.K. Bhuyian for help in explaining some of the technical aspects of the tea production process. Today I remember with great fondness and a tinge of sadness, the immense moral support and warm friendship of Rana Sen, Jugnu Ramaswami, Raj Chandavarkar, Arvind Das and Andrew Major, who were taken away from us before their time.

A generation of students whom I have had the privilege of teaching has taught me how to present ideas and tell stories in easy and simple ways. I sincerely hope I have lived up to their expectations. This book would not have been possible without encouragement, love and support from the late H.N. and Padma Agarwala, my in-laws, and their big-hearted extended family in Assam. Sanjay and Babita Khanna always provided me a home away from home on my research trips to the UK. Ben, Heeya, Shyamant and Renu have provided love, sustenance and strength. They have been a source of great joy and happiness, which has inspired me, at long last, to finish this work.

My special thanks to Maya Palit, Maya John and Indu Chandrasekhar at Tulika Books.

Introduction

This book presents the history of tea plantations in the Assam (Brahma-putra) Valley during colonial rule with a special focus on their labour force.[1] It explores the world of the Assam Valley tea plantations where more than two million migrant labourers produced tea under indentured servitude for an increasingly profitable global market. Migrant labour constituted the very core of plantation production in Assam. Having failed to coerce the local communities to produce tea commerically for them by traditional methods, the early British 'pioneers' adopted labour-intensive methods, instead of deploying the Chinese tradition of peasant-based production, which generated a demand for wage labour. The British capitalists set up huge plantations, creating a demand for a large labour force to produce tea for a growing global market. The issue of labour supply was beset with complications from the very beginning. Before the onset of colonial rule, Assam had suffered a serious demographic depletion on account of the Moamoria rebellion and the Burmese invasion, which par-tially constrained the availability of local labour.[2] The remaining local agrarian communities did not find the terms of employment and wages on plantations attractive enough. As a result, labour shortage became a regular lament of the tea planters, but they were unwilling to offer competitive wages to aug-ment the labour supply. Walter Rodney has argued that captialist plantations required a particular type of labour: 'The labor must be cheap and plentiful, and, even more important, the labor must be easily controlled. Unless labor can be provided under conditions that maximize the industrial control, you cannot have a functioning plantation system.'[3]

The planters found the local communities unwilling to become that 'par-ticular type' of labour, and labelled them 'lazy' and 'indolent'.[4] This necessi-tated the import of labour from outside Assam. In order to sustain the frenetic expansion of acreage under tea from the 1860s, planters mobilized the agrarian communities of Bihar, Bengal, Orissa and the United Provinces, consisting mostly of 'tribals and 'aboriginals' who were marginalized by the colonial land revenue policies. The migrant labourers were transformed into indentured 'coolies' for plantation production.[5] In this venture the planters received massive support from the colonial state in the form of a legal framework that facilitated the mobilization and exploitation of labour, capital accumulation, and a mass market with a standardized product. This was in sharp contrast to the Chinese system of tea production. The Chinese production process was based on small plots, domestic labour, very efficient but decentralized marketing through networks of mobile traders, and a fragmented market.[6]

How these migrant agrarian communities were transformed into 'coolies' is one among the several queries that are addressed in this book. The term 'coolie' was almost universally used for migrant labourers who had been mobilized from India and China to work on Dutch and British capitalist plantations in their overseas colonies, including Assam in India, during the nineteenth and twentieth centuries. Here, the story is narrated of how marginalized agrarian communities that were economically depressed as a consequence of colonial land revenue policies became a hunting ground for recruiters who transported them to Assam to work as 'coolies' under indenture contracts. While debating the 'voluntary' and 'rational choice' arguments, it may be worth remembering that the bulk of this labour migration to the Assam Valley plantations was sponsored by employers amidst complaints of coercion and abusive recruitment practices.[7] This is not to argue that all such recruiting was subject to fraud and abuse. There may have been other factors too that played a role in the migration toward Assam's plantations.[8] However, the substantial official evidence of coercion, deception and fraudulent practices during the process of recruitment does not conform to revisionist arguments of 'safety hatch' and 'voluntary' migration. The negligible size of 'free' and 'voluntary' migrants during one hundred years (1860s to 1960s) of migration corroborates the conclusion drawn by the Assam Labour Enquiry Committee of 1906: that the Assam Valley tea plantations were not an attractive or popular destination for employment. Upon arrival in the plantions, the 'coolies' were made to reside and work under coercive strategies of labour control and 'clockwork' industrial discipline. A remarkable feature of the sponsored migration to Assam was that women and children constituted nearly 50 per cent of the total labour force, unlike the migration of indentured labourers to British plantation colonies overseas, where they were a minority.[9] Women and children were paid less than the male labourers, which in the long run helped the employers to keep the wage bill low.

What happened in the Assam tea plantations is a part of a broader story of global history in modern times. Industrial capitalism and the colonization of Asia, Africa, the Caribbean and other parts of the world by the British empire triggered a massive mobilization of marginalized agrarian communities from the Indian subcontinent, to serve as labour both within and in overseas colonies. Between 1834 and 1937, over 30 million migrants from India are estimated to have gone to overseas British colonies like Burma, Ceylon, British Malaya, Mauritius, Fiji, the Caribbean and East Africa. Nearly 98 per cent of the total movement of migrants from India during the colonial period consisted of labourers.[10] The majority of these workers were employed under indenture contracts owned by British capital.[11] Slavery (in the Caribbean and Mauritius) was replaced by another form of servitude: 'coolie labour' under indenture and the *kangani/maistry* systems. The growing demand for raw materials and other tropical products in the west led to the setting up of modern plantations as agro-industrial enterprises by British capital in several colonies of the British empire, including India, during the nineteenth and early twentieth centuries. Sugar, rubber, coffee and tea emerged as the most significant plantation products in the Caribbean, Fiji, Mauritius, Malay and Ceylon, and in Assam, Bengal, northern Himalayas and southern parts of colonial India. The colonial state played a very important supportive role in providing land and procuring labour.[12]

The capitalist plantation complex in Asia differed from the much older Atlantic plantations in one important respect: it did not have a history of slave-based production. In the Caribbean plantations, slave labour was substituted by imported Indian indentured labour after the abolition of slavery. In pre-colonial Assam, there was a system of obligatory labour service by the peasants to the state. The state polity under the Ahom rulers was a quasi-feudal structure built on a largely tribal base. Obligatory labour was organized under the *paik* system in a hierarchical structure, by which adult males were obligated to offer service, including militia service, to the state for a certain part of the year. This system became the backbone of the state's militia. In the early seventeenth century this system was reorganized into the *khel* system, each with a hierarchy of officers. Slavery did exist but was not the dominant form of the production process in pre-colonial Assam.[13] The main similarity between these plantation systems lay in the export-oriented nature and industrial organization of agricultural production. Nineteenth-century Asian plantations were also similar to their Atlantic counterparts in that both utilized indentured labour, except in Ceylon and later Malay where labour recruitment was done under the *kangani* system, with labourers transported to the plantations over long distances and employed under contractually specific conditions.

There seems to be a certain fascination among researchers with the history of Indian migrant labour, particulary indentured labour that went to overseas colonial plantations, (those who went '*saat samunder paar*' – across the seven seas), which attracted, and continues to attract, the attention of historical, sociological and literary scholarship.[14] A popular discipline currently is diaspora studies, which keeps interest alive in the history of indentured labour in the British overseas colonies. On the other hand, the century-long servitude of migrant labour under the indenture and post-indenture regimes in Assam's tea plantations has remained on the margins of historical scholarship. In most studies of Indian indentured labour in British colonial plantations, mention of the Assam indenture system does not occur even as a footnote reference. The massive mobilization of millions of indentured labourers within British India who were recruited and transported to work in the tea plantations has been neglected. This book hopes to fill this gap for the northeast of the country, where more than 3 million migrant labourers were recruited and transported to Assam's tea plantions between the 1860s and 1947, and of these, over 2 million to the Assam Valley alone. A vast majority of these migrants worked in the plantations under conditions of generational servitude both during and after the indenture period. Even those who managed to move out into the neighbourhood or to villages around the plantations nevertheless remained in a dependent relationship with the plantations.

The two most important aspects of indentured servitude were: first, the provision that a breach of contract resulted in criminal prosecution, and second, the widespread penal sanctions granted to the planters.[15] One thing common to both the indentured and the *kangani* labour regimes was the inherent nature of unfreedom and dependency. In the Dutch capitalist plantations in Indonesia, as studies by Jan Breman and Ann Stoler have shown, contractual employment of Chinese 'coolie' labour was similar to servitude under indentured regimes in other colonial plantations.[16] In the early 1990s, a number of research articles on capitalist plantations in colonial Indochina, Malaya and India emphasized the nature of dependent labour relations enforced through labour laws and extra-legal coercion.[17] Another significant common feature of capitalist plantations in colonial settings was the immobilization of the labour force upon arrival in the plantations after they had been mobilized through employer-sponsored recruitment. It was the lack of freedom inherent in indenture, namely the inability of the worker to withdraw his or her labour power in bargaining over the terms of the contract or for higher wages, that led to it being viewed as a 'new system of slavery'.[18] These views are contested by revisionist historians who underplay the lack of freedom involved in indenture, and give primacy to the economic rationality of a system which, they argue, benefited employers and labourers alike. Galenson, for example, maintains that indenture was essentially a facilitating device that enabled labour to flow from low labour productivity areas (Asia) to high labour productivity areas (Caribbean or North America). It allowed the cost of migration to be worked out over the contract period 'in the form of advances against future labour'.[19] The powerful attraction of economic opportunity was sufficient to 'prompt many migrants over the course of three centuries to enter indentures giving up much of their freedom for a period of years in hope thereby to amend their estate'.[20] Emmer similarly argues that indentured emigration from India to overseas colonies was a result of rational and deliberate choices on the part of the migrants, prompted by hopes of bettering their future, an 'escape hatch' from social and economic oppression at home.[21] Although the revisionist view has modified the traditional notion of indentured emigration as a system based largely on ignorance of the migrant, it has little to say about the conditions that structured the indenture contract. These arguments emphasizing the benefits of indenture are similar to those advanced by contemporary defenders of the indentured system, notably planters and colonial officials. While revisionist scholarship is critical of the tag of 'slavery', contemporary colonial officials readily used the term for the indenture labour regime.[22] Marina Carter has argued that the nineteenth-century criticism of indenture stemmed from humanitarian concerns.[23] This may have been true of anti-slavery sentiments. However, the likes of Lord Curzon, the Viceroy, and many of his contemporaries in the imperial hierarchy, while equating indenture with slavery, were not moved by concern for Indian migrant labourers working in British capitalist plantations. They were committed to promoting the British capitalist enterprise in their empire. They considered indentured servitude on plantations to be a necessary 'evil' for the 'development and growth' of remote colonial wastelands by British capital, and for 'civilizing' 'junglis' and 'savages'.[24]

Considerable debate has been generated on the nature and emergence of these plantation systems. That they were agro-industrial enterprises set by European capitalists to produce for the global market and to make profits is accepted almost unanimously. It is about the nature of labour relations and mobilization that the descriptions and theoretical conceptions vary: from 'slavery', 'semi-feudal', 'pre-capitalist', 'free and unfree' and 'economic coercion', to 'intermediate non-classifiable position between feudal and capitalist' forms in the colonial 'plantation economies'.[25] The characterization of labour relations in these plantations has been central to the debate. One of the core issues concerns the nature of change that the migrant agrarian communities experienced during the course of their servitude in the plantations: were the newly transformed 'coolies' to be characterized as proletariat or semi-proletariat, or were they re-peasantised?

Discussions of everyday labour-lives and resistance against indentured regimes in the plantations, albeit underplayed by the revisionists, are an important contribution to the literature on the history of plantation labour. The authoritarian nature of the regimes supported by the colonial state, as well as the isolation and lack of mobility faced by the labourers, are seen as deterrants to collective and 'organized' labour resistance, and the formation of labour organizations.[26] The cultural and social diversity of the migrant labour communities was also considered to be a constraint on collective action.[27] In its absence, individual acts of passive resistance and accommodation were seen as alternative labour strategies. However, the perceived absence of collective resistance was due more to the nature of official reportage under indenture legislations than an account of actual reality. Actions such as desertions, gatherings, assemblies, the discontinuation of work and retaliatory violence were considered as criminal acts under the labour laws, and hence not recognized as collective resistance. Instead these actions were reported as acts of 'absconding', 'unlawful' assembly, 'riots' and 'assaults', and dealt with accordingly. The right to private arrest of 'absconding' labour conferred upon the planters under the indenture law often led to gross under-reporting of desertions, both individual and collective.[28]

Historically, there was a significant interest in indentured labour servitude in the public domain of colonial India. During the last two decades of the nineteenth century, the conditions of indentured servitude were known both among official and non-official circles. Calcutta's nationalist intelligentsia, the English and vernacular nationalist press, and the Indian National Congress expressed their concern about labourers in predominently foreign-owned enterprises, and championed their cause both inside and outside the legislative bodies.[29] A more adversarial position was adopted by Bengal's nationalists, and the Brahmo reformists Ram Kumar Bidyaratna and Dwarknath Ganguli, who published a series of articles in nationalist papers like *Sanjibani* and *Bengalee* from Calcutta between 1883 and 1887. They also visited Assam to gather first-hand information about the conditions of tea garden labourers. It was on the basis of these investigations that Bidyaratna's *Coolie Kahani* and Ganguli's *Slave Trade in India* stories appeared in Calcutta's nationalist newspapers.[30] These were followed by the publication of a book titled *Tea Garden Coolies in Assam* in 1894, by the Rev. Charles Dowding, an English missionary. Dowding's volume, a very radical critique by contemporary standards, was a reproduction of a fierce public debate he had conducted with representatives of the tea industry and their supporters.[31] In their writings, reformers and missionaries scathingly criticized the terrible working and living conditions, low wages, long hours of work, ill treatment at the work place and high mortality rates of labourers in the Assam tea plantations. In 1906, Ms H.B. Bonner of the Humanitarian League, London, published an equally damning critique of the Assamese plantation labour system. She cited official reports and communications to show that the high rates of sickness, mortality and desertions were a consequence of an abusive recruitment system, low wages and the hardship experienced by migrant labourers in Assam.[32]

During the 1920s and 1930s, Indian academics and labour activists began to take a serious interest in issues related to labour in the Assam tea plantations. Rajani Kanta Das published *Plantation Labour in India* while S.M. Akhtar completed a doctoral dissertation on the subject at the London School of Economics, a part of which was published as *Emigrant Labour for Assam Tea Gardens*.[33] Das's work is a detailed study based on official data on immigration, employment, wages, labour legislations, terms of contracts, etc. He used the official statistical data to study the growth of the Indian tea industry and labour employment. Akhtar's study concentrated on the history of the industry and its labour force in the nineteenth century. Both these studies, unlike those of Ganguly and Dowding before them, focused mainly on the oppressive and exploitative nature of labour relations on the Assam plantations. Around the same time, sympathetic trade unionists and political activists began to publish critical comments on various aspects of the lives of tea plantation labourers, their low wages, work conditions and lack of freedom of movement, labour legislations and labour organizations, etc. In 1924, N.M. Joshi wrote on the conditions of plantation labourers in Assam, drawing attention to the low wages they received and criticizing the employers for restricting their mobility and freedom. He demanded the removal of restrictions and political freedom for the labourers in Assam's tea plantations.[34] In a similar vein, Jatindranath Sarkar wrote about the terrible work and living conditions, and the exploitation of labourers in the Assam tea plantations, and critically engaged in a public debate with supporters of the tea industry on the history of its labour relations. He also drew attention to the extravagant lifestyle of the planters and the sexual abuse of women labourers.[35] In 1932, Diwan Chaman Lall, a member of the Royal Commission on Labour, published *Coolie,* a critical account of the wretched conditions of labourers in the 'slave' plantations of Assam.[36] A.V. Thakkar commented on the social diversity of labour communities in the tea plantations. He pointed to the lack of literacy and political organization of the labour force. He appealed to political parties and social organizations like the Congress, Hindu Mahasabha, Ramakrishna Mission, Arya Samaj, Harijan Sevak Sangha and Trade Union Congress to 'hear the distant cry of these tea coolies'.[37] These works represented the sympathetic concerns and propaganda put forward by activists and trade unionists. They were unable, however, to place the peculiarities of labour relations in Assam's tea gardens in relation to the power structures in the plantations under the domination of the planters. While the exploitative features of labour servitude were highlighted, a critical analysis of the mechanisms of economic and physical coercion, and the extra-legal authority exercised by the planters within the plantations remained outside the scope of these commentaries.

In the post-independence historical scholarship on modern Assam, despite a wealth of publications, the history of tea plantation labourers and the indentured labour regime occupies a small space. The work of a communist trade unionist, Sanat Kumar Bose, though limited in scope, was the only exclusive study of Assam's plantation labour.[38] Amalendu Guha's pioneering work on the history of modern Assam, despite the fact that its focus is not solely on labour, remains the only major study where the tea plantations and labour received significant attention.[39] Guha's emphasis is on the planters' power and influence in the province, around which issues of labour and resistance are discussed. Ramakrishna Chattopadhyaya's work critically examines the labour legislations enacted by the colonial state for regulating labour relations.[40] Mohammad Abu Siddique's work is a valuable contribution to the question of colonial policies with regard to: (i) providing huge tracts of land at highly favourable terms to the British capitalists and (ii) labour in the Assam tea plantations.[41] In Jayeeta Sharma's recently published work, which is a significant and important contribution to the historiography of modern Assam, plantation labour constitutes only a part of a larger study of the social landscape of the province.[42] A collection of brief essays by the labour historian Ranajit Dasgupta and other scholars on tea plantation labourers in North East India appeared in an edited volume in 1990.[43] More recently, Nitin Varma's published articles are a refreshing contribution to the history of labour resistance in Assam's tea plantations.

What accounts for this relatively low level of attention to plantation labour? Perhaps it is a consequence of the social and structural disconnect between the tea plantations, and the agrarian and urban society and economy of Assam. Tea plantations set up with the support of the colonial state as exclusive, enclaved enterprises by British capital grew at a spectacular rate, but provided no push to the development of the provincial economy and society. In fact it has been argued that the growth of plantations in many ways constrained the development of the agrarian and urban economy of Assam.[44] The ways in which the everyday lives of migrant labourers were structured by the plantation regime kept them isolated from the rest of Assam's agrarian society as well as the urban inteligentsia. This is in sharp contrast to the historiography of the indigo plantations and the peasant revolts in Bengal, where the production processes were deeply embedded in the agrarian society.

The employers of plantation labour, the tea companies and retired planters, on the other hand, showed a keen interest in publishing their own histories and memoirs. These publications provide valuable information on the technical and commerical aspects of the tea industry, and, to a lesser extent, its labour force. The Assam Company and Jorehaut Tea Company sponsored publication of their histories, written by Hinson Allan Antrobus.[45] The author traced the history of the early British 'pioneers', and narrated the details of the production processes, finances, machinery, marketing and management operations of the companies. In these company histories, there are only fleeting glimpses of labour: 17 and 8 pages, respectively, out of 490 and 363 pages on the Assam Company and the Joerhaut Tea Company. The instability of both local and imported labour due to 'abscondings', the high cost of labour recruitment, etc., were the issues that concerned the official historian. The coercive nature of labour relations, and the resultant stress and tensions, did not merit discussion. In 1967, Sir Percival Griffiths produced a comprehensive and authoritative official history of India's tea industry.[46] This work provides detailed information on almost every aspect of the Indian tea industry under the monopolistic control of British capital. Griffiths predictably viewed the issues of coercion, exploitation and dependency on the Assam tea plantations through the lens of planter paternalism. His perception of labour relations is similar to that of the planters and the colonial bureaucracy. It could not have been otherwise for he was a *burra sahib* himself.[47] Several memoirs, personal experiences, guides to youngsters from Britain seeking careers in Assam as planters and 'scientific' treatises on tea were published from the 1860s onwards by retired planters and colonial officials. These narratives are very useful for understanding labour relations and management strategies in the plantations.[48]

The existing literature does not provide a comprehensive account of the relationship between British capital and Indian labour in the Assam tea plantations. The histories of the tea industry and of the Assam and Jorhaut Companies by Griffiths and Antrobus respectively refrained from even commenting on the nature of labour relations, and refused to acknowledge the harsh realities of the plantation regime. This book is an attempt to provide an extensive description based on primary sources; but its ambition is to do more. As it lays stress on the negative features of the system much more than the positive ones, new questions arise about the specific roles of all the actors involved. After all, how could such a repressive system have lasted for such a long period? The answer is threefold: coalitions between the colonial state and the plantation owners; the attitude of the plantation management; and the attitude of the labourers. Regarding role of the colonial government, the sources are plentiful and a clear verdict can be given. Regarding the role of the management, the picture is mixed: the relatively few European staff members are clearly visible in the sources and unfortunately this provides a gloomy picture. The numerous Indian staff members and supervisors who occupied a place between the European sahibs and the large mass of workers are much less visible in the sources, but as far as possible their role will be discussed as well. As for the labourers, the main question addressed here is whether they, as the existing histories would want us to believe, simply suffered and at best tried to forget their miseries through the abuse of alcohol. Were they indolent or did they protest? This book shows that the latter is the case. First, it examines the practices employed in recruiting labourers, although it does not discuss at length their socio-economic conditions in the regions of their origin, for that would need a separate book.[49] Second, three types of protest receive attention: desertion by labourers before the end of contract and remigration to regions of origin; hidden protests á la Scott; and open collective action (although not in the classical trade union way).

The book seeks to cover a wide canvas by looking at the history of the tea industry, its labour force and the role of the colonial state in Assam. It book is divided into six main chapters. The first chapter traces the genesis and development of the tea industry from its inception in 1840 till the early 1860s. I examine the links between the colonial state and private British capital in fostering plantations in Assam in order to produce tea for a growing global market. During these two decades British corporate capitalists and individual 'pioneers' initiated the plantation enterprise in the Assam Valley with active assistance from the state. I look at the way in which the production process evolved through experiments with land, plant and labour, with the help of Chinese tea makers and local forest communites. The emphasis is also on the signicant role of the state and imperial science in setting up, sustaining and expanding tea plantations during the first twenty years. I examine the nature of speculative 'tea mania' and its consequences, leading to the emergence of the indenture labour system in the Assam tea plantations in the 1860s.

In the second chapter, the focus is on the process of labour mobiliza- tion in the recruiting districts and the nature of labour relations in the tea plantations in the Assam Valley. It deals with the operational aspects of the sponsored recruitment systems, and the transportation and employment of migrant labour in the tea plantations under indenture servitude from the 1860s up until its formal dismantling in 1926. The indenture labour regime in the Assamese tea plantations became notorious for low wages, high rates of sickness and mortality, confinement and desertions, physical coercion, and the negative reproduction of labour under a penal contract system. How did such a system survive and last so long? And did the formal dismantling of indenture mean free labour and the disappearance of the dependency relation- ship between planters and labourers? Why and how was such a large body of mobilized labour immobilized within the plantation complex? And finally, the question revisionist historians will not ask: why did the British capitalists shy away from the operations of the labour market, and instead adopt coercive strategies of production and labour control under the indenture system? This chapter seeks to provide answers to these questions.

The third chapter examines the nature of the power structure which determined the production organization and social relations within plantation complexes in the Assam Valley. The power structure evolved and operated at two levels: around the India Tea Association (ITA) as the apex body of the tea industry, and the omnipotent authority of the planter in the field. What sort of strategies were adopted by the ITA to influence the policies of the colonial state for promoting the interests of the tea industry vis-á-vis its labour force? The ITA also formulated the tea industry's policies with regard to its labour force and the formation of labour organizations. At the other level, I examine the extra-legal authority and coercive strategies employed by the planters in the everyday operations of the plantation, reinforced by the right to private arrest, in order to intensify the labour process and ensure uninterrupted production of tea. I try to analyse the nature of authority exercised by the planters over their labour force, and the mechanisms through which it was imposed and sustained. The tea plantations developed a power structure that was much like the one that existed under slavery in American plantations in the Antebellum era. The coercive strategies included residential confinement, isolation, disciplining and taming, to ensure that the labourers were available for work at all times and in all seasons. This task was achieved through the imposition of a hierarchical authority headed by the *burra sahib*, the British manager – the 'coolie-driver'. The chapter also investigates the process by which ordinary young British men were transformed into brutal, fearsome and omnipotent 'coolie-drivers' at the altar of monopolistic British capital, in order to extract labour for the production of tea for a global market.

The fourth chapter examines the role of the colonial state in providing assistance, from its inception till the end of colonial rule, for the setting up and growth of tea plantations in the Assam Valley. State assistance was crucial in providing vast tracts of forest land at favourable terms, building infrastructure and mobilizing labour. The most significant aspect of the role of the state was its attitude towards the planters vis-á-vis the labourers, as reflected in the labour laws. The critical question here is, how and why was the colonial state, while professing adherance to the doctrine of *laissez faire*, pushed to legislative intervention to regulate labour supply and labour relations in the tea plantations? How did these legislations, adopted to mediate between capital and labour, impact labour relations? An equally important question addressed here is to what extent the social and racial affinities of the colonial officials constrained the implementation of 'protective' provisions of the labour laws. The state often admitted the existence of genuine grievances of labour, like unhealthy living conditions, high rate of mortality, low wages, restrictions on freedom of movement, etc., and flagrant disregard of the labour laws by the planters. But no efforts were made to pressurize the employers to redress these grievances and comply with the labour laws. I show how the discriminatory attitude of the state provided legitimacy to the extra-legal authority imposed on the labour force by the planters.

The fifth chapter offers a critical analysis of the quantities of production, market prices, volume of exports and profitablity, acreage expansion, labour employment and wage payments in the Assam Valley tea plantations from the 1870s to 1947. The plantations experienced a massive growth in production, acreage expansion and labour employment during the last three decades of the nineteenth century, which followed an upward secular trend in the first half of the twentieth century. This chapter seeks to answer the following pertinent questions. While achieving a healthy growth rate, did the tea industry provide competitive wages for its labour force to enable it to live in good health and comfort, as was asserted by the planters and the colonial bureaucracy? While the indices of growth showed a healthy secular trend in per acre and per labour productivity, the trend of nominal wages showed only a minor increase or stagnation over this long period. Real wages actually declined or remained stagnant. Could this discrepancy be attributed to the constantly fluctuating prices of tea in the international market? In this context it is equally relevant to ask whether the declining and fluctuating market prices of tea also affected the profitablity of the Indian tea industry during this period. I examine the possibility of a connection between low wages and high rates of sickness and mortality among the labour force by raising another pertinent question: was high mortality a consequence of low levels of earnings, or was it a result of epidemiological factors as has been argued by some scholars?

The sixth chapter tells the tale of everyday labour life, and of resistance to the oppressive and dominant plantation regime by labourers who had been coerced into generational servitude. How did the 'coolies' respond to the indenture and post-indenture strategies of control and the dependency relationship imposed by the plantation regime? I analyse the forms of pro-test and the nature of labour politics which emerged in the Assam Valley tea plantations. One important issue in the long history of struggle and resistance was the very late emergence of labour organizations, which remained embry-onic till the end of colonial rule. This then raises the important question as to whether the authoritarian nature of the indenture regime, supported and legitimized by the colonial state, and the cultural diversity of the labour force were a deterrent to collective resistance. In this context, labour historians also need to debate whether trade unions are the only form of collective labour resistance. The evidence presented in this chapter shows that the lack of trade union organization or its late arrival did not mean the absence of collective resistance in the Assam Valley tea plantations, nor did the cultural diversity of the labourers deter them from putting up collective resistance against coercion by the employers. Equally important is the issue of women's participation in the collective resistance. I also examine the process of transformation of migrant agrarian communities into 'coolies', and how this impacted their lives. While focusing on their social origins, the chapter studies the patterns of mobilization and employment of migrant plantation labourers. An equally siginificant issue under examination here is whether this transformation of agrarian migrant communities working in conditions of unfree labour was proletarian in nature.

An area this book does not deal with directly relates to the links between the story of the tea plantations, which runs from the 1840s to the 1940s, and the social tensions in Assam in that period. These links are clear, but a separate and careful study of the post-independence labour history of the Assam tea plantations is needed before one can connect the present with the colonial past. I hope this book will serve as a first and necessary step towards this end, and as an encouragement to scholars to study the post-1947 story.

And finally, a few comments on the nature of the sources used for this study. The most important source of qualitative and quantitative information on the Assam tea plantations and their labour force are colonial documents in the state and central archives, and in public libraries spread across several locations – in Delhi, Kolkata, Assam and the UK. These include both published and unpublished documents generated by the provincial as well as central governments. Annual reports and Indian Tea Statistics routinely published detailed information on production, acreage, labour imports and exports, employment, wages, vital statistics, political developments, market prices, aggregate capital invested, etc. An important feature of these reports is that the quantitative information on wages, vital statistics and employment was provided by the employers to the government as per the requirements of the labour laws. The information so provided was simply reproduced in the annual reports by the Chief Commissioner without any verification as to its accuracy. There were some district officials who were less than satified with this process and often expressed their scepticism about the accuracy of the information, but to no effect. I have used this information despite reservations about its accuracy as it is useful to analyse long-term trends. Another set of important sources is the reports of various commissions of enquiry appointed by the colonial state during periods of crisis in the tea industry. The English and vernacular press published detailed information on issues arising out of political crises, and confrontation between capital and labour. Additional sources are papers of the Indian Tea Association, of British tea companies and of private individuals, available in the British Library, and in other public and university libraries and archives across the UK.

Notes and References

1 Five districts of Assam Valley, viz. Lakhimpur, Sibsagar, Darrang, Nowgong and Kamrup, were the tea-producing areas. Out of these, tea production was dominant in three: Lakhimpur, Sibsagar and Darrang. Surma Valley with Cachar and Sylhet as the other major tea-producing districts is not a part of this study. References to Assam in the book apply only to Assam Valley. The selection of Assam Valley for this study is purely arbitrary.
2 M'Cosh estimated the population of Assam Valley at 799,519 in 1837. See J. M'Cosh, *Topography of Assam*, Calcutta: G.H. Huttmann, Bengal Military Orphan Press, 1837, p. 129.
3 Walter Rodney, 'Plantation Society in Guyana', *Review*, IV, 4 (Fernand Braudel Centre, Bighamton, NY), Spring 1981, pp. 643–66.
4 Kacharis, a local community, were employed for clearing forests and opening plantations. They were considered 'troublesome' for not willing to be tamed and disciplined resident labour under the control of the plantation regimes. For more details about the Kachari

community, see Rev. Sidney Endle, *The Kachaires*, London: Macmillan and Co. Ltd., 1911.

[5] British planters in Jamaica, immediately after the abolition of slavery, decided to import Indian labour on indentured contracts because the former slaves were unwilling to continue working on the sugar plantations under conditions of unfreedom and low wages. Rodney, 'Plantation Society'.

[6] Robert Gardella, *Harvesting Mountains: Fujian and the China Tea Trade, 1757–1937*, Berkeley: University of California Press, 1994.

[7] For a detailed discussion on this, see below.

[8] For critical analyses, see Prabhu P. Mohapatra, 'Coolies and Colliers: Study of the Agrarian Context of Labour Migration from Chotanagpur 1880–1920', *Studies in History*, Vol. 1, No. 2, 1985, pp. 247–303; Lalita Chakravarty, 'Emergence of an industrial labour force in a dual economy – British India, 1880–1920', *Indian Economic and Social History Review*, Vol. 15, 1978, pp. 249–327.

[9] Tea plantations in Ceylon were the other example of sponsored mobilization of a significant number of children and women labourers under the *kangani* system.

[10] Kingsley Davis, *The Population of India and Pakistan*, New York: Russell and Russell, 1951; Prabhu P. Mohapatra, 'Eurocentrism, Forced Labour, and Global Migration: A Critical Assessment', *International Review of Social History*, Vol. 52, No. 1, 2007, pp. 110–15; Adam Mckeown, 'Global Migration 1846–1940', *Journal of World History*, Vol. 15, No. 2, 2004, pp. 155–89.

[11] Migrant indentured labour was also employed in the Dutch, French and Portuguese overeseas colonies.

[12] A. Kiefer, 'The Tea Industry of India and Ceylon: Its Development and Current State', *The Treatise of the Imperial Royal Geographical Society in Vienna*, Vol. IV, No. 3 (K.U.K.Hof-U. Universitats-Buchhandlung, Vienna), 1902.

[13] Amalendu Guha, 'The Medieval Economy of Assam', in Tapan Raychaudhuri and Irfan Habib (eds), *The Cambridge Economic History of India*, Volume I, Cambridge: Cambridge University Press, 1982, pp. 478–505.

[14] A brief list out of a rich and exhaustive literature: C. Kondapi, *Indians Overseas, 1839–1949*, Indian Council of World Affairs: New Delhi, 1951; Panchanan Saha, *Emigration of Indian Labour*, Bombay: Paople's Publishing House, 1970; K.L. Gillian, *Fiji's Indian Migrants: A History to the End of Indenture 1920*, Melbourne: Australian National University, 1962; Brij V. Lal, 'The Girmitiyas: The Origins of the Indian Fijians', *Journal of Pacific History* (Canberra), 1983; David Northrup, *Indentured Labor in the Age of Imperialism*, New York: Cambridge University Press, 1995; K.S. Sandhu, *Indians in Malaya: Some Aspects of Their Immigration and Settlement 1786–1957*, Cambridge: Cambridge University Press, 1969; Hugh Tinker, *A New System of Slavery*, London: Oxford University Press, 1974; Sunil S. Amrith, *Crossing the Bay of Bengal: The Furies of Nature and the Fortunes of Migrants*, Cambridge, Mass.: Harvard University Press, 2013; Patrick Peebles, *The Plantation Tamils of Ceylon*, London: Leicester University Press, 2001; Marina Carter, *Servants Sirdars and Settlers: Indians in Mauritius, 1834–1874*, Delhi: Oxford University Press, 1995; Munshi Rehman Khan, *Autobiography of an Indian Indentured Labourer 1874–1972*, translated by Kathinka Sinha-Kerkhoff, Ellen Bal and Alok Deo Singh, Delhi: Shipra, 2005; Gaiutra Bahadur, *Coolie Woman: The Odyssey of Indenture*, London: C. Hurst & Co., 2013; Peggy Mohan, *Jahajin*, New Delhi: HarperCollins, 2007.

[15] Malay plantations employed Indian labourers under indenture contracts till 1910 and then swiched to the *kangani* system already in operation in Ceylon. In Ceylon the indenture contract was not in operation, but a law enforcing penal sanction for non-compliance of work was put in place in the plantations. Here the dependency relationship was enforced through debt bondage under the *kangani* system. See Rana P. Behal, 'Coolies, Recruiters

and Planters: Migration of Indian Labour to the Southeast Asian and Assam Plantations during Colonial Rule', Crossroads Working Papers Series, No. 9, Bonn, July 2013.

[16] Jan Breman, *Taming the Coolie Beast: Plantation Society and the Colonial Order in Southeast Asia*, Delhi: Oxford University Press, 1989; Ann Stoler, *Capitalism and Confrontation in Sumatra's Plantation Belt, 1870–1979*, New Haven, CT: Yale University Press, 1985.

[17] Martin J. Murray, '"White Gold" or "White Blood"? The Rubber Plantations of Colonial Indochina, 1910–40', in E. Valentine Daniel, Henry Bernstein and Tom Brass (eds.), *Plantations, Proletarians and Peasants in Colonial Asia*, London: Frank Cass, 1992, pp. 41–67; P. Ramaswami, 'Labour Control and Labour Resistance in the Plantations of Colonial Malaya', ibid., pp. 87–105; Rana P. Behal and Prabhu P. Mohapatra, '"Tea and Money versus Human Life": The Rise and Fall of the Indenture System in the Assam Tea Plantations 1840–1908', ibid.; Ranajit Das Gupta, 'Plantation Labour in Colonial India', ibid., pp. 173–98.

[18] K.L. Gillion, *Fiji's Indian Migrants*, Melbourne: Oxford University Press, 1962; Hugh Tinker, *A New System of Slavery*, London: Oxford University Press, 1974; Rodney Walter, *A History of the Guyanese Working People, 1881–1905*, London: Heinemann Educational Books, 1981.

[19] David W. Galenson, 'The Rise and Fall of Indentured Servitude in the Americas: An Economic Analysis', *The Journal of Economic History*, Vol. 44, No. 1, 1984, p. 16.

[20] Galenson, 'The Rise', p. 24.

[21] P.C. Emmer, 'The Meek Hindu; the recruitment of Indian indentured labourers for service overseas, 1870–1916', in P.C. Emmer (ed.), *Migration: Indentured Labour Before and After Slavery*, Dordrecht: M. Nijhoff Publisher, 1986, pp. 187–207; P.C. Emmer, 'The Great Escape: The Migration of Female Indentured Servants from British India to Surinam 1873–1916', in Colin Clark, Ceri Peach and Steven Vertovec (eds.), *South Asians Overseas*, Cambridge: Cambridge University Press, 1990, pp. 245–66.

[22] See chapter 4.

[23] Carter, *Servants, Sirdars and Settlers*, pp. 1–2.

[24] See chapters 3 and 4.

[25] Jay Mandle, 'The Plantation Economy: An Essay in Defintion', *Science and Society*, Vol. 34, No. 1, 1972, pp. 57–60; George Beckford, *Persistent Poverty: Underdevelopment in Plantation Economics of the Third World*, London: Oxford University Press, 1972; Immanuel Wallerstein, *The Capitalist World Economy*, London: Cambridge University Press, 1980; Stoler, *Capitalim and Confrontation*; Tom Brass and Henry Bernstein, 'Introduction: Proletarianization and Deproletarianization on the Colonial Plantation', in Daniel, Bernstein and Brass (eds.), *Plantations, Proletarians and Peasants in Colonial Asia*, pp. 1–40; Tinker, *Slavery*; Breman, *Taming*; Murray, 'White Gold'.

[26] Murray, 'White Gold'; P. Ramasamy, 'Labour Control'; Doug Munro, 'Patterns of Resistance and Accommodation', in B.V. Lal, D. Munro and Edward D. Beechart (eds.), *Plantation Workers, Resistance and Accommodation*, Honolulu, 1993, pp. 1–44; Brij V. Lal, '"Nonresistance" on Fiji Plantations: The Fiji Indian Experience, 1879–1920', ibid., pp. 187–216; Carter, *Servants, Sirdars and Settlers*, pp. 193–235.

[27] Lal, 'Nonresistance', pp. 190–91.

[28] Also see Nitin Varma, 'Producing Tea Coolies? Work, Life and Protest in Colonial Tea Plantations of Assam, 1830s–1920s', unpublished dissertation, Humboldt University, Berlin, 2011.

[29] Bipan Chandra, *The Rise and Growth of Economic Nationalism in India*, New Delhi: People's Publishing House, 1966, pp. 361–79. They did not show the same concern about labour in industrial enterprises owned by Indian capitalists.

[30] Ramkumar Vidyaratna's articles were translated and presented in book form to Lord Ripon, the Viceroy, as a part of a memorandum to champion the cause of labour in the Assam

tea gardens by the Indian Association. Dwarkanath Ganguli's articles were compiled and published as *Slavery in British Dominion*, Calcutta: Jijnasa, 1972. See Sanat Bose, 'Indian Labour and its Historiography in Pre-Independence Period, *Social Scientist*, No. 143, 1985, p. 8.

[31] Charles Dowding, *Tea Garden Coolies in Assam*, Calcutta: Thacker, Spink & Co., 1894.

[32] Hypatia Bradlaugh Bonner, *Labour System of Assam*, London: Humanitarian League, 1906.

[33] Rajani Kanta Das, *Plantation Labour in India*, Calcutta: R. Chatterji, 1931; S.M. Akhtar, *Emigrant Labour for Assam Tea Gardens*, Lahore, 1939.

[34] N.M. Joshi, 'Labour Conditions in Assam', in Suresh Kant Sharma and Usha Sharam (eds.), *Discovery of North-East India*, Vol. 5, Delhi: Mittal Publications, 2005, pp. 1–7.

[35] Jatindranath Sarkar, 'Tea Garden Labour Labourers in Assam', *Modern Review*, December 1929, in Sharma and Sharma (eds.), *Discovery*, pp. 8–23.

[36] Diwan Chaman Lall, *Coolie: The Story of Labour and Capital in India, Volume II*, Labore: Oriental Publishing House, 1932.

[37] V.V. Thakkar, 'Harijan Manufactured in Tea Estates of Assam', *Modern Review*, March 1937, in Sharma and Sharma (eds.), *Discovery*, pp. 23–29.

[38] Sanat Kumar Bose, *Capital and Labour in Tea Gardens in Assam*, Bombay: All India Trade Union Congress, 1954.

[39] Amalendu Guha, *Planter Raj to Swaraj: Freedom Struggle and Electoral Politics in Assam*, New Delhi: Indian Council of Historical Research, 1977; revised edition, New Delhi: Tulika Books, 2006.

[40] Ramakrishna Chattopadhyaya, *Social Perspective of Labour Legislation in India: 1859–1932*, Calcutta University, 1987.

[41] Mohammad Abu Siddique, *Evolution of Land Grants and Labour Policy of Government: The Growth of the Tea Industry in Assam 1834–1940*, New Delhi: South Asian Publications, 1990.

[42] Jayeet Sharma, *Empire's Garden: Assam and the Making of India*, New Delhi: Permanent Black, 2012.

[43] Sebastian Karotemprel (ed.), *Tea Garden Labourers of North East India: A Multidimensional Study on the Adivasis of the Tea Gardens of North East India*, Shillong: Vendrame Institute, 1990.

[44] Amalendu Guha, 'Socio-Economic Changes in Agrarian Assam', in M.K. Chaudhury (ed.), *Trends in Socio-Economic Change in India 1871–1961*, Simla, 1967, pp. 569–622; Keya Deb, 'Impact of Plantations on the Agrarian Structure of the Brahmaputra Valley', Occasional Paper No. 24, Centre for Studies in Social Sciences, Calcutta, April 1979.

[45] H.A. Antrobus, *A History of the Jorehaut Company Ltd, 1859–1946*, London: Tea and Rubber Mail, 1948; H.A. Antrobus, *A History of the Assam Company*, Edinburgh: T. and A. Constable, 1957.

[46] Percival Griffiths, *The History of the Indian Tea Industry*, London: Weidenfeld and Nicolson, 1967.

[47] A retired British civil servant and a prolific writer, Griffiths had very close links with the tea industry as a political advisor to the Indian Tea Association during the late 1930s and World War II. His privileged position gave him access to the top circles of the industry and the government, and knowledge of the inner funtioning of the ITA and the tea companies' affairs. He was privy to decision-making processes in the industry on important issues like labour, trade unions, contemporary provincial politics and politicians, at a very crucial juncture of its history: World War II and the impending departure of the British from India.

[48] William Nassau Lees, *Tea Cultivation, Cotton and Other Agricultural Experiments in India, A Review*, Calcutta: Thacker, Spink & Co., 1863; Edward Money, *The Cultivation and Manufacture of Tea*, Calcutta: Thacker, Spink & Co., 1870; Samuel Baildon, *The Tea Industry in India: A Review of Finance and Labour, and a Guide for Capitalists and*

Assistants, London: W.H Allen & Co., 1882; George Barker, *Tea Planter's Life in Assam*, Calcutta: Thacker, Spink & Co., 1884; David Crole, *Tea: A Text Book of Tea Planting and Manufacture*, London: Crossby Lockwood and Son, 1897; F.A. Hetherington, *The Diary of a Tea Planter, 14 July 1907*, Sussex: The Book Guild Ltd., UK, 1994; Claud Bald, *Indian Tea*, Calcutta: Thacker, Spink & Co., 1922; Maurice P. Hanley, *Tales and Songs from an Assam Tea Garden*, Calcutta: Thacker, Spink & Co., 1928; C.R. Harler, *The Culture and Marketing of Tea*, London: Oxford University Press, 1933; Charles Reid, *Tea Manufacturing and Efficient Working Conditions*, Madras: The Madras Publishing House, 1934; W.M. Fraser, *The Recollections of a Tea Planter*, London: The Tea and Rubber Mail, 1935; Henry Cotton, *Indian and Home Memories*, London: T. Fisher Unwin, 1911; Bempfydle Fuller, *Some Personal Experiences*, London: John Murray, 1930.

[49] In general, these types of questions have been underplayed in South Asian migration history. Abundant descriptions of misery in regions of departure after all do not explain why certain regions saw many more labourers leave as migrants than others, and in particular why in such push areas, while some individuals and families left, the large majority stayed. See contributions on South Asia by Vijaya Ramaswamy and Sunil S. Amrith in Jan Lucassen and Leo Lucassen (eds.), *Globalizing Migration History: The Eurasian Experience (16ᵗʰ–21ˢᵗ Centuries)*, Leiden/Boston: Brill, 2014.

MAPS

OF THE FOLLOWING

TEA DISTRICTS

DARJEELING AND TERAI, JALPAIGURI AND DUARS, DARRANG

(COMPRISING MANGALDAI TEZPUR-BISHNATH), NOWGONG, GOLAGHAT,

JORHAT, SIBSAGAR, L. .HIMPUR, DIBRUGARH, CACHAR AND SYLHET

WITH

Complete Index to Tea Gardens.

Published by

THE INDIAN TEA ASSOCIATION,

CALCUTTA.

1930.

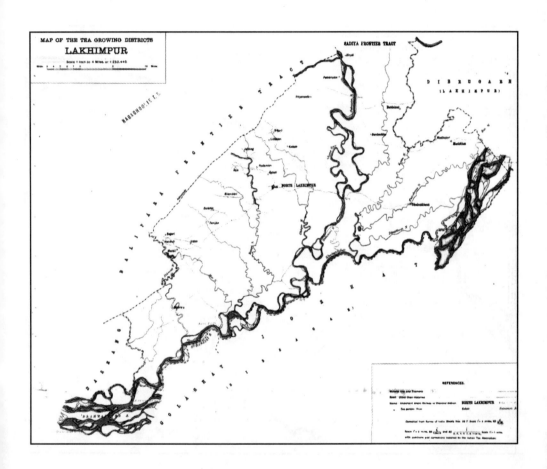

MAP OF THE TEA GROWING DISTRICTS
LAKHIMPUR
Scale 1 Inch to 4 Miles, or 1:253,440

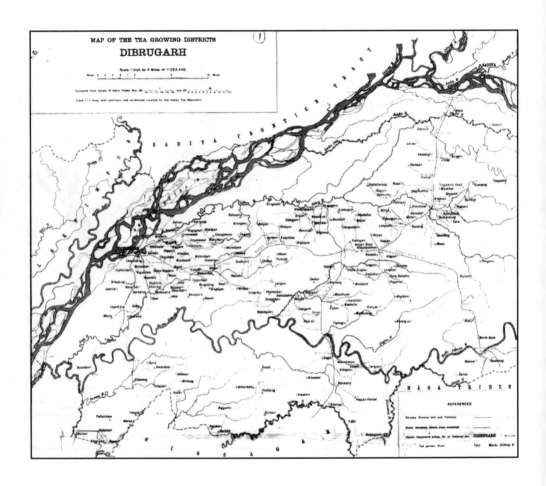

MAP OF THE TEA GROWING DISTRICTS

DIBRUGARH

Scale 1 inch to 4 Miles or 1/253,440.

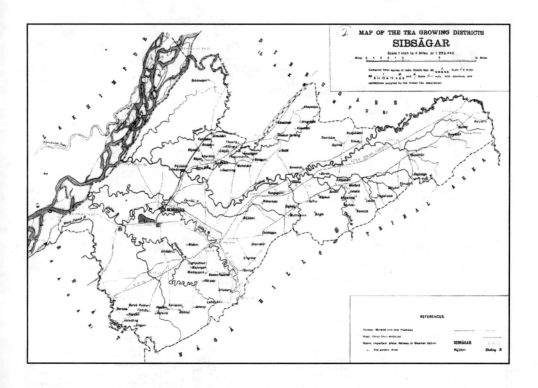

MAP OF THE TEA GROWING DISTRICTS
SIBSĀGAR
Scale 1 inch to 4 miles, or 1:253,440.

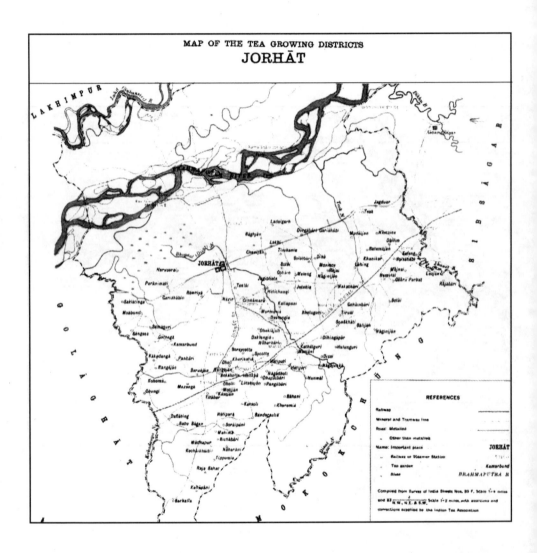

MAP OF THE TEA GROWING DISTRICTS
JORHĀT

MAP OF THE TEA GROWING DISTRICTS
DARRANG
COMPRISING
MANGALDAI – TEZPUR – BISHNÂTH

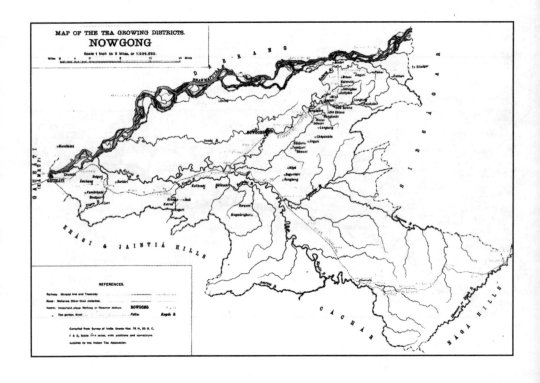

1

Genesis of Tea Production in Assam Valley

Chinese Tea and Indian Opium

The production of tea in Assam for consumption by the British market began only in 1840. Until that time, China was the sole supplier of tea to Britain. At the beginning of the eighteenth century tea consumption was confined to the upper class and the wealthy few of British society. But by the late eighteenth century tea had become an almost irreducible, everyday necessity for the poor and working class sections of that society.[1] Consumption of tea rapidly spread throughout Britain, increasingly replacing home-brewed beer, gin, milk and traditional infusions of indigenous plants.[2] Tea-drinking gripped the imagination of the British public to such an extent that it was officially declared the National Drink of England in 1784. This transformation in the consumption pattern of British society led to the commodification of tea as an article of international trade. In response to the growing demand at home, the East India Company purchased larger and larger amounts of tea from China: the quantity imported grew from 142,000 lbs in 1711 to 890,000 lbs in 1741, increased to 2,800,000 lbs in 1751, 4,9000,000 lbs in 1781 and then there was a massive jump to 15,000,000 lbs in 1791.[3]

The consumption-driven import of tea into England steadily grew despite very heavy import duties on tea throughout the seventeenth and eighteenth centuries. In 1724, import duty was levied at a rate of 13.93 per cent of the gross value; it was revised upward to 18.39 per cent in 1747 and again to 23.93 per cent in 1759. It has been estimated that during the years 1750–55, the rate of taxation on tea sales in England was in excess of 100 per cent of the net cost to buyers. Despite this steep rise in taxation rate, however, the demand for tea continued to increase, as reflected in the increased volume of tea imports.

Between the second and sixth decades of the eighteenth century, tea imports increased more than five-fold.[4] One of the reasons for the dramatic increase in imports between 1783 and 1785 was the passing of the Commutation Act (1784) by the British Parliament. This legislation, brought in partly to discourage smuggling caused by the high taxation rate, drastically reduced the import duty on tea – from 119 per cent to 12.5 per cent.[5] The consumption of tea skyrocketed from 5,857,882 lbs in 1783 to 15,000,000 lbs in 1785.[6] The Commutation Act granted the East India Company (EIC) full monopolistic rights 'to import sufficient tea to supply the domestic market' and 'to maintain in its warehouses a quantity equal to one year's consumption'.[7] In 1800, the East India Company bought 23.3 million lbs of tea, and after 1808, Britain purchased an average of 26 million pounds from China, twice as much tea as purchased by other countries, making the British probably the world's largest tea consumers after the Chinese.[8] The national drink brought huge profits to both private commercial enterprise in Britain and the British government. The EIC's profits soared and so did the government's revenues. The revenue accruing from tea to the British Exchequer averaged, in the last ten years of the EIC's monopoly, about £3,300,000 per annum. Tea imports from China to Britain in the eighteenth and nineteenth centuries accounted for about 10 per cent of the total revenue from import duties and the entire profits of the EIC.[9] By the last quarter of the eighteenth century, tea was well on its way to becoming the most important article of the East India Company's commercial exploits in the east and in the last years of its monopoly, the Company's exports to Europe and England consisted of tea alone.[10] During the years 1811–19 the Company's total imports into England was valued at £72,168,541, out of which the value of tea alone was £70,426,244. The total profit from tea ranged between £1,000,000 and £1,500,000 a year, according to various witnesses before the Select Committee of the House of Commons in 1830. The national drink of England was thus beneficial for all parties involved.[11]

Revenues from Bengal and from opium helped finance this enterprise.[12] The East India Company found a profitable though contraband market for opium in China, which also helped finance its tea imports into Britain. From the mid-eighteenth century onwards, once it established its hold over opium-producing areas in British India, opium exports to China became the EIC's major commercial activity. The Company became directly involved in the production of opium in India and its export to China.[13] Until the arrival of opium on the scene, the tea trade was financed by imports of silver bullion from Europe. As the Chinese barely consumed any European products, the balance of trade was very much in their favour till the arrival of opium.[14] Opium exports grew sufficiently to offset the balance of payments for the import of tea from China: from 1,000 chests in 1767 to 4,000 in 1800 and 19,000 in the 1820s, reaching a figure of 40,000 chests by 1839.[15] Duties on Indian opium exports accounted for 15 per cent of the East India Company's total revenue.[16] Opium dominated the private or 'country' trade, and by 1828, it constituted 55 per cent of all British imports into China, providing not only the wherewithal to pay for imported tea but also saving on the import of silver.[17]

The rapid growth of the coastal opium trade alarmed the Chinese government, as import of opium on such a large scale had far-reaching repercussions. It had begun to actively encourage large sections of the population to take to law-defying pursuits. Economically, the most conspicuous effect of the opium trade was the drain of silver spice, then China's main currency. As a consequence, Chinese commerce and finance were seriously affected. Furthermore, it encouraged corruption within local governments and the police force, and sapped the energy of the army. The lives of a large number of merchants, sailors, labourers and other occupational sections of the population were being rendered inactive, unproductive and useless.[18] More and more people were being drawn away from normal, socially productive careers. At this juncture, the imperial authorities in China decided to intervene. It was suggested that a great debate be held on how to cope with the situation, and the party that advocated a firm policy was put in power to crush the opium trade.[19] Suggestions to ban the opium and tea trade came from senior officials of the Imperial Chinese government.[20] For quite some time the Chinese government had been repeatedly issuing imperial edicts to stop the illegal opium trade but without success, because the trade was extremely lucrative for everyone involved, i.e both Chinese merchants and British traders.[21] Even though these prior efforts remained unsuccessful the growing tension in China was a major concern for the British, both in England and in India. In the late 1830s, the Chinese authorities threatened to take drastic action against the East India Company if the illegal traffic was not stopped.[22] The troubles in China over the opium question and the threat to the tea trade increased the momentum to search for an alternate source of tea supply, both within the British empire and elsewhere.[23]

Imperial Science and Early 'Pioneers'

The President of the East India Company's Board of Control and its Committee began deliberations on this subject from the early 1830s. Lord William Bentinck, the then Governor General of India, broached the subject of introducing the tea plant in the Himalayan regions of India in January 1834. The idea was brought to his notice at the time of his appointment as Governor General 'by a very intelligent gentleman of the name of Walker.'[24] Walker, in his memorandum, expressed concerns that were generally shared by many in Britain at that time: that the deteriorating Anglo–Chinese trade relations were threatening the supply of tea, which 'has become a luxury to all, and almost a portion of food to the common people'. 'Its use is so intermingled with our habits and customs, that it would not easily be dispensed with.'[25] He also pointed to its monetary significance for the British government, whose revenue from tea imports at that time was £4,000,000 a year. Considering this a matter of urgent 'national importance', Walker urged that 'some better guarantee should be provided for the continued supply of this article than that at present furnished by the mere toleration of the Chinese government, which, although the Chinese have at present a monopoly, it will be easy for us to destroy.'[26] The destruction of the Chinese monopoly, he proposed, could be accomplished if the East India Company was to undertake tea cultivation in those regions of India where the camellia and other plants similar to the tea plant are indigenous, with the application of the 'science of the Europeans'.[27] Walker's idea was not original. Long before him, Sir Joseph Banks and Dr Govan had recommended experiments in tea cultivation in the Himalayan regions. And Dr Forbes Royle had brought the subject to the notice of Governor General Amherst, Bentinck's predecessor.[28] The European scientific community and its establishments, in Europe as well as in the colonial world, had begun experimenting with the possibility of growing tea outside China, though not with any degree of success thus far.[29] However, it was the threat of stoppage of tea supply in the wake of the opium controversy that prompted the British East India Company to initiate serious action.

In accordance with the views of Governor General Bentinck, a Tea Committee was appointed in February 1834 to search for alternate locations in India for the production of tea for commercial purposes. The Committee, consisting of J.S. Pattle, J.W. Grant, R.D. Mangles, J.R. Calvin, J.R. Trevelyan, C.K. Robinson, Rob Wilkinson, R.D. Colquhoun, N. Wallich, Radhakunt Deb, Ram Comul Sen and G.J. Gordon, was a motley group representing opium traders from Calcutta, senior members of the Civil Service, British scientists and others.[30] Gordon, an opium trader based in Calcutta, was made the Secretary of this Committee. Through the Tea Committee the East India Company activated the whole network of imperial botanic gardens, along with medical, military and civil establishments of the British empire, to find ways and means of tea production in India as an alternative source of supply for the western markets.[31] Over the course of the next five years, the combined efforts of these establishments successfully set up nurseries for the commercial production of indigenous tea in Upper Assam. Most of these tea nurseries were then handed over to Assam Company, a British private enterprise set up in London in 1839 for the purpose of producing tea in India. Tales of the 'heroic' efforts and achievements of the 'pioneers' who opened tea plantations in the 'wilderness' of Assam are worth recounting in some detail.

Immediately upon its appointment, the Tea Committee issued a circular to various administrative and scientific establishments with a view to collecting information about the climate and soil of different localities in India, so that on receipt of the necessary information from China on these subjects, seeds and plants might at once be dispatched to those places found best suited for cultivation. At the same time, Gordon, the man with opium connections, was sent to China in July 1834 to procure tea plants and men skilled in tea cultivation and manufacturing.[32] The Tea Committee received favourable reports regarding soil and climatic conditions conducive to tea planting from Dr H. Falconer, Civil Surgeon, who was in charge of the Botanical Garden at Sharanpur, and Mr Trail, the Commissioner of Kumaon.[33] The most important breakthrough came with a report from Assam. In May 1834, in response to the circular, Sadiya-based Lieutenant A. Charlton and his Gauhati-based superior officer, Captain F. Jenkins, Agent to the Governor General in the North East, informed the Tea Committee that the tea shrub was found growing wild in Upper Assam, and sent samples of fruits and leaves of the tea.[34] Charlton reported to Jenkins that the Singphos and Kamptees, native communities of Upper Assam, 'are in the habit of drinking an infusion of the leaves' which they prepared through the process of boiling and sun-drying.[35] Members of the Tea Committee were ecstatic upon confirmation of this discovery, and they wrote to the Governor General in the same vein:

> It is with feelings of the highest possible satisfaction that we are enabled to announce to His Lordship in Council, that the tea shrub is beyond all doubt indigenous in Upper Assam being found there. . . . We have no hesitation in declaring this discovery, which is due to the indefatigable researches of Captain Jenkins and Lt. Charlton, to be by far the most valuable that has ever been made on matters connected with the agricultural or commercial resources of this empire. We are perfectly confident that the tea plant which has been brought to light, will be found capable, under proper management, of being cultivated with complete success for commercial purposes, and that subsequently the object of our labours may be before long fully realized.[36]

The Committee forwarded Jenkins' recommendations to the government with a request for one or more scientists to be sent to Upper Assam for further investigation, and to collect a variety of botanical, geological and other details. It also endorsed Jenkins' recommendation to import two or three Chinamen acquainted with the cultivation and manufacture of tea to help with the experimental operations. The government deputed a committee of three scientists to Upper Assam, which included Wallich (already a member of the Tea Committee), Griffiths, a botanist, and McClelland, a geologist, in March 1835.[37] During their travels this committee identified some of the forest sites at Koojo, Niggroo on the Booree Dehung river, inhabited by the Singphos,[38] Nuddooa and Tengrae communities in the Muttuk country, and at the foot of the Nagu range at Gubhroo in the territories of Raja Purandhar Singh. They were highly gratified upon discovering an abundance of tea shrubs and suitable soil, and were of the opinion that these jungles 'ought to be, without

delay, appropriated for the purposes of Government'.[39] Some of these areas
were outside the territories controlled by the British. The committee's original
brief was to select suitable sites within British territories, but the discovery of
a large number of new tea tracts in these areas whetted their appetite. 'I am
warranted in believing that we may get possession', Wallich wrote to Jenkins,
'not only of those forests, but of all the others I have mentioned . . . by adopting this measure, the number as well as sites of the intended plantations may
be considerably modified'.[40] He recommended that all the tracts enumerated
by them should be brought under British possession.

In the meantime, knowledge of the existence of tea plants in Assam,
acquired on the eve of the First Burmese War, had already increased the
importance of these regions for the British.[41] The Burmese invasion in the
1820s provided an excellent opportunity to the British government to intervene
in the political affairs of Assam, and to extend their control and influence
beyond the north-eastern frontiers. After expelling the Burmese from Assam
in 1826, the British established their military posts there but retained Raja
Purandar Singh, a scion of the Ahom royal family, as a puppet ruler. During
the decade of the 1830s, the British further extended their influence over large
parts of Assam. While attempting to set up experimental tea nurseries, as we
have seen above, members of the Tea Committee and other British officials
were already advocating the takeover of these territories. Having discovered
alternate sources of tea supply in Upper Assam, the British moved swiftly to
complete the territorial acquisition of Assam and other regions which were
still outside the boundaries of their expanding empire, where it would be
possible to cultivate tea. The puppet king, Raja Purandar Singh, was deposed
and Assam was annexed to the British Indian empire in October 1838.[42]
The establishment of Assam Company initiated a scheme of colonization
of wastelands in order to provide new avenues of investment for foreign
capital.[43] Its foundation as the first modern joint-stock industrial firm also
represented the beginning of a new stage of British economic activity in India.
It marked the change from the era of the East India Company's monopoly of
trade and appropriation of land revenue, to the era of exploitation of colonial
resources by the industrial capitalism of Great Britain. The opening up of
tea plantations as part of the first and biggest plantation industry owned by
British capital became a part of the process by which India was integrated
into world capitalism as a primary producer.

Wallich recommended that the government set up experimental stations
and that C.A. Bruce be appointed as superintendent of the operations. The
committee of three scientists had been assisted by Bruce during their excur-
sions and they were extremely impressed, Wallich in particular, by 'his intimate
acquaintance with the customs, languages, prejudices &.c. of many tribes that
inhabit the province . . . his extraordinary strength of constitution, which has

enabled him to encounter the fiercest jungles, at seasons when it would be fatal to any one else to come near them'.[44] In a similar vein, Jenkins, while supporting his candidature for the job of superintendent of government tea nurseries, enumerated his special qualifications as a man of great good temper, with a knowledge of the natives and extraordinary physical abilities to withstand any fatigue and exposure. And beyond these attributes was 'his zeal to forward by every means in his power the objects of Government'.[45] The government accepted Jenkins' recommendations and sanctioned the appointment of Bruce as superintendent of government nurseries at Sadiya in Upper Assam.[46]

Such eulogies made a legend of C.A. Bruce in the annals of Assam's tea plantations; he was considered one of the earliest 'pioneers' to convert the wild indigenous tea plant into a commercially viable commodity.[47] When his name was recommended to become the superintendent of tea nurseries in Assam, he was in command of gunboats in Upper Assam. A veteran of wars in the Isle of France and Java, he travelled to Assam to join his older brother Robert Bruce, who was already based in Jorhat. Robert Bruce had arrived in Assam in 1823 with a variety of merchandise to trade, and established contact with the Singpho chief, Beesa Gaum, in Upper Assam.[48] It was through this connection that he came to know of the existence of indigenous tea plants in those areas. C.A. Bruce in turn acquired this information and connections with the natives from his brother. He claimed – and this was uncontested by contemporary British officials and others in Assam – to be the first European to have penetrated the forests, discovered several of the tea tracts in Sadiya and other areas in Upper Assam, and collected specimens of soil, fruits and leaves.[49] He also established a reputation for his military exploits among the tribal communities of Upper Assam when, as a commander of gunboats, he successfully suppressed the uprising of Duffa Gaum and his followers.[50] From the official correspondence between Bruce, the Tea Committee, Captain Jenkins and Major White, it becomes clear that many of the chiefs of native communities were suspicious of the British and reluctant to divulge information on the existence of tea plants in their respective areas. 'I regret to mention', reported White,

> that Koochwo and Nugroo Gaums have as yet not made their appearance at Suddeya, for the purpose of treating regarding the tea forests discovered within their respective tracts of territory. I apprehend this is to be ascribed to some latent distrust on their part in consequence of their having been connected with the Dufla Gaum.[51]

Bruce travelled across the forested areas of Muttak and Sadiya in Upper Assam inhabited by the Singpho community, and sent information about his discoveries to Jenkins. 'There is plenty of tea in Rajah Purundhah's country', he reported, but he is too lazy to trouble himself about it. . . . The Singphos have known and drunk the tea for years, but they make it in different way from what the Chinese do. . . . These Singphos pretend to be great judge of tea. All their country abounds with the plant, but they are very jealous and will give no information where it is to be found, like the Muttuck people.[52]

He also reported the details of the methods he employed to 'persuade' these communities and their chief to provide him knowledge of indigenous processes of tea-making as well as the existence of tea tracts. Among the various 'means' he used to 'persuade' the reluctant and 'rude' Singphoes were 'gifts' of opium, firearms, and sometimes 'soft/sweet words' and promises of official favours from the British Commissioner, citing his proximity with the political power hierarchy. The Tea Committee gave a detailed account of how Bruce ingratiated himself with the reluctant chief at Ningrew on the Burra Dihing river with the offer of opium, sharing the smoke with them, and the promise of a double-barrelled gun and other firearms, and thus obtained information that tea was growing at Jugundoo, further down the river.[53] Bruce communicated details of his successful 'exploits' to Jenkins. At Rungah Ghurrah, Raja Burrah Sunna Putty, though reluctantly, provided him with an elephant and a few labourers to enable him to reach the village people of Tingry, where, he claimed, 'I lost no opportunity of gaining all the information I possibly could . . . although they had been strictly prohibited from giving me the information whatever. I told all these people that I had come to do their country good, by instructing them how to cultivate and manufacture tea; but I do not think any of them believed me.'[54] He asked for a supply of guns and pistols to be given as offerings to 'those gaums who may be favourably disposed to our objects'. Hugely impressed with the success of the 'means' of 'persuasion' employed by Bruce, the Tea Committee requested the government to supply him 'cheap double-barrelled guns and pistols, to be presented, at his discretion, to such native chiefs as may have it in their power, and may show inclinations favourable to our objects'. Bruce's mission was considered important enough by the government to sanction funds for this purpose.[55]

At the experiment stations Bruce was assisted by Chinamen who had been arranged to be sent by Gordon at the request of the Tea Committee. With their assistance and his own knowledge of indigenous methods acquired from the natives, Bruce evolved the process of tea cultivation and manufacture out of the indigenous plants of Upper Assam.[56] Based on his own experiences and keen observation of the tea-tract forests, he learnt and developed the seasonal production cycles of tea plants on the field – as also the process of pruning tea plants to productive and workable heights, and weeding and clearing the ground. He developed and noted down work categories of plantation agriculture, such as plucking, pruning, hoeing and clearing. One member of the committee of scientists, the botanist William Griffiths, was not very impressed with Bruce's work. Griffiths was upset that the imported Chinese tea plants, which he considered to be of primary importance to this project, were neglected and declined as a result. As for the importance of improving the Assamese plant, he raised the issue of necessary qualifications which he felt Bruce lacked since he was not a botanist. He was not impressed with the overall performance of the tea nurseries because these were 'directed by a person who was bred up to a seafaring life, and whose long residence in Assam has been devoted entirely to mercantile pursuits, and the command of gun-boats'.[57]

However Jenkins and Wallich were staunch believers in Bruce's abilities and their support for him was accepted by the British government. Bruce's detailed account of the manufacture of black tea, developed by him with the help of Chinese assistants, was lauded as 'highly creditable to the zeal and intelligence of the gentleman' by the government.[58] They were all elated when the first batch of tea manufactured in the Assam nurseries was sent to and sold at a very high price in the London market, in January 1839.[59] Detailed information about the tea experiments and Bruce's report were published in the contemporary British press, creating an awareness and atmosphere to attract private capital to the tea venture in India.[60] Around this juncture, the government reminded the Tea Committee of the injunction of the Court of Directors with regard to the strictly experimental nature of the operations that were now in progress at public expense: 'Those operations it was never intended to extend beyond the point of ascertaining that marketable tea could be grown and manufactured in British India.'[61] In reply, while assuring the government of the strictly experimental nature of the operations, the Tea Committee also urged them to consider

> that the experimental operations now in progress at the tea tracts in Assam require, not only time and careful preservation to any degree of perfection, but likewise to be carefully preserved, in order to encourage private speculation, whenever it may be deemed advisable to commit the future extension and profitable success of this experimental trial entirely to individual enterprise. This view seems to us to be in perfect accordance with the original intention of the Government . . . and distinctly founded on the principle, that the Government are eventually to withdraw entirely from all further prosecution of the scheme, and, as soon as it may appear to be expedient, to entrust its future success to private speculators, but not earlier.[62]

The arrival and sale of tea in the London market marked the end of governmental involvement and the entry of private British capital in Assam, for the production of tea for the world market and the establishment of a viable alternative to the Chinese monopoly. Since this project was proposed to be taken up within British India, the tea-growing areas of Assam and other parts which were still outside its boundaries were annexed, on some pretext or the other, and made a part of the British Indian empire.

Immediately after the first sale of Assam tea in London and the news that the government wished to encourage the entry of private enterprise for tea production in Assam, a number of capitalists, both in Calcutta and London, approached the authorities for detailed information about existing planta-tions and the possibilities of transfer to them.[63] A memorial was submitted by London merchants to the East India Company requesting information on the possibility of commercial cultivation of tea in Assam so that they could form an estimate of possible gains from such an enterprise.[64] The deputation of memorialists who met the Directors of the East India Company reported an 'extremely satisfactory' response, and this encouraged the formation of private companies for the purpose of cultivating tea in India.[65] The Assam Company was formed in London on 14 February 1839 with a capital of £500,000 in 10,000 shares of £50 each.[66] Around the same time the Bengal Tea Associa-tion was formed with the approval of the government; this was a joint stock company with a capital of Rs 10,00,000, organized by the partners of Carr, Tagore and Company.[67] Very soon the Assam Company approached William Prinsep of the Bengal Tea Association to arrange a 'junction of interests'.[68] The idea appealed to Prinsep. He felt a joint venture might prove more effec-tive in persuading the government to hand over the established tea gardens. The Assam Company, in return, accepted the condition that the direction in Calcutta would be independent of London, and that preference on the Lon-don Board should be given to returning members from Calcutta. The Bengal Tea Association agreed to merge with the Assam Company under the latter's name.[69] The Calcutta branch of the company was allotted 2,000 shares, which were distributed among 78 shareholders. Of these 280 were held by Indians, including 100 each by Dwarkanath Tagore and Motilal Seal. Prinsep was the first secretary of the Committee of the Calcutta branch. However this partnership did not survive very long due to constant conflict between the two branches. London controlled the majority of the shares and it dwarfed the power of the Bengal group; hence the control of events shifted to London. In 1866 they succeeded in abolishing the Calcutta Board.[70]

The Assam Company immediately established contact with Jenkins to gather information about the status of tea nurseries and other related issues. The Bengal Committee reported 'most satisfactory replies to several ques-tions regarding the means to be taken up for carrying into early effect the object of the Company', which included information about the importance of Bruce, a copy of Bruce's report on the tea localities in Upper Assam, the nature of labour requirements, existing transport infrastructure and sundry requirements of day-to-day nature.[71] This was valuable information which helped the company in framing its application for the transfer of government plantations. The government liberally transferred to the Assam Company the services of C.A. Bruce, the superintendent, and two-thirds of its own establishments, plantations and lands free of rent for ten years.[72] When the Chairman of the East India Company complained that Governor General Auckland had given away too much to the Assam Company, the latter replied that he hoped the government would soon withdraw from all interference, adding, 'and it seems to me to be of immense importance that we should attach whatever we can British capital to our sail'.[73]

Before Bruce joined its operations the Assam Company had sent J.W. Masters as its superintendent to Nazira, from where he commenced operations such as searching for tea plants in the neighbourhood and submitting applications to the government for grants of land for cultivation.[74] *Laissez-faire* orthodoxy was hardly reflected in the colonial government's attitude towards the planters when it came to providing state assistance for their private enterprises.[75] It made special rules of land grants whereby the planters got land at nominal prices. These grants, made under the 'Waste Land Rules' of 6 March 1838, were 'distinct from the ordinary rules for the occupation of plots of agricultural lands'.[76] Wastelands were offered on a forty-five year lease to applicants on the condition that a quarter of the area must be cleared within five years, failing which the land was liable to resumption. The terms of these land grants were extremely liberal even though they meant sacrifice of public revenue. According to these rules, one-fourth of a grant was to be held revenue-free in perpetuity. The remaining portion of the grant was to remain revenue-free for an initial period of five to twenty years, varying according to the nature of the wasteland concerned: i.e. for five years if the land was under grass, ten years if under reed and high grass, and twenty years if under forest. On expiry of this period, revenue was to be assessed at 9 annas per acre for the next three years, after which the rate was to be Rs 1–2 an acre for twenty-two years.[77] The special rules fixed the area of land granted at a minimum of 100 acres, and applicants were required to be in possession of capital on stock worth Rs 3 per acre. It was probably expected that Europeans would avail of the concessions only under these conditions. In the official discourse it was couched in welfare rhetoric, as the primary object of the government was supposed to be 'the general improvement of the province with benefits – moral as well as physical – which must result to its inhabitants from the introduction of foreign enterprise, capital and skill'.[78] In 1854 the revision of these rules made these grants even more liberal and attractive for the European planters, providing for a 99-year lease. It also raised the minimum land area limit to 500 acres (reduced to 200 acres later on).[79] A quarter of the grant was to be revenue-free in perpetuity and the remaining three-fourths was to be revenue-free for the first fifteen years. At the end of this period, the land was to be assessed at 3 annas per acre for another ten years and for the next 74 years at 6 annas per acre.[80]

Initially, the Assam Company was the major beneficiary of these special rules; but after about a decade, several other individuals also applied and acquired lands for tea cultivation. It is interesting to note that in the first twenty years of their evolution, tea plantations were opened up in Assam by both corporate companies and individuals. The first private garden in Assam owned by an individual was opened by Colonel Hannay near Dibrugarh, in Lakhimpur district, in 1850–51. Mr Mills, a judge at the Saddar Court, founded three private gardens in Sibsagar and six near Dibrugarh on his arrival in Assam in 1853.[81] The Assam Company was the major tea company. The early years of its operations were troublesome; the inexperience of European assistants, the strained relationship between the Calcutta and London branches, and the high mortality of staff and labour due to the unhealthy conditions of areas around the tea tracts threatened to derail the project.[82] However, after the early hiccoughs of the 1840s, the Assam Company – as well as other individual investors – settled down, and began to expand their acreage and quantities of manufactured tea. The revision of land grant rules in 1854 proved attractive to the planters. Applications for grants increased and several new tea gardens were opened up. The figures in Appendix Tables 1.1 and 1.2 show the acreage ownership and tea production by individual planters and companies in the Kamrup and Lakhimpur districts of Assam Valley during 1852–59. The figures reflect a slow but steady increase in acreage and production of tea in the decade of the 1850s. The Assam Company in particular experienced steady expansion and growth from 1853 onwards (see Table 1.1 below).

For the period 1858–59, Jenkins, now promoted to the post of Colonel, reported detailed statistics on the number of tea gardens, factories, acreage,

TABLE 1.1
Assam Company: Acreage under Tea, Production, Profits and Dividends, 1853–60[83]

Year	Acreage	Production (lbs)	Profits (£)	Dividends (%)
1853	2,921	366,687	13,261	6
1854	3,313	478,258	20,640	7
1855	3,493	583,094	11,480	8
1856	3,838	944,199	25,077	9
1857	4,261	707,132	13,008	10
1858	4,466	766,998	29,790	12
1859	4,636	810,680	18,311	12
1860	4,726	880,154	21,530	10

production and names of proprietors. In Sibsagar, the largest tea district, thirty-one tea gardens had been opened up by this time with a total area of 18,574 acres, which produced 15,39,458 lbs of tea in 1858. Similarly, the district of Lakhimpur reported the opening of fourteen tea gardens with a total area of 14,038 acres producing 2,82,689 lbs in 1859. Darrang district had only three gardens with a total area of 3,196 acres producing 23,280 lbs in 1859. Nowgong district reported the opening of fourteen gardens with a total area of 11,034 acres which produced 48,000 lbs in 1859. Kamroop district had eleven gardens with an area of 12,207 acres, but produced only 6,160 lbs of tea. Thus, by 1859, Assam Valley districts witnessed the opening of a total of 68 tea gardens covering 54,859 acres of land by planters, out of which 7,599 acres had been cleared for cultivation; and 12,05,689 lbs of tea had been produced in that year.[84] While the ownership pattern showed dominance of the Assam Company, there were a significant number of individual proprietors and joint-stock concerns which included the names of George Williamsons, J.E. Todd, Spears, Jenkins, Hassack, Nuthall, Colonel Reid, Colonel Hannay, A.C. Campbell and Co., W. Stafford, M/s Higgs, Melang and Sevenoaks, M/s Warren and Jenkins, J.N. Martin, H. Partridge, H. Herriot, H. Birkinyoung, Stewart, A. Michel, R.D. Cameron, J.P. Wise, William Becher, Lyall and Bruce.[85] Some of them, like Williamson and Birkinyoung, were to become major figures in the history of Assam's tea industry. Some among them, like Colonel Hannay, Commandant of 1st Assam Light Infantry, Williamson and G. Barry of Serajganj, managed their own gardens.[86] These men came from a wide range of backgrounds. Edward Money, a contemporary tea planter, remarked: 'tea planters in those days were a strange medley of retired or cashiered army and navy officers, medical men, engineers, veterinary surgeons, steamer captains, chemists, shop-keepers of all kinds, stable-keepers, used-up policemen, clerks, and goodness knows who besides!'[87] The steady growth of the industry became evident when another joint-stock company, the Jorehaut Tea Company, was incorporated in 1859, with a capital of £60,000 divided into 3,000 shares of £20 each.[88] This company showed profits from the very first year of its trading, declaring dividends amounting to 5 per cent in 1860 and 11 per cent in 1861. Encouraged by this success, it increased its capital in 1862 by £20,000.[89]

Labour Supply Concerns

The opening of new plantations and the expansion of older ones generated a demand for labour. The growing acreage under tea cultivation and rising production of tea could be sustained only by increasing the labour supply. From its very inception in the Assam Valley, the issue of labour was a subject of intense concern, comment and discussion among the planters, the state and all others connected with the tea industry. In the beginning, at the government tea nurseries, the process of tea cultivation and manufacture was carried on with the help of Chinese tea makers whom Gordon had sent from China.[90] Clearing of forests and the erection of bamboo and thatched buildings were effected by employing local labourers, mostly from the indigenous *Kachari* community.[91] Bruce, although successful in extracting information from the Singphoos, was unable to persuade them to work for him or make tea for the market. He exasperatedly reported to Jenkins:

> I am sorry to say that I cannot get the Singpho to do as I wish; they work how and when they please. They are under no control, and wish not to work at all. . . . The Singphoos are all under their own petty chiefs, so coolies cannot be had, and these men will not work for any as long as they have sufficient opium and rice of their own.

Jenkins, while informing Wallich about Bruce's complaint regarding the apathy of the Singphoos, offered a solution which was almost prophetic in nature; he suggested that they encourage 'the emigration of more industrious races from Chota Nagpore or elsewhere'.[92] Anticipating the take-over of government plantations, the Assam Company sought to import labour from China for its tea-producing operations in Assam, using the services of Dr Lumqua, a Chinese physician from Calcutta, as interpreter.[93] Bruce had been working with the Chinese tea makers and, with their help, he had converted the wild indigenous tea plant into a marketable commodity. More Chinese men were brought in to work as labourers in early 1840. However these men were found to be troublesome and this experiment of importing workers from China turned out to be a complete fiasco.[94] The Assam Valley was a very sparsely populated region when the Assam Company commenced its operations in the 1840s and, as a consequence, shortage of labour was a serious problem. Efforts made to procure labour locally were not very successful, for low wages and growing competition from government infrastructure projects rendered plantation employment an unattractive option.[95] For clearing the jungles, however, the tea planters did manage to procure the services of the Kachari tribal community, reputed for their skills in this work. But they were not willing to reside in the enclosed plantations or work on the field for low wages under close supervision.[96] The failure to procure local labour necessitated the search for labourers from Bengal through *sirdars* and agents who were mostly fortune-seeking Englishmen. These efforts constantly ran into trouble, however, with the recruited labourers deserting soon after arrival on the plantations, or not reaching their destination even when sent by boats from the recruiting areas, thereby causing a loss of money paid as advances.[97] In February 1842, Bruce reported that out of 500 labourers brought by Sirdar Modoo Hazaree from Rangpur, 80 ran away. In June 1842,

Parkers complained that a party of 100 labourers sent up by steamer never reached. And in October 1842, Masters reported the desertion of labourers from his sub-division.[98]

With the impetus in growth of tea plantations following the liberalization of land grant rules in 1854, the labour supply issue became even more complicated. Cheap availability of land for tea cultivation consequent to the revision of land grant rules induced the planters to expand their acreage and production far beyond the extent of labour availability. Jenkins was already warning that the planters had planted more land with tea plants than could be properly farmed, and that the 'little labour we have is wasted in useless extension of plantations'.[99] The Secretary of State for India, in the meantime, was enquiring if 'success has attended the cultivation of this plant, as it seems likely to prove much use in civilizing and giving security to these wild districts'.[100] In response, the local officials of these 'wild districts' reported that the expansion of tea cultivation remained hampered because of the shortage of labour. The prospects of rapid progress, they informed their superiors, were not very encouraging on account of the 'deficiency' of labour, and remedial measures were suggested. As an explanation for this deficiency, the stereotype of 'lazy and indolent' natives was already gaining currency among the planters and the colonial bureaucracy in Assam.[101] Opium consumption and subsistence farming which provided easier access to food were considered to be the cause of lethargy and lack of 'industriousness' among the natives. They recommended the prohibition of opium cultivation in Assam to discourage its consumption. They also reported that the planters were unable to induce the local ryots, who were 'well off', to work in the plantations.[102] Captains Rowlatt, Comber, Lloyd and Holroyd, Collectors of Kamrup, Darrang, Nowgong and Sibsagar districts respectively, recommended raising land revenue 'as a means of throwing labor into the hand of the Planters by compelling the ryots to seek for employment in order to pay their revenue'.[103] Colonel Jenkins, their superior officer, supported their recommendation of prohibiting opium cultivation. He did not concur, however, with their suggestion to raise the government assessment on land, nor did he share their stereotypical perception of the natives. He felt that the 'theme of want of industry and energy among the Assamese' was 'fallacious', and attributed the ryots' unwillingness to work in the plantations as wage labour to the abundant availability of very fertile land, the 'simple habits of the people' and the 'customs of the country'. He reminded his superiors: 'Before we occupied the country hired labour was almost unknown, or confined to the Cacharees, or other rude tribes unconverted to Hinduism'.[104] The indigenous Kachari community had provided labour on the tea plantations, but they were 'difficult to manage, exceedingly jealous of ill-treatment, and who at Nazira, have lately shown a dangerous spirit of combination and mutiny'.[105] On a practical note, he feared that any steep enhancement in assessment would have the effect of 'decreasing the quantity of land cultivated, to the certain loss to the Government'.[106] The government, despite initial hesitation in the light of Jenkins' reservations, responded favourably to the planters' demand. A 15 to 30 per cent increase in land revenue rates on dry crop lands in four districts – Lakhimpur, Sibsagar, Darrang and Nowgong – was ordered.[107] The opium ban was implemented in 1860 – however, without banning the lucrative sale of north Indian opium, which was a very profitable source of income for the government.[108] Jenkins was convinced that the only way to overcome the problem of labour shortage in the tea plantations was to import labourers from other parts of British India, and strongly recommended this as follow-up action.[109]

The planters approached the government for assistance in procuring labour from Bengal. Williamson, one of the important and influential figures among the planters in Assam, wrote in November 1859:

> as to the measures which the Government could adopt to assist the Tea Planters in extending the cultivation of the tea plant, I think a moderate increase in the land revenue would in some degree tend towards this object and might be carried out without detriment. A decrease in the Opium cultivation would also cause a greater number of labourers to work on Tea plantations. A steady flow of emigrant labor in the province is, I think, the principle means by which the cultivation of the Tea plant can be extensively increased. An emigration scheme to be successful would require to be conducted under the auspices of Government and a fund for the purpose provided by the Tea Planters.[110]

A Tea Planters' Association was formed in December 1859 for the purpose of lobbying with the government on matters of labour. They requested setting up of a government emigration agent and demanded that imported labourers should be engaged for five years. To deal with the problem of runaway labourers, they urged the government to amend the law for cognizance of a breach of contract. They also expected provision of infrastructure for the transportation of labourers by placing a sufficient number of steamers and flats on the Brahmputra river to keep up regular monthly communication.[111] The district officials in the Assam Valley worked in close collaboration with the planters and provided them with all possible assistance, including recommending their demands to superior officers. On the issue of labour supply, Captain Holroyd, the Collector of Sibsagar, wrote to Colonel Jenkins, Commissioner of Assam: 'every assistance should be given by the Government to the planter in bringing emigrants into the province, and this I think can be best done by organizing under Government patronage a sound system of emigration'. He was convinced that if sufficient labour was made available, 'the Assam Tea planter would soon become in a position to increase greatly the field of his operations, and the trade and prosperity of the province be in like measure advanced'.[112]

The government of Bengal, however, had a different perception of the labour problem in the Assam tea plantations. The Lieutenant Governor believed that the problem was not inadequate availability of labour but the lack of competitive wages offered by Assam planters, which was the main reason they were unable to attract sufficient labour from Bengal. Here, it may not be out of place to reproduce at length the communication of the government of Bengal to Jenkins, summing up its position on this matter.

> This is work in which men, women and grown children of a whole family can be employed; and it is therefore most favourable for the importation of labour at a moderate charge, and the fixing of a new labouring population in the neighbourhood of Tea plantations. It is also found that the profit of Tea cultivation is such as richly to repay an adequate expenditure in increasing it. This state of things indicates the propriety of high wages; and the generally scanty population of Assam, its remote position, and its difficulty of access for poor people from populous parts of India, indicate the expediency of having resort to a systematic course of proceeding in the importation of labor from other parts of India. But it is not for Government but for those immediately interested in the Tea Plantations of Assam, to apply themselves to this and as to other requirements of their position. If they do so, they may be sure that whatever Government can legitimately do to facilitate their endeavours, will be readily done.[113]

It was pointed out that in remote and scantily populated Assam, labour could be attractive only if the wages offered were higher than that prevalent in Bengal.[114] The planters were not too pleased with this response of the government of Bengal pointing to 'shirking' of responsibility and neglecting to augment the supply of labour from other areas. William Nassau Lee, a planter and spokesperson of the tea industry, was scathing in his criticism. After all the British Indian government had 'induced' English capitalists to invest large sums of money and effort in a project of 'Imperial' importance, and therefore it was expected that facilities would be provided by it. It was a severe blow to the 'credulous' capitalist that the government of Bengal had ignored all its responsibilities and refused to take any action whatsoever, 'which was nothing short of abandoning the prerogatives of the Government, and shifting its highest duties and responsibilities from their legitimate and proper resting place, to the shoulders of a few tea planters'.[115] Thus the supply and retention of labour in the newly opened up tea plantations in Assam remained a problem in the first two decades. However, the use of physical coercion and extra-legal means to control and tame labour, characteristic features of the later indenture system, did not appear to be in practice during this period.

The concern over losing labourers and jeopardizing production at this stage of its enterprise drew caution from the Assam Company's management. Even while not offering higher wages to prevent labour from deserting, the company's Directors instructed the superintendent of its plantations in Upper Assam that 'they positively forbid any violence on the part of the assistants to the natives of the country or to the coolies of the Association and on any such case being formally reported immediate dismissal will most assuredly be the penalty'.[116] All this was to change with the dramatic events of the 1860s.

'Tea Mania': A Speculative Boom

The success and rapid progress of the two tea companies and individual tea planters attracted further capital. However, it was the publication of Lord Canning's Resolution offering wasteland grants at very lucrative terms in October 1861 that triggered off events in the form of a wild speculative boom, or 'tea mania', as it has been described by the official historian of the Indian tea industry.[117] The Resolution aimed at the inclusive interests of the European speculators as the Governor General 'confidently expects that harmony of interest between permanent European settlers and the half-civilized tribes by whom most of these waste districts, or the country adjoining them, are thinly peopled, will conduce to the material and moral improvement of the Queen's Indian subjects'.[118] It sanctioned the alienation of wastelands in fee-simple and redemption of land revenue of wastelands already granted on leasehold tenures. The land was offered at a fixed price of Rs 2–8 to Rs 5 an acre. Later, in August 1862, these rules were modified at the insistence of the Secretary of State for India, and came to be known as 'fee-simple' rules under which the land was to be sold through public auctions. All unassessed wastelands free of any proprietary claims were made available for sale, and payment could be made in instalments within ten years of the completion of sale. The size of the lot for purchase was not to exceed 3,000 acres, but any individual buyer could buy any number of lots. The rules required the demarcation and survey of each lot before sale. However these precautionary measures were found to be very inconvenient by the speculators and pressure was mounted to remove them. The government, in its anxiety not to appear as creating any obstacles to the 'progress of industry', quickly relaxed these conditions. It also removed the conditionality of showing means to cultivate wastelands while seeking grants.[119] This generated a massive rush for grants and resulted in reckless speculation, land-grabbing and over-extensions. It was reported that applications poured in for grant of 558,078 acres in Cachar district alone, while other tea districts too experienced a similar rush.[120] The official historian of the Indian tea industry described these developments as follows: 'A madness comparable in intensity with that of the South Sea Bub-

TABLE 1.2
Jorehaut Company: Acreage under Tea, Production and Dividends, 1860–65[124]

Year	Acreage Granted	Acreage under Tea	Crop (lbs)	Dividends (%)
1860	2,919	716	118,949	5.00
1861	6,000	778	193,476	8.70
1862	8,539	1,021	262,260	13.00
1863	–	1,373	295,224	36.00
1864	22,920	15,61	270,948	34.00
1865	22,920	1,931	327,050	12.00

ble seized men's minds, and normally level headed financiers and speculators began to scramble wildly for tea shares and tea lands.'[121] The tea industry experienced very rapid expansion and raised expectations of high profits. In 1862, Lee reported, there were 160 tea plantations in Assam owned by 60 companies and individuals. Of these owners, five were joint-stock companies, fifteen were private companies and the rest were individuals.[122] Over the course of next three years, thirty-eight and twenty new tea companies were registered in Calcutta and London respectively.[123] The recently incorporated Jorehaut Company did exceedingly well during the 'tea mania' years. (See Table 1.2 above.)

The Assam Company had acquired a massive grant of 33,365 acres in 1840 itself, which it expanded in acreage. It steadily expanded its crop and declared handsome dividends during the 'tea mania' years of between 12 to 25 per cent.[125] Joint-stock companies mushroomed overnight and speculators fraudulently sold non-existent or under-prepared tea gardens at extravagant prices to unsuspecting and ignorant investors in England. The *modus operandi* of the speculator was to gain possession of one or more lots of wasteland, bring a portion of it under some sort of a semblance to tea cultivation in the shortest period possible, and then sell it to joint companies or other investors who were keen to make quick fortunes.[126] Greedy to make quick money, the agents on the spot often misled the promoters of the companies by lumping together one or two really good gardens with three or four inferior jungle-tracts, and selling the lot to the company at prices that were two or three times higher their actual value.[127] Other forms of fraud also prevailed. Often money was invested in 'gardens' that never existed. Tea companies with or without land sprang up overnight and shares rose to dizzy heights. Lands were cleared without any consideration of their suitability for cultivation or availability of labour.[128] Colonel Edward Money, in his prize-winning essay, reported that a small garden of 30 to 40 acres was often sold to a company as 150 or 200 acres.

It was done over and over again. The price paid, moreover, was quite out of proportion even to the supposed area. Two or three lakhs of rupees (£20,000 or 30,000) have often been paid for such gardens, when not more than two years old, and forty per cent of the existing area, vacancies. The original cultivator 'retired' and the company carried on.[129]

Edgar, a Bengal civilian, described this period as a dishonest and reckless era in tea planting. 'The evils of this reckless speculation', he reported, 'in waste lands were greatly aggravated by the inadequacy of the provisions for demarcation and survey made in the Assam rule.'[130]

The 'tea mania' boom busted in 1866 and the tea industry went deep into crisis. By the end of 1870, 56 out of 65 companies registered up to 1866 went into liquidation. Over one million pounds were lost by speculative investors in India and Britain within five years.[131] The Assam Company sustained losses in 1865 and 1866, and could not pay dividends for the next four years.[132] The Jorehaut Company also failed to declare any dividends in 1867. The land under tea began to lapse into jungle and, in some cases, tea gardens were formally abandoned. The shareholders, lacking confidence, sold their holdings quickly at whatever price they could get, and thus deepened the crisis. 'One distressing feature connected with these mushroom companies', Campbell reported with anguish,

> was the ruin, misery, and destitution in which they involved numbers of young men whom they engaged in England and sent to Assam, and who, when collapse came, found themselves suddenly turned adrift in a most inhospitable country without a penny or a friend; some died, others had literally to beg their way out of Assam.[133]

In many cases, the families of these young men lost their investments as they had been duped into buying shares of these companies in England. However the worst sufferers were the migrant labourers who had been mobilized from other parts of British India and transported to Assam to work on the rapidly expanding plantations.

The newly launched 'coolie trade', for which the impetus was given by the actions of speculators, was a flourishing business for the recruiters and contractors in Calcutta, but resulted in the misery, disease and death of countless migrant labourers both during transit and in the tea districts. The recruited labour was sent to Assam via Calcutta by river transport, a journey that often took more than a month. No proper facilities for food, water, sanitation and medical care were provided during the passage. The result was starvation, disease and consequently a high rate of mortality during transit. The description of the recruitment and transportation of migrant labourers by William Nassau Lee, a staunch defender of the planters and no sympathizer of labour, is comparable to the horrors of slave ships carrying African slaves across the Atlantic.[134] He wrote:

Coolies were contracted by private parties as so many sheep or bullocks, the contractor receiving a certain sum for those who arrived in the district and for those who died en route but not for deserters. . . . False representation, corruption, oppression of every and the worst description were used to swell the numbers of contractors' recruits. The old and decrepit, the young and tender, the halt, the maimed, and the blind – nay even the infected, the diseased, and the dying, were pressed into the service of these most degraded of crimps. There was no Government Protector, no Medical Examiner. On arriving at the depots, these unfortunate creatures were located in filthy places, with pestilential vapours which were deadly to human life. The cesspools caused many to contract the germs of distemper and disease and in this state they were placed in gangs on board boats to be sent to the final destination. Here crowded and huddled together and compelled to live in a state of uncleanliness. As might be expected, cholera and other malignant diseases broke out with fearful effect. In some instances, ten per cent of these wretched victims were carried off in as many days. In others, mortality rates reached to forty or fifty per cent during the three week voyage. With some truth it may be said that the horrors of the slave trade pale before the horrors of the coolie trade of Assam and Cachar in the years 1861–62.[135]

The Bengal government acknowledged that:

The system under which the Tea Plantations of Assam and Cachar are supplied with labourers from Bengal has attracted the serious attention of Government during the year. It was reported that in almost every shipment of labourers from Calcutta a fearful amount of mortality occurred from Cholera and other diseases during the journey. In one case the mortality was said to have reached even to fifty per cent.[136]

The situation did not get any better for the migrants after their arrival in the tea districts. Lee's description of equally painful experiences for them at their destination does not find any fault with the planters. His narrative continues:

Yet is the worst not told. The dead feels no pain – let us follow the living. Arrived at their destination, many urged that they were unequal to field labour, that they had been engaged as artisans, menial servants – nay priests of temples, at treble the rates of wages they were offered. But the planters had contracted for coolies, – had paid for them, as such – they had signed contracts to serve as such for three or five years – they were able bodied – they must work. But what of the weak, the halt, the maimed, and the blind? Rejected by the planters as useless, they were turned adrift, to find their way, penniless, hundreds of miles to their village homes, or, more probably, to starve – to die![137]

A Special Commission appointed in July 1862 to conduct investigations into the whole affair presented a horrible picture of labour life in the tea plantations. The Commissioners found the prevalence of great abuses in the coolie trade, which was regarded as an ordinary commercial transaction between a native contractor and the planter: 'all parties considering duty and responsibility discharged when the living are landed, and the cost of the dead adjusted'.[138] The Commission reported the complete absence of any regulatory system of supervision, including medical attendance, at all points of recruitment, transit depots and transportation. These revelations in turn warranted state intervention, and the Bengal Native Labour Act III of 1863 was passed by the Bengal Legislative Council for the regulation of emigration to the districts of Assam, Sylhet and Cachar. It provided that recruiters should be licensed; that every intending emigrant should be produced before the Magistrate of his own district; that he should be medically examined for his fitness to work in the tea districts; and that the contract of service, which could not exceed four years, should be explained to him and executed in the presence of the Superintendent of Emigration. The steamers and boats carrying labourers to the tea districts were also to be licensed. But the Act failed to provide any protection to the labourers once they arrived in the tea gardens.[139] The legislation was meant to provide 'protection' to prospective migrants against deception by contractors, and to lessen mortality during transit and on arrival in tea districts. It failed miserably on both counts, as is clear from the later official reportage.

In 1868, the Bengal government appointed W. Ainslie, H. Stewart Reid and J.M. Cunningham as Commissioners to enquire into the status of the tea industry in Assam, Cachar and Sylhet. On the basis of the evidence collected at Calcutta and in the tea districts, the Commissioners presented an appalling picture of the migrant labourers, both during transit and on arrival in the tea plantations. Most of the labourers for the Assam plantations were recruited from Chota Nagpur, lower Bengal, Bihar and southern parts of the North Western Provinces. They reported practices of deception of the migrants by the recruiters, extremely poor hygenic and sanitary conditions, and a high rate of mortality at the transit depots as well as during the river voyage to Assam.[140] The migrants were promised higher wages and a better life in the plantations. During transit, at the depots, they were guarded like prisoners. Things did not improve upon arrival on the plantations, where

> they found themselves set down in the midst of a swampy jungle far from human habitation where food was scarce and dear, where they have seen their families and fellow labourers struck down in numbers by disease and death, and where they themselves prostrated by sickness and have been able to earn less than they could have in their home. This is no fanciful picture; it has occurred in many instances and when to the ills we have described, the labourer has had to serve a hard master, it is not to be wondered at that he was thoroughly discontented and miserable.[141]

The Commissioners' findings of the 'pitiable' and 'truly deploreable' life

TABLE 1.3
Statement of Death Rates in Tea Gardens in Upper Assam, 1865–66[143]

Name of Garden	Half year	Ratio of deaths per 1,000 during the half year
Nagapholee	2nd of 1865	162.36
Doomdooma	"	223.30
Rungolating	"	288.88
Wilton	"	161.49
Moran Company's	"	246.49
Gilladharee	"	393.61
Rungajan	"	234.32
Cherido	2nd of 1866	365.44
Deopani	"	351.98
Tiphok	"	217.38

and conditions of labour in the tea gardens presented the most severe indictment of the tea industry during the 'tea mania' period:

> In the mad race of speculation, when fresh clearances were made, and acre upon acre covered with tea, to meet the terms of contract entered into with the promoters of new, or to satisfy the shareholders in old companies, no one has suffered more than the unfortunate labourer, for the opening out of new Tea Cultivation has been too often synonymous with disease and death.[142]

The Commissioners supported their remarks with figures of mortality in several tea gardens (see Table 1.3).

Campbell, Assistant Commissioner of Barpeta district in 1872, reported the lack of proper accommodation or medical help for the newly arrived labourers in the gardens. Not accustomed to this kind of work, climate and diet, the migrants fell prey to serious illnesses and succumbed to death. 'In one extreme case the mortality in the garden was so excessive that the manager deserted it, leaving the dead unburied and the dying without help.'[144] For the survivors matters were made worse when they were subjected to gross ill-treatment at the hands of the planters. While presenting his report on tea cultivation plantations in 1873, J.W. Edgar remarked: 'The mortality among immigrants into the tea districts in the early days of the industry is generally understood to have been great; but few people, I believe, realize how appalling it actually was.'[145] He reported that between May 1863 and May 1866, about 84,915 labourers were imported into the Assam tea gardens. But the returns for 1866 showed only 49,750 as working on the gardens. The remaining 35,165 had either died or deserted. 'All must have died during the three years or have absconded and not been caught, and it is a terrible certainty that the greater number of the latter must have died of hunger or exhaustion in the jungles.'[146] Both the Commissioners of 1868 and Edgar were emphatic that the number of imported labourers during these years far exceeded the supply of food available for them, and attributed much of the sickness and high mortality to want of food sufficient in quantity and variety. Assam, being predominantly a province dependent on subsistence agriculture, did not produce surplus food, and the poor means of communication meant that the import of food could not keep pace with the sharp increase in demand due to the large number of labourers brought into the province.[147]

Both Edgar and Campbell held the government's wasteland policy responsible for encouraging the 'tea mania'. 'There can be no doubt that the reckless speculation and insane attempts to extend cultivation led to the depression of the tea industry in 1866 and that the following years were very much encouraged by the way in which waste lands were dealt by the Government.'[148] Edgar lamented the fact that the government, despite being aware of the situation in the tea gardens, did not insist on the district officers protecting the labourers under the existing law. Campbell felt that by providing wastelands without either demarcations or surveys to the speculators, the government had 'materially hasten[ed] the catastrophe in tea'.[149] Lee, the planter, also held the government culpable for the 'catastrophe in tea' during the 'tea mania' years, but from a different perspective altogether. He was, as pointed out earlier, critical of the Bengal government for ignoring the recommendations of the district officials and the planters' appeals for assistance in mobilizing labour from outside the province.

> The results of this inaction on the part of the Government of Bengal, were very lamentable. Situated in a country in which it is a notorious that no important operation, if new, can be undertaken with the remotest chance of success, without Government supervision and support, the planters, thus abandoned, were driven back on their own resources.[150]

Matters were made worse for the planters, he complained, by the Public Works Department's entry into the labour market of a province already 'strained to the utmost limit', pushing wages up: 'the crying want of the province was a sufficiency of labour, it behoved the ruling authority to use every exertion to increase rather than to diminish the supply'.[151] In desperation, the planters turned to large-scale import of labour through the agency of 'villainous' native contractors whose supplies were unfit for labour. They were dying in large numbers, causing a loss of investment and restricting extensions. Many of the survivors deserted, breaking their contracts and aggravating the planters. Lee quipped, 'Ill-feeling naturally arose.'[152] This was his rationalization for the ill-treatment of imported labourers by planters on the tea plantations. Lee, while giving this graphic account of the suffering of migrant labourers at the depots and during transit, was silent about their treatment at the hands of the planters in the plantations.

The 'tea mania' boom came and went, but the tea industry survived. Campbell could state the revival of confidence among planters by 1869. He reported the improvement of the quality of tea which had suffered during the reckless speculation years, and, as a result, better prices, profits and declaration of dividends.[153] The prospects of tea cultivation began to improve. However, small and individual owners lost control of the management of their tea plantations. Even if many of them remained owners of plantations, their names disappeared from official reportage. The post 'tea mania' years ushered in an era of corporatization of the tea industry, and the management of tea plantations came under the monopolistic control of managing agency houses in Calcutta with their headquarters in the UK. The operation of bigger companies stimulated the amalgamation of smaller gardens into larger-scale enterprises. The Assam Company was the first to initiate this process by appointing Schoene, Kilburn and Company as their managing agents in 1867.[154] This recovery and stability of the tea industry after the disastrous speculative boom period was closely linked to the setting up of an indentured labour regime in the Assam plantations, following the passing of Act VI of 1865 by the Bengal government.

Notes and References

[1] John Burnett, *Liquid Pleasures: Social History of Drinks in Modern Britain*, Florence: KY, USA: Routledge, 1999, p. 52.

[2] Ibid.

[3] Ibid., p. 53.

[4] For further details, see B.R. Mitchell and Phyllis Deane, *Abstract of British Historical Statistics*, Cambridge: Cambridge University Press, 1962, pp. 266–91; K.N. Chaudhury, *The Trading World of Asia and the English East India Company 1660–1760*, Cambridge: Cambridge University Press, 1978, pp. 388–94.

[5] Burnett, *Liquid Pleasures*, p. 53.

[6] Michael Greenberg, *British Trade and the Opening of China 1800–42*, Cambridge: Cambridge University Press, 1969, p. 3; Chun Wai Tang (Kenny), 'A Global Technological Diffusion – Traditional Chinese Tea Technology and Its Contribution to Modern Tea Production in the 19th Century', unpublished Master's dissertation, Simon Fraser University, USA, October 2008.

[7] Hoh-Cheung Mui and Lorna H. Mui, 'The Commutation Act and the Tea Trade in Britain 1784–1793', *The Economic History Review*, New Series, Vol. 16, No. 2, 1963, pp. 234–35.

[8] Immanuel C.Y. Hsu, *The Rise of Modern China*, New York: Oxford University Press, 1995, p. 149.

[9] Greenberg, *British Trade*, p. 3.

[10] Ibid., pp. 3–4.

[11] Ibid.

[12] For the development of tea trade, and the triangular system of settlements between India, China and England, see ibid.

[13] Frances Moulder, *Japan, China and the Modern World Economy*, Cambridge: Cambridge University Press, 1977, p. 100.

[14] Hsu, *The Rise*, p. 150.

[15] Moulder, *Japan*, p. 102.

[16] Hunt Janin, *The India–China Opium Trade in the Nineteenth Century*, London: McFarland & Company, Inc., 1999, p. 37.

[17] Susan Naquin and Evelyn Rawski, *Chinese Society in the Eighteenth Century*, New Haven, CT: Yale University Press, 1987, p. 233.

[18] Increase in spending on opium caused a stagnation in the demand for other commodities, with a consequent general sluggishness in the market. The constant inflow of opium also caused a continuous outflow of silver. Hsu, *The Rise*, p. 172.

[19] Hsin-pao Chang, *Commissioner Lin and the Opium War*, Cambridge, Mass.: Harvard University Press, 1964, pp. 29–32.

[20] Chang, *Commissioner Lin*, pp. 98–99.

[21] Janin, *Indo–China*, p. 50; Moulder, *Japan*, p. 105.

[22] Greenberg, *British Trade,* pp. 196–215.

[23] A. Kiefer, 'The Tea Industry of India and Ceylon: Its Development and Current State', in *The Treatise of the Imperial Royal Geographical Society in Vienna*, Vol. IV, No. 3, 1902, Vienna: K.U.K. Hof-U. Universitats-Buchhandlung. I am grateful to Dr Felicitas Hentschke of Re:Work, International Research Centre, Work and Human Lifecycle in Global History, Humboldt University, Berlin, for translating the German text into English for me.

[24] Copy of Papers Received from India Related to the Measures Adopted for Introducing the Cultivation of the Tea Plant within the British Possessions in India, Parliamentary Papers, 1839, p. 5.

[25] Ibid., p. 7; William Nassau Lees, *Tea Cultivation, Cotton and other Agricultural Experiments in India, A Review*, Calcutta: Thacker, Spink & Co., 1863, p. 2

[26] Parliamentary Papers, 1839, p. 11.

[27] Ibid.

[28] Lees, *Tea Cultivation*, p. 2; Harold H. Mann, *The Early History of the Tea Industry in North-East History of India*, Calcutta: The Calcutta General Printing Co., 1918, p. 4.

[29] Parliamentary Papers, 1839, pp. 8–15.

[30] Ibid.

[31] According to Lucile H. Brockway, the British botanical gardens under the auspices of Royal Botanical Gardens at Kew in London played a critical role in generating and disseminating useful scientific knowledge which facilitated transfer of energy, manpower and capital on a worldwide basis and unprecedented scale during the nineteenth century. Lucile H. Broakway, 'Science and Colonial Expansion: The Role of the Royal Botanical Gardens', *American Ethnologist*, Vol. 6, No. 3, 1979, pp. 449–65. Also see Jayeeta Sharma, 'British science, Chinese skills and Assam tea: Making Empire's Garden', *Indian Economic and Social History Review*, Vol. 43, No. 4, 2006, pp. 429–55.

[32] Parliamentary Papers, 1839, p. 27.

[33] Ibid., p. 21; Lee, *Tea Cultivation*, p. 13.

[34] Ibid., pp. 32–36.

[35] Charlton to Jenkins, 17 May 1834, Parliamentary Papers, 1839, p. 35.

[36] Parliamentary Papers, 1839, p. 32.

[37] Ibid., p. 38.

[38] For more details on this community, see M'Cosh, *Topography of Assam*.

[39] Parliamentary Papers, 1839, p. 58.

[40] Ibid., p. 66.

[41] The British got their first opportunity of political intervention in Assam when the Moamaria Revolt broke out against the Ahom kings in the late eighteenth century. For details, see E.

Gait, *A History of Assam*, Calcutta: Thacker, Spink & Co., 1906; S.K. Bhuyan, *Anolo-Assafnese Relations 1771–1826*, Gauhati: Lawyer's Book Stall, 1949.

⁴² The process of annexation, however, was not peaceful and uncontested. For a detailed account, see H.K. Barpuzari, *Assam in the Days of the Company 1826–58*, Shillong: United Publishers, 1963, pp. 142–57; Rebati Mohan Lahiri, *The Annexation of Assam, 1824–54*, Calcutta: Firma K.L. Mukhopadhyay, 1975; N.K. Barooah, *David Scott in North-East India 1801–31: A Study of British Paternalism*, New Delhi: Munshilal Manoharlal, 1972. Apart from Assam, other areas where the possibility of tea cultivation existed, viz. Cachar, Coorg and Mysore, were also annexed to the British dominions on one pretext or the other.

⁴³ For further details, see Amalendu Guha, 'Colonization of Assam: Years of Transitional Crises, 1825–40', *Indian Economic and Social History Review*, No. 2, June, 1868, pp. 125–40.

⁴⁴ Parliamentary Papers, 1839, p. 68.

⁴⁵ Ibid., p. 71.

⁴⁶ Ibid., p. 69.

⁴⁷ Lees, *Tea Cultivation*, pp. 25–26; Mann, *Early History*, pp. 13–14.

⁴⁸ Anonymous, *Assam: Sketch of its History, Soil, and Productions: with the Discovery of the Tea Plant, and of the Countries Adjoining Assam*, London: Smith, Elder and Co., 1839, p. 21.

⁴⁹ C.A. Bruce, *Report on the Manufacture of Tea, and the Extent and Produce of the Tea Plantations in Assam*, Calcutta: Bishop's College Press, 1839. In his report Bruce acknowledged the assistance, in the discovery of tea tracts, of 'A Dewaniah . . . who was well acquainted with the leaf, as he had been in the habit of drinking tea during his residence with the Singphos' (p. 4). The reference here is to Maniram Dewan, who was later employed by the Assam Company to help Bruce with the production of tea.

⁵⁰ Parliamentary Papers, 1839, p. 91.

⁵¹ From Major A. White, Political Agent, Upper Assam, to Captain F. Jenkins, 30 May 1836, Parliamentary Papers, 1839, p. 69.

⁵² Parliamentary Papers, 1839, p. 114.

⁵³ Tea Committee to W.H. Macnaghten, Secretary to Governor-General, 6 August 1836, Parliamentary Papers, 1839, p. 77.

⁵⁴ Bruce to Jenkins, 1 October 1836, Parliamentary Papers, 1839, p. 85.

⁵⁵ Ibid., p. 79.

⁵⁶ C.A. Bruce, *An Account of the Manufacture of the Black Tea as now practice in Suddeya in Upper Assam*, Calcutta: G.H. Huttmann, Calcutta Military Orphan Press, 1838.

⁵⁷ Parliamentary Papers, 1839, p. 105.

⁵⁸ R.D. Mangles, Officiating Secretary, GoI, to the Tea Committee, 30 October 1837, Parliamentary Papers, 1839, p. 115.

⁵⁹ Ibid.; Lee, *Tea Cultivation*, p. 27; Mann, *Early History*, p. 16.

⁶⁰ *Chambers' Edinburgh Journal*, 9, 417, January 1840, pp. 2–3; *Penny Magazine of the Society for the Diffusion of Useful Knowledge*, 9, 50, February 1840, pp. 59–71.

⁶¹ Parliamentary Papers, 1839, p. 94.

⁶² Ibid., p. 96.

⁶³ Lee, *Tea Cultivation*; Mann, *Early History*, p. 19; H.A. Antrobus, *A History of the Assam Company*, Edinburgh: T. and A. Constable, 1957, p. 35.

⁶⁴ Assam Company Papers (hereafter ACP), Ms. No. 9924, Vol. 1, p. 1, London Minute Book, 12 February 1839, Guildhall Library, London.

⁶⁵ Antrobus, *Assam Company*, p. 37.

⁶⁶ ACP, Ms. No. 9924, Vol. 1, p. 11, London Minute Book, 14 February 1839; Antrobus, *Assam Company*, p. 37.

⁶⁷ *Englishman*, 29 June 1839, cited in Mann, *Early History*, p. 19; B. Blair Kling, *Partners*

in Empire: Dwarkanath Tagore and the Age of Enterprise in Eastern India, California: University of California Press, 1976, p. 145; Antrobus, *Assam Company*, p. 39.

[68] *Bengal Harkaru*, 31 May 1939, cited in Kling, *Partners*, p. 147.

[69] Mann, *Early History*, p. 20; Kling, *Partners*, p. 147; Griffiths, *The History*, p. 62.

[70] ACP, Ms. No. 9925, Proceedings of the Committee in Bengal, Vol. 1, p. 9; Kling, *Partners*, pp. 147, 153–54; Antrobus, *Assam Company*, p. 154; Kalyan K. Sircar, 'A Tale of Two Boards: Some early management problems of Assam Company Limited, 1839–1864', *Economic and Political Weekly*, Vol. XXI, Nos. 10–11, 1986, pp. 453–59.

[71] ACP, Proceedings of the Committee in Bengal, pp. 6–12 and 24–25.

[72] Lee, *Tea Cultivation*, p. 28; Antrobus, *Assam Company*, pp. 44–46.

[73] Auckland Private Letter Book, Vol. XII, 11 July 1840, British Museum Additional Manuscripts 37700, cited in Kling, *Partners*, p. 151.

[74] Antrobus, *Assam Company*, p. 46.

[75] S. Bhattacharya, 'Laissez-Faire in India', *Indian Economic and Social History Review*, Vol. II, No. 1, 1965, pp. 1–22.

[76] B.H. Baden Powell, *The Land Systems of British India*, Oxford: Clarendon Press, 1892 (reprint, Delhi, 1974), Vol. III, p. 410; Amalendu Guha, *Planter Raj to Swaraj: Freedom Struggle and Electoral Politics in Assam 1826–1947*, New Delhi: Indian Council of Historical Research, 1977, p. 13; Barpujari, *Assam*, p. 212; Mohammad Abu Siddique, *Evolution of Land Grants and Labour Policy of Government: The Growth of the Tea Industry in Assam 1834–1940*, New Delhi: South Asian Publications, 1990, p. 11.

[77] Baden-Powell, *The Land Systems*, p. 412; Guha, *Planter Raj*, p. 13.

[78] Revenue and Judicial Letters from India and Bengal, 14th March 1837, No. 5, cited in Barpujari, *Assam*, p. 235.

[79] Guha, *Planter Raj*, p. 14; Siddique, *Evolution*, p. 19.

[80] Siddique, *Evolution*, p. 19.

[81] Reports on the Tea and Tobacco Industries in India, 1874, pp. 32–33.

[82] Mann, *Early History*, pp. 22–29; Lee, *Tea Cultivation*, pp. 27–30.

[83] Antrobus, *Assam Company*, pp. 407–08.

[84] Papers Relating to Tea Cultivation in Bengal, *Selections from the Records of the Government of Bengal*, No. *XXXVII*, Calcutta: Bengal Military Orphan Press, 1861, pp. 33–35.

[85] Ibid.

[86] Lee, *Tea Cultivation*, pp. 30–31. H.A. Antrobus, *A History of the Jorehaut Company Ltd, 1859–1946*, London: Tea and Rubber Mail, 1948, pp. 19–24.

[87] Edward Money, *The Cultivation and Manufacture of Tea*, Calcutta: Thacker & Co., 1870, p. 2.

[88] Antrobus, *Jorehat Company*, p. 13.

[89] Ibid., pp. 37–39.

[90] Parliamentary Papers, 1839, p. 62.

[91] Antrobus, *Assam Company*, pp. 374–75.

[92] Ibid.

[93] Parliamentary Papers, 1839, p. 62.

[94] ACP, Ms. No. 9925, Vol. 1, pp. 87–144.

[95] ACP, Ms. No. 9925, Vol. 4, Proceedings of Calcutta Committee, 18 July 1846, 13 March 1847 and 18 July 1847, pp. 1014–136.

[96] ACP, Ms. No. 9925, Calcutta Committee Minute Book, Vol. 5, 15 February 1850, p. 111, and Vol. 7, 4 January 1854.

[97] ACP, Ms. No. 9925, Vol. 2, August 1841–July 1844, pp. 350–474.

[98] ACP, Ms. No. 9925, Vol. 2, 1842, pp. 392–441; Kalyan K. Sircar, 'Labour Management: First Twenty Years of Assam Company Limited (1839–59)', *Economic and Political Weekly*, Vol. XXI, No. 22, 1986, pp. M38–M43.

[99] Papers Relating to Tea, 1861, p. 25.

[100] Extract from a Dispatch from the Secretary of State for India, 26 May 1859, Papers Relating to Tea, 1861, p. 1.

[101] Lee, *Tea Cultivation*, p. 328.

[102] It was reported that *duffadars* (labour recruiters) sent to the villages to recruit ryots as labour in the gardens were causing alarm to the Darrang *mauzadars*. The latter agreed among themselves not to let *daffadars* enter their villages because they were 'seducing' young men with drinks and forced advances to take them away from their families and fields. Papers Relating to Tea, 1861, pp. 2–25.

[103] Ibid., p. 24.

[104] Ibid., pp. 3–4.

[105] Ibid., p. 26.

[106] Ibid., p. 24.

[107] Barpuzari, *Assam*, p. 205; Guha, *Planter Raj*, p. 9. But even this increase in land revenue did not induce local peasants to seek employment as labourers in the tea gardens. One possible explanation for this could be the fact that taking up land for cultivation, though still at subsistence level, was more lucrative to the peasants, both from the social and economic point of view, than serving as manual labourers in the tea gardens. Moreover, land was in abundance and easily available for cultivation in the sparsely populated province of Assam.

[108] Guha, *Planter Raj*, p. 9.

[109] Papers Relating to Tea, 1861, p. 25.

[110] Lee, *Tea Cultivation*, p. 333.

[111] Papers Relating to Tea, 1861, pp. 57–62.

[112] Ibid., p.32.

[113] Communication from E.H. Lushington Esq., Officiating Secretary to GoB, to Jenkins, 20 January 1860, Papers Relating to Tea, 1861, p. 39.

[114] Ibid., p. 40.

[115] Lee, *Tea Cultivation*, p. 331.

[116] ACP, Ms. No. 9925, Vol. 2, August 1841–July 1844, p. 112.

[117] Percival Griffiths, *The History of the Indian Tea Industry*, London: Weidenfeld and Nicolson, 1967, pp. 61–69; Radhey Shyam Rungta, *The Rise of Business Corporations in India 1851–1900*, Cambridge: Cambridge University Press, 1970, pp. 94–108.

[118] 'The Sale of Waste Lands and Redemption of Land-Tax in India', *Fraser's Magazine for Town and Country*, 67, 397, January 1863, p. 3.

[119] Papers Regarding the Tea, Parliamentary Papers, Calcutta, 1874, pp. 15–17.

[120] Papers Regarding the Tea, 1874, p. 1.

[121] Griffiths, *History*, p. 96.

[122] Lee, *Tea Cultivation*, p. 32.

[123] Rungta, *Business Corporations*, p. 97.

[124] Antrobus, *Jorehaut Company*, p. 47

[125] Antrobus, *Assam Company*, p. 408.

[126] Papers Regarding the Tea, 1874, p. 33–36.

[127] Often a speculator started forming a company while the land was barely scratched. The company was to 'start by buying the lands he had scarcely finished clearing as accomplished tea garden, and what still remained of undeniable waste, at a cost out of all proportion . . . to what it was worth'. *Friend of India*, 9 June 1874, cited in Rungta, *Business Corporations*, p. 97.

[128] Papers Regarding the Tea, 1874, pp. 17–20.

[129] Edward Money, *Cultivation and Manufacture of Tea*.

[130] Papers Regarding the Tea, 1874, p. 16.

[131] Rungta, *Business Corporations*, p. 103.

[132] Antrobus, *Assam Company*, p. 409.

[133] Papers Regarding the Tea, 1874, p. 34.

[134] Marcuse Rediker, *The Slave Ship: A Human Story*, New York: Penguin Books, 2008.

[135] Lee, however, held only the native recruiters, *arakatis*, responsible for this state of affairs. The European recruiters did not invite such remarks. In fact he cited an official commendation of one Mr Banneritze's recruitment agency. (Lee, *Tea Cultivation*, p. 338.) This did not necessarily mean that he was exaggerating the details in order to malign the native recruiters as the official reports were equally revealing.

[136] Annual Report on the Administration of the Bengal Presidency for the Year 1861–62, cited in Lee, *Tea Cultivation*, p. 340.

[137] Lee, *Tea Cultivation*, p. 339.

[138] Report of the Commissioners Appointed to Enquire into the State and Prospects of Tea Cultivation in Assam, Cachar and Sylhet, 1868, p. 25. (Hereafter Commissioners, 1868.)

[139] Report of the Assam Labour Enquiry Committee (hereafter RALEC), 1906, Appendix A, p. 136.

[140] Commissioners, 1868, p. 25.

[141] Ibid., p. 36.

[142] Ibid., p. 49.

[143] Ibid., p. 54.

[144] Papers Regarding the Tea, 1874, p. 35.

[145] Ibid., p. 21.

[146] Ibid.

[147] Ibid., p. 22; Commissioners, 1868, p. 60.

[148] Papers Regarding the Tea, 1874, p. 18.

[149] Ibid., p. 35.

[150] Lee, *Tea Cultivation*, p. 334.

[151] Ibid., p. 335.

[152] Ibid.

[153] Papers Regarding the Tea, 1874, p. 36.

[154] ACP, Ms. No. 9924, Vol. 9, 27 May 1867; Daniel Houstan Buchanan, *The Development of Capitalistic Enterprise in India*, London: Macmillan Company, 1934 (reprint, 1966), p. 58.

2

Emergence of the Indenture Regime

As we saw in the last chapter, availability of land and capital presented no obstacles to the British for using Assam's wastelands to set up tea plantations. However, mobilization of labour for the fast-expanding tea industry was a critical problem. Assamese peasants, stigmatized as being naturally 'indolent', 'lazy' and largely addicted to opium, could not be mobilized to work on the tea plantations.[1] Nagas and Kacharies cleared up the jungle tracts, but they were found to be too independent to be disciplined, and were unwilling to live on the plantations. Assam was sparsely populated and did not have enough agricultural labourers to meet the growing demand for plantation labour. This led to a search for an alternate source of labour from outside the province. The unwillingness of Assamese peasants and the corresponding absence of a labour market were frequently cited as reasons for long-distance recruiting, but there is no doubt that the high wages demanded by the local labourers was an important trigger. In 1861, a manager of the Jorhat Tea Company reported to his superior that large-scale importation of labour was a *sine qua non* for expansion, considering that local labourers were demanding higher wages and would not agree to work at existing rates, given the high standard of *nirik* (tasks) set in plantations.[2] The Commission of Enquiry reported in 1868 that local wages had doubled since the 1850s and even if local labour was now available, the high price it commands would materially affect the profits of tea cultivation. The wages were increasing because of growing employment by the Public Works Department in the province.[3] Thus the need for cheap and pliant labour in a strict work regime weighed more in the consideration of the planters than the availability of local labour *per se*. However, the argument of absence of a labour market was a constant refrain of the planters in their efforts to secure the active support of the colonial state for establishing and maintaining indentured recruitment along with a vigorous penal contract system in Assam. The colonial state was pliable in providing all possible assistance for mobilizing migrant labour to the planters, despite the knowledge that it was not the absence of a labour market but the abysmally low wages offered in the plantations which failed to attract the local labour. The Commissioners in 1868 reported that the earnings of labourers working in the tea gardens were very small. During their visit to one of the gardens they found that twelve men earned an average of less than Rs 3 in the month of September, and out of this they had to purchase rice at Rs 2 per maund. Sixteen women labourers earned an average of only Rs 1–8 each during the same month. There were reports of a similar nature in the other tea gardens they visited.[4]

The origin of colonial state intervention in the establishment of a penal contract system has to be placed in the context of the rapid expansion during the speculative boom period of the early 1860s, when the appalling conditions of fraudulent recruitment and unsanitary transportation of labourers led to high mortality rates and large-scale desertions from the plantations. The planters had rebuffed the advice of the Lieutenant Governor of Bengal to offer competitive wages in order to attract migrants from outside Assam, and instead initiated a process of assisted migration from the neighbouring provinces, i.e. recruitment through native professional recruiters, *arakatis*, who operated in districts of eastern India.[5] The system of recruitment that developed under this arrangement was full of abuses, leading to tragic consequences such as serious illnesses and high mortality among the migrants who had been mobilized by these private recruiters. The scale of mortality and desertion was considered serious enough by the colonial authorities to warrant state intervention, departing from its avowed policy of non-intervention in matters of labour relations, in the form of the Bengal Native Labour Act III (B.C.) of 1863, with the objective of regulating the emigration system to Assam, Cachar and Sylhet.[6] This legislation introduced a licence system of recruitment, stipulating that migrants be produced before a magistrate in their home districts and undergo a medical examination to test their fitness to work, before agreeing to the five-year labour contract. The terms of the legislation were to be explained to the migrants before executing the contract in the presence of the Superintendent of Emigration. The Act also provided for the licensing of steamers and boats carrying labourers to Assam.[7] However, as pointed out earlier, the legislative intervention failed to redress the problem of high mortality and the large number of desertions.[8] The planters were concerned not so much with the human misery suffered by the migrant labourers but the financial losses caused by desertions, a constant source of anxiety for them.

Prior to the enactment of indenture legislations, the actions of the planters for recovering runaway labourers and the harsh punishment meted to them on recovery were illegal, and in violation of the existing law dealing with default of contracts. Under the existing provisions, a labourer breaking his/

her contract could be punished only by a judicial authority under Section 492 of the Penal Code, which provided for one month's imprisonment in the case of defaulters who had been imported – and there was no provision for the arrest of runaways without a warrant.[9] The flagrant violation of the law and resort to extra-legal methods by the planters were generally overlooked by most district officials despite their knowledge, as Edgar and the 1868 Commission reported, of the most inhuman and cruel treatment of labourers by the planters. The Assam Company had organized an establishment of *chapprassies* and *burkandauzes* to pursue the runaways, capture and bring them back to the gardens, in violation of the existing provisions of law. One incident of taking cognizance of these violations in May 1864 by R.P. Davis, the Superintendent of Police in Sibsagar district, provoked a strong and angry reaction from the Assam Company. The police officer had apprehended two employees of the Company and fined them Rs 5 for illegally 'capturing' 'absconding' labourers, one of whom was working at his residence. In defence of his action, Davis informed his superior that one of the 'captured' men had complained of ill treatment and beatings, which he personally verified on physical examination.[10] J. Smith, the Superintendent of Assam Company, wrote a very angry letter to the Commissioner of Assam protesting against the action of the police officer. While not denying the illegality, he asserted that a system of capturing 'absconders' had been put in place by several tea gardens across Assam and Cachar because, in the 'interests of all concerned in the welfare of the country . . . a proper control should be exercised over imported labour'.[11] He was unable to comprehend the action of the Sibsagar police officer as this system was both recognized and encouraged by his counterparts in other districts. He demanded 'protection' of the Company's investment in the import of emigrant labour. This incident triggered off a series of communications among the colonial bureaucracy seeking increased and urgent government intervention. Alarmed by the increasing desertions by emigrant labour in the Assam tea plantations, A. Aden, Secretary to the Government of Bengal, informed the Government of India that relations then existing between the planters and imported migrant labourers were on a 'most unsatisfactory footing', and a 'serious and growing evil has sprung up which must be dealt with vigorously and promptly'.[12] It was argued that government intervention should proceed beyond the existing law (Act III of 1863) and start regulating the interests of the planters as well as of the labourers after their arrival in the tea plantations. It was suggested that government intervention, instead of ceasing with the migrants' arrival, should continue for the duration of their contract on the plantations. H. Hopkinson, Commissioner of Assam, believed that the existing law, by which the planters had to seek magisterial help to recover absconders, was 'scarcely fair' to them; therefore there was a need to provide 'protection' of their interests, otherwise they will be 'compelled to have recourse to measures which are confessedly illegal'.[13]

These recommendations and suggestions were based on the presumption of 'protection' of the interests of planters as well as of labourers. As the planters had incurred 'considerable' expenses on imported labour, some effective steps were required to prevent 'such breaches of contract by the labourers as are now . . . daily occurrence'.[14] The act of breaching their contracts by labourers, it was admitted, was due to the fact that the wages actually received by the migrants were often far below their expectations and obtainable in the neighbourhood of their homes. As a consequence, the migrant displayed 'careless indifference to the interest of the master . . . sullen idleness and apathy, constant attempts to abscond, and sometimes even violence to the employer'.[15] The remedy suggested was payment of a secure minimum wage at a monthly rate. At the same time, it was suggested that the law be amended to 'compel' the 'protected' labourer to perform his work and that a penalty should be imposed for wilful neglect, breach of contract or absconding.[16] These suggestions and recommendations were to become the foundation stones of indenture legislations for regulating labour relations in the Assam tea plantations during the next half a century, beginning with the Assam Contract Act VI of 1865. The Bengal government thus legalized the 'illegal' acts of planters, and instead of strictly enforcing the existing law to deal with the issue of desertions, enacted a law which empowered the planters with right of arrest of runaway coolies without a warrant.

The new labour legislations introduced the system of indenture contract, which remained in force in the Assam tea plantations, with periodic modifications, till the first decade of the twentieth century. The penal contract system stipulated minimum monthly wages, Rs 5 for men and Rs 4 for women; a three-year contract term; a nine-hour work day; and the appointment of an inspector of labour empowered to cancel the labour contract on complaints of ill treatment. The main provision of the Act was the sanction for breach of contract by labourers: planters were given powers to arrest 'absconding' labourers without a warrant within the limits of the district. Non-compliance with the contract by labourers was considered a criminal offence punishable by imprisonment. The period of imprisonment if convicted under this provision was to be added to the terms of the contract.[17] The grant of such extraordinary powers to the planters and the introduction of penal clauses were justified on grounds of the 'exceptional' circumstances of Assam: poor means of communication, remoteness and isolation of plantations from the administrative centres, made worse by the 'tardiness' and 'inefficiency' of the police. The labourers, it was argued on the other hand, were ensured a minimum wage, housing and medical facilities, and subsidized rice. They were obliged to continuously stay and work in the garden for the period of their contract. The rationale for residential compulsion in the plantation was to protect the planters' investment in the recruitment and transportation of labour, and for fulfilment of their contractual obligations.

Act VI of 1865 was amended in 1870, and again in 1873. The first amendment provided for cancellation of contracts in the case of deserting labourers who had undergone imprisonment for six months. The 1873 amendment was meant to encourage free recruitment for the Assam tea gardens. The Bengal Act VII of 1873 introduced for the first time provisions for recruitment by licensed garden *sirdars,* and also for recruitment outside the Act on short-term, one-year civil contracts.[18] However, given the overwhelming preference for penal contracts by the planters, the innovation of the 1873 Act remained practically unused. For the next eight years, only 17 per cent of the migrants were recruited to Assam under this Act.[19]

The official enquiries carried out in 1868 and 1873 revealed that statutory minimum wages for indentured labour in Assam were not paid, recruitment abuses flourished, and appalling transportation, living and working conditions continued, resulting in high mortality of labour. The labour 'protective' provisions of the Act often remained unimplemented. Section 4 of the Act VI of 1865 provided for a minimum monthly wage of Rs 5 for a man, Rs 4 for a woman and Rs 3 for a child for all imported labourers, unless it was proved before a magistrate that they had wilfully absented themselves from or neglected their work. The Bengal government's instructions were clear: the first duty of the labour protector was 'to see that all labourers are paid their full wages according to contract, and that none of them received less than the minimum wages prescribed by section IV of this Act'.[20] The Commissioners reported that the planters interpreted these wage figures as minimum 'rates' subject to the completion of a daily *nirik* (task), the schedule of which was fixed by them, thus introducing the concept of piece rates instead of conforming to the provision of the Act. The office of the Protectorate remained ineffective with the excuse that many of the staff lacked knowledge, and the long distances to the plantations were an impediment to regular inspections.[21]

Having observed its operation in Assam for nearly eight years as an official, Edgar remained sceptical about the effectiveness of the new legislation (Act VI of 1865) in preventing desertions or reducing mortality. He reported that mortality in the first eighteenth months after its introduction was very high, and the number of deserters who were not arrested was very large. The provision of appointing special protectors of labour remained ineffective in preventing labourers from suffering ill treatment at the hands of planters. On the contrary, it became worse as the planters often displayed intense irritation at the 'interference' of the protectors; their 'periodical visits to the gardens exasperated the planters while doing very little good to the coolies'.[22]

Labour Process in the Tea Garden:
Rationale for Residential 'Compulsion'

At this stage, it is pertinent to ask why the labourers were compelled to reside in the plantations throughout the period of their indenture contract and even afterwards? An understanding of the nature of the labour process adopted by the planter for cultivating and manufacturing tea will explain the rationale behind this compulsion. The frenetic pace of expansion of the tea plantations between 1860s and 1900, starting with the years of the 'tea mania', generated a huge demand for labour; this, in the absence of adequate local supply, necessitated the import of migrant labour from other parts of India. The most important characteristic feature of the plantations which emerged during this period was the requirement of compulsory residence for labourers and other managerial personnel within the tea estates. The compulsion to reside in the garden was linked with the labour process involved in the cultivation and manufacture of tea that was developed and adopted in the Assam plantations. A short description of this labour process and its links with the organization of production will help understand the logic of the compulsion to keep resident labourers on the tea estates.

The process of tea cultivation and manufacture in Assam was evolved in the first two decades through experimentation with Chinese and indigenous methods of using manual labour. C.A. Bruce, upon being appointed the Superintendent of the Government Tea Experimental Station in Upper Assam, learnt and adopted tea cultivation and manufacturing methods from the native Singphos in the Muttuck country, with the help of Chinese tea makers. He learnt about the various stages and seasons of tea cultivation and manufacturing from the Singphos: pruning of plants which were growing wild, hoeing for clearing weeds, digging of the ground, plucking of leaves, and then the process of converting fresh leaf into tea.[23] Most of these stages involved manual labour, and the Singphos produced tea for self-consumption at their own leisure and convenience. Unable to 'persuade' the Singphos to produce tea for the market, Bruce brought seeds from these areas, planted them in the government's experimental station, and followed their methods of production with the help of hired Chinese tea makers and local labourers.[24] Thus, unlike the organization of Chinese tea production, which was predominantly based on the use of peasant household labour, the Assam plantations began producing tea for export with the help of hired labour.[25] The cultivation and manufacturing methods adopted by Bruce, which were almost entirely dependent on manual labour, were further refined and modified later on by other planters in order to increase productivity. The production of tea involved two processes: agricultural and manufacturing. The cultivation process went through different stages and seasons: site selection and clearance; production and sowing of seed; establishment of nurseries; transplanting; digging, weeding and hoeing; pruning; and, finally, plucking.[26]

Nurseries and Transplanting

The geographical locations of tea plantations in the Assam Valley were heavily forested areas. After selection and clearing of the jungle site, the production process began at the nurseries where the tea seeds were carefully sown and reared in special seed-beds prepared for this purpose. After the plants had grown in the nurseries for several months, they were transplanted. The transplanting was generally done during rainy weather so that the plants would have the best opportunity to take root in the new environment. The hot and humid climate of Assam was conducive for the growth of the tea plant, and within three to six years it became fully productive. In the tea gardens located in the plains, the tea plants survived for a very long time, remaining productive for over 6–70 years.

Plucking

Plucking constituted the most significant task in the tea production process, and was performed mostly during the summer months between April and September. The work of plucking began once the new shoots developed five leaves and a bud in addition to a small leaf at the foot of the shoot, known as the sheath leaf or *jhannum*. Plucking was considered a skilled task, and

Women workers plucking tea under supervision

was mostly performed by women and young girls. They carried a basket on their backs, supported by a strap round the forehead: into this the leaves were thrown while plucking with both hands from the bushes. Plucking time was a very busy time in the gardens, and all available hands had to be put to this work. Plucking had a very strong element of continuity in the production process. A week or two after the first flush had been plucked the second flush appeared as shoots growing from the axils or nodes, as they were called, between the leaves left on the first shoot and the stem of the shoot. Ordinarily, this second flush was taken when it was possible to let two leaves remain on the new shoot. After the bud and two leaves of the second flush had been plucked the third flush came within a short time, and so on. Thus plucking had to go on almost continuously from the time of the first flush in April or early May into the month of August or September. During this period the factory too was kept busy manufacturing the leaves that were brought in. In the aftermath of the plucking season began the cold weather tasks of treating the tea bushes and soil for the next season's crop. The season of cold weather lasted from November to March.

Pruning

The first task to be taken up after the bushes ceased to flush was pruning. Regular pruning prevented the tea plant from growing into a full-grown tree and kept it as a low, leafy bush. The bush height was maintained at a height of 2 to 2.5 feet, within reach of the labourers' hands for plucking. Although pruning stunted the growth of the plant, it did not make it less healthy. The purpose of pruning was to encourage flushing and to gain as large a bearing as possible, and this was attained by removing all the dead or injured wood. The tea plant could not be left without pruning indefinitely, for with each season left unpruned the leaf would become smaller and more difficult to gather, and flowers would be produced at the expense of leaf. Pruning was conducted between December and January every year. If pruning was not done in these months, the crop would be lost.

Hoeing

Hoeing was crucial for cleaning of the soil around the bushes which, because of the rain, scorching heat and being trodden by pluckers' feet, got caked; in addition, it attended to overgrowth of weeds. To maintain a healthy bush, clearing of weeds and grass was crucial. Consequently, the soil was required to be 'single'-hoed at least once a month and often more frequently, especially between the months of May and September. Double-hoeing of the soil had to done immediately after the pruning task was over. Child labour was used for cleaning the stems of the bushes and adjacent grounds with the aid of bamboo stakes (*koorpies*).

Digging and Cutting 'Nullahs' (Drains)

The digging and cutting of drains was another important task, and also the heaviest work in the garden. Drainage received very careful consideration, as a proper fall for the water was of paramount importance. Stagnant water was considered fatal to the proper growth of tea and therefore tea land had to be protected from inundation. Drains had to be well-maintained and kept clear of obstructions in order to drain water and prevent inundation. Crole commented that 'Drain digging is about the hardest work that coolies have to perform, and it tries the constitution of even the strongest and most robust.'[27] Besides cutting drains, deep digging work was carried out around the plants once a year, after the end of rainy season. This work was done by using a straight garden fork with a short handle. In addition to the annual digging, a light forking was sometimes required to clear the soil of weeds which could grow during the spring and early summer rains. Apart from work directly related to the tea plant, the labourers were also put to the task of building and repairing roads, bridges, wells and coolie huts within the gardens on a regular basis. These were important tasks in the gardens where infrastructure, housing, etc., were in constant need of repair and maintenance due to the harsh tropical weather conditions.

Manufacturing

The manufacturing process began after the plucking of the green leaf was done. In the early decades, the manufacturing tasks were also performed manually. After plucking, the green tea leaf went through several processes on the way to becoming the final product. These involved withering, rolling, fermenting, drying and firing, sorting and final heating, before packing. Most of these tasks were performed in the factory. From the 1870s onwards machinery and technology were introduced, which was crucial for raising the productivity of tea to larger scales in order to meet the growing export demand. Though manual labourers continued to be used in the factories, with the adoption of mechanization of the manufacturing process, they were reduced in number.

Withering

Withering, an important process by which water from the leaf was taken out, was carried out after the green leaf came from the garden. For this the leaf was exposed to air for a considerable period of time, which resulted in physical and chemical changes. The process involved hoisting the green leaves up to lofts built for this purpose, where they were thinly spread on trays. A gang of children was often employed for this work under close supervision, to ensure tender handling. The length of the withering process varied with the temperature and the state of the leaf.

Rolling

After withering came the process of rolling. The rolling operation broke up the cells of the leaf, and set free the juice or sap in the leaf. Rolling had to be done in such a way as to bruise and distort the cells in order to liberate the juices, and thereby facilitate the next process, fermenting.

Fermenting and Drying

The freeing of its juices prepared the tea leaf for the next process: fermentation. The fermentation process was a natural one which brought about certain chemical changes in the leaf under conditions arranged in the fermenting room. This room was generally separated from the factory, for it was considered important to keep the temperature low. During fermentation the colour of the leaf changed considerably, turning from green to yellowish copper. From the fermenting room the tea was taken back to the factory for drying. The purpose of this operation was to draw out all the moisture from the leaf without ridding it of its juices or essential oils and other properties, which give it its chief value. Once it was fully dried, the tea was sorted, sifted and packed as the final product for marketing.

While tea cultivation continued to be primarily based on manual labour, the manufacturing process began to be mechanized in the 1870s. Machines for rolling, withering, fermenting and drying appeared in the tea factories, and their technology was upgraded from time to time. The increasing productivity of tea resulting from mechanization helped to keep the tea industry profitable in the face of fluctuating and declining market prices. Edward Money, award-winning author of an essay on tea, was very perceptive about the advantages of mechanization in this context. He wrote:

> But though Tea prices may, and we think will, improve, it is not likely we shall ever again see the rates obtainable formerly. This being so, it is probable that only those plantations in the future will pay that produce Tea cheaply. How is this to be done? . . . We allude to the use of machinery, which does much now, and will do more and more as each year passes, to reduce the cost of production.[28]

The relentless push for an increase in tea production during the last three decades of the nineteenth century bore positive results through a combination of new planting as well as raised production from already mature acreage.[29] This was done by intensifying the cultivation process and organizing the work cycle in the manner of an industrial organization, and, at the same time, by mechanizing the process of manufacture. For the sustenance of this production organization, it was imperative that labour was available at all times and during all seasons. This could only be achieved by making the labourers stay in clusters within the plantations, called coolie lines, from where they could be easily mobilized to work, from sunrise to sunset every day. To utilize the maximum amount of sunlight for work, the planters put the garden clock ahead of the rest of Indian subcontinent by one hour, and daily life and work were scheduled on 'garden time'.[30] The intensification drive certainly increased the volume of tasks demanded of labour. David Crole observed:

> In Upper Assam, at any rate, coolies accomplish much more work now than they did twenty or thirty years ago. The daily task ('nirikh') for such work as hoeing, for instance, has increased from 25 to 30 per cent. More than what used to be demanded of coolies. This has been brought about by more efficient supervision.'[31]

The tea plantations in the Assam Valley were designed to extract maximum labour at minimum cost, through low wages and long hours of work.

Minimum Wage vs. Piecework[32]

The wage paid to labour was linked to the performance of various tasks. This, as pointed out earlier, was in violation of the minimum wage fixed under Act VI of 1865. In order to earn their daily wage (*hazira*), the labourers had to complete a standard daily task (*nirik*). Payment for work over and above the standard task amounted to what was called *ticca* (or overtime work). The *nirik* was not determined by a fixed number of hours put in daily by the labourer, but by the work assigned to him/her by the planters based on what they considered to be a reasonable day's labour. There was an understanding in planter-officials' circles that the coolies worked on a primitive, natural notion of time, which enabled this shift from time-wage to task-wage. The 1865 Act fixed a minimum wage subject to completion of nine hours of daily work and six days of work in a week. However, in practice, the wages were determined on the basis of piecework. The Act of 1882 legitimized this practice by making the payment of wage subject to the completion of a daily task, though the daily wage figures of Rs 5, Rs 4 and Rs 3 for men, women and children respectively remained on the statute book. The schedule of the tasks and the rates of payment for the tasks were determined by the planters, though they were required under Section 115 of the Act to put them up at a place accessible to labourers, in both English and Bangla. In practice, the task rates varied across different gardens and remained outside any regulatory system. Section 115 of the Act remained totally ineffective as the district officials were both sceptical and unwilling to enforce it. In 1883, Williams, Deputy Commissioner of Darrang, informed the Chief Commissioner that 'it is a perfect waste of time to make managers put up a schedule of work. On a large garden the tasks vary very much according to the season of the year and the quality of the coolie.' The Chief Commissioner was in agreement with his subordinate's opinion and did not see any value in enforcing this section of the law.[33] In 1891, again, the district officials expressed a similar sentiment:

'in no garden is the task schedule book prescribed by Section 115 properly kept up, and in my mind it appears a most difficult thing to do'. Another official reported that 'A schedule of tasks is sometimes stuck up in the office of teahouse, but it is often in English, and not in Bengali as required by Section 115. I do not think this provision of the law is of much use.'[34] Luttman Johnson, Commissioner of Assam Valley Districts, called the schedule of tasks in the tea garden a 'sham', and was definite that 'no amount of inspection will improve wages'.[35] He confirmed that the district officials had not enforced this section of the Act in practice.[36]

The ineffectiveness of even the limited regulatory provisions that were meant to ensure a fair daily task and wage schedule allowed the planters to extract maximum work at less than minimum wage, by allocating heavy tasks which the labourers were unable to complete during the work day. There were complaints to this effect from Sibsagar district, but the district officials refused to take cognizance of these.[37] The inspections specially carried out by district officials under the orders of Chief Commissioner Henry Cotton in 1900 revealed a large number of incomplete *haziris* in the garden books.[38]

Sickness and Mortality

The expanding acreage and production of tea intensified the recruitment drive to bring in larger numbers of migrant labourers. The number of migrants imported into Assam was 31,897, 34,283 and 34,283 in 1876, 1877 and 1878 respectively.[39] The total strength of migrant labour in the tea districts increased from 135,809 in 1876 to 157,219 in 1877 and 179,216 in 1878.[40] The journey up to Assam Valley via river steamers on the Brahmaputra continued to take a severe toll on the migrant labourers. The Sanitary Commissioner of Assam, Dr DeRenzy, reported 'lamentable mortality among the coolies in transit' to the tea districts of Assam. He reported that the average death rate among labourers in transit to Assam was 2.1 per cent, as compared to the death rate of 1.97 per cent among migrants going to overseas colonies of the British empire. The difference, he remarked, may not appear very great, but 'it is necessary to remember that the Assam coolie death-rate occurred on a passage of an average length of 16 days, while the death-rate of colonial coolies occurred on a passage of an average length of 60 days'.[41] By way of comparison, he concluded that the 'death-rate of Assam coolies on the passage will be 47.8 and that of the colonial coolies as 11.98 per cent'.[42]

The number of tea gardens in the Assam Valley districts increased from 275 in 1876 to 317 in 1878.[43] The opening up of new gardens also took its toll on labour life. The official reports on immigration continued to record a high incidence of mortality and desertions in the tea gardens. In 1875, the percentage of desertions was 9.78. (This proportion included women deserters who accounted for 4.02 per cent). The death rate for Assam in 1876–77 was reported as 8.1 per cent. The Deputy Commissioner of Darrang district reported a death rate of 9.17 per cent and a desertion rate of 6.22 per cent in 1877.[44] In 1878, the Chief Commissioner described mortality among tea labourers as a very serious issue; the death rate in the Assam Valley districts of Lakhimpur, Sibsagar, Darrang and Nowgong were 7.35, 7.72, 9.64 and 11.09 per cent respectively.[45] Local officials and the planters attributed the high mortality to the arrival of 'unfit' and sickly labour from Calcutta. In January 1876, the Inspector of Labour, Upper Assam, reported a severe level of sickness among the labourers in the Hulunguri and Desai tea estates of Dibrugarh district. On arrival in the garden and after inspecting the batch of sick labourers he commented: 'A more pitiable sight I have seldom witnessed. In Hulunguri there was scarcely a coolie of the new batch that was fit or ever likely to be fit for hard manual labour.'[46] For this state of affairs the office of the Superintendent of Emigration in Calcutta was held accountable, and explanations were called for. In response, Dr Grant, the Superintendent, denied any laxity in inspections in his establishment, and blamed the garden management for the sick conditions of the labourers. He argued that these labourers for both the gardens had been selected in a healthy state, with the authorized agents of the gardens in Calcutta considering them fit for labour. After their arrival in the gardens no effort was made for several months to find out the state of their health. He held the unhealthy conditions in the gardens and the negligence of the gardens' management responsible for the labourers' poor health.[47] While this blame game between Grant and provincial bureaucrats continued for several years, the inherent 'unfitness' of the recruited immigrants remained a frequently cited reason for the high mortality rates in the Assam tea plantations. In continuation of the debate, Dr Grant further elaborated his diagnosis of high mortality among migrant labourers in Assam's tea gardens, in 1880. The selected migrants, he asserted, were sent aboard ships in a healthy state, and it was the unsanitary conditions both during the onward land journey to the tea gardens and at their work places which rendered them too sick and feeble to perform manual labour.[48]

Dr Grant's own establishment may not have been faultless, but the reports of the Sanitary Commissioners of Assam for 1877–84 and the evidence presented by them were supportive of Grant's criticism of the tea garden management. In his report of 1877, Dr DeRenzy had held local causes, i.e. bad water, damp floors and a general lack of cleanliness, rather than the climate, as being responsible for excessive sickness and high mortality among tea garden labourers.[49] The Sanitary Commissioner's findings during his tour of the tea gardens in 1878 presented a very dismal picture of the labourers' health, in sharp contrast to the general refrain of 'coolies being well fed and in comfort' in most official labour reports. The high mortality and considerable amount of sickness among the labourers, he reported, were due to insufficient intake of nitrogenous and oleaginous diet, as they could not afford to purchase food articles which were sources of oil and nitrogen. He found many of them in a stage of 'extreme emaciation' and 'advanced starvation'.

> Every particle of subcutaneous fat had disappeared, the skin was dry and hard, the muscles were wasted to an extraordinary degree and the tout ensemble was that of hide-bound skeletons. This language may sound exaggerated, but it really not so. The cases I refer to were very numerous, and mostly came under my observation in the districts of Upper Assam.[50]

Because of their financial inability to purchase dal, ghee or oil, the main element of nitrogen in their food, rice became the mainstay of their diet as it was supplied to them at subsidized rates by the garden management. Rice satisfied their sense of hunger but it did not provide a sufficient amount of nitrogen to keep them healthy. What was the nitrogen sufficiency for a healthy human diet? He drew a comparative picture to provide a satisfactory answer.

> ... poorly-fed operatives in England consumed about 135 grains of nitrogen a day, and that labouring convicts in Assam jails are allowed 136 grains a day, we may assume that this is the minimum quantity necessary. Probably about 250 grains a day would suffice for a man doing moderate work. Irish farm labourers consume about 349 grains a day. As a result of many enquiries, I have come to the conclusion that in many cases coolies try to live on 112 grains a day, and in some cases as little as 84 grains a day.[51]

The second important element of diet was carbon, which was required in starch and fat through milk, butter, oil, meat, fish, *ghee*, etc. He particularly referred to the high rate of mortality among labourers from the North West Provinces, for whom *ghee* was an important element in their diet, and which they could not consume sufficiently because of its high cost. Rice was the source of starch and the subsidized volume of ten *chittacks* a day per labourer was inadequate for this. And because of the high market price of rice, the labourers could not afford to purchase it to supplement the quantity of subsidized rice. The subsidized quantity was far short even in comparison with the diet of labouring convicts in jails, which was also ten *chittacks* of rice a day, but, in addition, they were given two *chittacks* of dal or the same of fish, and every Sunday two *chittacks* of meat, and also two *chittacks* of vegetables, and one-third of a *chittack* of oil. The convicts' allowance was just sufficient to keep the prisoners, whose labour was by no means as heavy as that of the tea coolies, in reasonable health.[52]

The Sanitary Commissioner also reported that the water supply in the tea gardens, even on some of the larger properties, was highly unsatisfactory: 'there can be no doubt whatever that bad water causes an immense amount of coolie sickness and mortality. The deaths caused by cholera, dysentery, and diarrhoea are almost all due to this one cause'.[53]

DeRenzy's successor Eteson, Deputy-Surgeon-General and Sanitary Commissioner, Assam, attributed the excessive mortality of labourers in tea gardens to the sudden changes taking place in their living conditions after their arrival in the plantations. His close observation of labour life in the Assam tea gardens for over fifteen months convinced him that DeRenzy's reported diagnosis was absolutely correct.[54] He further attributed the conditions of everyday living in 'coolie lines' as important factors of the high rates of sickness and mortality. He reported 'miserably insufficient' bedding used by labourers to sleep.

> The sites of the coolie lines or village cannot always be either high or well drained: the ground is generally damp; the *machans*, made of bamboo, are used as fire-wood, and the coolie sleeps on the ground with a few tattered rags beneath, and a poor old blanket to cover him. I am describing now the condition of the new hands, among whom the 'terrible mortality' is persistent. It is impossible that health and strength can be maintained under such conditions.[55]

Push towards Unregulated 'Free' Labour

During the period of indentured labour, three major features characterized the growth of the tea industry. First, rationalization, which took the form of an increased transfer of control over the management of tea gardens to the British managing agency houses, a process initiated by Assam Company placing its gardens under the management of Schoene, Kilburn and Company. The operations of the bigger companies stimulated the amalgamation of a number of smaller gardens into large-scale enterprises under managing agents, and by the end of the century, the seven top managing agency houses controlled nearly 61 per cent of all tea gardens. Second, much of the expansion of the tea industry after 1870 was financed not by Britain's home savings but rather by the investments of British residents in India, and by the undistributed surplus and ploughed-back dividends of older companies already in the field.[56] And third, in contrast to the pre-1865 expansion, a large part of the expansion of the tea industry during the indentured labour period up until the end of the century took place in a context of steadily falling prices; between 1880 and 1900, tea prices fell by half (see Chart 2.1 and Appendix Table 2.1). All these features had an important bearing on the structure of recruitment for the development of a labour system in the Assam plantations.[57]

Between 1865 and 1882, when the tea industry grew steadily, recruitment continued to be under the supervision of the government while a penal contract system came into being in Assam. The planters' persistent complaint was the high cost of recruitment, which they attributed to the restrictions imposed

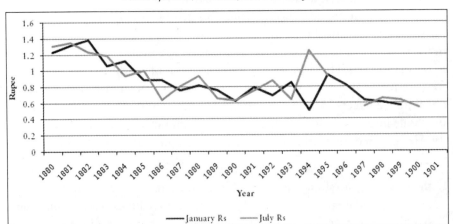

CHART 2.1
Prices of Tea in Calcutta, 1880–1901, per lb

under the law. District officials of the recruiting districts were singled out for putting obstacles in the way of recruitment of labour for the Assam tea gardens. It was pointed out that the cost of bringing coolies up to Sibsagar district had increased from Rs 35 per head in 1875 to between Rs 66 and Rs 84 in 1878. Similar or, in some cases, even higher estimates were reported in Dibrugarh and Darrang districts.[58] The trigger for the next round of changes in the legislation and labour system was provided by the slow but steady downward drift of prices from 1878 onwards. The planters now launched a campaign for drastic cost-cutting measures combined with rapid expansion. Since labour was a main component of their production costs, the Indian Tea Districts' Association (ITDA), in a memorandum to the Government of India in April 1880, stated that the 'future of the tea industry hinged on the main-tenance of an adequate supply of coolie labour at a cost calculated to leave a fair margin of profit on the capital invested'.[59] The Association complained that the greatest hindrance to the expansion of the tea industry was the 'exces-sive cost of recruitment largely due to the stringency of labour laws'.[60] In the opinion of the planters, the three-year contract period was too short to allow them to recover the cost of recruitment and outlay on health care; they also complained that time-expired coolies not subject to penal sanctions became 'complete masters of the situation' due to competition for their labour power, and left in search of higher remuneration. They sought harsher punishment for 'offences' and defaulting on contract by coolies. They complained about and demanded the removal of 'restrictions' on their privilege of private arrest of runaway labourers. The existing rules permitted the arrest of a deserter without warrant only at a distance of ten miles beyond a magistrate's court, and the deserter had to be taken immediately to the nearest police station to be produced before the magistrate. Yet another demand of the planters, seeking official sanction for wage payment based on piecework, was that the words 'at the rate of' before Rs as wages were to be inserted in the contract.[61] The planters concluded by demanding the abolition of all governmental regulations on recruitment, extension of the term of penal contract from three to five years, and greater control over time-expired labourers.[62]

Opinions were sought from the district officials about the ITDA's demands for suitable amendment to the existing Labour Emigration Act VII of 1873. Recognizing the contradictory nature of the demand for deregulated emigration alongside a vigorous penal system in the labour districts, the Government of India suggested that the true remedy for the difficulties of the tea industry lay in 'free emigration and free labour'.[63] However, the Assam planters strongly opposed the suggestion of a non-penal labour system: a leading planter from Assam wrote that the absence of any labour market in Assam placed the planters so completely in the hands of his coolies that the majority of them would prefer to work under the unamended 1873 Act rather than allow any change in the penal system. In fact the planters demanded *additional* penal powers, aimed largely against time-expired labourers engaged under short-term contracts of Act XIII, which the planters felt had inadequate penal provisions. For instance, under the 1859 Act there was no right to private arrest without a warrant, and prosecution automatically terminated the labour contract. The reason for the planters' demand for greater penal powers over time-expired labourers was the growth of the labour market resulting in competition among planters for time-expired labourers: by 1880 a 'bonus' system had developed, with such workers being paid between Rs 12 and Rs 24 when re-engaged.[64] Absence of legal control over time-expired labourers also enabled them to seek preferred employment in favourably situated and healthy gardens, rather than in the remote and unhealthy gardens of Upper Assam. Furthermore, the planters were afraid that lack of adequate control over time-expired labourers would – as it often did – lead to a mass refusal to work. The Mangaldai Tea Planters' Association, for example, observed that 'old coolies who are in the know . . . will not only meet the demand for labour by a distinct refusal, but will incite other coolies to do the same'.[65] Another planter argued for the entire labour force to be put under penal contract, citing the need for absolute control over labourers during the rainy season when the heaviest tasks (hoeing, planting and plucking) were performed, and when refusal to work by old labourers was most common.

There were, however, a few dissenting voices among local officials and even some planters, against extension of the term of contract. They pointed out that it would result in inefficient work by a disheartened labour force and an increased death rate due to greater application of the Act in unhealthy gardens. Major Boyd warned that 'it is likely to induce increased mortality by tying coolies for a longer period'.[66] Consequently, there would be a greater incentive for the labourers to desert, and the managers would be tempted to overexploit them. All this, the dissenters argued, would raise rather than lower labour costs for the planters. A.E. Campbell, Deputy Commissioner of Sibsagar, in fact recommended an increase of the monthly wage in the fourth and fifth years, to Rs 6 and Rs 7 respectively, as a solution to prevent desertion. However, these dissenting voices and the recommendation of higher wages were brushed aside by the Chief Commissioner of Assam. He fully supported the planters' demand for more powers of control, and suggested that they be freed from any restriction on their private right to arrest without a warrant.[67]

The Government of Bengal appointed a Commission headed by Mr Mackenzie along with two other official members, which included representatives of Calcutta's agency houses and planters. The Commission agreed with the planters in their demand for deregulation of recruitment, but 'in the interest of "gardens" which cannot have the garden *sirdar* recruiting and must depend on professional assistance', it insisted that the system of licensed contractors and recruiters should continue under government supervision as before.[68] On the question of penal contracts, Sir Stuart Bayley, Chief Commissioner of Assam and later a Member of the Viceroy's Council, put forward the argument of exceptionality of circumstance of Assam for its retention: 'circumstances of tea gardens are still so far exceptional as to require exceptional treatment and exceptional legislation to regulate the relations between the planter and his labour'.[69] As a result of lobbying by planters and the bureaucracy, the planters' demands were met in full. 'In deference to the almost unanimous wish of the tea planters' and against the objection of some of the district officials, the Commission proposed extension of the period of contract to five years. For local labour contracts, planters now merely had to file the papers of the contract within one month, without having to present the labourer in front of a magistrate; and instead of the 'cumbersome' procedure for endorsement of days of unlawful absence, they had to provide only a list of defaulters to the Inspector of Labour on his annual visit. All restrictions on the power of arrest, such as requiring a warrant if the magistrate's court was within ten miles of the plantation, were lifted; moreover, planters could now delegate the power of arresting deserters to others.

With regard to labour, the Commission re-introduced the statutory minimum wage of Rs 5 for men and Rs 4 for women for the first three years of the period of contract, with provision for an increase of Re 1 over the last two years. However, the minimum wage was made conditional on completion of the daily task, thus formally legitimizing the piece-work payment that had already become a standard practice on the plantations. Inspectors were permitted to reschedule the daily work load if it was judged to be too heavy; and the government was given powers to close down a garden if mortality rates were high and could be shown to be the result of inadequate sanitary arrangements.[70] With a few minor changes, all the suggestions of the Commission were accepted by the government and made into law: the 1882 Labour Districts Emigration Act I was passed without much difficulty in the Governor General's Council. The 1882 Act remained the major legislative device for the regulation of recruitment of labourers and the labour system in Assam until 1901, being modified slightly in 1893 when the maximum term of contract was reduced to four years. The major features of the Act, namely deregulated emigration and freedom for local contracts, were clearly designed to serve the needs of the planters to regulate an expanding labour force. By strengthening planters' control over time-expired labour, the legislation thwarted the development of an embryonic labour market.

It is crucial to locate Act I of 1882 in the context of the strategy adopted by planters in the face of two important developments in the world market: first, the need to attain the pre-eminent position in exporting tea to the UK market where the main rival was China; second, the steady yet fluctuating decline of tea prices from 1878 onwards. The planters' two-fold response was to expand production at an unprecedented scale while simultaneously attempting to cut costs of production, a strategy described in the Indian Tea Association Report of 1884 as reduction of expenditure 'by a more economic use of the labour available and by getting better work from the coolies'.[71] To meet the growing demand of exports, planters were constantly under pressure from the tea companies and their agents to increase production. Monetary incentives such as bonus and commissions on profits, as well as fear of being rendered unemployed on failure, fuelled the drive for intensification of the labour process, expansion of acreage by clearing jungles and to keep up with higher production targets. Hetherington, a young planter, noted that his senior manager Dunlop received £7,700 as profits and £400 as commission from his employer, The Imperial Tea Company.[72] His diary contains a large number of entries recording his anxieties and concerns about production figures. While financial gains functioned as an incentive, 'non performance' could lead to unemployment for the planters.[73] For the managers, the security of their jobs, personal financial gains and further promotions became synonymous with ensuring uninterrupted production and steady growth of profits for the tea companies. W.M. Fraser, a retired planter, recollected that while developments in clearing of forest lands for gardens were everywhere in evidence about his time, 'it was in 1894 that the contagion spread'. He recorded that more than 150,000 acres of tea were planted during the next three years in Assam, the Surma Valley and the Dooars (in north Bengal). Not only was new land broken in to a vast extent, he remembered, but there was also great activity in the nature of purchase and amalgamation of existing estates to form new companies:

TABLE 2.1

Acreage, Production and Average Strength of Labour Force Employed in Tea Plantations in Assam Valley, 1885–1900[77]

Year	Acreage under Tea	Tea Production (lbs)	Labour
1885	108,017	32,625,619	157,073
1890	131,280	48,144,401	224,908
1895	155,095	56,733,295	298,467
1900	204,985	75,283,500	388,607

TABLE 2.2

Tea Imports into Britain[78]

Year	Indian Tea (lbs)	Chinese Tea (lbs)
1883	58,000,000	111,780,000
1884	62,217,000	110,843,000
1885	65,678,000	113,514,000
1886	68,420,000	104,26,000
1887	83,112,000	90,508,000
1888	86,210,000	80,653,000
1889	96,000,000	61,100,000
1890	101,770,882	73,743,124
1891	109,637,790	62,283,778
1892	111,711,261	57,050,708
1893	115,022,926	56,208,958
1894	118,379,650	43,762,974
1895	123,361,870	40,083,864
1896	127,720,415	35,299,730
1897	134,729,401	28,760,297
1898	139,545,011	27,077,759
1899	142,329,277	34,814,281
1900	153,581,439	21,315,538

While the jungle, forest, bamboo, *sunn* and *ekra* [indigenous construction materials] grass was cut into to make more room for tea plant, Agency Houses in London, Glasgow, and Calcutta were busy turning land syndicates into gardens, established gardens into companies and companies into still bigger companies. The bones of the industry were stirring with a vengeance.[74]

After the passing of Act I of 1882, the tea industry experienced phenomenal growth in Assam: between 1880 and 1900 acreage under tea increased by 120 per cent, while the production of tea quadrupled. The major part of this growth took place in the Assam Valley (see Table 2.1). Indian tea acquired a leading position in the world market, outstripping Chinese tea in 1888 for the first time; and its share of the British market increased from 27 per cent in 1880 to 54 per cent by 1901[75] (see Table 2.2). In the phase of the downward drift of prices, such growth was made possible by importing no less than one million persons into Assam during the period in which Act I was in operation.[76] By keeping wages below even the statutory minimum level, the strengthened penal contract system aided the intensification of labour that contributed to reducing production costs. We now turn to the history of emigration and the structure of recruitment during the period of indenture.

Labour Recruitment under Indenture

Long-distance recruiting was practically coterminous with the inception of tea plantations in Assam. The Assam Company initially relied on European contractors to supply them with labour; these contractors worked through paid native agents who did the actual recruiting from the districts of Bengal and Bihar.[79] The phenomenal expansion of tea gardens during 1860–65 saw a proliferation of native Indian recruiting contractors who supplied the tea planters with thousands of labourers from Chotanagpur, Bihar and eastern United Provinces. In the 1860s, the planters also sent out coolies from their gardens to recruit labourers from their home districts. This system was known as garden *sirdari*. After the passing of the 1863 and 1865 Acts, both these forms of recruitment came under government supervision: recruits had to be registered in their districts of recruitment, medically examined, and their conveyance to Assam had to follow health regulations laid down by the government. Although the 1882 Act, which introduced the system of free or deregulated emigration, was designed to encourage private recruitment through garden *sirdars,* an immediate result was an increase in unregistered recruitment by unlicensed contractors, which outstripped registered recruitment by a ratio of 4 to 1.[80] This development was facilitated by the emergence of the 'Dhubri contract' system. Instead of registering emigrants at the district headquarters where they also signed a contract, as was done earlier, the unregistered emigrants were taken straight to Dhubri in Goalpara district of Assam, from where a regular steamer service transported them to the tea gardens. Goalpara, which did not have a single tea garden, had been declared a labour district under the new Act; it was here, nearly 400 miles from their homes, that a vast number of recruits under the unlicensed system were made to sign their contracts in front of a magistrate who, by all accounts, made only perfunctory inquiries as to the willingness of the coolies to emigrate to Assam.[81] F.H. Tucker, a police officer appointed to investigate charges of fraud and kidnapping connected with recruiting coolies for the Assam tea gardens, reported that there was a great deal of slackness in the registration of coolies at Dhubri and that the provisions of the Act were generally not followed.[82]

Unregistered emigration and Dhubri contracts became the standard practice for recruitment of indentured labourers in the era of deregulated emigration. The first casualties of the new recruiting system were the older agencies of licensed contractors and recruiters. In 1882 there were about twenty licensed contractors and 1,000 licensed recruiters in the field, but by 1890 they had all but vanished from the recruiting districts of Chotanagpur and Santhal Parganas; many licensed contractors and recruiters were reported to have gone over to unlicensed recruiting.[83] There was a similar decline in the number of licensed tea garden recruiters (*sirdars*); they were recruiting only about two labourers per head in 1895, as compared to about ten per head in 1882.[84] The manager of the Jorhat Company complained in 1889: 'We have to send away 100 garden *sirdars* for 300 or 400 coolies required. Formerly we calculated on getting 15 to 20 coolies for each *sirdar*.'[85] In many cases, garden *sirdars* went to work for the local agents of Calcutta's managing agency houses, who were also unlicensed contractors. Thus many *sirdari* recruits were in reality unlicensed contractors' labourers, and the garden *sirdar* often acted as a chaperone for these recruits on their journey to a specific tea garden. This system, known as 'mixed *sirdari*', was very common in the Assam Valley and Cachar.[86]

The deregulated recruitment system had at its base the *arakati,* or the village recruiter, and at its apex the large labour recruiting firms of Calcutta controlled by managing agency houses (Begg and Dunlop, Balmer and Lawrie) who also had a great many tea gardens under their control.[87] The village *arakati* was not in any sense a creation of the 1882 Act; there is much evidence to show that he played a crucial role even in the phase of controlled emigration. In 1877, the magistrate of Ranchi, the largest coolie-recruiting district, noted that most of the recruitment under the licensed recruiting system and garden *sirdari* was actually done by *arakatis,* who received Rs 2 to Rs 5 per coolie supplied.[88] In November 1882, Ware Edgar, now Officiating Commissioner of the Chota Nagpur Division, reported that a great number of 'coolie-dealers' (*arakatis*) had acquired a notorious reputation as 'bad characters', 'deceivers' and 'cheaters' of labourers among local agents, police officers, missionaries and district officials.[89] Seven years later, the village *arakati* was still variously described as 'belonging to the very class of people who emigrate as labourers and live and move among them', or, in more uncharitable terms, as a 'notoriously bad character', being 'as a rule the scum of the country, ex-convicts, burglars, thieves, dacoits and notorious badmashes'.[90] The sphere of operation of the *arakati* was usually a small group of villages around a weekly market or *haat*. His success lay in being in close touch with the village, or, as a contractor put it, 'to know the wants and inclinations of the people'.[91]

Above the village *arakati* was the *sudder arakati,* who normally resided in the major towns of the recruiting districts and often fixed deals with local agents of the coolie contractors. The function of the local agent was to finance the *sudder arakati* through cash advances and to confirm the suitability of the recruits. The labourers would then be sent to depots which dotted these major towns or railheads, whence they were sent with contractors' escorts to the forwarding depot at Dhubri. Accordingly, this system involved three to four distinct levels of transaction, and officials often disparagingly referred to the *arakati* recruitment and transfer of coolies through various intermediaries as the 'sale system'.[92] The boom in unlicensed recruitment led to proliferation of these professional recruiters on an unprecedented scale. In 1890, by a conservative estimate, no less than 5,000 *arakatis* were said to be operating in Ranchi district alone.[93] By 1895, the Bengal Labour Commission found that the coolie contractors in Purulia, the major recruiting station in Chotanagpur, each had about 500 to 1500 *arakatis* on their books, and there were no less than fourteen labour contractors in the town.[94]

The high density of *arakatis* could only be explained by the increasing profits of the recruitment business. In 1877, *arakatis* received between Rs 2 and Rs 5 per head for each coolie supplied to the contractors. In 1883, immediately after the promulgation of the 1882 Act, the price paid to village *arakatis* nearly doubled, to Rs 10 per head. By 1888 it was reported that *arakatis* got Rs 20 per coolie supplied to the *sudder arakatis,* who in turn received Rs 50 to Rs 60 per head from the depot owners and local agents of the contractor.[95] The high rates paid to *arakatis* also affected the prices of garden *sirdari* coolies. Many tea gardens and their managing agents complained bitterly in 1889 about the practice of garden *sirdars* selling their labourers to *arakatis,* since the price they received was invariably much higher than the commission paid by the tea gardens.[96] The profits of recruitment at the lowest level were replicated at all stages of the coolie transactions, the net result being a steady increase in the costs of recruitment to planters. For example, one Mr Driver, a former agent for some Calcutta firms, and a Ranchi *arakati* collected Rs 40 each per pair (male and female) of labourers from the Raneeganj agent. The Ranchi *arakati* in turn paid Rs 20 to 25 to the village *arakati* as his share.[97] The rising cost of recruitment was cited as the primary reason behind the planters' demand for deregulated emigration, yet the results were contrary to their expectations. In 1875, the cost of importing labourers in Sibsagar district of Assam was reported to be Rs 35 per head.[98] By 1889, evidence suggests that the cost of recruitment had more than doubled, with a leading contractor estimating it to be about Rs 90–100 per head.[99] In 1895, the best labourers – tribals from Chotanagpur – were costing the planters nothing less than Rs 150 per head, the average cost for an average labourer being estimated at Rs 130.[100] The massive famines which occurred in the recruiting districts during 1897 and 1900 led to a slight decline in the price; yet even in the famine years the price did not fall below Rs 100 per head.

The cost of labourers otherwise varied according to region and caste, the overwhelming favourite among the planters being tribal labourers from Cho-tanagpur – referred to in recruiting parlance as '1st class jungley'.[101] The next in terms of preference were the so-called 'semi-aboriginal castes'; and the least preferred were labourers from Bihar and the United Provinces, who were to be had from contractors at half the rate of tribal coolies from Chotanagpur. Between 1880 and 1900, of the 710,000 adult coolies recruited for the tea gardens of Assam, no less than 46 per cent were from Chotanagpur, while only 21 per cent were from the congested plains of the United Provinces.[102] The cost of recruitment in Assam contrasted unfavourably with that in the Dooars gardens of northern Bengal, where in 1895, unlicensed garden *sird-ars* recruited coolies at a cost of Rs 6 per head while the same labourer cost Assam planters Rs 60. The host of middlemen spawned by the deregulated emigration system shared roughly Rs 40 to Rs 120 between them, depend-ing on the class of labourers supplied, and the Bengal Enquiry Commission did not mince words in describing them as 'doing the work of hunting and offering the spoils of the chase to the planters but at an enormous cost'.[103]

In a sense, the metaphor of hunting is not inappropriate for the *arakati* system of recruitment: 'The essence of hunting is snaring and violence, and these two are the favourites of the *arakatis*', observed an official in 1895.[104] Thus, while the immediate results of deregulated emigration were welcomed unabashedly by planters and officials in Assam as having made 'emigration simpler and more popular', they evoked a cry of disapproval from officials in the recruiting districts. The first reports concerning the increased abuses associated with deregulated emigration came from the Chota Nagpur Division, where the Commissioner reported, in 1882, a great increase in the enticing of minors away from the protection of their guardians and the abduction of married women. Missionaries in Chotanagpur supplied the Commissioner with 50 documented cases of kidnapping and abduction in 1882, and the Deputy Commissioner of Ranchi and Manbhum reported another 100 cases of abduction of women.[105] The Deputy Commissioner of Lohardugga was convinced that 'the enactment of Act I of 1882 has immensely facilitated the abduction of women and children'. The Deputy Commissioner of Ranchi felt the only solution to prevent kidnappings and deception in the recruitment system was to repeal Act I of 1882; he advocated direct government interven-tion in matters of sanitation and health in the tea gardens. On the basis of these observations, the Bengal government reported in 1885 that the district officials 'unanimously condemned the free emigration system as affording the greatest facility of wrong-doing'.[106] Similarly, in Chotanagpur, 262 cases of kidnapping, cheating and wrongful confinement were filed in 1888, while the Commissioner received some 500 complaints of missing persons.

Yet these cases were said to represent gross underestimates of actual abuses, since 'in the majority of the cases the complainants are themselves in the dark about the *arakatis* who caused such trouble and therefore consider it futile to undertake the cost and journey to the police station or magistrate'.[107] There were reports of unwilling victims being kept under lock and key in secret depots, and then being spirited away to Dhubri where they had no choice but to sign a labour contract. In a note submitted to the Lieutenant Governor of Bengal in 1899, Father Hoffman, a Jesuit missionary stationed at Chotanagpur, listed the typical methods of *arakati* recruitment. They included loans advanced to potential victims, tempting young men with liquor and women, and kidnapping young girls and marrying them off in the depots, a system known as 'depot marriages'.[108] The high profits of early recruiting lured a significant number of freelance Europeans and Indians. An example is John Henry Lawton, a dismissed soldier, who with his posse of armed peons set up a business of 'coolie raiding' on highways along which gangs of labourers recruited by *sirdars* of the Dooars gardens travelled to Jalpaiguri. Lawton posed as a government official with his retinue and ordered the labourers into specially constructed temporary depots, from where they were taken to Assam. He was prosecuted for five such cases of 'coolie raiding' in 1888 alone, a year in which a special police officer was appointed to investigate thirty-two such cases.[109] The Bengal Labour Enquiry Commission noticed the existence in 1895 of a new set of men called '*daffadars*', armed musclemen from the United Provinces, who had inserted themselves in the recruiting business between the *arakatis* and the contractors.[110] The depredations of *arakati* recruiting caused near-panic in many recruiting districts. A magistrate in Hazaribagh district noted in 1889 that

> the fear of recruiting in this district is very great, and it is not too much to call it a terror. People even fear to go to their several *haats* and *bazars* for fear of them. Hardly since the days of *thugee* has there been such widespread fear of travelling.[111]

Similar reports of widespread fear of recruitment for Assam were received from Santhal Parganas and Ranchi.[112]

By making emigration to Assam unpopular, *arakati* recruitment and its related host of intermediaries no doubt contributed directly to the increasing cost of recruitment. However, the most important reason for the existence of the *arakati* system, as well as the rising cost of recruitment, was the ever-increasing demand for labour that emanated from the operation of the penal contract system in Assam Valley. The question to be asked is: despite the migration of one million persons over the last two decades of the nineteenth century, why did the tea garden labour force amount to only 400,000 workers in 1900?[113] The Special Report on the Working of Act I of 1882 also commented that the total labour force of the province did not increase equally with the increase in importation.[114] Planters and the government alike justified the existence of the penal contract system in terms of a chronic labour shortage in Assam. However, as we will see below, the cause of this shortage lay in the penal contract system itself.

The Labour System under Indenture

A characteristic feature of the tea plantation labour system in Assam was extensive use of the penal contract. In this context, the 1882 Act marked the watershed. Prior to this only 22 per cent of the labour force came under penal contract. By 1891, at its height, 55 per cent of the labour force was contracted under the 1882 Act, and another 40 per cent under Act XIII of 1859.[115] Widespread use of the 1882 Act during the period in which the tea industry expanded immensely strengthened the planters' power in relation to their work force. This expansion was carried out under the statutory minimum wage provision of the Act (in effect, the maximum wage paid), since the major function of penal sanctions was to keep down wages by preventing the operation of a labour market. It did so by checking competition among planters for scarce labour and by preventing workers from taking advantage of this situation.

The passing of the 1882 Act was followed by the opening of new gardens in remote and unhealthy areas of Assam. Thousands of *arakati* labourers were hastily assembled in newly opened gardens without adequate health protection, availability of provisions or safe drinking water, which resulted in increased mortality rates within the year. As a medical official noted, 'Anybody of experience who saw the ground would know before the garden opened that it was a question of tea and money versus human life.' But other officials were certain that it was a direct consequence of the application of the new Act and its stringent provisions. 'The Emigration Act', wrote an official, 'no doubt operates to keep down the scale of wages. Unhealthy gardens could not be opened out without its aid. It would be too expensive. Free coolies would demand the wages sufficient to compensate them for the risk they run or would desert.'[116]

The working of the penal labour system often came under criticism from the emerging nationalist press. In 1887, D.N. Ganguly, assistant secretary of the Indian Association, published a series of articles in the *Bengalee* depicting the abysmally low wage rates and bad working conditions in the Assam gardens, a situation that he compared to slavery.[117] The government's reaction was to dismiss these criticisms as orchestrated by 'perambulating philanthropic Babus and garden sea [*sic*] lawyers', and 'a mere handful of obscure and disreputable men representing nobody but themselves'.[118] An interesting insight into the working of the penal labour system at this time is provided by a confidential report on Assam written by a group of Santhal tribal headmen in 1894. They had been taken on a tour of the Assam tea gardens by the president of the

Indian Tea Association, J. Buckingham, the purpose being to create a favour-able impression among Santhals and to encourage them to migrate to Assam: 'on their return they could give a report to their fellows which would dispel the distrust and dislike felt towards emigrating to Assam.' The tour lasted seventeen days, during which they visited twenty-seven gardens and personally interviewed 216 labourers, visited the coolie lines, and inspected the work-ing conditions in the gardens. The Santhal headmen and an accompanying British official submitted separate reports of their visit to the Government of Bengal.[119] Predictably, the official report described the working conditions of the gardens in glowing terms. In his report, J.A. Craven, the official who headed the deputation, praised the management for giving moderate tasks, 'perfect' sanitary arrangements, and wrote that the 'coolie is too well off to think of returning to his own country to revert to the mahajan and life of slavery'.[120] By contrast, the report of the Santhals was highly critical of the labour system in the tea gardens. It is almost certain that they had been taken to twenty-seven of the best run gardens in Assam, and their criticism of the labour system is thus all the more incisive.

The first point they made in their report concerned the insufficient wages. The monthly rate of Rs 5 per man and Rs 4 per woman was considered by the workers themselves to be too low, given the high price of rice in the gardens. The daily wage of three annas (3/16th of a rupee) was similarly considered inadequate in relation to the heavy work load, which left no opportunity to earn overtime. Wages were only about half of what the Santhal migrants could earn by working on road construction in Chittagong (where the monthly rate was Rs 9), and lower than that paid in the Dooars gardens of Bengal.[121]

The second point in their report dealt with the general working conditions in the gardens. They found conditions of work unacceptable in twenty-three out of the twenty-seven gardens they visited. In these gardens labourers were not allowed any sick leave, and prolonged illness was penalized by a cut in pay. In most gardens the non-completion of tough work schedules was punished with fines and substantial pay-cuts. Flogging men and women was common in every garden, either for non-completion of work, or for disobedience and desertion. Women were not allowed any rest after giving birth to a child, and were 'required to work within six days of delivery'. In contrast to Craven's claim, the tribal headmen reported that labourers were unable to return home even after fifteen or twenty years, because they did not have enough money and their wives and children were still working out the contract.

Feeling slighted, Buckingham wrote to Carstairs, the Deputy Commissioner of Santhal Parganas who had helped in selecting Santhali headmen for the deputation, rubbishing their report which 'have not a vestige of truth' and claiming that he should not believe their assertions.[122] Carstairs, empathizing more with the Santhali deputationists, remarked that their statements may not be recorded as a proof of facts but he believed they were 'not invented'.[123] In short, the report indicted the penal contract system in Assam for not providing workers with a living wage, and pointed out that the low wage levels were maintained by the use of force, both legal and extra-legal. Many of the claims made by the Santhal headmen were subsequently confirmed by the detailed investigation into wages in Assam during the famous controversy of 1899–1900, initiated by Henry Cotton, Chief Commissioner of Assam. Cotton showed that through the whole period of indenture, up to 1900, the average wage remained well below the statutory minimum of the 1882 Act, the highest being only about Rs 4.75 for men and Rs 3.75 for women. More importantly, while wages in the tea gardens had stagnated for thirty-five years since 1865, between 1875 and 1900 the price of foodgrains increased by 100 per cent. Wage levels in the tea gardens also compared extremely unfavourably with that of agricultural labourers outside the gardens, amounting to only about half the latter.[124]

Non-Reproduction of the Plantation Labour Force

Along with a low living wage and also as a consequence of it, the plantation system in Assam was characterized by a persistent problem of work force reproduction. Throughout the period in which the indenture and penal contract system was in operation, labour force mortality constantly outstripped the birth rate, with the result that the net reproduction rate was negative. Between 1882 and 1901, the average annual death rate for adult labourers was 3.93 per cent. More significantly, over the same period, the death rate of labourers recruited under the 1882 Act was 5.4 per cent.[125] In other words, one in every four of the adult labour force recruited under the 1882 Act did not survive the full period of the contract. Labourers recruited under the 1859 Workman's Breach of Contract Act had a much lower death rate, the annual average for the period being 3.07 per cent, while that for the non-tea-garden population of Assam of a comparable age group was only 2.4 per cent.[126]

The high death rate among tea plantation workers in Assam drew repeated criticism – from the nationalist Indian press and from independent missionaries like Charles Dowding.[127] From the official immigration reports, Dowding estimated in 1892 that '57,000 people, more than one-eighth of the whole garden population Assam, were dying at the rate of 10 per cent per annum'. Referring to the high death rate in the tea gardens, he drew a parallel in order to make his point:

> Take a garden with a population of 700 or so. This would make a fair size village at home. With a death-rate a shade over 7 per cent this would mean a funeral a week, for every week in the year; or two funerals a week, for six months in a year; or if it

were an epidemic, a funeral, every other day, for nearly four months in the year.[128]

Sometimes even the officials were constrained to admit this reality. Charles Elliot, Chief Commissioner of Assam, when faced with death rates of 37.8 and 41.3 per cent respectively in 1882 and 1883, admitted that 'terrible mortality' in tea gardens was 'a blot on his administration'.[129] It became evident that the local government had failed abysmally to enforce the sanitary measures provided under the Labour Immigration Act. Of the 725 gardens officially declared unhealthy (those with more than 7 per cent mortality of the labour force) between 1882 and 1892, only 50 gardens had been inspected by the officials; and of these, only ten gardens were mildly penalized. The standard response of the tea planters was to blame the high mortality rates on 'bad batches' or 'unsuitable coolies' supplied by the contractors,[130] and the coolies themselves for bringing with them diseases like anchylostomasis or the infamous 'coolies anaemia' and cholera contracted in their home districts[131] – explanations designed to delink mortality from the penal contract labour system. A special enquiry conducted by the Assam government in 1889 into the causes of mortality in 107 gardens concluded that 'unacclimatized' new coolies were most liable to suffer from disease and death. This new explanation became a stock argument for planters and officials alike in defence of the penal contract system, since they could claim that the death rate was independent of the system under which the coolies worked.

The problem of high death rates was thus sanitized and made a natural condition, rather than a direct consequence of the penal contract system. Replying to Dowding's criticism of the Assam labour system, Henry Cotton, Chief Commissioner of Assam, wrote in 1897:

> Unfortunately, the fight of civilization against nature demands its victims no less than war against a human enemy and land cannot be reclaimed from jungle except at the price of comparatively high mortality amongst the pioneers of cultivation. . . . But the cost of life and treasure has never been allowed to count in the balance and the victories of peaceful industry must continue to claim their victims.[132]

The 'victories of peaceful industry' were however gained at a cost; ironically, even here the official sympathy lay not with the coolies who died but with those who had paid for them – the planters. Thus William Ward, Cotton's predecessor in Assam, justified penal powers for the 'hapless' planters because 'it seems right to give him [the planter] something more for the cost he incurs, the *inferior article* he has to put up with, and the consequent risks he runs in losing by death or desertion the coolies he has paid for'.[133] Hence, the labour force mortality was attributed to the labourer being an 'inferior article'. As a planter wrote in reply to Charles Dowding's criticism, 'They do not die from diseases engendered by local conditions of gardens. They die from diseases which are induced by their own inherent faults.'[134] The labourers were sick and unhealthy because many of them would 'starve themselves to save money', was one of the official explanations.[135] In the Malayan plantations too, the colonial officials and British planters blamed the Tamil migrant labourers for their own sufferings and high mortality: 'the filthy habits of the natives as regards conservancy are too well known to require explanation'.[136]

Accordingly, attempts to explain the high death rates in the tea gardens in Assam avoided any reference to the operation of the penal contract system, and how this enabled planters to intensify the labour process while paying workers below-subsistence wages. There is however much evidence to show that the mortality pattern was intimately connected with the rigours of the penal contract system operating under the 1882 Act. The special enquiry of 1889 noted that 'many unhealthy gardens owe their unhealthiness, in a great measure, to the insufficiency of labour force and to the fact that the greatest pressure on the coolies to work is exercised during the rains, which is also the most unhealthy time of the year'.[137] It also showed that, due to these labour shortages, the enforcement of penal sanctions in the unhealthy gardens coincided with a stricter work regime, and that the death rates mounted when coolies were not allowed sick leave.[138] A large number of deaths attributed to anchyolostomasis in 1888, the civil surgeon of Lakhimpur reported, were because the 'number of coolies palpably suffering from it are allowed to go on working or trying to work, until it develops into an incurable stage'.[139] In 1889, when the death rate was as high as 6.4 per cent among labourers recruited under the 1882 Act, only 5 per cent of the total working days were granted as leave of absence due to illness. New gardens opened in unhealthy and remote sites invariably employed labourers under the 1882 Act. When there was a proposal to repeal this Act in 1897, planters unanimously opposed it as, 'without the penal contract, the labour required for starting new ventures cannot be obtained'.[140]

Overwork and undernourishment remained the most common causes of death among labourers. Non-Act labourers invariably obtained a higher wage, which in no small measure contributed to the differential mortality levels between the two groups. The Deputy Commissioner of Sibsagar noted in 1894:

> Most of the new coolies have little or nothing to live on besides their bare wages. Bearing in mind the fact that the wages they earn are usually below the average, I think, it is impossible to avoid the conclusion that coolies for some time after they arrive must find it difficult to subsist.[141]

Similarly, by 1899 Henry Cotton was coming round to the view that a considerable number of deaths among 1882 Act labourers was due to the abysmally low wages they earned and the consequent malnourishment. During the controversy over the wage question in 1900–01, Cotton showed from the wage data of a number of tea gardens that the high death rate correlated with low average wages and high daily tasks set for 1882 Act coolies.[142] It was in the context of a penal contract system characterized by low wages, an intensified work regime and grossly inadequate health care, therefore, that the impact of the so-called hostile influence that the labourers brought with them was magnified to epidemic proportions.

The penal contract system systematically militated against a normal rate of reproduction by the labour force. Thus the birth rate for women employed in the tea gardens over the period 1880–1901 averaged only 86 per 1,000, as compared with an average of 127 births per 1,000 women in the non-tea-garden population of Assam.[143] This trend continued into the early years of the twentieth century. The Assam Labour Enquiry Committee also reported that the birth rate in the tea plantations continued to be lower compared to the figures in the province (see Table 2.3). Moreover, during the last two decades of the nineteenth century the birth rate declined steadily, the overall effect being a persistent negative rate of net reproduction among the tea garden work force (Tables 2.4 and 2.5).

The low birth rate was attributed by medical opinion to the widespread

TABLE 2.3
Comparative Birth Rates in the Tea Gardens and Province of Assam[144]

Year	Of Total Population		Of Adult Female Population	
	Tea Gardens	Province	Tea Gardens	Province
1900	27.6	34.96	89.2	102.4
1901	29.1	33.98	93.2	101.8
1902–03	30.8	34.21	98.6	102.5
1903–04	28.9	35.57	93.4	125
1904–05	28.4	35.55	92.1	124.9

TABLE 2.4
Birth and Death Rates in Assam Tea Gardens[145]

Year	Birth rate per mille	Death rate per mille
1880	31.3	35.2
1881	36.6	37.8
1882	39.1	41.3
1883	34.3	43.2
1884	32.2	43.2
1885	32.6	36.8
1886	29.0	39.8
1887	28.2	36.2
1888		39.8

TABLE 2.5
Birth and Death Rates in Assam Valley Tea Gardens, 1885–1900[146]

Year	Birth Rate per mille	Death Rate per mille
1885	29.2	37.3
1890	22.7	38.8
1895	21.8	33.9
1900	26.0	33.3

practice of abortion among women labourers.[147] The medical officer of Nazira observed in 1906 that 'the amount of abortion on some gardens is appalling; on some gardens 65 per cent of pregnant women do not give birth to living children'.[148] The Assam Labour Enquiry Committee reported that there were a large number of abortions and attributed these to the 'conditions of life on the gardens'.[149] The reason for abortions was ascribed to the woman 'not wanting her earning interfered with' or, as the Indian Tea Association concluded, to the 'weakness of marriage ties amongst the coolies'.[150] It is impossible to escape the conclusion that the abortions were due to absence of maternity leave coupled with low wage levels, which compelled women to work throughout their pregnancy and immediately after childbirth. Women workers under the 1882 Act contract suffered especially, since they were made to work continuously during the plucking season and barely had any rest time. Low birth rates and high death rates were both outcomes of the low wage penal contract labour system. The labour force in the Assam tea gardens was as a result constantly depleted, necessitating greater recruitment of fresh labour each year. The situation did not improve even in later years. Dr Charles Forsyth, the medical officer of Bengal United Tea Company's garden in Tezpur, informed the Assam Labour Enquiry Committee 1921–22 that 'abortions are fairly frequent' among the 'coolies' in the tea gardens. [151]

The low rate of reproduction was compounded by high child mortality in the plantations, though the official reports were generally silent on this issue. There are, however, rare glimpses of the lives of children in the Assam Valley tea plantations during the indenture period from reports made by district officials like Dr Whitewell, the civil surgeon of Dibrugarh. During his inspection of the Sessa garden in that district in 1884, he found a high rate of child mortality. He reported:

> The conditions of child-life in a tea-garden are altogether so unfavourable that the wonder is how so many children succeed in passing childhood stage. A coolie woman gets a variable amount of leave for her confinement. After that, if the infant is not strangled at birth, she must either take it out to her work, or leave it behind, with no one to look after it. In the former case tied to its mother's back or left in the nearest drain, it is exposed to the extreme of heat and cold, to wind and rain;

in the latter the child gets half starved and so paves the way to a death from some bowel-disorder, or succeeds in cutting short its career by a fall or a role into the open fire. So alive are coolie women to these facts that, to avoid the trouble of bringing up their children under such circumstances, abortion is frequently resorted to, and *daes*, who produce it, often find their business a very profitable one.'[152]

These observations were corroborated by some other district officials also.

The planters' efforts in response to these developments in 1880 and 1900 only aggravated the situation. Their strategy of intensification and expansion of production was based largely on coercion of fresh emigrants, which in turn militated against a positive rate of reproduction of the labour force. It is in this contradiction that we must seek the causes of the tremendous pressure exerted on the structure of recruitment to supply an ever-increasing number of workers for the Assam plantations.

Dismantling of the Indenture System

A crisis erupted in 1900 when the Chief Commissioner, Henry Cotton, published his annual report on labour immigration into Assam. Cotton's annual report of 1900, in sharp contrast to the earlier annual reports, presented an altogether different picture of labour relations and labour life. It linked the high rates of mortality among tea plantation labourers to their low wages.[153] The report showed that not only were the wages paid to the labourers below the statutory minimum rates, but, in several cases, the higher amount applicable for the fourth and fifth years was not paid.[154] Cotton also reported cases where rice had not been provided at the statutory rate and subsistence allowance not paid to sick labourers.[155] His report regarded relations between employer and labourer as being far from cordial; in fact ill feeling was clearly growing. Ten cases of 'riots' had been reported in that year alone.[156]

District officials conducting inspections reported several cases of grave abuses by the management in the gardens. Captain Cole, Deputy Commissioner of Darrang, noted that a large number of labourers earned so little that 'they would inevitably starve if the management did not provide sufficient rations and enter the cost of the same as an advance against the coolie'.[157] Captain Asher Leventon, the civil surgeon at Sibsagar, reported that a majority of the labourers did not receive a full month's *haziri* (wage) at the Latabari tea estate; the result was a large number of outstanding 'advances' against them in the books. He was not impressed with the manager's explanation of 'laziness' on the part of labourers who were getting enough food to live and were therefore satisfied.[158] J.C. Arbuthnott, Deputy Commissioner of Sibsagar, commenting on the low wages, wrote:

Comfort is hardly compatible with a starvation wage, and the condition of the labourers, which is practically that of slaves, can hardly be satisfying, except to the owners, who naturally in their own interest supply them with food while gradually increasing the debt against them, in order that the period of bondage may be interminable.[159]

He described the conditions of labourers in the Latabari tea garden as 'legalized slavery' and recommended strong action against the employers.[160] The inspection report of the Nagora tea garden in Sibsagar district revealed a similar state of affairs. The Commissioner of Assam Valley attributed the high rate of mortality on the garden to 'inefficient' wages paid to the labourers.[161]

Endorsing the findings of the district officials, the Chief Commissioner of Assam reported to the Government of India that the labourers were hopelessly burdened with advances and their condition was 'in no appreciable degree distinguishable from servitude'.[162] Following the recommendations of the district officials, Henry Cotton banned employment of Act labourers in the inspected gardens. However he was rebuked for this by his seniors and, acting on a representation made by the Indian Tea Association (ITA), J.J. Woodraff, advocate general of Bengal, gave his verdict against Cotton and his order was suspended.[163]

Cotton's report received a hostile reception from the planters. The ITA, which wielded much political clout in the province and in London, organized protest meetings and mounted pressure on the colonial and home governments through memorials and deputations to the Secretary of State for India and the Viceroy.[164] The Anglo-Indian press in India and *The Times* in London launched blistering attacks on Cotton, which acquired a personalized tone when the nationalist Indian press came out in his support.[165] The situation was further aggravated when Cotton proposed an increase in the minimum statutory wages of labourers through the Assam Labour and Emigration Bill introduced in the Central Legislative Assembly. This provoked a very angry reaction from the tea lobby, and led to very unpleasant and bitter public exchanges between him and the planters.[166] Their powerful opposition in the Legislative Council against the wage hike successfully curtailed the wage increase to only half a rupee a month, along with several other changes in the existing law on labour immigration in Assam. Cotton lost his job, but the public exposure of the abuse of the labour system and the failure of the 'free' recruitment system under Act I of 1882 initiated the process of dismantling the indenture system. However it still took two-and-a-half decades to remove it from the statute book because of opposition from the planters.

The penal contract labour system and *arakati* recruitment, which had grown alongside it, were substantially transformed during the first decade of the twentieth century. The first component to be affected was the system of 'free' or deregulated emigration; by closing about 90 per cent of the main recruitment areas to unlicensed recruiting, Act VI of 1901 drastically curbed the *arakati* system.[167] Under section three of this Act, the government reverted to the previous system of supervision and registration, an important innovation being the special concessions granted to the centralized recruiting agency, the Tea District Labour Supply Association. The planters were now forced to take on direct responsibility of recruitment in order to avail themselves of these concessions. The second important legislation was Act XI of 1908, which was enacted on the recommendation of the Assam Labour Enquiry Committee of 1906. Under this Act, the power of private arrest given to planters in the Assam Valley was withdrawn. Unlicensed recruiting was also abolished. These two legislative actions of the colonial state effectively dismantled much of the penal contract labour system. But complete abolition of recruitment by licensed contractors and special penal legislation took place only in 1915.

'Indenture' without Indenture and its Final Demise

The withdrawal of penal clauses under Act VI of 1901 and of the power of private arrest in 1908 became matters of serious discussion within the ITA circles. The planters resented the loss caused by the withdrawal and argued that Act XIII (which was still in force) alone could not provide the required control over their labour force.[168] The Enquiry Committee of 1906 suggested that better treatment of labourers by the planters and the availability of adequate wastelands to settle the immigrants would be sufficient to keep the labour force under 'control'. The planters did not agree. W.T. Cathcart of the Assam branch of ITA retorted: 'the majority of imported labour is not the thrifty settler, but of a type naturally indolent, who will work with a little judicious handling, but from whom some sort of security against enticement and outside influence is necessary to safeguard the employer from loss of his heavy recruiting expenses'.[169] It was further argued that Act XIII applied to the province only by executive order and could easily be withdrawn.[170]

Alternate strategies by planters of curbing labour mobility within the tea estates included a proposal for 'Labour Rules', which came under discussion among various branches of the Indian Tea Association.[171] They came to the conclusion that an 'agreement binding proprietors to protect themselves against the enticement' was of vital necessity, and 93 per cent tea gardens in the Assam Valley signed it.[172] It was also decided to seek state legitimacy for this agreement through legislation. The ITA sent a memorial to the Government of India in 1912 demanding the introduction of a new legislation against 'enticement' of labour 'before some return has been received for the cost of importing' by the importers. And to prevent migrant labourers from leaving the garden to settle on government land, the memorial further demanded that no land should be settled with anyone who had not been an inhabitant

for at least four years in Assam.[173] Obligingly, the Assam government initiated a detailed and lengthy process of drafting a Bill against Enticement of
Labour.[174] District officials, judicial officers and planters were involved in
year-long consultations for framing the Bill. In the meantime, the Colonial
Office's suggestion that Messrs Mcniell and Chimanlal visit the Assam tea
gardens to compare labour conditions there with those of other colonies was
successfully warded off.[175] The officials were aware that such a Bill will be
'open to unavoidable objection that the freedom of the coolies is somewhat
fettered', which had been pointed out to them by 'Native Gentlemen' who
were consulted.[176] The 'Native Gentlemen', Mr Barua, Mr Mazid and Mr
Chanda, raised objections to the proposed Bill even though they had a 'large
interest' in tea.[177] Ignoring this, the Assam government went ahead with the
final framing and passing of the Assam Labour Enticement Bill by the Legislative Council, which was promptly approved by the Government of India.[178]
However, the Secretary of State for India refused to sanction the Bill on the
ground that it involved 'principles' which could not be accepted.[179] The 'Bill
will impose heavy restrictions on freedom of immigrant and is an objectionable extension of jurisdiction of Criminal Courts', he stated.[180] The Secretary
of State demurred because he was worried that it would be in the face of the
strong anti-slavery public sentiments in Britain.[181]

However, Act XIII of 1859 was still operational in the tea gardens, and the
planters resorted to contract labourers, both immigrants and time-expired
labourers, under this Act in larger numbers.[182] The provisions of the Immigration Labour Acts applied only to newly recruited labour. Time-expired or
locally recruited labourers were increasingly contracted under the Workman's
Breach of Contract Act XIII of 1859 since it was extended to Assam in 1864.[183]
Consequently, all the labour contracted under the Immigration Labour Acts
was referred to as Act labour, while the rest of the labour force, including
those contracted under Act XIII of 1859, was termed as non-Act labour in
official reports. Act XIII of 1859 functioned as an important supplement to
the indenture contract in the tea gardens and acquired special significance once
the penal clauses were repealed from the legislation in 1908. The operations
of Act XIII were beyond any regulatory system and were essentially geared
towards holding the labour force within the tea plantations after they had
completed their indenture contract period.[184] Colonial officials were fully
aware of this and admitted that it was 'totally indefensible on principle', but
were complicit in its continuation. The contracts were unwritten, unregistered
and unverifiable. Besides, there were no protection provisions for labour even
on paper, nor were there any obligations imposed on the employer beyond
that of paying daily wages for work done. The contracts under this Act were
meant to be short-term, for a year at the most, but often were enforced for
up to 939 days.[185]

Charles Elliot, the first Chief Commissioner, was the first to suggest the withdrawal of its operations in 1882 and again in 1885. He considered it a 'bad Act, one-sided and unfair in its operations, and liable to be misunderstood and misused'.[186] However, for fear of exciting 'violent opposition' from the planters, its actual removal was not recommended. W.E. Ward, Chief Commissioner, observed in 1887: 'These evils are further intensified by the fact that no limit is now placed on the term of a contract under Act XIII . . . also provides no safeguard for the labourer.' He was in favour of its repeal in the Assam tea gardens, but thought it would be 'inexpedient to raise a storm of indignation about our ears' from the planters.[187] Another Chief Commissioner, Quinton, enumerated some of the abuses in the working of Act XIII: use of the Act by employers to evade sanitary regulations; possible separation of husband and wife due to their inability to redeem or cancel the work contract; and the indefinite period in the contract as expressed in terms of number of days, often in a large number of cases.[188] He was informed by the Deputy Commissioner of Darrang that the planters often manipulated the operations of the existing legislations to escape being caught on the death rate issue: by placing their coolies under Act XIII, for instance, as it lowered the death rate as compared to Act I of 1882. For similar reasons some gardens put the Kacharies under Act I of 1882, because deaths among them were low and this brought down the average death rate of Act I labourers.[189] However he too, like his predecessors, did not advocate abrogation of the Act and commented: 'If a penal law is to be maintained at all, perhaps Act XIII practically works better, so far as enforcement of labour is concerned'.[190] It was the widespread labour rebellion in the Assam tea plantations in 1921–22 which finally ended the indentured labour system, with Act XIII of 1859 being abolished in the year 1926.[191]

Despite the staggered demise of the penal contract and indentured labour system, the critical importance of the legislations of 1901 and 1908 should not be minimized. The number of 1882 Act labourers in Assam declined rapidly after 1901, indicating a shift in the pattern of labour recruitment and the contract system. Between 1900 and 1910, the number of Act labourers declined from 133,000 to only 23,000, constituting merely 5 per cent of the total labour force.[192] Similarly, though restricted unlicensed recruiting through *arakatis* continued till 1908, the major burden of recruiting was taken over in 1902 by the Tea District Labour Supply Association, under whose auspices *sirdars* recruited for their respective gardens.

The transformations in the system of labour recruitment for the Assam tea plantations were undoubtedly due to a reversal in the policy of the colonial state, beginning with Act VI of 1901. Until then, state policy towards the tea industry was essentially set in a gradualist framework. Special labour legislation was considered a transitory measure, necessitated by the absence of a labour market in Assam, and designed to promote the ultimate objective of 'genuinely free emigration and free labour'. In the sphere of recruitment, the transition was conceived as one from state-supervised emigration to privately assisted emigration, and finally, to completely unassisted emigration. The penal powers of the planters were justified as necessary in the phase of assisted emigration and an insufficiently developed labour market; they would be rendered unnecessary by a fully developed labour market and free, unassisted emigration. In 1891, these policy assumptions were clarified by the Government of India in the following words: 'there is a tendency towards the development of free emigration from the assisted to the unassisted form and when this system has reached a sufficiently advanced form, free labour properly so called shall be rendered practicable'.[193] The Chief Commissioner of Assam was more specific as to the conditions under which the penal contract could be abolished when he wrote in 1886: 'The time when the planters in the upper districts of Assam Valley can do without such a contract can only come when ten million acres of cultivable land in that valley are taken up and the population has increased from 2'/2 million to 7'/2 millions of people.'[194] Thus the ultimate goal of the colonial state policy, 'really free emigration and absolute liberty of contract', obviously lay very much in the distant future.

Within the narrative of colonial discourse, this reversal of policy is generally ascribed to the realization by an increasing number of colonial state personnel that special labour legislation had failed in its objective of developing genuinely free emigration and free labour in Assam. For example, Charles Elliott and Stewart Bailey, who as heads of the Assam administration had ardently defended the 1882 Act, became its bitter critics when they came to head the Bengal administration, after becoming aware of the enormity of abuses under the 'free' emigration system. Similarly, Henry Cotton, who began his tenure as Chief Commissioner of Assam by sending troops to apprehend runaway coolies from the Assam Bengal railway constructions, eventually became extremely critical of the labour system in Assam, especially the tendency to pay abysmally low wages to contract workers. The findings of the Bengal Labour Enquiry Commission of 1896 and the Assam Labour Enquiry Committee of 1906 were crucial in this regard. The former conclusively demonstrated that *arakati* recruitment under the free emigration system of Act I was extremely unpopular in the recruiting districts and a major factor in the rising cost of recruitment. The latter supplied the arguments from the points of origin, with twenty-eight of the thirty-one witnesses it examined in the recruiting districts citing the existence of the penal contract as the most important cause for the absence of a free flow of labour into Assam.[195] These findings then became the basis for the 1901 and 1908 legislations.

However, realization by the colonial state of the increasing distance between policy goals and practical results is not entirely adequate as an explanation, and fails to account for the timing of the policy changes in the first decade of the twentieth century. Moreover, it begs the question: why were the practical results of colonial state policy so different from its avowed objectives? The real nature of colonial state interventions, and the changing relations between the plantation economy and the colonial state, cannot be fully comprehended purely within the parameters of colonial policy. The legislations of 1901 and 1908 were enacted when the tea industry was undergoing a severe economic crisis, with prices plunging to an all-time low between 1895 and 1906. Much of the crisis was caused by overproduction due to acreage expansion in the previous decades. Profits and dividends were under threat for the first time since the depression of 1865–70. Intervention by the colonial state was thus intended to rationalize the structure of recruitment and the labour system in order to overcome the inbuilt contradictions of the plantation system in Assam, the most acute form of which was the tendency towards overproduction. The legislations of 1901 and 1908 thus indicated a shift in the strategy of the colonial state, from provision of a constant supply of cheap labour to ensuring the long-term viability of the plantation system as a whole.

The major contradiction affecting the plantation system during the indenture period arose from the necessity of expanding production by increasing the acreage planted under tea, in response to the declining tea prices of the last two decades of the nineteenth century. The exceptional labour legislations aided the planters by providing a vast number of labourers who were paid wages much below the market rate. Yet, precisely because of the penal contract and its accompanying low wages, the labour supply remained largely independent of the wage rate and dependent on the capacity of the *arakati* recruitment structure. While penal labour legislation held down wages by not allowing the operation of the labour market, competition for labour among planters gave rise to a 'recruiters' market'. What the planters gained by paying below-market wage rates might have been offset to a great extent by the rapid rise in the premium paid to the recruiters. Planters' responses to the rising cost of recruitment reinforced intensification of the labour process, in effect pushing wages below the level at which labour power could be reproduced. This had a direct effect in terms of increased mortality and desertion rates, which raised the real cost of labour further and induced greater dependence on *arakati* recruitment. This contradiction of the plantation system, of an expansionary phase based on payment of low living wages, was expressed, paradoxically, in the high cost of cheap labour.

At another level, the same contradiction was manifested in the delinking of the social reproduction of plantation labour power from physical reproduction of the work force. Low wages and intensification of the labour process accordingly contributed significantly to a combination of high mortality and low fertility. Throughout the phase of indenture, and especially in its last two decades, the planters' main concern was ensuring an adequate supply of labour for the expansion of production rather than the long-term goal of building a resident work force. Until the end of the nineteenth century, planters actively discouraged the grant of plots of land to time-expired labour, fearing a reduction in the supply of labour. Low wages and high work norms enforced by the penal sanctions led to an exhaustion of fresh emigrant labour, and the negative rate of work force reproduction contributed directly to planter dependence on the *arakati* system and the high cost of recruitment it entailed.

Resistance on the part of the labour force to the indenture system was also an important factor in hastening its formal demise. In the recruiting districts, resistance manifested itself in the immense unpopularity of the *arakatis* and in growing opposition to the penal contract, while in the plantations, resistance took the form of desertion and other modes of opposition to work intensification.[196] Despite the best efforts of the planters, therefore, labourers – and especially time-expired labourers – persisted in operating a fledgling labour market. In the end, the indenture system fell largely because of its inherent contradictions. It became economically untenable and politically costly to maintain. It was altered in a phase of acute crisis, when the colonial state stepped in to rationalize the labour system. The gradual dismantling of indenture marked the transition from a system based on physical coercion of labour to one based on its rational exploitation. In one sense it was an immensely successful system, in so far as it laid the foundation of the tea industry by permitting a large expansion in the acreage under tea; yet this success was achieved at the expense of no less than half a million deaths, and in the end this proved a little too much even for a system that looked at 'coolie' deaths merely as 'depreciation *en bloque*'.[197] However the forms of dependency did not disappear altogether with legal dismantling of the indenture system in the Assam tea plantations. Planters were preparing to adapt to this new contingent situation, and adopted new strategies to control and discipline their labour force.

Notes and References

[1] Percival Griffiths, *The History of the Indian Tea Industry*, London: Weidenfeld and Nicolson, 1967, p. 101; Assam Company Papers (hereafter ACP), Ms. No. 9925, Vol. 1, July 1840, London Minute Book, Guildhall Library, London, p. 154.

[2] Griffiths, *The History*, p. 73.

[3] Report of the Commissioners Appointed to Enquire into the State and Prospects of Tea Cultivation in Assam, Cachar and Sylhet, Calcutta, 1868, Appendix (hereafter Commissioners, 1868); Griffiths, *The History*, p. 103.

[4] Commissioners, 1868, p. 50, para 105.

[5] In response to the Lieutenant Governor's suggestion to offer higher wages for attracting migrant labour, a Committee of Tea Planters of Lukhimpur district passed a resolution stating that a higher rate of Rs 5 (Rs 4–8 being the current rate paid) should not be offered

to the 'imported coolies'. See Papers Relating to Tea Cultivation in Bengal, *Selections from the Records of the Government of Bengal No. XXXVII*, Calcutta: Bengal Military Orphan Press, 1861, p. 61.

6 See chapter 1, p. 46.

7 Report of the Assam Labour Enquiry Committee (hereafter RALEC), Calcutta, 1906, Appendix A, p. 136.

8 Commissioners, 1868, p. 35.

9 Papers Regarding the Tea, Parliamentary Papers, Calcutta, 1874, p. 23.

10 Home Department Proceedings, Government of India, November 1864, National Archives, New Delhi, p. 683.

11 Ibid., p. 681.

12 Ibid., p. 679.

13 Ibid., p. 681.

14 Ibid., p. 679.

15 Ibid.

16 Ibid.

17 Rajani Kanta Das, *Plantation Labour in India*, Calcutta: R. Chatterji, 1931, pp. 31–32; RALEC, 1906.

18 E.A. Gate, *Assam Immigration Manual*, Calcutta, 1893, pp. iv–v.

19 S.M. Akhtar, *Emigrant Labour for Assam Tea Gardens*, Lahore, 1939, p. 60.

20 Commissioners, 1868, p. 64.

21 Ibid., pp. 68–72.

22 Papers Regarding the Tea, 1874, p. 24.

23 C.A. Bruce to Captain F. Jenkins, 1 October 1836, Parliamentary Papers, 1939, pp. 84–85. C.A. Bruce, *An Account of the Manufacture of the Black Tea as now practiced in Suddeya in Upper Assam*, Calcutta: G.H Huttmann, Calcutta Military Orphan Press, 1838.

24 Parliamentary Papers, 1939, pp. 109–14.

25 Robert Gardella, *Harvesting Mountains: Fujian and the China Tea Trade, 1757–1937*, Berkeley: University of California Press, 1994, p. 45.

26 For detailed descriptions of the processes of tea cultivation and manufacture, see Edward Money, *The Cultivation and Manufacture of Tea*, Calcutta: Thacker & Co., 1870; David Crole, *Tea: A Text Book of Tea Planting and Manufacture*, London: Crossby Lockwood and Son, 1897; J.C Kydd, *The Tea Industry*, London: Humphrey Milford, Oxford University Press, 1921; C.R. Harler, *The Culture and Marketing of Tea*, London: Oxford University Press, 1933.

27 Crole, *Tea*, p. 62.

28 Money, *Cultivation and Manufacture of Tea*, p. 255.

29 See chapter 5.

30 See chapter 6.

31 Crole, *Tea*, p. 49.

32 For a detailed discussion on the wage question, see chapter 5.

33 Report on Labour Immigration into Assam for the Year 1883. (Hereafter Assam Labour Report.)

34 Special Report on the Working of Act I of 1882 in the Province of Assam during the years 1886–1889, Department of Revenue and Agriculture, Government of India, Emigration A, Nos. 6–14, November 1891, p. 220. (Hereafter Special Report, GoI, 1891.)

35 Department of Revenue and Agriculture, Government of India, Emigration A, Nos. 1–5, July 1888.

36 Ibid.

37 Special Report, GoI, 1891, p. 228.

[38] Department of Revenue and Agriculture, Government of India, Emigration A, Proceedings – Nos. 6–8, File No. 90 of 1901, pp. 145–47. For details, see chapter 5.

[39] Department of Revenue and Agriculture, Government of India, Emigration A, Nos. 4–6, December 1878.

[40] Department of Revenue and Agriculture, Government of India, Emigration A, Nos. 12–19, November 1879.

[41] Annual Sanitary Report of the Province of Assam for the year 1878, para 21.

[42] Ibid.

[43] Department of Revenue and Agriculture, Government of India, Emigration A, Nos. 4–6, December 1878. For more details on migration, see chapter 6.

[44] Assam Labour Reports, 1875–1878.

[45] Assam Labour Report, 1878. For more details on mortality, see chapter 5.

[46] Department of Revenue and Agriculture, Government of India, Emigration A, Nos. 1–4, September 1876.

[47] Ibid.

[48] General Department, Inland Emigration, Government of Bengal, File Nos. 7–6, November 1880.

[49] Assam Sanitary Report, 1878; Department of Revenue and Agriculture, Government of India, Emigration A, Nos. 32–35, November 1880.

[50] Ibid., para 2.

[51] Ibid., paras 7–8.

[52] Ibid., paras 12–16.

[53] Ibid., para 38.

[54] Assam Sanitary Report, 1884, paras 49–50.

[55] Ibid., para 54.

[56] Amiya Kumar Bagchi, *Private Investment in India*, Cambridge: Cambridge University Press, 1972, pp. 161–62, 176; John S. Gladstone, *History of Gillanders, Arbhuthnot and Company and Ogilvy, Gillanders and Company*, London: Gladstone Family Records, Clwyd Record Office, Howarden, UK, 1910, pp. 93–94.

[57] Rana Behal and Prabhu P. Mohapatra, '"Tea and Money versus Human Life": The Rise and Fall of the Indenture System in the Assam Tea Plantations 1840–1908', in E. Valentine Daniel, Henry Bernstien and Tom Brass (eds), *Plantations, Proletarians and Peasants in Colonial Asia*, London: Frank Cass, 1992, pp. 146–50.

[58] Department of Revenue and Agriculture, Government of India, Emigration A, Nos. 30–32, November 1880.

[59] Immigration into Assam, Government of Bengal, File No. 30– 17/15, August 1880.

[60] Ibid.

[61] General Department, Inland Emigration, Government of Bengal, November 1879.

[62] Assam Labour Report, 1880.

[63] Department of Revenue and Agriculture, Government of India, Emigration A, Nos. 20–23, June 1880.

[64] The 'bonus' was actually a system of advances that planters introduced to attract time-expired labour. The advances were, of course, subject to deduction from the future earnings of the labourers.

[65] Department of Revenue and Agriculture, Government of India, Emigration A, Nos. 68–72, December 1880.

[66] Immigration into Assam, Government of Bengal, File No. 30– 17/15, August 1880.

[67] Department of Revenue and Agriculture, Government of India, Emigration A, Nos. 68–72, December 1880.

[68] Department of Revenue and Agriculture, Government of India, Emigration A, Nos. 30–32, November 1880.

[69] Department of Revenue and Agriculture, Government of India, Emigration A, Nos. 68–72, December 1880.

[70] Department of Revenue and Agriculture, Government of India, Emigration A, Nos. 1–15, August 1881.

[71] Griffiths, *The History*, p. 123.

[72] F.A. Hetherington, *The Diary of a Tea Planter, 14 July 1907*, Sussex: The Book Guild Ltd., 1994, p. 151.

[73] W.M. Fraser, *The Recollections of a Tea Planter*, London: The Tea and Rubber Mail, 1935, p. 40. Writing about unemployed planters, he said, 'at that time there were always in Calcutta in the cold weather twenty or thirty planters searching for jobs', failing which many 'whacked the bottle'.

[74] W.M. Fraser, *The Recollections*, pp. 25–26.

[75] Griffiths, *The History*, pp. 120–29.

[76] Assam Labour Reports, 1880–1900. For long-run trends of production, acreage expansion, labour employment and export in the Assam Valley, see chapter 5. For details on import of labour, see chapter 6.

[77] Annual Reports on Tea Culture in Assam, 1885–1900; Assam Labour Reports, 1885–1900.

[78] John Weatherstone, *The Pioneers 1825–1900: The Early British Tea and Coffee Planters and Their Way of Life*, London: Quiller Press, 1986, p. 30.

[79] ACP, Ms. No. 9925; Griffiths, *The History*, p. 64.

[80] Report on Inland Emigration from Bengal, Government of Bengal, 1883, Calcutta, p. 3.

[81] Assam Labour Report, 1887, pp. 2–3; Griffiths, *The History*, p. 276.

[82] East India: Assam Coolies, Parliamentary Papers, 1889, p. 51.

[83] Special Report, GoI, 1891.

[84] Report of the Labour Enquiry Commission of Bengal, Government of Bengal, Calcutta, 1896, para 66.

[85] Special Report, GoI, 1891, para 24.

[86] Special Report, GoI, 1891, para 19; Assam Labour Report, 1884, p. 3.

[87] Griffiths, *The History*, p. 295.

[88] General Department, Government of India, Emigration A, Nos. 22–23, January 1878.

[89] Revenue and Agriculture, Government of Bengal Proceedings, Nos. 4–5, October 1883, para 6.

[90] Department of Revenue and Agriculture, Government of India, Emigration A, Nos. 6–31, September 1889, para 14.

[91] Ibid.

[92] Revenue and Agriculture, Government of Bengal Proceedings, Nos. 4–5, October 1883, para 2.

[93] Special Report, GoI, 1891, pp. 24–25.

[94] Labour Enquiry Commission, 1896, Appendix.

[95] Special Report, GoI, 1891, pp. 24–25.

[96] Department of Revenue and Agriculture, Government of India, Emigration A, Nos. 6–31, September 1889.

[97] Government of Bengal Proceedings, Revenue and Agriculture, Nos. 4–5, October 1883.

[98] Department of Revenue and Agriculture, Government of India, Emigration A, Nos. 68–72, December 1880.

[99] Special Report, GoI, 1891, p. 25.

[100] Labour Enquiry Commission, 1896, para 76.

[101] Ibid., para 73.

[102] Assam Labour Reports, 1877–1902. For more details, see chapter 6.

[103] Labour Enquiry Commission, 1896, paras 73, 85.

[104] Department of Revenue and Agriculture, Government of India, Emigration A, Nos. 9–10, April 1897.

[105] Department of Revenue and Agriculture, Government of India, Emigration A, Nos. 2–6, November 1883; Department of Revenue and Agriculture, Government of India, Emigration A, Nos. 4–5, October 1883.

[106] Department of Revenue and Agriculture, Government of India, Emigration A, Nos. 15–17, August 1886.

[107] Department of Revenue and Agriculture, Government of India, Emigration A, Nos. 9–19, November 1899.

[108] Ibid.

[109] Department of Revenue and Agriculture, Government of India, Emigration A, Nos. 4–7, November 1888; Department of Revenue and Agriculture, Government of India, Emigration A, Nos. 3–4, July 1889; Department of Revenue and Agriculture, Government of India, Emigration A, Nos. 6–14, July 1890; Special Report, GoI, 1891.

[110] Labour Enquiry Commission, 1896, para 76.

[111] Special Report, GoI, 1891; Department of Revenue and Agriculture, Government of India, Emigration, Nos. 2–9, February 1899.

[112] Department of Revenue and Agriculture, Government of India, Emigration A, Nos. 9–19, November 1899; Department of Revenue and Agriculture, Government of India, Emigration, Nos. 2–9, February 1899.

[113] RALEC, 1906, p. 83.

[114] Special Report, GoI, 1891, p. 165.

[115] Assam Labour Report, 1891: Special Report, GoI, 1891, paras 110–11.

[116] Assam Labour Report, 1883, para 15.

[117] Dwarkanath Ganguly, *Slavery in British Dominion*, edited by Sris Kumar Kunda, Calcutta: Jignasa, 1972: reprint of thirteen articles published in the newspaper *Bengalee* between September 1886 and April 1887.

[118] Special Report, GoI, 1891, p. 239.

[119] Department of Revenue and Agriculture, Government of India, Emigration B, Nos. 1–3, September 1894.

[120] Ibid.

[121] Ibid.

[122] Ibid.

[123] Ibid.

[124] Proceedings of the Central Legislative Council (hereafter PCLC), 1901, Vol. XL, Calcutta, pp. 94–96.

[125] Assam Labour Reports, 1882–1901.

[126] Special Report, GoI, 1891, p. 97.

[127] Ganguly, *Slavery*, 1972; Dowding, *Tea Garden*.

[128] Dowding, *Tea Garden*, p. vi.

[129] Special Report, GoI, 1891, para 189.

[130] Assam Labour Report, 1884, p. 29.

[131] Dowding, *Tea Garden*.

[132] Department of Revenue and Agriculture, Government of India, Emigration A, Nos. 28–29, September 1897, para 6.

[133] Department of Revenue and Agriculture, Government of India, Emigration A, Nos. 3–11, April 1893.

[134] Dowding, *Tea Garden*, p. 50.

[135] Special Report, GoI, 1891, para 180.

[136] Sunil S. Amrith, *Crossing the Bay of Bengal: The Furies of Nature and the Fortunes of Migrants*, Cambridge: Harvard University Press, 2013, p. 128.

[137] Special Report, GoI, 1891, para 264.

[138] Ibid., para 252.

[139] Ibid., para 280.

[140] Department of Revenue and Agriculture, Government of India, Emigration A, Nos. 11–13, April 1897, Appendix D.

[141] Assam Labour Report, 1894, p. 35.

[142] PCLC, 1901, pp. 94–96.

[143] Assam Labour Reports, 1882–1901.

[144] RALEC, 1906, p. 82.

[145] Department of Revenue and Agriculture, Government of India, Emigration A, Nos. 36–39, December 1888, p. 39.

[146] RALEC, 1906, p. 86.

[147] Special Report, GoI, 1891, pp. 273–74.

[148] RALEC, 1906, p. 83.

[149] Ibid., p. 84.

[150] Ibid., p. 86.

[151] Evidence Recorded by the Assam Labour Enquiry Committee, 1921–22, p. 8.

[152] East India (Assam Coolies), Parliamentary Papers, 1889, pp. 72–73.

[153] Assam Labour Report, 1900, p. 3; Department of Revenue and Agriculture, Government of India, Emigration A, Nos. 1–5, November 1901. For more details on Cotton controversy, see chapter 4.

[154] Assam Labour Report, 1900, p. 8.

[155] Ibid., p. 10.

[156] Ibid., p. 22.

[157] Department of Revenue and Agriculture, Government of India, Emigration A, Proceedings – No. 6, November 1901, p. 941.

[158] Department of Revenue and Agriculture, Government of India, Emigration A, Proceedings – Nos. 6–8, 1901, p. 145.

[159] Ibid.

[160] Ibid.

[161] Government of Assam, Revenue B, Proceedings – No. 526/535, August 1901, p. 4.

[162] Department of Revenue and Agriculture, Government of India, Emigration A, No. 6, November 1901, p. 939.

[163] Department of Revenue and Agriculture, Government of India, Emigration A, Proceedings – Nos. 6–8, File No. 90 of 1901, pp. 122–36.

[164] The Report of the Indian Tea Association, 1900, p. 6; Rana P. Behal, 'Power Structure, Discipline and Labour in Assam Tea Plantations under Colonial Rule', in Rana P. Behal and Marcel van der Linden (eds), *India's Labouring Poor: Historical Studies c. 1600–2000*, Delhi: Foundation Books, 2007, pp. 145–55.

[165] *The Englishman*, 14 January, 11 and 23 February, 7 March, 1901; *Capital*, 21 February 1901; *The Times* (London), 29 August and 2 September, 1902; Rana P. Behal, 'Coolie Drivers or Benevolent Paternalists? British Tea Planters in Assam and Indenture Labour System', *Modern Asian Studies*, 44, 1, 2010, pp. 46–50.

[166] *The Englishman*, 7, 14 January, 11, 12, 19 February, 1901; *The Times* (London), 29 August, 2 September, 1902.

[167] Assam Labour Report, 1902, p. 2.

[168] Detailed Report of the General Committee, Indian Tea Association (hereafter ITA Report), Calcutta, 1909, p. 46.

[169] Ibid., p. 49.

[170] Ibid., p. 101.

[171] ITA Report, 1908, p. 9.

[172] Judicial Department, Government of Assam, Immigration A, Nos. 1–36, December 1913.

[173] ITA Report, 1912, p. 10.

[174] Judicial Department, Government of Assam, Immigration A, Nos. 1–36, December 1913. Bill to provide against the enticement of tea-garden coolies in Assam.

[175] Department of Commerce and Industry, Government of India, Emigration B, Nos. 29–31, January 1914.

[176] Department of Commerce and Industry, Government of India, Emigration B, Nos. 31–32, November 1914.

[177] Ibid.

[178] ITA Report, 1914, p. 81.

[179] Ibid.

[180] Department of Commerce and Industry, Government of India, Emigration A, Nos. 33–35, February 1915.

[181] Under such a law labourers would have been reduced to a status of slavery since hiring of any labour from another garden by any employer would be illegal.

[182] Assam Labour Report, 1915, p. 3.

[183] RALEC, 1906, p. 136.

[184] For a detailed and nuanced analysis, see Prabhu P. Mohapatra, 'Assam and West Indies, 1860–1920: Immobilizing Plantation Labour', in Douglas Hey and Paul Craven (eds), *Masters, Servants and Magistrates in Britain and the Empire, 1562–1955*, University of North Carolina Press, 2004, pp. 455–80.

[185] Special Report, GoI, 1891, para 110.

[186] Department of Revenue and Agriculture, Government of India, Emigration A, Nos. 15–17, August 1886.

[187] Department of Revenue and Agriculture, Government of India, Emigration A, Nos. 1–5, July 1888. Note on the proposal to repeal Act XIII of 1859.

[188] Special Report, GoI, 1891, para 119.

[189] Ibid.

[190] Ibid.

[191] For details, see chapter 6.

[192] Assam Labour Reports, 1900–1910.

[193] Department of Revenue and Agriculture, Government of India, Emigration A, Nos. 2–8, June 1892.

[194] Department of Revenue and Agriculture, Government of India, Emigration A, Nos. 2–8, June 1886.

[195] RALEC, 1906, p. 27.

[196] See chapter 6.

[197] Dowding, *Tea Garden*, p. vi.

3

Dominance and Dependency: Planters and Their Power Structure

The Assam tea plantations, as a modern agro-industrial enterprise producing for the world market, were arguably the largest employer of migrant labourers, who were mobilized in tens of thousands every year for a long period between the 1850s and 1947. As pointed out earlier, Assam's plantation workers were employed under a contractual penal system as indentured labourers with a statutorily fixed minimum wage, number of hours of work, and obligation to work for the duration of the contract ranging from three to five years. Beginning with a combination of joint-stock companies and individual proprietors, the tea industry, from 1870 onwards, came under the monopolistic control of British managing agencies in Calcutta with their headquarters in Britain. Over the course of four decades, some of them acquired control over a very large acreage of land (Table 3.1). These firms retained their monopoly over the tea industry throughout the period of British colonial rule, and continued to enjoy dominance even two decades after India's independence. From Table 3.2 it will be seen that even as late as 1942, 84 per cent of the tea estates

TABLE 3.1
Tea Acreage under Control of Managing Agency Firms in Indian Tea Plantations[1]

Name of Agency	1895	1933
Finlay, Muir and Co.	35,321	72,322
Williamson, Magor and Co	35,321	48,024
Octavius Steel and Co	18,497	48,936
Begg, Dunlop and Co	17,466	31,441
Macneill and Co	16,218	30,634
McLeod and Co	11,578	33,460
Jardine, Skinner and Co	11,276	16,562
Balmer, Lawrie and Co	11,120	26.549
Shaw Wallace and Co	8,738	29,600
Duncan Brothers	7,094	65,177

TABLE 3.2

Number of Tea Gardens and Acreage under Tea Cultivation under the Control of
Managing Agency Firms in the Assam Valley in 1942[4]

	European Managing Agencies: Tea Gardens under their Control, 1942	Number of Tea Gardens	Acreage under Tea
1.	Williamson, Magor & Company	43	34,213
2.	James Finlay & Company Ltd.	30	29,849
3.	Begg, Dunlop & Company	19	22,790
4.	Balmer, Lawrie & Company	37	28,651
5.	Planters Stores & Agency Company Ltd.	31	20,413
6.	Mcleod & Company Ltd.	19	16,199
7.	Octavins Steal & Company	23	15,010
8.	Kilburn Burn & Company	13	13,646
9.	Macneill & Company	17	11,308
10.	Shaw Wallace & Company Ltd.	14	9,340
11.	R.G. Sham & Company Ltd.	11	8,849
12.	Andrew Yule & Company	16	7,453
13.	Gillanders Arbuthnot & Company	10	7,674
14.	Duncan Brothers & Company Ltd.	7	4,797
15.	Barry & Company	5	3,421
16.	Tea Estates India Ltd.	6	3,545
17.	George Henderson & Company Ltd.	3	2,516
18.	Jardin Skinner & Company	1	703
19.	Williers Ltd.	3	736
20.	Kettlewell Bullen & Company Ltd.	2	964
21.	Martin & Company	2	885
22.	Devenport & Company Ltd.	1	549
23.	G. Lochen & Company	1	486
	TOTAL	314	240,452
	Total Number of Tea Estates in Assam Valley	373	
	Total Acreage under Tea in Assam Valley		269,044

with 89 per cent of the acreage under tea in the Assam Valley was controlled by the European managing agency houses. The Indian Tea Association (ITA) represented 92 per cent of tea acreage in Assam and 78 per cent in the province of Bengal in 1948.[2] At the all-India level, thirteen leading agency houses of Calcutta controlled over 75 per cent of the total tea production in 1939.[3]

The nature of organization and relations of production in this massive enterprise is the concern of this chapter. It analyses the power structure and authority established by the planters, and how this determined labour relations in the Assam tea plantations. It was a subject widely discussed and debated by contemporary and later defenders and opponents of the plantation labour system.[5]

Writing about labour relations in the Assam tea plantations during the indenture era, Sir Percival Griffiths, the official historian of the Indian tea industry, argued that benevolent paternalism gradually emerged as the guiding force that shaped the planters' attitude towards their labour force during the course of the nineteenth century. Since Assam was a wholly strange place for the migrant labourer who came from great distances to work on the plantation, he was placed in a relation of complete dependency vis-á-vis the manager. The manager occupied a special position in almost every aspect of garden life. He was the provider of accommodation, subsidized rice and space for recreational activities to the labourers, and also acted as arbitrator of their internal feuds.

> Such a system developed a sense of responsibility and brought out the best in any naturally humane manager. . . . Their methods were rough and ready and sometimes included personal chastisement, but there is little doubt that the lot of a tea garden coolie was better than that of the ordinary Indian landless labourer at that time.[6]

Interestingly Griffiths recognized that this relation of total dependency could lead to managerial excesses, as it did in the early phase of the industry, especially during the 'tea mania' of the 1860s. Describing the powers and status of the manager of a tea plantation, he wrote:

> He was . . . clad in the authority of the ruling race during the heyday of British power – the unquestioned king of a garden population geographically isolated from more advanced element of society. If the unscrupulous European adventurers who flocked to the tea industry during the boom of the sixties had continued to form an important element in the managerial personnel, circumstances would indeed have led to a reign of tyranny. Fortunately, tea-garden managers in the last few decades of the last century were drawn from a better class of society and so the system which grew up was as a rule not tyranny, but paternalism.[7]

Obviously Griffiths located the coeval development of paternalism and rationalization of the tea industry in direct opposition to the managerial tyranny of the irrational phase of 'tea mania'. The term 'paternalism' had been used by Genovese in another context, to describe Southern American slavery of the antebellum era. Paternalism in the Old South, Genovese argued, grew out of the necessity to discipline and morally justify the system of exploitation. It did encourage kindness and affection, but it simultaneously encouraged cruelty and hatred. In the Southern plantations 'both masters and slaves, whites and blacks, lived as well as worked together. . . . Southern paternalism developed a way of mediating irreconcilable class and racial conflicts; it was an anomaly even at the moments of its greatest strength.' With the growing need for reproduction of labour after the closing of the African slave trade, the paternalistic features were reinforced.[8]

Contemporary colonial officials, even those who were not critical of the planters and fully supportive of the British capitalist venture in Assam, were less sanguine in their assessment of the nature of labour relations under the indenture system. J.B. Fuller, senior official of the Government of India and later Chief Commissioner of Assam, observed in 1901:

> The truth is of course that serious abuses must occur under a labour system which is something of the nature of slavery, for an employee who can be arrested and forcibly detained by his master is more of a slave than a servant and that these abuses are the price which has to be paid for the great advantages which has resulted from the establishment and growth of the tea industry in Assam.[9]

Viceroy Lord Curzon, who forced Henry Cotton out of his job to appease the planters, was similarly equivocal in his assessment of the indenture labour system:

> It is an arbitrary system, an abnormal system. . . . But it has been devised not in the main in our interests but in the interests of an enterprise with which the Government of India could not but sympathize, namely, the effort to open up by capital and industry the resources of a distant and backward province.[10]

The law member of the Viceroy's Council, Sir Thomas Raleigh, did not dwell on the development aspects; he was much more forthright about the immediate motives while participating in the 1901 debate on the Assam Labour and Emigration Bill in the Central Legislative Council:

> The labour-contract authorized by this Bill is a transaction by which, to put it rather bluntly, a man is often committed to Assam before he knows what he is doing, and is thereupon held to his promise for four years, with a threat of arrest and imprisonment if he fails to perform it. Conditions like these have no place in the ordinary law of master and servant. We made them part of the law of British India at the instance and for the benefit of the planters of Assam . . . the motive power in this legislation is the interest of the planter, not the interest of the coolie.[11]

Lord George Hamilton, Secretary of State for India, was even more candid in a private communication to Lord Curzon:

> I agree with you that the present labour system is a modified version of slavery, and reacts prejudicially upon the masters. It is only justifiable on the plea that without it the tea plantations could not be worked, as outside the half savage tribes from whom the coolies now come, it would be difficult to induce the ordinary Hindu to volunteer.'[12]

Contemporary non-official critics of the labour system in the Assam tea plantations also characterized it as a system of slavery. Dwarkanath Ganguli, an important Brahmo Samaj activist and joint secretary of the Indian Association in Calcutta, wrote a series of critical articles in the Calcutta newspaper *Bengalee*, based on the investigation he made during his visit and stay in Assam.[13] Another strong critic was the English missionary Rev. Charles Dowding, who described the indenture labour system in the Assam tea plantations as 'thinly disguised slavery'.[14] Contemporary supporters and critics of the Assam tea plantations, both were unanimous in their assessment – though from differing perspectives – that the indenture labour regime established there in the ninteenth century was not very different from slavery.

In what follows, I will argue that the characteristic features of labour relations under the indenture system in the Assam tea plantations were not shaped by 'paternalism', as defined by Genovese and by Griffiths. On the contrary, these relations, as reflected in the actions and attitude of the tea planters, were marked by features akin to the Atlantic slave plantations. Walter Rodney emphasized the particularity of the labour regime in the modern plantations. He argued that the system could function only because labour was cheap, plentiful and employed under conditions of maximum industrial control.[15] The other similarity between the two plantation systems was the export orientation and industrial organization of agricultural production. However, unlike the older South American and Caribbean plantations, Assam did not have a history of slave-based production. And unlike Caribbean planters who transited from managing slave production to indenture-based production, European tea planters in Assam had no prior experience of managing slave-based production. Contrary to Griffiths' assertion, the early planters of Assam were transfomed into 'coolie drivers' precisely during the period when the tea industry developed into a corporate business organization producing for the world market. Here was a case of coexistence of an 'irrational' and inhuman labour regime producing for the benefit of a modern and 'rational' corporate world.

The early British planters, the 'pioneers', started to arrive in the province from the 1840s as employees of tea companies or as individual proprietors. Many of them had already been in India, and came to Assam attracted by the prospects of government-promoted plantations to produce tea for the international market. The generous offer of wastelands at throwaway prices and extremely favourable terms for private capitalist enterprise presented huge opportunities to fortune hunters. These men came from a wide range of backgrounds. They gave up their prior vocations to take up tea cultivation. Available information, though sketchy, about this 'strange medley' of 'pioneers', provides some insight into their diverse backgrounds and activities.[16] Colonel Hannay, a military officer posted on the Burmese border, was involved with the enterprise from its early stages when the Tea Committee was touring Upper Assam in search of the tea plant. He gave up his army job to become a planter by purchasing the last of the government plantations and expanded his operations by opening up new plantations in the 1850s.[17] John Berry-White was a medical doctor turned planter who set up a joint venture with Duncan Macneil. He moved to London from Assam and set up a partnership there, J.B. Barry & Son, to import and sell tea.[18] Dr O'Brien was another medical doctor who set up two small gardens, Beheating and Ghooronia, in Sibsagar district.[19] J.H. Williamson, the joint owner of Cinnamara and Oating tea gardens, was the captain of a government-run inland river steamer which transported troops but was permitted to conduct private trade with local communities en route the Brahmaputra river.[20] George Williamsons, the co-founder of Jorehaut Tea Company, was earlier working as a superintendent of Assam Company's gardens, where he was accused of abusing his privileges by unauthorized use of tea seeds and labour from the Company's resources to set up the Jorehaut Company along with his cousin.[21] Another planter, James Warren of Assam Company, along with his brother Walter, set up the Beesakopi and Hansara tea gardens in Doom Dooma in Upper Assam.[22]

The planters' own perception of their daily lives on the plantations, as depicted in the (auto)biographical works of retired planters, was one coloured by misery, loneliness and hardship. There was much moaning and groaning about the secluded, 'desultory' lives of 'self denial' in the 'dreadful' and 'unhealthy' climate of Assam.[23] Fear of untimely death due to cholera, malaria and other diseases was a constant refrain in the planters' tales. The pioneers' work of opening up plantations in Assam was seen as a heroic and 'civilizing' task, converting hundreds of 'thousands of acres of virgin soil, now lying waste and uncultivated' into rich and highly productive crops of tea which were to provide employment to hundreds of thousands of 'starving people, paid, for the most part, by foreign gold'. The plantation enterprise was expected to bring prosperity to the province, make 'miles of malarious and deadly jungle disappear, and our fine healthy young hill colonies connect by broad high ways with the *termini* of the great arterial lines of railroads, and thus with the ports of Calcutta, Bombay, Karachi, and Madras'.[24]

Some among the colonial bureaucracy were however much more forthright about the reality of this grand 'vision': 'The tea interest in Assam is essentially a class interest, more so even than the cotton interest in Bombay, and it should not be confounded with the general interest of the people of Assam.'[25] In the early years, the main task was to clear the wild, 'malaria ridden' forests of Assam where indigenous tea plants grew most thickly. A sizeable crop of tea could then be obtained from the tea clearings in the following year. These small plots, no more than patches of 200 by 400 yards of cleared jungle, were then built up to form tea *baris* (nurseries), which in turn became the first tea gardens. Setting up plantations was considered hazardous and time-consuming, with very 'primitive' means of communication available. Hostile neighbouring tribal and hill communities, wild animals and poisonous snakes, the unhealthy climate and diseases, the lack of adequate medical facilities, etc., often caused the untimely demise of the planting 'pioneers'.[26] Social isolation and seclusion added to their miseries:

> White women were as scarce as white elephants during early years. A few managers were married, but rarely an assistant. There was nothing of course to stop a newly arrived assistant from dreaming of a fair one with chestnut hair and green eyes that he had left back in the country.[27]

Natives were considered too 'desultory', 'unenterprising' and of 'low intellect' to be worthy of socializing with the white planters. The labourers were considered to be of 'lowest intellect' and the 'worst nightmare' for a planter to have to deal with every day of their entire life in the plantations. However, since they were an integral part of life in the plantation and crucial to tea production, the planters, despite their loathing for them, had to deal with them.

The issue of labour was problematic from the very inception of the tea industry in Assam. The adoption of a labour-intensive process of production for the fast-expanding plantations required a continuous and adequate supply of labour, which was not easily available. Planters and government officials alike complained about the 'deficiency of labour'.[28] Unable to procure local labour, mostly because of their unwillingness to offer competitive wages, the planters turned to importing labourers from neighbouring Bengal. After a first decade of uncertainty, the steady growth of tea plantations during the 1850s whetted the appetite of the planters, and they began to seek bigger fortunes and embarked upon an ambitious expansion plan overlooking the constraints of labour supply. Colonel Jenkins' warning that this expansion was not 'judicious and prudent' given the limited 'means of procuring labour in the Province' did not dampen the expansionist drive of the planters.[29] The inadequacy of labour supply was compounded by the general instability of labour employed in the tea plantations. The local Kacharis, while being excellent workers for clearing the tropical forests, were unwilling to accept permanent resident employment in the plantations. The labourers imported from neighbouring Bengal often deserted on arrival when they discovered that the wages were too low, along with harsh working and living conditions and an inhospitable climate.[30] However, the acreage under tea continued to expand, and production seems to have increased during the early two decades without resort to any significant degree of coercion of the available labour; there is no evidence to the contrary, at least for this period. To prevent jeopardy to their enterprise at this early stage, the Directors of Assam Company in fact specifically instructed the garden management to desist from coercive treatment of the labour force, as it could adversely affect production and future recruitment.[31]

European tea managers and their assistants
(courtesy National Anthropological Archives, Smithsonian Institution)

The structure of the planters' power hierarchy based on coercion and extra-legal authority, aided and abetted by the colonial state, which was to dominate production relations in the Assam tea plantations for long, evolved in the 1860s with the introduction of the indenture system at the height of the speculative boom of the 'tea mania' years. Over the next couple of decades this power structure developed and operated at two levels. At the top level, the tea companies, with their headquarters in Britain and managing agents in Calcutta, instituted a centralized authority in the form of an apex body in 1881, the Indian Tea Association. This apex body, manned by senior executives of the tea companies and retired officials of the Indian Civil Services, functioned as a lobbyist for the industry in the corridors of power, on the one hand, and as a planner and implementer of strategies of production organization and labour policies in the plantations, on the other. This power structure was bolstered by the industry's social and political connections with the colonial authority to influence policies on matters of labour, particularly for preventing legal impediments against the use of extra-legal and coercive forms of labour control in the plantations. The ITA used its organizational connections and political clout to influence the colonial state, and its policies on matters concerning recruitment, transportation and legislation. Remarkably, it also displayed the cunningness to adapt to the exigencies of changing legislative and political situations in the region, and manipulated them to the industry's advantage. However it was the nature of the power structure and production relations which evolved within the plantation complex that played a crucial role in ensuring and sustaining the planters' domination and control over labour for over more than a century. From the very beginning, given its labour-intensive production processes, the tea industry's major pre-occupation was labour.

At the ground level, these strategies and policies were enforced through a hierarchical power structure centered around the managerial authority of European planters and their native assistants. The key emphasis throughout was on immobilizing labour within the plantation complex after their arrival there, and, at the same time, on curbing their contact with the outside world – both aimed at preventing the formation of collective labour organizations. The authorities at both levels operated in tandem, and strategies and policies prepared by the apex body were implemented with a remarkable degree of success. In what follows, we shall try to trace the story of how this power structure evolved and functioned in Assam Valley's tea plantations.

The dramatic expansion of plantations and its sustenance demanded a stable labour force and a regular supply of large numbers of labourers. The destabilization caused by increasing desertions among migrant labourers threatened the growth of the newly set up plantations, as well as the loss of capital invested in their recruitment and transportation. The requirement of labour stability was also linked to the production processes that were operational in the tea plantations. Tens of thousands of the mobilized labour force were immobilized within the spatial confines of plantation enclaves as a substitute for the labour market mechanism. The frenetic increase in acreage and production in the face of declining tea prices could only be sustained through stable and cheap labour. The logic of all this demanded a docile and disciplined labour force which had to be kept under control and prevented from desertion by all means including violence and intimidation.

The 'tea mania' era witnessed growing incidents of ill treatment and physical coercion of the labour force by the planters. Edgar was the earliest civil servant to observe and critically report on this development:

> The miseries of the early immigrant were in too many instances cruelly aggravated by the ill-treatment of their employers. At one time the feelings of the planters as a body towards their labourers was most deplorable. The best men looked on them as a thankless, discontented lot, for whose good it was almost useless to do anything, and whom it was impossible not to dislike; while among the worst sort of planters this feeling of aversion deepened into a mingling of hatred and contempt that led in some instances to acts of revolting cruelty, and in far more cases than has ever been publically known to systematic and gross ill-treatment.[32]

Instances of labourers being tied and flogged by planters as punishment for not performing their share of daily tasks appeared in an official report for the first time. 'I have reasons to believe', Edgar reported, 'that this practice was almost universal in Cachar when I went there in 1863, and I had on excellent authority that it was at least equally common in Assam.'[33] Edgar, one among the few British officials who were critical of the indenture system, tried to find reasons for this behaviour of the planters, and his explanation became a standard one to be used in all future official reportage: namely, that the planters had invested capital on the recruitment and transportation of immigrants who were expected to perform labour in return; and that on arrival these labourers were found 'unfit' to work or were deserting in large numbers, thus threatening the very survival of the enterprise. Going beyond this explanation and presenting a psychological profile of planter behaviour, Edgar argued that the planter, who himself was suffering the 'miserable' weather and consequent sickness but still stuck to his work, expected his labourers also not to 'shirk' work and run away. He had paid for them and was going to extract work from them by any means at his disposal. 'Some such line of reasoning as this led to the practice of tying up and flogging coolies, who were really physically unfit for work of any kind, when the amount of daily task did not come up to what the manager considered they ought to do.'[34]

Non-compliance of the contract in the form of desertion by labourers was considered the worst 'crime', which ought to be treated with severe punishment aimed as a deterrent and at taming the 'jungley coolie'. Serious efforts were made to prevent desertions. Edgar reported that hill men were specially employed to track down 'absconders' with a promise of a reward of Rs 5 per head. Dogs also seem to have been specially trained for this purpose – a practice reminiscent of slaves tracked down by dogs in British-owned plantations in Jamaica during the seventeenth century.[35] The worst fate awaited those who tried to desert but failed to do so. If the 'absconder' (an epithet planters used for the deserting labourer) was caught, he was tied up and flogged – and the reward paid to his capturer was deducted by way of fine from his future earnings. But severe flogging often meant no future earnings: 'often runaways enfeebled by their sufferings in the jungles, died under or from the effect of the floggings they received when caught'.[36]

Edgar's report was not the only one. In March 1866, Captain T. Lamb, Deputy Commissioner of Darrang, reported gruesome flogging of labourers by Dunne, the assistant manager of Seerajooli tea garden of Assam Tea Company. R. Donald, the senior manager, had ordered Dunne 'to give a jolly good welting to the ringleaders' who had run away and were brought back after being caught. Lamb's account, recorded in his Mofussil Diary, spoke of extreme physical cruelty – 'the unfortunate men had had their backs cut to pieces with a cane, oil and salt had been rubbed into the wounds'[37] – by Dunne, who was already implicated in a case of flogging a young labourer who died the next day from its effects. Very often such cases remained unknown and unreported because of the enforced isolated existence of the labour communities in the Assam Valley tea plantations.

With the amalgamation of tea gardens under the management of agency houses and the impressive growth of the tea industry from the 1870s onwards, the entire geographical landscape of Assam Valley was transformed. Tens of thousands of acres of jungles and wastelands were converted into private estates, inhabited by Indian labourers and clerical staff, and European managers and assistant managers. Through mergers of small gardens, large units averaging 1,200 acres in size emerged as the typical plantation in the late nineteenth century. Most of these gardens were physically isolated and deliberately excluded from urban settlements, as well as from surrounding rural areas through fencing. The isolation and secluded existence of the plantations further exacerbated the demographic gap between the European planters and the migrant labourers. By the end of the nineteenth century, there were approximately 1,000 European planters living among a population of over half a million labourers. These vast tea gardens, with resident indentured labourers compulsorily settled in 'coolie lines', provided the milieu for the exercise of virtually unlimited powers by the planters over the labour force. Physical coercion became integral to the assertion of authority of the *sahibs* over the labourers in daily life on the plantations during the indenture regime, in order to keep labour docile, disciplined and intimidated.[38]

The extraordinary power of private arrest of runaway labourers bestowed upon the planters by the indenture legislations provided legitimacy to the extra-legal authority that planters exercised over indentured labourers. This also began to shape the attitude of European planters, both as individuals and as a class, towards labour. The planter in this regime was no mere employer of wage labour. He occupied a pivotal position around which revolved the lives of the entire plantation community: of assistants, supervisory staff including clerks, *sirdars*, *muharrirs*, *jamadars*[39] and labourers. Behind the assertion of such authority was an assumption of the inherent inferiority of the labouring classes as sub-human beings. In the worst cases they were compared to animals, as the planter T. Kinney did: 'Assam imports . . . a number of curious and expensive animals known as Act I coolies.'[40] Terms like 'coolie', 'primitive', 'jungly', 'slothful', 'scoundrel', 'absconder', etc., emerged in the planters' vocabulary while referring to labourers. Such perceptions began to spread among European planters sometimes at the very outset of their journey, even prior to taking up their posts in the Assam plantations. Describing his woes of steamer travel en route to Assam, John Carnegie, a young British arrival, bitterly complained of 'mosquitoes . . . and worse than all we have 500 coolies on board the dirtiest brutes in creation swarming with lice and one had cholera last night, what with coolies, mosquitoes and lice I shan't be sorry when this is at an end'.[41] His brother Alexander, also en route to Assam to take up a job as an assistant in a tea garden in Tezpur, wrote to his parents of his experience with the 'coolies': 'We had awful work driving the coolies, we rode up and down the line and had to shove them on exactly as nigger drivers in America.'[42] Between the time he arrived and became assistant manager, Alexander had already imbibed and assumed the attributes of authority and power of the master:

> I am now in a jungle, a sort of small king among the niggers. Counting women and children I have charge of about 450 people, an awful queer lot the most of them are. They are always getting ill and I am doctor and have made some wonderful cures of dysentery and spleen, they all have more or less enlargement of spleen. I have a large store of medicine here and some recipes and every morning I have to administer oil of castor to a lot of them. I have a splendid recipe for spleen and have cured a lot of chaps and dysentery too, two of them are dead but they die here very easily so they don't think much of that. . . . They not only died, they absconded in a tiresome way.[43]

The practice of flogging as a form of disciplining and taming labourers soon became a regular feature of the Assam Valley tea plantations. The public display of such brutal punishment was also meant to act as a deterrent against desertions. To the planters it appeared quite natural that labourers who deserted or disobeyed should be flogged. After all the company had invested so much money in bringing them to the gardens. A letter from W.A. Stoddard, manager of the Maphock Tea Estate in Sibsagar district, to the government in 1872 revealed this attitude. Suggesting methods of dealing with defaulting labourers, he wrote: 'that it be enacted all agreement labourers after punishment for default be returned to their employers to complete their contracts with the terms of absence added on', and that on a second offence any once convicted labour should be whipped. 'The stick has a greater terror for those innate thieves and scamps.' He added that flogging was useful, 'especially without hurting the man much, the quiet, firm systematic way the government floggings are conducted'.[44]

That such 'tyranny' was not confined only to 'unscrupulous European adventurers' of the 1860s, as Griffiths asserted, is clear from the observations and comments of later British officials. At the turn of the twentieth century, Henry Cotton, Chief Commissioner of Assam, reported the case of a woman labourer who was flogged for trying to escape from the garden. Another woman was flogged on suspicion of helping others to escape. He also came across a case where labourers were confined for a number of days in a 'prison-house' in the tea garden and mercilessly beaten. The arms of three of the labourers were broken as a result of the beating by the manager.[45] Similarly, Sir Bampfylde Fuller, the next Chief Commissioner of Assam, observed:

On some gardens there was a good deal of flogging, and I will mention two cases which had some interesting features. In one of them a woman was stripped and flogged. Her husband brought a criminal charge against the garden overseer. He was acquitted by an Indian Assistant Magistrate on the score that he acted under the orders of his European manager. . . . The other case was still more serious. A coolie who had been flogged with a stirrup leather, under the direction of a young European assistant, was killed by the punishment. He suffered from an enlarged spleen, and this was ruptured.[46]

As late as the 1920s, a British trade union delegate reported: 'we witnessed a group of men, women and children working away together, while five yards away was a planters' young assistant proudly hugging the whip'.[47]

Flogging was not the only means of punishment used to deter desertion, defiance of authority and 'shirking' of work by labourers. In daily life at the workplace and at the *sahib*'s bungalow, physical beatings and the showering of abusive language became a 'natural' routine for the planter to enforce discipline and as punishment. Writing about runaway labourers to his parents in England, a young planter Alexander recounted that

four of the coolies were caught, and brought in this morning, they got a great mauling from the overseers and are put to double work for the next month, at least I said so today but in about a week I will let them do the same as the rest, this is an awful bore when they run away.[48]

Writing towards the end of the nineteenth century, David Crole, a retired planter, observed:

Coolie men are easy to manage, as a rule. Now and then, there happen to be half-a-dozen rascals in some *chillan* (gang), and they make a good deal of trouble; but as the planter does not often bother to wear the kid gloves on his iron hand, and as he is vested also with a good deal of power and authority partly by law, but mostly by coolie tradition and his own self-assertion, he is generally quite able to cope with any tendency to 'kick over the traces' on the part of men's gangs, at all events.[49]

George Barker, another planter, recalled his recipe for dealing with 'shirking' labourers in his garden during the 1880s: 'Various forms of punishment – from a good thrashing to making him do two or three times the amount [of work] over again – are inflicted.'[50] In the case of malingering labourers, 'the wrath of the sahib when he places his hand on the cool unfevered wrist of an impostor is justifiable, and the judicious application of the cane quickly convinces the coolie that he has made a mistake in imagining that there could be anything the matter with him'.[51] Reminiscing about his days in the plantation in the 1890s, planter W.M. Fraser wrote about an instance of a senior manager chastising women labourers for faulty leaf-plucking, 'The ground become strewn with bad leaf, while from one woman to the other went the admonishing Thomson, his tongue and hands fully employed.'[52] Unlike the prevailing practice in the Ceylonese and Malayan plantations where *kanganies* (counterparts of *sirdars*) functioned as communication mediators between the planters and the labourers as the former did not know Tamil, the British planters evolved '*coolie-baat*' (coolie-talk), a creole version, which became the language of command and of everyday communication directly with them.

These attitudes were also acquired by younger European planters in the process of becoming 'coolie drivers' on the plantations. F.A. Hetherington, a new arrival, after spending a few months as an assistant under the tutelage of a senior planter, recorded this interesting episode in his diary on 1 August 1901:

> Went round the new lines plucking and nearly caused a riot by clouting three women, one of whom happened to be Moorali Sirdar's wife. They were plucking into *kapre*, which was strictly forbidden. The punishment was in accordance with Dunlop's ways, but I was too new to inflict it myself. With one accord the women complained to Godwin and Dunlop pitched into me. A few days before he had censured me for not punishing them, so neither way could I do right. Am getting sick of the place and feel inclined to chuck up the job. I can't hit it off with the coolies.[53]

He did not 'chuck up' the job, of course, but worked for ten years as a planter; and, in due course, beating recalcitrant labour came naturally to him. On 11 July 1902, he recorded 'thrashing' his two bungalow servants Nando Lal and Kaddo for some trouble, the cause of which he found out only later: 'Investigating the case at the office and found them only partially guilty . . . so my thrashing was considered sufficient punishment and they were restored to the bungalow once more, instead of going to hoe on hard day.'[54] In November 1902 he recorded flogging a labourer who had quarrelled and beaten up his wife; and after the flogging he went socializing, attended a farewell dinner and 'had a jolly evening'.[55] By May 2003, Hetherington had adapted himself to the role of a 'coolie driver' very smoothly. On 28th May, when he found a field labourer's performance of the hoeing task unsatisfactory, 'My wrath, which had been accumulating, burst forth and I hammered Behari.' The next evening, he gave Behari a bottle of rum: 'It is the best way to deal with a coolie: half kill him when he plays the fool and then show him how kind you can be if you like.'[56]

When their harsh treatment of labourers and extra-legal practices invoked angry public criticism, the planters and their supporters provided a series of justifications. First, they argued that the existing penal laws as a means of maintaining 'order' and 'contentment' among the tea garden labourers were wholly inadequate. Even the power of private arrest bestowed by legislation in the person of the manager was not considered enough.[57] Secondly, they cited the 'tardiness' and 'inefficiency' of the police, and the distance of the magistrate from the gardens, as reasons for the ineffectiveness of the existing laws. Therefore, it was argued, 'in the interests of all parties, it is absolutely necessary that an undivided principle of authority should primarily and visibly repose in the person of the manager'.[58] In order to keep under control a labour force that varied from 300 to 1,000 in one estate, it was further argued, the manager wielded extra-legal authority 'on his own responsibility with the consent of the labour force'.[59]

The need to wield extra-legal authority also arose out of a fear of the possibility of violent militancy of the labour force in the gardens. Through the history of tea plantations in Assam, there have been a number of cases of spontaneous militant revolt by labourers against the harsh and inhuman treatment meted out to them by the planters. Such violent revolts sometimes resulted in the death of managers and assistant managers.[60] This fear regarding personal safety was further aggravated by the fact that the planters were vastly outnumbered by the labour force. The Indian Tea Association expressed the fear in a memorandum to the government: 'There are on the average 400 coolies to one white man; large numbers of the tea gardens are isolated and the planter's control rests mainly on his prestige. Instances of organized rebellion and attack on the managers are numerous to indicate that manager's authority is none too secure.'[61] It was argued that 'The coolie who strikes a planter strikes authority and deserves to be punished with the full measure of severity with which this offence has been visited by every law maker since the beginning of history, and which is still demanded by the circumstances of India.'[62] The government of course was a willing supporter of the planters. It gave legitimacy to their extra-legal authority. Many of them were appointed honorary magistrates with powers to deal with petty cases, both criminal and civil, involving labourers.[63]

The rationale for the use of extra-legal methods, unacceptable in the 'civilized' west, was well articulated by Barker: 'Coolie management is the planters' worst trouble. All the other work is of most pleasing kind, but coolie driving rapidly multiplies a manager's grey hair.'[64] To the planters, the 'coolie' presented the lowest level of human intellect for company, and stood for everything that was disagreeable and undesirable about life in the plantations. Samuel Baildon, a retired planter, advised new young planters to be 'patient' while dealing with the 'intellectually low condition' of the 'coolie' because,

> while he undoubtedly possess a head, the nature of its contents is still an unsettled question as regards brains (if they have any) . . . coolies should not be expected to grasp the gist of an order directly it is spoken. It requires great patience to be thus forbearing, I well know; but when it is remembered that coolies are looked upon generally as the dubious possessors of brain power. Young planters should hasten

them judiciously, but never hurry them. It is possible to make one's life a constant jar and dissatisfaction, by allowing oneself to be worried and vexed unceasingly by the stupidity of the coolies.[65]

Barker's lamentation expressed strong feelings: '*AH* me! What a host of past troubles that one little word "coolie" conjures up! The climate is not all that one could desire, the insects are infamous; the coolie is worse than either, and makes the two former feeble by comparison with his own powers of inflicting torture.'[66] To western liberal critics of the plantation regime he responded with the argument that eastern labourers were different from their counterparts in Europe. He asserted that after years of personal acquaintance with their 'idiosyncrasies', he was convinced that

> The coolies, both men and women, are lazy and require a great deal of looking after. Hot days are conducive to this spirit of idleness, and many small parties of coolies have to be routed out from under the grateful shade of the nearest tree, where they are to be found stowed away, enjoying the rest from toil.[67]

Native labour, he argued, was unresponsive to higher wage inducement: 'Even the prospects of an increase to their income will not allure these people, so curiously are they constituted. . . . A native troubles not about future, for he can always obtain employment, and if the worst comes, his people will support him in declining days.'[68] Barker was expressing a view shared by the highest in the colonial hierarchy. On the issue of applying western standards in the Indian context, Lord Landsowne, the Viceroy, in his farewell dinner speech delivered at Royal Exchange, Calcutta, protested vehemently against the practice of pouring 'inordinately strong doses of Western nostrums' down Indian throats – 'There is a tendency to apply British standards to such questions as the employment of labour in mines, in factories, and the tea gardens.'[69]

The planters' notion of the labouring class in their gardens was akin to that of the white masters regarding their black slave labourers in the Caribbean colonies and during the antebellum era in the Southern states of the USA. Their views were well articulated in *The London Times* in 1902, in a series of articles written in defence of the tea planters during their conflict with Henry Cotton. The author of these articles pointed out that the Assam tea garden labourers have been recruited from 'jungly' races that could not be mobilized for competition. The reasons given for this were the 'obscure forces of custom and sentiment' in the labourers' lives, because of which they were 'blindly rooted to their homes'. Only starvation caused by famines could move them.[70] Referring to the scandals and abuses associated with recruitment during the past forty years, the author of the articles blamed, apart from the private contractors, the 'jungly' recruit himself:

> The jungly character, primitive but not honest, and always cheating, but always

out-cheated, lent itself readily to further these abuses. Not the recruiter only, but the recruit, his friends and family, the constables and petty underlings, the headmen and the watchmen, all these ignoble savages were reveling in the Orgy of Fraud.[71]

But after coming to the tea gardens, he argued, they were 'well-fed' and lived in 'comfort', and achieved 'permanent prosperity'. However, in order to reach such a state, they had to go through the 'troubles' of a long journey, acclimatization, fever, sickness and homesickness. These 'troubles' were not considered too serious as ultimately, he argued, the rewards were to follow. Similar justifications in defence of slavery in the British-owned Caribbean plantations were put forward by a resident of St Christopher in the 1650s, who wrote that Negro bondage was really a blessing for the Africans; they had suffered so much neglect and warfare in their native habitat that they 'prefer their present slavery before their former liberty, the loss whereof they never afterwards regretted'.[72]

Towards the end of the nineteenth century, Buckingham, a senior planter and Chairman of the Assam branch of the Indian Tea Association, echoed similar claims:

> The tea industry has not only been the means of saving and civilizing thousands of natives of India, but also kept them from perishing miserably from starvation and disease; and at the same time it is gradually developing the resources of the one of the richest provinces of the Empire.[73]

The Chairman of the Assam Labour Board described the process of recruitment for the Assam tea gardens as a 'famine relief measure' in the recruiting districts.'[74]

In answer to propaganda by the nationalist press against the living conditions in the plantations, the author of *The London Times* article retorted that once a labourer came to Assam, he did not want to go back: 'After arrival on the gardens there ensues a great and genuine conversion. The coolie "suffers a tea-change". After a little time the kidnapped youth and the abducted woman will have to be rekidnapped and reabducted before you can induce them to return.'[75] This was of course simply not true. Most labourers simply did not have enough money to go back. Henry Cotton noted:

> . . . this 'tea-change' is a pure delusion. Emigrants do not return to their homes, first, because they are under a penal contract to serve for a term which ordinarily extends to four years, and if they were to attempt to return within that period they would be guilty of desertion and sentenced to a term of rigorous imprisonment. They often do try to escape – there are annually many thousand desertions recorded and not infrequently these hapless deserters perish miserably in the jungle or pass the remainder of their lives in slavery among the savage hill tribes to whom they have unwillingly escaped.[76]

The planters' eagerness to present a picture of a the labourer enjoying a most comfortable life was not unconnected with the very real problem of recruitment.[77] By depicting the condition of the labourer as 'comfortable' and 'secure', they hoped to attract labour as well as to neutralize the nationalist propaganda. Interestingly, the apologists of slavery in South America also painted a stereotypical picture of 'happy and contented' bondsmen as a form of propaganda to counter the abolitionists' image of wretched slaves.[78] For the apologists of black slavery, the harsh, exploitative side of it disappeared almost entirely: the white master became a 'parent' or 'guardian', and the slave a child who, on the basis of 'common humanity', was submitted to the 'family circle' and subjected to family government.[79] In Assam, the tea planter became the arbiter of the social life of the labour force isolated in 'coolie lines'. Barker remembered fondly the times when on account of some quarrel in the 'coolie lines', the *jamadar* (headman) would bring the 'delinquents' to his bungalow in order to punish the 'evil-doer': 'The sahib acts as judge and jury, and sits in judgment.'[80] The author of the articles in *The Times* boasted:

> . . . each individual coolie lives his life under the direct daily personal supervision of an English Sahib. The Sahib was the only one who was directly interested in coolie's personal welfare, and who is always on the spot. The Sahib watches the condition of his labourers with his own eyes, he hears their complaints with his own ears, he pays their wages to them with his own hand. Hard is his life and scanty his reward.[81]

This 'sacrifice' on the part of the *sahib*, it was claimed, saved the labourer from the 'fierce battle of millions, amid storms and stress of varying seasons', and brought him 'into the constant shadow of prosperity and peace. . . . He is protected from famine, from fraud, from violence, from usury, from all manner of external ill. For him and for his life alone, among the poor of India, the problem of life is solved.'[82]

For the chairman of the Indian Tea Association, the tea gardens existed 'mostly for the benefit of the coolie. Shareholders have had nothing; the manager toils for a salary that allows him to save nothing; yet the coolie continued happy in the knowledge that he has exchanged the fear of famine for a certain livelihood and modest savings.'[83] These 'toiling' managers drew a monthly salary between Rs 800 and 1,000 plus 5 per cent commission on net profits, as compared to the labourers' monthly wage of Rs 5 for men and Rs 4 for women, at the turn of twentieth century.[84] Along with a cash salary, the planters enjoyed perks and privileges that could have been the envy of even the better paid civil servants. By the 1880s, the managers' bungalows 'were like palaces compared to those in the dark old days'.[85] The planters used labourers for domestic chores. Barker recounted the members of his bunga- low staff: *kitmutgar* [*khitmadgar* – one who serves] or waiter/butler; bearer to look after the bedroom; *khansama* [cook] and his assistant; two or three *paniwallahs* [water carriers]; the *mater* [*mehtar* – sweeper]; two *chowkidars* [watchmen]; *punkah-wallahs* [fan pullers]; *sysces*; *malee* [gardener]; *moorgie-wallah* [to look after the chickens]; *gorukhiya* [cow-herd]; and a few others.[86] The seclusion and social isolation of the 'pioneering' days had given way to an active social and sporting life. Hetherington's diary is full of entries depicting a life of high pleasure, entertainment and socializing among the planters – constant rounds of visiting each other, dinners and dance parties, church services, club evenings, hunting and sports. The list of favourite sports played by the planters included polo, bridge, cricket, billiards, angling and hunting. Unlike in the early days, white women were no longer scarce. Planters were staying longer periods in their jobs, and bringing their wives with them or getting married once their contracts were renewed.[87]

Among the managers, security of job and prospects of promotion became synonymous with ensuring uninterrupted production and a steady growth of profits for the tea companies. The drive for intensification of the labour process and constant supervision to prevent labourers from running away reinforced the elements of physical coercion, violence and extra-legal methods that had been adopted by the planters for controlling labour in the period of the 'tea mania'. The tea companies considered desertions as a financial loss on account of managerial failure in the gardens. James Finlay & Company's instructions to its Estate Department on this issue were to

> impress on Managers the absolute necessity of keeping their labour if their gardens are to be profitably worked, and they must understand that the proper handling of their labour force will be regarded as an essential point in considering a Manager for any promotion that they may be going, or even his continuance in his charge. An undue proportion of abscondings will be carefully noted against a Manager.[88]

This attitude of the companies further pressurized the planters to resort to coercive methods as a deterrent against desertions. Such extra-legal action was not confined just to the workplace or to the prevention of desertions, but permeated the entire social life of the labour force isolated in 'coolie lines' within the plantation complex. George Barker fondly recalled sitting in judgment every morning on cases of 'coolie' 'delinquency' reported to him by the *jamadar* (headman in the 'coolie lines') and meting out punishment to 'evildoers'.[89] Planters also devised extra-legal mechanisms to prolong the period of indenture servitude. Labourers were often coerced or tricked into renewing their contracts after the expiry of the original period of five years. A Bengal government official reported in 1888 that he was shocked to find a planter organizing a polyandrous marital union between five 'time-expired' 'coolies', i.e. labourers who had completed their contract period, and a single woman. In return each man had to agree to re-engage in the same garden for a five-year period. 'The disposal in marriage of all imported female coolies', he noted, 'is regarded as a matter entirely within the jurisdiction of the manager.'[90] Barker recounted the difficulties in getting the 'low caste' labourers to renew their contracts (*bundibus* in Assamese): they gave 'as much trouble as they possibly can before signing a new *bundibus*. Long separation from their relations' sweet society, a longing to return to their own country, illness or perverseness, and a thousand and one things, makes the renewal of agreements a time of suffering for the planter.'[91] Crole's observations reveal the nature of such 'persuasion' adopted by the 'suffering' planter:

> I have known cases where the planter has cunningly arranged so that the wife's original four years' agreement expires before the husband's new agreement is fully served, and then the wife is told she must also take anew contract for two years or else leave the garden, and of course she has to submit to the former. Then when husband's contract is worked out he is again forced to renew it, owing to his wife's term not yet being expired. And so the business is worked on the principle of a 'little more bread for my cheese and a little more cheese for my bread'.[92]

His sense of outrage obliged him to describe this practice as 'selling of women (for that is what it comes to when shorn of all quibbling), and trading on the affections of the simple-minded unfortunates who consider they are in the power of the Sahib, would rebound little to the credit of planting community'.[93]

Fuller, who became the Chief Commissioner of Assam after the sacking of Henry Cotton, also discovered that planters had developed strategies of keeping labour on the garden far beyond the period of their contracts. In his confidential note he recorded:

> From the facts that have come to my notice it appears that gardens are commonly guarded by chaukidars. Under the law the coolie's indenture terminates in four years, but there are a great many planters who would feel it be a grievance if a coolie left them after 20 years' service, and, as a matter of fact, four years' service is not sufficient to recoup a garden for the high original cost of the coolie. Every kind of expedient – good or bad – is practised in order to induce the coolie to renew his contract.[94]

As a consequence, the majority of the migrant labourers who were under indenture contracts in the Assam tea gardens became, in due course, permanent residents over generations. Fuller was candid in his observations when he commented, 'The idea that an employer of labour can forcibly detain his coolies seems to be prevalent throughout all classes in the province, and it is not without reason that Assam is known as a "prison land".'[95] He was however well aware of Cotton's fate before him and was therefore, at the same time, very careful and conciliatory towards the planters:

I wish to disavow here any intention of condemning garden managers, the majority of whom work their labour force with a good deal of kindness. The practices which I condemned are the result of an environment which owes its origin to legislation undertaken more than a generation ago in view of special difficulties that attended the engagement and control of foreign labour in Assam.[96]

One of the remarkable features of the tea industry, as pointed out above, was its ability to adapt to the exigencies of changing legislative and political situations in the region, and to manipulate them to its advantage. For example, the withdrawal of penal provisions and the power of private arrest in 1908 was seen as a threat to or dilution of its control and dominance over the labour force. The Indian Tea Association immediately activated its branches to successfully lobby with the government to adopt new means and strategies to perpetuate the basic dependency of labour relations and the isolation of labour. They demanded that, in the absence of the power of private arrest, provision should be made for expediting the issual of warrants against 'absconding' labour, and they complained that Act XIII (which was still in force) alone could not afford the necessary control over the labour force.[97] The government obliged and appointed special magistrates to address the first issue.[98] On the second issue, the Enquiry Committee of 1906 had suggested a way beyond the dependency relationship for controlling labour. To keep labour under 'control' and prevent desertions, it recommended better treatment of labourers by the planters and the use of available wastelands to settle the immigrants as an incentive. Initially the planters were reluctant to offer land for private cultivation to their labourers. Instead of accepting the suggestion of the Enquiry Committee, they demanded that rules be framed prohibiting imported labourers, unless they had been residents for four years in Assam, from holding government land.[99] They feared that the imported labourers would be tempted to take up government land for independent cultivation and desert garden employment, hence the conditionality of four years' residence.[100] However their fears were unfounded. Most government officials in the province were unanimous in their view that imported labourers were rarely in a position to take up land on their own account until the expiry of four years of service in a garden.[101] The Chief Commissioner argued that it was beyond the means of newly imported tea garden labourers to settle on government land immediately after their arrival. A cultivator taking up wasteland in Assam needed sufficient resources to survive for a year or two without getting any return from the land. Moreover, he was charged land revenue at full rates from the day he took over the land. No tea garden labourer would be able to satisfy these conditions unaided; he would have keep earning wages until his savings was sufficiently high to pay for his upkeep.[102] The Enquiry Committee of 1906 also observed, 'the fact that a revenue free term is not allowed and that full rates are charged for land newly taken up, operates as a powerful check on the exodus from the estate.'[103]

The planters now adopted the strategy of using land to tie down labour on the tea garden while declaring it to be an incentive to supplement their income. They had vast acreage under their control which was unutilized. The Assam Valley plantations had so far used only one-third of the total land granted to them for tea cultivation. The state government assisted the planters in the implementation of their new strategy by granting land on special terms specifically for this purpose. This grant was seen as a part of the government's policy to encourage colonization of wastelands and, at the same time, 'to help gardens to retain their labour force'. Planters could thus allot small plots of lands to labourers for private cultivation, but on condition of their continued work in the gardens. Planters were empowered to evict labourers for non-compliance of this condition.[104] Subsequent official reports considered such grants of land to labourers as an important 'concession' which supplemented the earnings of labourers and as a source of 'popularity'.[105] The Royal Commission remarked: 'The garden worker is essentially an agriculturist, and he desires for the possession of a holding which he can cultivate with the help of the Members of his family.'[106] However the labourers had to pay rent on such land without any occupancy rights and the grants were conditional on continuation of their employment.[107] Planters were empowered to evict them for non-compliance;[108] the land could also be taken back on 'disciplinary' grounds.[109] Besides, the size of these land-holdings was very small, averaging between one-fourth to half an acre per worker, and was hardly a source of additional earnings.[110] The Assam Labour Enquiry Committee in 1921–22 did not consider the cash value of crops as a 'concession'.[111] While private cultivation did not contribute significantly towards the total earnings of the labour force, in the face of constantly declining real wages their dependence on such land for survival increased. Even for those who could escape from garden work, alternate employment was not a real option; work in other industries, such as might have existed, required different skills. Thus, given the low level of garden wages, these lands provided labourers an extra source of subsistence and often tied them to garden employment for long periods, sometimes generationally.

Another significant practice which sustained severe forms of dependency in production relations was the partial payment of wages in kind, in the form of rice at subsidized rates. This was first introduced in the indenture contract and remained in vogue till well after Indian independence. The general impression of the material conditions of labour projected by the planters and the colonial state was one of 'comfort' and 'well-being'. It was further pointed out that the cash wage did not represent the total earnings of the labourer since it was supplemented by grants of cultivable land for private cultivation as well as by the provision of cheap, subsidized rice.[112] In reality, however, as was often revealed in colonial documents themselves, this subsidy was merely a subsistence device for the bare minimum maintenance of labourers on the gardens. Planters were often guilty of non-compliance in paying minimum statutory wages, and the real wages of tea garden labourers did not rise or remained stagnant during most of the period of colonial rule. Since the statutory minimum cash payment was highly inadequate even as subsistence wage, and even that was not fully paid, the labourers and their families were forced to depend on the planters for subsidized rations for their daily survival.[113]

A third practice that perpetuated dependency was payment of 'advances' or 'bonus' for renewal of contracts with 'time-expired' labourers under the Workman's Breach of Contract Act XIII of 1859.[114] It was asserted that these were popular incentives for labourers contracted under this Act.[115] In reality, these advances or *girmit* (agreement) money, given both in cash and kind, were to be recovered from the labourers' wages. Given the extremely low level of their earnings, the advances became a source of indebtedness and bondage. 'It would not be unfair to hold', noted the Enquiry Committee of 1921–22, 'that the indebtedness of the labourer affects his freedom.'[116] The Royal Commission (1931) found that 'before the abolition of Act XIII of 1859 an outstanding advance, whatever its nature, was no doubt used as an argument against the grant of a discharge certificate, and to that extent the indebtedness of the labourer may be said to have affected his freedom'.[117] Similar methods of binding and controlling the labour force by employers through a system of advances were also used in the Ceylon tea plantations during colonial rule.[118]

The dismantling of the last vestiges of the indenture system deprived the planters of legislative support and legitimacy of running an overtly coercive labour regime. Newer strategies needed to be put in place to deal with the changing official attitude consequent upon growing awareness of prevailing abuses, and to counter the display of aggressive labour militancy in the tea gardens during 1921–22. The planters now proceeded to work out their own internal system, which effectively curbed labour mobility within the tea districts. An elaborate set of rules were drawn up by the ITA in 1929 to discourage enticement of labour from within the tea gardens, which became the basis of the Revised Brahmaputra and Surma Valley Labour Rules and were agreed upon by the tea companies.[119] These rules prohibited tea garden managers from deliberately 'enticing' or employing labourers from other gardens. Rule No. 2 unambiguously laid down that

> no subscriber to these rules shall employ directly or indirectly or harbour or detain any coolie (whether under contract or not) who has been imported by another concern, within the period of 3 years after importation, it being understood, however,

that no claim under this rule shall be made or entertained unless duly formulated within two calendar years after the coolie has left the importing concern.[120]

For arbitration of disputes, an internal court was to be constituted by the ITA branch committee on receipt of written complaints. Breach of rules was punishable by fines varying from Rs 300 to Rs 1,000.[121] D.V. Rege, appointed to enquire into conditions of labour in the plantations in 1946, reported that though these rules were terminated by mutual consent of the planters with effect from 14 September 1938, they reverted to the practice within a year. In 1939, an agreement with identical provisions, known as the Brahmaputra and Surma Valley Local Recruitment Agreement, was signed by the planters.[122] But in order to make the agreement more effective it was stipulated that if an estate employed an 'enticed' immigrant from another estate, the former had to pay a transfer fee of Rs 75 for the first year, Rs 50 for the second and Rs 25 for the third to the garden from which he had been moved.[123] Thus, even after the withdrawal of indentured contract and Act XIII of 1859, the planters still managed to restrain labour mobility and a labour market within the plantations.

One of the most effective means of sustaining the spatial isolation of plantation labour was through control over the freedom of movement of the labour force. Most of the labourers working and living within the garden were employed under the penal contract system and, as already pointed out, kept under close surveillance. Life within the plantation under this system was perceived by most of them as a *phatak* (literally, jail) – a perception based on their experiences. As the Deputy Commissioner of Lakhimpur ruefully noted: 'Every form of punishment however mild and whether really done for the coolie's good or not is designated as phatak.'[124] The power of private arrest was often used against captured runaways and recalcitrant labourers, who were held within the plantation-erected *phatak*. Hetherington, a young planter, recorded in his diary on 23 January 2003 that one of his garden 'coolies', Gora, 'returned from Tezpur, having been flogged by Brown and kept in futtock on the garden for a week'.[125] For the labourer, the *phatak* symbolized the indenture regime based on a penal system. The Assam Chief Commissioner, J.B. Fuller, was convinced that the labourers commonly regarded the whole plantation system as a *phatak*.[126] Successive official enquiry committees and commissions commented disapprovingly on this imposed immobility of labourers and their isolation as an irrational system, but no action to dismantle it was seriously considered.

The planters' logic in resorting to such immobilization was also to 'protect' these 'ignorant' and 'illiterate' labourers from influence and exploitation by 'outsiders'. On the question of 'outsiders' and 'outside influence', they had developed a siege mentality bordering on paranoia.[127] They considered the entire area of the plantation as their private property, and therefore anyone from outside who wished to go through the gardens had to seek prior permission of the manager.[128] While asserting such a claim, they often betrayed their strong racial prejudices not only towards the labourers, but also against the local people living outside the plantation area. The planters controlled vast areas of land in the province, including also public pathways; and they reserved the right to open such pathways for the use of the public. One of the Indian members of the Assam Legislative Council bitterly complained that many tea garden managers demanded *salam* (salute), closing of umbrellas, and dismounting from cycles or horseback, of people passing through the gardens.[129] Indian members also complained that tea garden roads and sometimes even a Local Board road were blocked by the *chowkidars* of the planters, and they were not allowed to pass through because they were the '*kala admi*' (black-skinned men).[130] The planters claimed the right to prevent outsiders from entering the gardens in the exercise of their right to private property.[131] The Royal Commission was not impressed, though, and remarked: 'We do not regard as satisfactory the existing position where workers are largely isolated from outside influence and any member of the public may be effectively prevented from approaching the workers' lines except with the manager's permission.'

As for the planters' argument of the danger of outsiders exploiting the 'illiterate' and 'ignorant' labour force on the tea gardens, the Royal Commission commented that 'this is a risk to which every industry in India is exposed, and we think it better to face it than to continue a policy which inevitably gives rise to suspicion and is liable to be abused'. They recommended that steps should be taken to 'secure public contact with workers' dwellings on all plantations'.[132] Planters in the Ceylon tea gardens adopted similar methods to isolate their labour force from the 'mainstream of political and trade-union developments in the rest of the country. A strict surveillance was maintained on plantations and trespass laws prevented "outside agitators" from having access to the labour force at its place of work.' [133]

Omeo Kumar Das, the Congress MLA from Assam Valley, was the first to publicly contest this position of the planters. In November 1937, he informed the Secretary of the Assam Legislative Assembly of his intention to move the Assam Tea Garden Labourers' Freedom of Movement Bill, and sent a communication to that effect to all concerned, including representatives of the ITA. In a statement of the objects and reasons for the intending Bill, he argued:

> It is generally felt that freedom of movement of tea garden labourers is limited in a manner unheard of in any other industry. They are not allowed to go out of the estate whenever they want to do so. It is a common practice to engage night chowkidars to keep watch over the lines and prevent labourers from leaving the

estate. The impression has been created in the minds of labourers that they have no right to go out of the gardens of their own free will. This constant restraint on their right of free movement has reduced them to a state of slavery.

Through this Bill, Das intended to put an end to the forced isolated existence of labourers in the tea gardens: 'Removal of obstructions will help to establish contact with the outside world which is absolutely necessary for their moral and economic advancement.'[134] The immediate response of the planters was anger and protest against these 'allegations'. F.W. Hockenhull, the ITA representative, threatened further action unless the objectionable expressions were removed from the letter. In the conference called to discuss the Bill, he arrogantly dismissed the charges: 'So far as the letter is concerned in which the conditions of the tea garden labourers is so described, it is sheer nonsense. We are not here to talk about nonsense.'[135] As to the complaint of preventing outsiders' entry and free movement, the ingenious explanation given was that 'the access to outsiders was only denied for the consideration of contagious disease they might bring to the gardens'![136]

At the same time, to cushion the impact of the Bill introduced by Das and to prevent matters escalating into a public debate, the planters made a show of terminating the Assam and Surma Valley Labour Rule. They further assured that no restraint would be placed on labourers attending any meeting outside the gardens. But if outside contact was attempted inside the garden, managerial permission would be required. The Bill was withdrawn as the planters' representatives managed to convince the Congress Ministry that the grievances would be removed.[137] The assurance was not honoured, however. Rege reported in 1946 that the old practice of *chowkidars* keeping a watch and the requirement of managerial permission were still in place. 'Even in cases of marriages, the consent of the manager concerned is generally taken to save trouble.'[138] It was only after independence in 1947 that rules were framed under the plantation code to guarantee freedom of movement in the tea gardens.

The Indian Tea Association

The tea industry acquired cohesiveness and became a well-organized business lobby with the formation of its apex body, the Indian Tea Association (ITA), in 1881 in London, with branches in Calcutta and Assam. Its first chairman and vice chairman were Sir T. Douglas Forsyth (retired Commissioner of Punjab) and Henry Hopkinson (retired Commissioner of Assam), respectively. Other members included planters, representatives of tea companies, bankers and ex-army officers of the British Indian empire.[139] By the beginning of the twentieth century, the ITA and its branches had become an important European pressure group, which successfully influenced government policy affecting the industry in particular and the province of Assam in general. European planters formed the chief body of non-officials who were asked by the government to participate in local committees set up for purposes of developing local communications, etc. Similarly, until 1915, most of the local boards were heavily loaded with ex-officio and elected European planter members.[140] In 1906, a Legislative Council was established as a result of the 1905 settlement which constituted East Bengal and Assam into a Governor's province. The new Council was dominated by Europeans; they accounted for practically two-thirds of its membership.[141] When the question of its enlargement came up with the Morley-Minto Reforms of 1909, the ITA, backed by the Bengal Chamber of Commerce, succeeded in pressuring the government to allocate two seats to the tea interests in the Council.[142] In 1912, when the Assam Legislative Council was constituted, the tea industry alone was allocated three out of eleven elected seats;[143] however, no representation was given to labour. The Assam Legislative Assembly constituted under the Act of 1935 had seven European and two Indian planter members, representing only 1,319 voters. On the other hand, tea garden labour, representing 34,279 voters, was given only four seats.[144] The European group continued to be influential in the provincial government even after a 'popular' ministry was formed in 1937. The official historian of the tea industry acknowledged rather uncomfortably that the European group counted for a great deal in Shillong, and indeed found itself called on to 'play an embarrassingly prominent part in the making and unmaking of provincial governments'.[145] The ITA's views, expressed through deputations, memorials and representations, as well as behind-the-scene contacts with officialdom, received the most privileged considerations by the colonial state. In 1901 the Chief Commissioner of Assam, Henry Cotton, recommended an increase in the monthly wages of labourers in the plantations, and also undertook some corrective administrative measures on the basis of inspection reports by district officials. The ITA's campaign through the Anglo-Indian press and lobbying with senior government officials in Calcutta led to trouble for Cotton from his superiors, and marred his future prospects in the Indian Civil Services.[146]

There were exceptions: the rejection of the Anti-Enticement Bill, which had been cleared by both provincial and central governments after hard lobbying by the ITA, in 1914 by the Secretary of State for India; and the withdrawal of Act XIII of 1859 in 1926.[147] But these did not mean that the ITA was becoming unimportant. For example, when the planters were confronted with the new realities of labour protests assuming collective forms like strikes and a labour exodus during 1921–22, the ITA successfully lobbied with the Assam government to use its propaganda and law enforcement machinery to suppress labour militancy. The government immediately responded and appointed a special officer to supervise the propaganda work.[148] At the same time, complying with the planters' request, the government detailed a number of platoons of the Assam Rifles to assist the civil police in suppressing a strike on the Dibru-Sadiya Railway and an outbreak of rioting among tea garden labourers in the Assam Valley.[149] Further, most of the revolts were ruthlessly suppressed by the local police, and by court prosecutions and convictions of varying terms of rigorous imprisonment.[150] Here are some examples cited in the official report. In Sonaguli and Kacharigaon tea gardens, thirteen and twenty-six labourers, respectively, were convicted and sentenced to various terms of rigorous imprisonment. In Dhandai, Bamgaon and Khairabri tea gardens, 65, six and twelve labourers, respectively, were arrested; of them, forty-nine were sentenced to rigorous imprisonment. In Barkathani tea garden two labourers were convicted – one ran away and the other was sentenced to two years' rigorous imprisonment on the charge of assaulting a manager. The 'ringleaders' in the Amguri and Borsilla tea gardens were prosecuted and directed to execute bonds of Rs 50 each with two sureties to keep the peace for six months, and in default to undergo six months of simple imprisonment. In Suffry tea garden, the sub-divisional officer came with the Assam Rifles and forced the labourers to disperse.[151]

That the ITA's clout had in no way diminished was clear when the Government of India, before passing the Tea Districts Emigrant Labour Act XXII of 1932, sent copies of the draft Bill to the ITA for their views on its provisions. This was followed by several interviews and meetings between planters' representatives and government officials. Consequent to these discussions, the recommended amendments were accepted in the draft of the Bill.[152] The tea industry had been constantly complaining against restrictions and government control over its recruitment and transportation of immigrant labourers, and lobbied for modifications in the legislation. Following the recommendations of the Royal Commission and the ITA, the Government of India passed the Tea District Emigrant Labour Act (XXII of 1932) and repealed Act VI of 1901. Under this Act the government appointed a Controller of Emigrant Labour, whose main job was to supervise recruitment and the transportation of labourers to the Assam tea gardens according to the regulations specified in the Act.

In the latter part of the 1930s the political climate in Assam, as in other parts of India, began to change with growing nationalist political activities and the formation of elected provincial governments under the Government of India Act, 1935. The arithmetic of electoral politics in Assam prevented the formation of a stable single-party government, and ushered in an era of short-term, multi-party coalition governments. The European group acquired a balancing position between Congress and non-Congress groups.[153] The ITA's main concern at this juncture was to prevent any legislative action by any of the coalitions in power that it considered inimical to the tea interests. With

Sir Percival Griffiths (a retired civil servant and later the official historian of the Indian tea industry) as its political adviser, the ITA prepared strategies to manipulate and support those political groups in the formation of the government that it considered amenable and easy to influence. Their basic approach on this issue was summed up in the following excerpt from a communication sent by the chairman of the ITA, Calcutta:

> It seems to me to be of vital importance for the industry to realize the dangers which lie ahead, and to do everything possible to consolidate its position. If with a friendly Government we can do anything, which will prevent hostile Legislation, either being introduced if Congress returned to power, or if introduced being effective against tea interests, a great step in the right direction will have been made.'[154]

As part of Griffiths' action plan to deal with the political situation in Assam, it was decided to support the coalition led by Muhammad Saadulla to form the government instead of the Congress, in return for certain considerations. Abdul Matin Chaudhury was expected to be the new Minister of Labour. As the chairman of the ITA acknowledged, 'we have in fact cultivated him for sometime past', and he was seen as a guarantee against any legislation hostile and detrimental to the industry. Saadulla was reported to have given his 'personal assurance that he will not introduce any Legislation which directly affected the Tea Industry without full consultation with us, as his object is to be guided by those who control the tea industry'.[155]

The years between 1937 and 1940 also witnessed an upsurge of labour unrest and the emergence of trade unions.[156] The Government of Assam expressed its anxiety over the 'frequency of strikes and disturbances on the tea gardens in several parts of the province'.[157] The ITA made anxious representations to the government, drawing its attention to the need for urgent action in order to maintain law and order.[158] As a result, the Government of Assam appointed a Tea Garden Labour Committee to investigate the causes of the recent strikes and disturbances. The members of the Committee were K.C. Ghosh, ICS, as chairperson; F.W. Hockenhull of the ITA; Baidyanth Mukherjee, representing the Indian plantation owners; A.K. Chanda, MLA from the Surma Valley; and Debeswar Sarma, MLA from the Assam Valley representing labour.[159] The terms of reference of the Committee were as follows: (1) to determine the root cause of recent strikes and other manifestations of discontent on tea gardens in Assam, and particularly whether there were economic grievances either generally in the district concerned or in the affected estates; (2) what measures were required in order to remove the root cause or causes of the said strikes; and (3) whether and if so what forms of organization were desirable for enabling labourers on tea gardens to communicate their grievances to the management in such effective manner as will remove any doubt that their interests are secure, and to procure settlement of such grievances, if any, by negotiation. The ITA, suspicious of the Congress and clearly unhappy with the appointment of two labour representatives, used its proximity with the colonial bureaucracy to delay and thwart the operations of this Committee from the very outset.[160] In a letter to the Chief Secretary of the Assam government dated 26 May 1939, the ITA chairman protested against the appointment of the two MLAs on the Committee, alleging that they were 'biased' against the industry and were personally involved in fomenting labour disturbances in the tea gardens.[161] The ITA was willing to cooperate with the Enquiry Committee only if it was carried out by persons 'acceptable to the tea industry', failing which it threatened to withdraw its participation. It carried out the threat and withdrew from the Enquiry Committee when its objections did not elicit a positive response.[162] Thus the Committee folded up even before it could start to work.

Growing labour militancy and the emergence of trade unions in the tea gardens clearly emerged as a major concern for the ITA. Ever since the early 1920s, relatively more organized forms of labour resistance like strikes in the Assam Valley tea gardens had been seen as the work of outside agitators.[163] The same refrain dominated the industry's perceptions in the late 1930s when early signs of trade unions appeared on the scene. Under these circumstances, the industry initiated discussions within the tea circles to think of strategies in order to control and counter the growing militancy, and the emergence of collective modes of organized labour protest. One strategy was suggested by A.C. Turnstall, Assistant Chief Scientific Officer of Tocklai tea research centre at Jorhat, in June 1939. In his proposal to the ITA entitled 'A Contribution Towards the Solution of Problem of Tea Garden Education', Turnstall attempted a psycho-analytical explanation of the problem of growing labour troubles, and suggested a concrete plan for its solution. A summary of his proposal is instructive of the prevailing attitudes and perceptions amongst members of the European community in Assam Valley's tea circles. He argued that the 'tea garden coolies require some sort of education to protect them from unscrupulous and dishonest agitation'. The existing schools in the tea gardens, though increasing in number, were not 'conducive to industrial peace'. The educational curriculum of these schools, he felt, rendered students of the labour community 'especially susceptible to agitation of the worst type'. He believed, citing the recent Digboi experience as an example, that offers of high wages and better amenities were no safeguards against strikes. He was convinced that the unrest was not due to any serious grievances, but because the strikers 'suffer from a feeling of inferiority which give them an ill-defined sense of grievance'. Agitators find such people easy prey. His remedial solutions were more in the nature of long-term planning for the future.[164] 'The only sure remedy for labour unrest of this kind is to somehow or other, replace the feeling of inferiority by one of self-respect and self-reliance.' And this could be achieved by adopting the principles of Baden Powell's scout movement and training the younger generation of tea garden labourers on these lines.

A detailed note on its planning and execution was submitted along with the proposal. 'It is important', Turnstall recommended, 'to get, from the beginning, the right type of scoutmaster with the right type of training'.[165] One such person had already been taken by him under his wings. R.C. Mohanta, one of the younger sons of a respectable *adhikari* (chief) of a small *satra* (a Vaishnavaite monastery) in a village in Jorhat, was put into the 'right type of training' to become a 'King's Scout'. After completion of his schooling and keeping the above object in view, young Mohanta was sent for further training to the US and the British Boy Scout headquarters. This entailed an adventurous international tour for him via Burma, Southeast Asia and Japan, to the USA and Britain.[166] On his return to Assam, Turnstall suggested that Mohanta be a scout master, under his supervision, to organize training camps in the tea gardens.[167] The proposal did not elicit a favourable response from the ITA hierarchy, which was busy evolving its own strategies to come to terms with the emerging trade union movement in and around the plantations of Assam Valley.

By the late 1930s there were indications of emerging trade union activity in and around the plantations; during 1938 and 1939 there was talk of the formation of trade unions in the tea gardens. To begin with, the ITA was opposed to the very idea of such trade unions. It argued that the conditions on the gardens were fundamentally different from those in industrial concerns: 'In most gardens, labour is simple and primitive; and if unions are started they would most probably be run by outsiders. In such cases the prevailing opinion is that they should be discouraged.'[168] The top brass of the ITA, as pointed out earlier, were paranoid with the fear of 'outside influence'. The tea garden managers were instructed not to negotiate with or entertain any outsider who 'professed either to represent the labour or to be interested in their welfare'.[169] The stereotypical perception of labourers was once again brandished to discourage them from forming trade unions: 'The sublime ignorance of the labour as to what is really meant by unions was almost equalled by that of the outside agitators who attempted to form them.' It was argued that the labourers had no notion of politics and political parties, as they 'did not know whether they had joined the Congress Party or a Trade Union, or had taken out an insurance policy'.[170]

However, by 1939, confronted with the new situation of spreading nationalist and, more alarmingly, communist activities, the ITA began to review and modify its position. Instead of outright opposition, it decided to follow a policy of conditional recognition of unions in the tea gardens. Percival Griffiths prepared and communicated detailed instructions to the superintendents and managers on the terms of conditionality, which were aimed at constraining the formation of labour unions in the tea gardens. For formal recognition of a union, it was laid down that only permanent labourers residing in the gardens could be enrolled as members and its executive members should be from amongst them, with a maximum of two persons from outside as members. No union would be allowed to represent more than one garden. A strike could not be called without a prior ballot with a minimum of two-thirds of votes cast and approved by 50 per cent of voters. Thereafter an advance notice of fourteen days was compulsory. The union was to maintain its accounts, which were to be audited at least once a year by a government auditor. Several conditions laid emphasis on discouraging outside intervention. The intention behind the new policy was

> that Managers having done their best to prevent a Union being formed, would perforce change their attitude once such a Union had been established, and would in fact as far as possible become the guide of those running the Union in the hope that, by so doing, undesirable influences would be kept out of the Union.[171]

This policy remained on paper for a while as the Government of India imposed the Defence of India Rules in September 1939, which suppressed, for the time being, the embryonic trade union movement in Assam. Four labour unions that had been formed in Lakhimpur district were moribund by May 1940. The jubilant ITA was supremely confident that they would be 'struck off the rolls for failure to submit their accounts for the past year'.[172]

The most important aspect of ITA's adaptation and adjustment to the new political situation, in accordance with the interests of the tea industry, was its shifting position with regard to the emerging trade unions during the 1940s. From complete opposition to the very concept of trade unions on the tea gardens, it shifted its stance to conditional recognition – this, at a time when uninterrupted tea production became the priority to meet the growing demand for war efforts. These developments forced the ITA to implement its earlier proposal: trade unions were here to stay, but under the leadership of those who would be acceptable to the industry. 'It would be idle to pretend', wrote Griffiths in July 1945, in his notes on post-war planning of trade unions in the tea gardens,

> that sufficient labour leaders of the right type are likely to be forthcoming. In practice, if the Trade Union Movement develops in the Tea Industry – as indeed in other industries in this country – it is almost certain to fall under the control of people who can reasonably be described as agitators.[173]

He went on to analyse the current situation facing the tea industry: 'We know that hasty development of Trade Unions may well mean a period of difficulty and even convulsion in the Tea industry; we equally know that undue opposition to them may merely make things worse.'[174] In the face of this reality, what was the industry supposed to do? It was decided that the industry would recognize those unions which were willing to accept its conditions: no affiliation to the Communist Party; white-collar staff and labourers were not to belong to common unions; and, finally, one-third of the garden labour force had to be paying members.[175] The formation of a clerical staff union together with labourers and *sirdars* was not really welcomed by the industry. One such union had been formed by the efforts of two senior clerks in the superintendent's office, which included clerical staff, factory staff, garden overseers and labourers as its members. While, as per the ITA's recent policy, forming a union was no longer an offence, the idea of a joint union of clerical staff and labourers was neither acceptable nor allowed by it. 'It was intolerable to think that clerks', it was argued, 'who had access to wage books, confidential correspondence etc., should be in a position to work in concert with the labour against the Management.' The ITA issued a circular to agency houses advising them that any attempt by Indian clerical staff, including *mistries*, *mohurrirs,* to join labour unions should not be tolerated.[176]

The ITA remained hostile to Communist-dominated trade unions: 'with irresponsible and unrepresentative unions, organized by communist agitators, whose avowed aim is the expropriation of our estates, we have had and will have nothing whatever to do'.[177] Earlier, the ITA had aligned with non-Congress groups when it felt that the Congress was hostile towards the tea industry in matters of labour and trade unions. However, with the growth of Communist-backed unions, which was seen as a bigger threat, an alliance with the Congress seemed prudent. The ITA's labour adviser, H.F. Clark, reported to its labour sub-committee in December 1946 that the Congress Ministry in Assam was acutely aware of the spreading Communist influence in the province, and was keen to promote labour unions under the Congress umbrella.[178] A Congress labour cell was formed under the leadership of Robin Kakoti and Bijoy Bhagawati (later the head of the Indian National Trade Union Congress – INTUC) to work in the tea gardens. In May 1947, the Assam branch of INTUC was formed with Kamakhya Prashad Tripathi as its president.[179] Thus, at the dawn of independence, the Congress-led INTUC emerged as a dominant substitute for Communist unions. The joint secretary of the Communist AITUC (All India Trade Union Congress) complained of mounting hostility and attacks from INTUC sponsors and the Congress government in Assam. According to him, the government machinery was freely used to build up INTUC and for disruption of AITUC. The Congress government in Assam had 'put behind the prison bars more Trade Unionists within a month (the vast majority of them being detained without trial) than even within a year of the worst days of direct British rule'.[180] Naturally, under these circumstances, the Congress was acceptable to the ITA:

The outstanding development in labour organization during 1947 was undoubtedly the growth of the new Indian National Trade Union Congress, formed in May by leaders of Congress Party to counteract the disruptive influence of the communist dominated All-India Trade Union Congress. In contrast to the direct action policy of the latter body, the new organization purports to encourage the settlement of labour dispute through the medium of conciliation and arbitration machinery . . ..'[181]

Following an agreement between Robin Kakoti of INTUC, Gopinath Bordoloi, Assam's Chief Minister, and the ITA, the latter agreed to allow free access in the tea gardens to such INTUC organizers as were accredited by Kakoti.[182] The INTUC on its part assured the ITA that its activists would conform to 'legitimate' trade union activity and would not upset the existing labour–management relations.[183] The INTUC was to dominate the tea garden labour unions and their politics for over half a century after independence in Assam Valley.

The geographical isolation of the tea plantations from the more advanced areas of the province, the labourers' compulsion to reside in the gardens under the penal contract, and their total dependence on their employers for even the simple amenities and necessities of life provided an opportunity to the planters to establish unquestioned control over the labour force. They frequently resorted to coercion, both physical and economic, to perpetuate this dependency. The exercise of extra-legal authority helped to maintain planters' dominance over the labour force for most of the period under study. They succeeded in preventing the formation of labour organizations by curbing labour mobility within and outside the plantation complexes, and the enforced isolation of labourers through constant surveillance and the penal contract system. The colonial state overlooked the frequent resort to extra-legal methods by the planters against their labour force, and provided legitimacy and reinforced their extra-legal authority through legislative devices. In the next chapter, we shall examine the role of the colonial state in greater detail.

Notes and References

[1] W.M. Fraser, *The Recollections of a Tea Planter*, London: The Tea and Rubber Mail, 1935, p. 42.

[2] S.R. Deshpande, *Report on an Enquiry into the Cost and Standard of Living of Plantation Workers in Assam and Bengal*, 1948, p. 64.

[3] Plantation Enquiry Commission Report, 1956, p. 23.

[4] Tea Directory and Tea Areas Handbook, 1942.

[5] Rana P. Behal, 'Coolie Drivers of Benevolent Paternalists? British Tea Planters in Assam and the Indenture Labour System', *Modern Asian Studies*, Vol. 44, Part 1, January 2010, pp. 29–51.

[6] Percival Griffiths, *The History of the Indian Tea Industry*, London: Weidenfeld and Nicolson, 1967, p. 376.

[7] Ibid.

[8] Eugene D. Genovese, *Roll, Jordon, Roll: The World the Slaves Made*, New York: Pantheon Books, 1972, pp. 4–6.

[9] Department of Revenue and Agriculture, Government of India, Emigration A, Proceedings – No. 6, File No. 90 of 1901, p. 2.

[10] Proceedings of the Central Legislative Council (PCLC), 1901, Vol. XL, p. 139.

[11] Ibid., p. 133.

[12] Secretary of State for India's letter to Lord Curzon, 26 August 1903, Letter No. 59, Curzon Papers, Microfilm, Acct. No. 1632, National Archives, India. Original Mss Eur. F. 111/161, Oriental and India Office Collection (OIOC), British Library, London.

[13] Dwarkanath Ganguly, *Slavery in British Dominion*, edited by Sris Kumar Kunda, Calcutta: Jignasa, 1972: reprint of thriteen articles published in the newspaper *Bengalee* between September 1886 and April 1887.

[14] Charles Dowding, *Tea Garden Coolies in Assam*, Calcutta: Thacker, Spink & Co., 1894, p. 31.

[15] Walter Rodney, 'Plantation Society in Guyana', *Review,* IV, 4, Spring 1981, pp. 643–66.

[16] Also see chapter 1.

[17] Parliamentary Papers, 1839, p. 55; Papers Relating to Tea Cultivation in Bengal, *Selections from The Records of the Government of Bengal No. XXXVII*, Bengal Military Orphan Press: Calcutta, 1861, p. 13. Also see chapter 1.

[18] Tweedy Papers, Centre of South Asian Studies Archives, Cambridge University, UK; Stephanie Jones, *Merchants of the Raj: British Managing Agency Houses in Calcutta Yesterday and Today*, London: Macmillan, 1991, p. 28.

[19] R. Palmer Papers, Centre of South Asian Studies Archives, Cambridge University, UK.

[20] H.A. Antrobus, *A History of the Jorehaut Company Ltd, 1859–1946*, London: Tea and Rubber Mail, 1948, p. 22.

[21] Assam Company Papers (ACP), Ms. No. 9924, 1858–65 and Ms. No. 9935, 1862–66; Antrobus, *Jorehaut*, p. 19.

[22] Jones, *Merchants of the Raj*, p. 50. Some of these individuals and their concerns flourished and grew into larger amalgamated corporations later on.

[23] George Barker, *Tea Planter's Life in Assam*, Calcutta: Thacker, Spink & Co., 1884, p. 3; Samuel Baildon, *The Tea Industry in India: A Review of Finance and Labour, and a Guide for Capitalist & Assistants*, London: W.H Allen & Co., 1882; T. Kinney, *Old Times in Assam*, Calcutta: Star Press, 1896.

[24] William Nassau Lees, *Tea Cultivation, Cotton and other Agricultural Experiments in India, A Review*, Calcutta: Thacker, Spink & Co., 1863, p. 3.

[25] Lt. Colonel H. Hopkinson, Agent, Governor General, North East Frontier, and Commissioner of Assam, May 1866, Coolie Trade, Parliamentary Papers, 1867, p. 8.

[26] John Weatherstone, *The Pioneers 1825–1900: The Early British Tea and Coffee Planters and Their Way of Life*, London: Quiller Press, 1986, Chapter III.

[27] Ibid., p. 77.

[28] Papers Relating to Tea, 1861.

[29] Ibid., p. 24.

[30] ACP, Ms. No. 9925, Vol. 2, 1841–1844.

[31] See chapter 1.

[32] Papers Regarding Tea, 1874, p. 22.

[33] Ibid. p. 23.

[34] Ibid.

[35] Richard Dunn, *The Rise of the Planter Class in the English West Indies, 1624–1713*(USA: University of North Carolina Press, 1972), p. 248.

[36] Papers Regarding the Tea, Parliamentary Papers, 1874, Calcutta, p. 23.

[37] Coolie Trade, Parliamentary Papers, 1867, p. 3.

38 Rana P. Behal and Prabhu P. Mohapatra, '"Tea and Money versus Human Life": The Rise and Fall of the Indenture System in the Assam Tea Plantations 1840–1908', in E. Valentine Daniel, Henry Bernstien and Tom Brass (eds), *Plantations, Proletarians and Peasants in Colonial Asia*, London: Frank Cass, 1992, pp. 142–43.

39 They were the native field staff in the plantation social hierarchy who assisted the European planters. *Sirdars* were labourers who had risen in the hierarchy. The *sirdars* were supervised by Assamese *muhurrirs* (generally pronounced as *moories*) who acted under a head, or '*burra muhurrir*', who was answerable for the whole conduct of the outdoor work. David Crole, *Tea: A Text Book of Tea Planting and Manufacture*, London: Crossby Lockwood and Son, 1897, p. 8.

40 Kinney, *Old Times*, p. 11.

41 Letters of John and Alexander Carnegie to their parents from Tezpur and other Assam tea plantations, 1865–66, Mss. Eur/c/682, 5th letter, dated 17 February 1866, OIOC, British Library, London (hereafter Carnegie Letters); Alan Macfarlen and Iris Macfarlen, *The Empire of Tea: The Remarkable History of the Plant that Took Over the World*, New York: The Overlook Press, 2004, pp. 148–50.

42 Carnegie Letters, 20 February 1866.

43 Carnegie Letters, 4 April 1866.

44 Papers Regarding the Tea, 1874.

45 Henry Cotton, *Indian and Home Memories*, London: T. Fisher Unwin, 1911, p. 266.

46 Bempfydle Fuller, *Some Personal Experiences*, London: John Murray, 1930, p. 118.

47 A. Purcell and J. Hallsworth, *Report on Labour Conditions in India*, General Council, Trade Union Congress, London, 1928, p. 35.

48 Carnegie Letters, 22 March 1866.

49 Crole, *Tea*, p. 206.

50 Barker, *Tea Planter*, p. 130.

51 Ibid., p. 267.

52 Fraser, *Recollections*, p. 15.

53 F.A. Hetherington, *The Diary of a Tea Planter, 14 July 1907*, Sussex: The Book Guild Ltd., 1994, p. 24.

54 Ibid., p. 59.

55 Ibid., p. 71.

56 Ibid., p. 92.

57 *The Times* (London), 2 September 1902, p. 6.

58 Ibid.

59 Ibid.

60 Rana P. Behal, 'Forms of Labour Protest in the Assam Valley Tea Plantations 1900–1947', *The Calcutta Historical Journal*, Vol. IX, No. 1, July–December 1984; Rana P. Behal, 'Boundaries and Shifting Forms of Resistance: Labour in Assam Tea Plantations during Colonial Rule', in Herausgegeben von Elisabeth Hermann-Otto, unter Mitarbeit von, Marcel Simonis und Alexander Trefz (eds), *Sklaverei und Zwangsarbeit zwischen Akzeptanz und Widerstand*, Zurich: Georg Olms Verlag Hildesheim, 1911, pp. 427–51; Nitin Varma, 'Producing Tea Coolies? Work, Life and Protest in Colonial Tea Plantations of Assam, 1830s–1920s, unpublished dissertation, Humboldt University, Berlin, 2011.

61 Department of Revenue and Agriculture, Government of India, Emigration A, Proceedings Nos. 6–8, File No. 90 of 1901, p. 6.

62 *The Times* (London), 2 September 1902, p. 6.

63 Ibid.

64 Barker, *Tea Planter*, p. 171.

65 Baildon, *The Tea Industry in India*, p. 74.

66 Barker, *Tea Planter*, p. 153.

[67] Ibid., p. 138.

[68] Ibid.

[69] Dowding, *Tea Garden*, p. viii.

[70] *The Times* (London), 29 August 1902, p. 6.

[71] Ibid.

[72] Richard Dunn, *The Rise of the Planter Class in the English West Indies, 1624–1713*, University of North Carolina Press, 1972, p. 246.

[73] Dowding, *Tea Garden*, p. xiii.

[74] The Report of the General Committee of the Indian Tea Association (hereafter ITA Report), Tocklai Tea Research Centre, Jorhat, Calcutta, 1918, p. x.

[75] *The Times* (London), 29 August 1902, p. 6.

[76] *The Times* (London), 2 September 1902, p. 6

[77] For details, see Behal and Mohapatra, 'Tea and Money', pp. 150–55.

[78] For example, a contemporary, Thomas R. Dew, argued that servitude had been a necessary stage of human progress and hence could not be regarded as an evil in itself. Underlying the argument was the assumption that the black slave, referred to as 'Negro', was undoubtedly inferior to the white American. It was further argued that the black slave was better off in slavery than he had been in Africa – he got better food, better clothing, and some 'kind' and 'valuable' attendance when he was sick: 'It was no wonder then that he had developed a happy disposition.' George H. Frederickson, 'Slavery and Race: The Southern Dilemma', in Allen Weinstein and Frank Otto Gatell (eds), *American Negro Slavery: A Modern Reader*, London: Oxford University Press, 1973, pp. 225–32.

[79] Frederickson, 'Slavery and Race', p. 235.

[80] Barker, *Tea Planter*, p. 171.

[81] *The Times* (London), 2 September 1902, p. 6.

[82] Ibid.

[83] *Capital* (Calcutta), 23 August 1900.

[84] Ibid.

[85] Weatherstone, *Pioneers*, p. 80.

[86] Barker, *Tea Planter*, pp. 99–100.

[87] Hetherington, *The Diary*.

[88] James Finlay & Company Papers, UGD 91/139, Glasgow University Archives, Glasgow, UK, 27 September 1900.

[89] Barker, *Tea Planter*, p. 171.

[90] Department of Revenue and Agriculture, Government of India, Emigration A, Proceedings, Nos. 2–9, February 1889.

[91] Barker, *Tea Planter*, p. 173.

[92] Crole, *Tea*, p. 205.

[93] Ibid.

[94] Department of Revenue, Government of Assam, A, Nos. 77–117, August 1904, p. 4.

[95] Ibid.

[96] Ibid.

[97] ITA Report, Calcutta, 1908, p. 6.

[98] Department of Commerce and Industry, Government of India, Emigration A, Nos. 7–8, January 1908, p. 1.

[99] ITA Report, Calcutta, 1912, p. 10.

[100] Department of Revenue, Government of Assam, Nos. 315–26, File No. S-186-R, December 1912, p. 15.

[101] Ibid., pp. 18–20.

[102] Ibid., pp. 36–7.

[103] Report of the Assam Labour Enquiry Committee (RALEC), Calcutta, 1906, p. 70.

[104] Department of Commerce and Industry, Government of India, Emigration B, No. 3, September 1906.

[105] Griffiths, *The History*, p. 302; Report of the Royal Commission on Labour in India (hereafter Royal Commission), 1931, p. 384.

[106] Royal Commission, 1931, p. 384.

[107] Report of the Tea Districts Emigrant Labour Act (XXII of 1932), 1937, p. 15. (Hereafter RTDELA.)

[108] Department of Commerce and Industry, Government of India, Emigration B, No. 3, September 1906.

[109] RALEC, 1921–22, p. 24.

[110] See chapter 5.

[111] RALEC, 1921–22, p. 24.

[112] Griffiths, *History*, p. 297.

[113] Rana P. Behal, *Wage Structure and Labour: Assam Valley Tea Plantations, 1900–1947*, NLI Research Studies Series, No. 043/2003, V.V. Giri National Labour Institute, NOIDA, India, 2003.

[114] 'Time expired' referred to labourers who had completed their contract.

[115] Griffiths, *The History*, p. 281.

[116] RALEC, 1921–22, p. 74.

[117] Royal Commission, 1931, *Written Evidence, Assam and Dooars*, Vol. VI, Part I, p. 22.

[118] Rana P. Behal, 'Coolies, Recruiters and Planters: Migration of Indian Labour to the Southeast Asian and Assam Plantations during Colonial Rule', Crossroads Working Papers Series, No. 9, Bonn, July 2013; Rana P. Behal, ' Transporting and Transforming Agrarian Communities: Indian Migrant Labourers in South-East Asian and Assam Plantations under the British Imperial System', in Henryk Alff and Andreas Benz (eds), *Tracing Connections: Explorations of Spaces and Places in Asian Contexts*, Berlin: WVB, 2014, pp. 159–85; Vijaya Samaraweera, 'Masters and Servants in Sri Lankan Plantations! Labour Laws and Labour Control in an Emergent Export Economy', *Indian Economic and Social History Review*, Vol. XVIII, No. 2, April–June 1981, pp. 123–55.

[119] ITA Papers, October 1929, Mss. Eur 174/Bay 1/shelf 2.

[120] Ibid.

[121] Ibid.

[122] Dattaraya Varman Rege, *Report on An Enquiry into Conditions of Labour in Plantations in India*, 1946, p. 28.

[123] Ibid.

[124] Special Report, Government of India, 1891, p. 240.

[125] Hetherington, *The Diary*, p. 77.

[126] Department of Revenue, Government of Assam, A, Nos. 77–117, August 1904.

[127] For more details, see chapter 6.

[128] *Assam Legislative Council Proceedings*, 1927, Vol. VII, No. 5, pp. 40–103.

[129] Ibid., p. 1249.

[130] Ibid.

[131] Rege, *Report on An Enquiry into Conditions of Labour*, p. 29.

[132] Royal Commission, 1931, p. 378.

[133] Samaraweera, 'Masters and Servants', p. 22.

[134] General and Judicial Department, Government of Assam, Immigration B, Nos. 34–63, September 1939, pp. 48–49.

[135] Ibid., p. 81.

[136] Ibid., p. 79.

[137] Ibid., p. 49; Assam Administrative Report, 1938–39, p. ii; Amalendu Guha, *Planter Raj to Swaraj: Freedom Struggle and Electoral Politics in Assam 1826–1947*, New Delhi: Indian

Council of Historical Research, 1977, p. 243; *Assam Legislative Assembly Debates*, 1938, Vol. II, pp. 820–21.

[138] Rege, *Report on An Enquiry into Conditions of Labour*, 1946, p. 28.

[139] ITA Papers, Ms. Euro F 174/1.

[140] Guha, *Planter Raj*, pp. 30–31.

[141] Ibid., p. 75.

[142] ITA Report, 1909, pp. 144–46.

[143] ITA Report, 1912, p. 6; Guha, *Planter Raj*, p. 82.

[144] Guha, *Planter Raj*, p. 220.

[145] Griffiths, *The History*, pp. 527–28.

[146] Department of Revenue and Agriculture, Government of India, Emigration A, Proceedings, Nos. 6–8, File No. 90 of 1901, pp. 122–36.

[147] After the withdrawal of penal clauses from the Immigration Labour Act in 1908, the ITA submitted a memorial to the government asking for a new legislation against 'enticement' of labour in the tea gardens in Assam. The Secretary of State for India rejected the Bill on the ground that it involved 'principles' which could not be accepted. The growing anti-slavery sentiments prevailing in Britain could explain this response.

[148] ITA Report, 1921, p. 5.

[149] Financial Department, Government of Assam, Immigration Branch B, Nos. 20–112, March 1922, pp. 105–07.

[150] Assam Labour Report, 1920–21, p. 2.

[151] Ibid.

[152] ITA Report, 1932, p. 10.

[153] Guha, *Planter Raj*, pp. 216–36; Basudev Chatterji (ed.), *Towards Freedom, 1938*, New Delhi, 1998, chapter on the Assam Ministry.

[154] ITA Papers, Circular C. 159, 20 November 1939, Mss Eur F 174, Bay/H.

[155] ITA Papers, Mss. Eur F174, Bay/H, 17 November 1939.

[156] For further details, see chapter 6.

[157] General and Judicial Department, Government of Assam, Immigration Branch B, File No. 118, GIM. 49/47, 1939, p. 167.

[158] ITA Report, 1939, p. 26.

[159] AICC Papers, File No. P1-12, TL No. 1020, 1939, p. 3, Nehru Memorial Museum and Library, New Delhi; *Amrita Bazar Patrika*, 29 May 1939; General and Judicial Department, Government of Assam, No. 118-GIM-49/47, 1939, p. 167.

[160] ITA Circulars 92 and 115, ITA Papers, Mss Eur F/174/Bay/H, 1939.

[161] General and Judicial Department, Government of Assam, File No. 118-GIM 49/47, 1939, p. 137.

[162] Ibid.; ITA Report, 1939, p. 28.

[163] See chapter 6.

[164] ITA Papers, Circular No. 87, 12 June 1939, Mss. Eur F 174/Bay/H, pp. 1–5.

[165] Ibid.

[166] A copy of the typescript entitled 'Note on the general plan of Mohanta's education', private collection of Mohanta family, Jorhat, Assam. I am grateful to Mr Jayraj Mohanta, the son of late R.C. Mohanta, for allowing me access to this collection. A copy of this is also part of the ITA Papers collection in the British Library, London.

[167] ITA Papers, 12 June 1939, pp. 1–5. The Mohanta episode lies buried as an unnoticed tale in the British Library records. For the Mohanta family, however, it acquired a folklorist aura, a narrative tradition of recounting the adventures of R.C. Mohanta. Turnstall arranged for Mohanta to travel through the forested areas of Southeast Asia, the Far East and America, finally ending up in Europe to participate in the International Boy Scout Meet. During World War II, he joined Lord Mountbatten's commando force in the British Indian army that was

trained and operated in the Southeast Asian jungles. After leaving the army, he joined the tea industry as an assistant manager, and in due course earned the reputation of being one of the toughest tea planters in Assam.

[168] ITA Report, 1937, ITA Papers, p. 37.

[169] ITA Papers, Mss. Eur F174/2070, Labour Matters: January 1940 to December 1941.

[170] Ibid.

[171] ITA Papers, Mss. Eur F 174/Bay 2 (C), 11 April 1939.

[172] ITA Papers, Mss. Eur F 174/Bay, 1940.

[173] Post War Planning: Notes by the Political Advisor, Circular No. 164, 21 July 1945, ITA Papers, Mss. Eur F/174, Bay 2 (G) 2.

[174] Ibid.

[175] Griffiths, *The History*, p. 391; Guha, *Planter Raj*, p. 293.

[176] ITA Papers, Mss. Eur, F174/2070, Labour Matters: January 1940 to December 1941.

[177] ITA Report, 1946, p. XIV.

[178] ITA Papers, 2 December 1946, Mss. F 174/ Bay 2 (G).

[179] Guha, *Planter Raj*, p. 296.

[180] AITUC Papers, TL No. 4, File No. 47, 1947–48, Nehru Memorial Museum and Library, New Delhi.

[181] ITA Report, 1947, p. 41.

[182] ITA Circular to Garden Managers, No. L.D. 600, dated Dibrugarh 21 July 1947, cited in Guha, *Planter Raj*, p. 297.

[183] Ibid., p. 296.

4

The Role of the Colonial State

Tea plantations in Assam began as a state enterprise. Following the Anglo-Chinese tension over the issue of illegal export of opium into China by the East India Company, which threatened to stop the tea supply to Britain in the early decades of the nineteenth century, the search for an alternate source of tea production was initiated by the British in India. A series of initiatives including the import of tea plants, seeds and tea makers from China, and setting up tea nurseries were launched using state revenues, and involving scientific establishments and the colonial bureaucracy during the 1830s.[1] The success of these initiatives in setting up early plantations to produce tea commercially brought in private British capital. Two-thirds of the newly set up plantations were handed over to the newly incorporated, London-based Assam Company in 1839, free of charge! From then on, the colonial state was fully committed to supporting and assisting private British capital to produce tea for the world market. To ensure unhindered growth of this new enterprise under private British capital, the colonial state deposed the puppet ruler Purandhar Singh, and Assam was formally annexed to the British Indian empire.[2]

Having handing over the plantation establishment to British capitalists, the colonial state provided all possible assistance to them to further develop and expand it. It began by making vast tracts of wastelands available to them. The formal annexation of Assam made it easier for the British government to provide land at cheap and favourable terms for commercial cultivation of tea in that province. A series of special Land Grant Rules were promulgated from 1838 onwards, which gave access to vast expanses of wasteland as well as ordinary land at extremely cheap rates and on liberal terms to private British capitalists. The conditionality of these grants for special crops, like tea, debarred the growers of traditional crops access to the lands. The grants also displaced a large number of tribal communities who had traditionally owned these lands.[3] Such a policy encouraged tea planters to acquire land far in excess of their requirement. The amount of land in the Assam Valley under planters' control rose from 54,859 acres in 1859 to a staggering figure of 1,112,196 acres by 1900.[4] However, the area under tea cultivation never exceeded one-third of the total area, at most, as is evident from Charts 4.1, 4.2, 4.3 and 4.2, and Appendix Table 4.1.

The excess land acquired by the planters provided materials and space for the construction of 'coolie lines', planters' bungalows and houses of office staff in the plantations. The planters made use of the excess land to tie down labour to the tea gardens, by allotting small-sized plots to them for private cultivation to supplement their low wages.

State assistance was particularly critical in the matter of mobilization of labour for the plantations. As pointed out earlier, unstable and inadequate

CHART 4.1
Total and Operation Area under Tea in Lakhimpur, 1888–1947

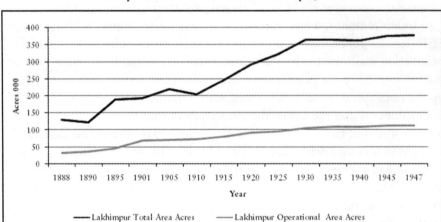
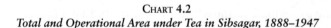

CHART 4.2
Total and Operational Area under Tea in Sibsagar, 1888–1947

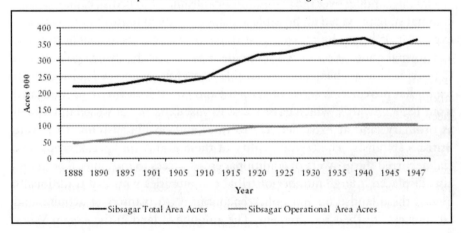

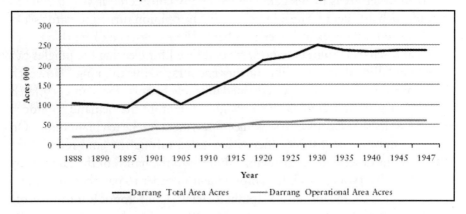

CHART 4.3
Total and Operational Area under Tea in Darrang, 1888–1947

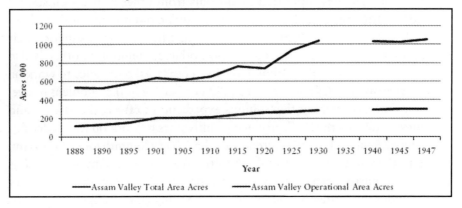

CHART 4.4
Total and Operational Area under Tea in Assam Valley, 1888–1947

labour supply was a constant source of anxiety for the planters from the very inception of the tea industry in Assam. This is clear from the correspondence and discussions between the Directors of Assam Company and officials in the tea gardens. They spent a lot of time and effort on procuring labour both locally and from neighbouring Bengal territories, and on keeping them on the gardens. Superintendent Mornay informed the Directors on 18 December 1849 about labourers deserting the gardens. Wage cuts and overwork appear to have been the reasons for desertion.[5] Another Company official, Herriot, informed the Directors in 1851 that his efforts to procure a supply of labourers from Darrang district succeeded in getting only ten men because the wages in other districts were Rs 3 per month, and 'when that rate is to be obtained so near homes it cannot be expected they will go to a distance for the same'.[6] There were several such communications from Herriot on different dates informing the Directors about the efforts for and difficulties of labour supply. In one of these, he suggested the possibility of acquiring labourers through European agents in other areas of Bengal. The Company considered it worthwhile to appoint such an agent.[7] Thus, increasingly, the opinion turned towards seeking imported labourers in larger numbers. The experience of working with the local Kachari labourers, who were employed for clearing the jungles but were found difficult to discipline, further encouraged this thinking.[8] However, the labour supply from Bengal remained unstable because the planters offered wages that were not competitive enough – therefore the demand to induce native Assamese peasants into seeking employment on the tea plantations. On their prompting, the district officials suggested raising the land revenue for what Jenkins described as 'throwing labour into the hands of the Planters by compelling the ryots to seek for employment in order to pay their revenue'.[9] Making a case for the increase, Captain Rowlatt, Collector of Kamrup, wrote as follows to the Commissioner of Assam: 'the want of labour is undoubtedly caused by the low rate of assessment levied on the lands generally throughout the Province'. He was supported by officials from other districts on similar grounds.[10] However F. Jenkins, the Commissioner, did not accept their diagnosis of 'indolence' and 'lazy' natives, nor was he willing to support their suggestion to raise the land revenue.[11] Some other contemporary officials also had a slightly different perception of the local peasants' reluctance to work on the tea gardens. J. Edgar, for instance, did not believe in the 'indolent native' theory, and was critical of the 'ruinous expedient' of raising the rate of land revenue for 'driving the food-producing cultivators to work on tea gardens'.[12] In a similar vein, C.J. Lyall, secretary to the Chief Commissioner of Assam, wrote to the Government of India that 'the Assamese peasant is well off as a rule, and, partly perhaps from the tradition of the system of compulsory labour under the former indigenous rulers, he thinks it an indignity to labour on other fields than his own, or on the roads'.[13] Notwithstanding the dissenting views of these officials, the government went ahead with the revenue increase.

With the expansion of acreage under tea and the planters' refusal to offer competitive wages despite the suggestion of the Lieutenant Governor of Bengal, the labour problem became very acute by the late 1850s.[14] Assamese peasants, despite being burdened with the increase in land revenue imposed by the government, could not be 'induced' to take up employment in the tea plantations. When the demand for labour rose dramatically with the massive expansion of tea plantations during the speculative 'tea mania' period, the planters turned to private recruitment agencies in Calcutta. These agencies utilized the services of professional native recruiters (*arakatis*) operating in the districts of eastern India who forwarded the recruited migrants by rail to Calcutta, from where they were sent to Assam by the river route. However, successful mobilization of labour through these agencies came at the cost of very high mortality among the migrants during the voyage and upon reaching Assam – a tragic consequence of the 'coolie trade' during the 'tea mania' years. A Special Commission appointed in July 1862 to conduct investigations into the whole affair presented an appalling picture of the miseries, mortality and desertions among migrant labourers, and the prevalence of much abuse in the 'coolie trade.'[15] These revelations prompted state intervention in the form of the Bengal Native Labour Act III of 1863. The legislation was meant to provide 'protection' to prospective migrants against deception by contractors, and to lessen mortality during transit and upon arrival in the tea districts. The legislative intervention failed miserably on both counts, however, and the Bengal government passed another legislation, Act VI, in 1865. Thus began the saga of legislative enactments, which became a regular feature of colonial policy for regulating labour recruitment and labour relations in Assam tea plantations.

The question to ask at this stage is, why did the colonial state decide to intervene legislatively in the face of its professed policy of *laissez faire*? The question is relevant in the context of state intervention, as the penal contract system was introduced through labour legislations in the 1860s and 1880s. These legislations laid the foundations of the indentured labour regime in the Assam tea plantations.[16] The official justification for the labour legislations and penal contract system was put forward by a senior official of the Assam government in paternalist tones: labour legislation was important for the 'protection' of emigrant labourers going to the Assam tea gardens because they were 'extremely ignorant' and to ensure that they were not 'imposed upon'. Since these emigrants had to travel long distances, government supervision was necessary in order to prevent 'overcrowding, disease and consequent mortality'. Because of the climate and unfamiliar diet in the new country, the emigrants were liable to serious illnesses, often fatal in their results. Therefore it was necessary to provide provisions of the 'requisite comforts, medical attendance and other appliances for his well-being' which would be enforced by law. At the same time, it was argued, some regulations were required to effectively enforce the provisions of contract between labour and capital as 'demanded by justice'. After all the employers had spent a lot of money on importing the labourers and providing them the 'comfort' that was required by the law.

> The employer is compelled by law to guarantee the coolie a minimum wage; and it is only equitable that the law should provide him with the means of obtaining the due fulfilment of the contract by the coolie, whose only capital is his labour, and who ought not to be allowed capriciously to withdraw himself from the service of the employer. . . . A penal labour law and government protection to the labour are thus correlative terms.'[17]

Thus these legislations, at one level, were couched in the language of a paternalist concern of the colonial state for the 'helpless' and 'ignorant' migrant natives; and at the same time, at another level, they criminalized labour relations in the Assam tea plantations by introducing the penal contract system. But the spirit of paternalist concern was conspicuously absent in the actual implementation of the law, for the interests of the employers were given priority over those of the labourers. The planters constantly defied the provisions concerning labour welfare, but the state rarely took action against them. On the other hand, 'protection' of labourers remained a policy on paper. One of the Indian members of the Central Legislative Council, Ram Bahadur, complained that under the influence of the planters, the government was constantly adding penal laws to the list of legislations, while it neglected the provisions of labour protection.[18]

Under the initial legislations of 1863 and 1865, the 'protective' provisions for labour included payment of minimum wages of Rs 5, Rs 4 and Rs 3 per month for men, women and children, respectively. These were fixed monthly wages and deductions could only be made for absence from work or idleness, on conviction before a magistrate. The legislations provided for the appointment of Protectors of labour, who were empowered to suspend or cancel the contracts of labourers on grounds of ill-health or ill-treatement by employers. Later the nomenclature was changed from Protector to Inspector. Contracts could also be cancelled if a garden was declared unfit for human habitation by a committee. The employer was bound to notify the Protector/Inspector if a labourer in his service wished to make a complaint, failing which a fine of Rs 500 could be imposed. The provisions in support of the employers included imprisonment of labourers for non-compliance of the contract. The term of the contract was fixed for five years in 1863, then reduced to three years in 1865 and raised again to five years in 1882. Absence from work, negligence or idleness was punishable with a fine, including forfeiture of wages. The act of desertion carried a severe penalty of three months' imprisonment and this period was added to the period of the contract. The most arbitrary provision provided in the 1865 legislation was the one that empowered planters with the right of private arrest of an 'absconding' labourer without a warrant if he/she was found in the same district and not in the service of another employer. The employer was however bound to hand over such an arrested labourer to a police officer or a magistrate within forty-eight hours, failing which he was liable to pay a fine of Rs 500.[19]

Various government-appointed enquiry commissions/committees to investigate conditions in the Assam tea gardens, as well as the official annual reports on immigrant labour regularly reported the dismal failure of the labour legislations, particularly with respect to implementation of the labour 'protection' provisions. The 1868 Commission reported high rates of mortality among migrants during the journey to the tea gardens, and overworked, ill-fed and sick labourers without proper medical facilities living in overcrowded conditions in the gardens, lacking proper housing and drinking water.[20] Similarly, the provisions of the law requiring an employer to notify the Protector/Inspector of the completion of a contract were generally ignored. Nor did any employer ever give a notice to the Protector that a labourer wished to make a complaint. The provision for providing compensation to labourers on account of wage arrears was never adhered to. The conditionality attached to the power of private arrest – that arrested deserters were to be handed over to the police or produced before a magistrate – was habitually ignored. The provision of a statutory minimum fixed wage was constantly violated by the planters. This was acknowledged by district officials in their reports at regular intervals.[21] The wage data published in the annual labour reports on Assam clearly showed that the wages paid were often below the statutory minimum. The Enquiry Committee of 1906 observed that the adoption by the planters of a piecework mode of wage payment, i.e. payment on the basis of a fixed task or 'haziri', was the reason why labourers in the Assam tea plantations earned much less than the minimum wage, and in many cases 'wages earned were insufficient to keep the coolie in health'.[22]

Recruitment

While passing Act I of 1882, the government contemplated that it would encourage free immigration. The planters complained of the high cost of recruitment, and, attributing this to the restrictions imposed by the existing law which governed recruitment for Assam, Act VII of 1873, demanded amendments.[23] Their memorial to the government demanded extension of the labour contract period from three to five years, simplification of regulations and conditions, and instructions to local officials in the recruiting districts 'to co-operate in a friendly spirit' in recruitment of labour.[24] Fitzpatrick, the Chief Commissioner of Assam, thought that it was time for the emigrants to come to Assam without the 'stimulus and aid' of the professionals and *arakati* recruiters. However it was soon admitted that 'the free recruiting system has undoubtedly given rise to a not inconsiderable number of cases of forcible kidnapping and fraudulent enticement of labourers'.[25] But almost in the same breath, these were dismissed as 'exaggerated' reports. The prevalence of such 'abuses and evils' was rationalized as 'more or less incidental to any system of emigration'.[26]

Here, the perceptions of the civil servants of Assam differed from that of their counterparts in Bengal, an important catchment area of labour for the Assam tea plantations. While the latter reported very critically about the abusive practices of the professional contractors and their 'under trappers' in the recruiting districts, the former were often dismissive of these charges as 'unsubstantiated'.[27] The Government of India invariably backed the Assam government on this issue. Within a year of the passing of Act I of 1882, A.P. MacDonnell, Secretary to the Government of Bengal, informed the Government of India that due to 'free recruiting' and the dismantling of the regulatory system under the new Act, serious abuses like kidnapping and abduction of women by unlicensed recruiters were reported by district officials from the recruitment areas. The Deputy Commissioner of Manbhum reported that labourers recruited under the free system did not go through medical examinations, nor were they registered or brought to the headquarter station. In many cases the new recruits were marched directly to Raneeganj, from where they were sent by rail to Assam via Dhubri.[28] Similarly, officials from other districts reported that many of the recruiters lured the migrants to go to the Assam tea gardens with false promises of high wages, cheap rice supply and light work.[29] The Chief Commissioner of Assam, however, did not give much credence to these reports. While acknowledging that unprotected women were often taken away against their will and turned into prostitutes, it was argued that the emigrants were generally attracted to the 'high wages' and 'admirable arrangements' made for securing their comfort in Assam. 'They are in many ways better off there than in their own houses.'[30] This was to become a stock argument for years to come among the planters, the colonial bureaucracy and the revisionist scholarship, when confronted with the unpleasant realities of labour life in the plantations during the indenture regime.

The Bengal officials were very critical of the 'free recruitment' system operating under Act I of 1882 in the districts of Santhal Parganas, Hazaribagh, Lohardagga, Beerbhum, Bankura and Midnapur. They argued that in the absence of an official regulatory system, 'free' emigration was 'affording greatest facilities for wrong doing', and 'enticing away women and young people – better cover for illegal proceedings'.[31] Among the Bengal officials, J. Ware Edgar, starting with his early posting in Cachar and his report on Assam and Bengal tea plantations in 1874, remained the most vocal critic of the recruitment system for Assam plantations during his long career. In 1882, after the passing of Act I of 1882, as Commissioner of the Chota Nagpur Division, he reported in great detail about the hierarchical structure of notorious *arakatis* and other professional recruiters in the Bengal countryside, and their involvement in the flourishing 'coolie trade' under the 'free' recruitment system for the Assam tea plantations. His report, based on information provided by local officials and Christian missionaries, revealed a sordid picture of deception, fraud and 'sale' in the recruitment of migrants.[32] Expressing his strong disapproval of the employers and their recruitment system, he warned that 'there are very grave dangers in the attempt now being made by some employers to evade the law in recruiting districts, and take advantage of it in the labour districts'.[33] Again in 1889, as Chief Secretary, Government of Bengal,

Edgar was instrumental in the appointment of F. Harrington Tucker, a police officer, as special officer to investigate into charges of fraud and kidnapping connected with the recruiting of labourers for the Assam tea districts.[34] The tea planters of Dooars had complained about the kidnapping of labourers recruited for their district, and claimed that they were being taken away to Assam by the professional recruiters. Tucker's investigations in the recruiting districts confirmed the prevalence of many 'evil malpractices'. He reported about the involvement of native and Eurasian recruiters in the enticement of men and girls with false promises of 'well paid' jobs and 'well-to-do' husbands. Referring to their *modus operandi*, he wrote: 'Assuming various disguises by which they induce men and women to join them in pretended enterprises and somehow getting them under pecuniary obligations and taking them to recruiting depots, and there making them over to contractors who ship them off to Assam.'[35] His investigations convinced Tucker that so long as the 'free recruitment' under Act 1 of 1882 existed without any official control over the *arakatis* and sub-agents, the abductions and malpractices would continue: 'The whole thing is now a trade and a very paying one.'[36] Tucker was also critical of the 'great slackness' in compliance of the provisions of the Act concerning registration at Dhubri. He found that the contractors' depots at Dhubri, 'into which every abducted coolie is placed before registration, are well manned by peons, arakatis, &c., who keep the inmates in order by threats etc., and bring them out, thoroughly cowed, to be registered'.[37] At the end of Tucker's appointment period, Edgar recommended extension for further investigation.[38]

These sordid tales of the recruitment system were not palatable to the Government of India and Government of Assam, and the former was reluctant to extend Tucker's tenure. It argued that his investigations showed 'very small cases of oppression and fraud' and were of 'trivial character', and, therefore, concluded that 'no such abuses exist'.[39] Tucker's efforts were belittled and rebuked through comments such as:

> Mr Tucker's position appears to be much like that of an outpost on behalf of the Bengal tea planters, to assist them against the Assam planters in their competition for coolies labour. . . . Considering that his reputation and his Rs. 80 per mensem are dependent on the number and blackness of the malpractices he brings to light . . .[40]

This apathy and lack of serious concern allowed abuses and malpractices to flourish in the recruitment system under Act I of 1882, and the Assam plantations remained an unpopular destination in the recruitment districts. R. Macleod, officiating Superintendent of Emigration in Calcutta, reported in 1891 that the unlicensed recruitment system under Act I of 1882 had paved the way for serious abuses like 'falsification of the description' of intending emigrants when they were produced before the registering officers. And since the registering officers were not from the same district, they were not in a position to verify their descriptions.[41] The Bengal Labour Commission of 1896 and the Enquiry Committee of 1906 reported the continuation of abuses and malpractices in recruitment for Assam: 'There is same tale of deception, of false inducements, of entrapping people'.[42] Sir Bampfylde Fuller confidentially observed:

> The coolies are virtually treated as prisoners for the date of engagement, being closely confined in depots, clothed in a special dress, fed on cooked food, and, finally, transferred to garden agents at so much per head. Arrangements such as these are obviously suited only to the dregs of the labour market.[43]

The consequences of this were acknowledged by Sir Charles Rivaz in the Imperial Council:

> a horde of unlicensed and uncontrolled labour purveyors and recruiters sprang into existence, under false pretences, ignorant men and women, chiefly from the most backward districts of Bengal and Central Provinces, to allow themselves to be conveyed to Assam, and by practically selling these people to the planters for the purpose of being placed under labour contract.[44]

To overcome these problems, the Government of East Bengal and Assam appointed an Enquiry Committee in 1906. There was now growing realization in official quarters that the extraordinary power of private arrest vested with the planters and other practices of an extra-legal nature were becoming a deterrent in mobilizing migrant labour. The Lieutenant Governor, Bampfylde Fuller, believed that indiscriminate use of private arrest by the planters had 'produced in the minds of the ignorant labour force a feeling of helplessness and unprotected bondage . . . the existence of this feeling was mainly responsible for the marked unpopularity of service in Assam'.[45] The investigations of the Enquiry Committee confirmed the above view. Therefore, as a measure to boost labour supply, the government repealed Sections 195 and 196 of Act VI of 1901, in 1908.[46] Although the object of the measure was to attract more labour, the planters opposed it on the ground that there would no longer be any security against the enticement and desertion of labour. Yielding to the protests of the planters, the government appointed a number of special magistrates empowered to issue warrants for the arrest of 'absconding' labourers.[47] As pointed out earlier, the repeal of penal provisions from the Act of 1901 did not mean the complete dismantling of the indenture system, as long as Act XIII of 1859 remained in force.[48]

Towards Monopolistic Control

One important development in the late nineteenth and early twentieth centuries was the tendency towards centralization and monopolistic control over recruitment by planters, who had already formed the Tea District Labour Supply Association in 1892 and the Assam Labour Association earlier. It appears that Charles Elliot, late Lietenant Governor of Bengal, also wanted to ensure the establishment of a centralized agency by the tea industry, for the purpose of taking the whole business of recruitment into its own hands. The Indian Tea Association (ITA) wanted, in addition, a ban on recruiting by any other channel. The Lieutenant Governor of Bengal was not in favour of this: 'It is impossible for Government to confer a monopoly of this kind and to force all gardens to join such an association'. Instead, he suggested as an alternative the abolition of 'so-called free emigration' in his letter of 29 December 1896 to the Government of India.[49] The Bengal Labour Commission of 1896 then recommended the setting up of a central agency for recruitment purposes, as 'innumerable abuses have grown up round the present system of free recruiting, and . . . drastic measures are needed to purge it from the scandalous reputation it has acquired'.[50] The planters welcomed this and immediately held a meeting to discuss and consider the possibilities of setting up such an agency.[51] The ITA and its Assam branches were very pleased with the proposal of Henry Cotton, the Chief Commissioner, to implement this recommendation and willingness 'to give it all the moral support in his power'.[52] A meeting of tea company representatives and planters was held in the Bengal Chamber of Commerce on 29 March 1897, to consider a scheme for the formation of a Centralized Recruiting Agency for Tea Gardens and Other Concerns in the districts of Assam, Cachar and Sylhet. The ostensible purpose was to provide a labour force at reasonable costs, with greater certainty and dissociated from abuse, etc.[53]

In 1917, the Assam Labour Association and the Tea District Labour Supply Association were amalgamated to form the Tea Districts Labour Association.[54] By the 1920s, this Association had established its agencies all over the recruiting districts. Most of the *sirdari* recruitment was controlled by these agencies. After the passing of Act VI of 1901, the emphasis was on greater encouragement to the *sirdari* system of recruitment. Under Section 3 of this Act, local governments were empowered to prohibit unlicensed recruiting in any area, subject to the sanction of the central government. Secondly, a special class of garden *sirdars* was created who could recruit without registering their recruits within notified areas. And finally, local governments were given the discretion to relax any provisions relating to recruitment by *sirdars* working under approved agencies of the Association.[55] The effectiveness of these measures is clear from the figures which show that out of 26,664 immigrants sent to Assam during 1902–03, no less than 22,746 were imported through the agency of the Tea District Labour Supply Association (TDLSA). The Chief Commissioner observed that 'this Association appears to have enjoyed practically a monopoly of the recruiting business'.[56] Again, in the Amendment Act

CHART 4.5
*Assisted Emigrants sent by Tea District Labour Association
to Assam Valley Tea Plantations, 1934–47*

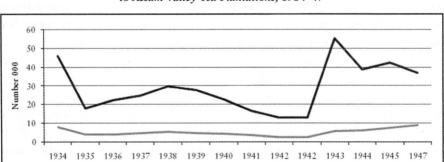

of 1908 (which modified Act VI of 1901), recruitment by unlicensed contractors was forbidden and facilities for recruitment by garden *sirdars* working under local agents of the TDLSA were increased.[57] Following this, new areas of recruitment were opened up in Madras Presidency. The Governments of Madras, Bengal and the Central Provinces granted concessions to *sirdars* working under the TDLSA.[58] Finally, in 1915, the system of recruitment by contractors was completely abolished by the Assam Labour and Emigration (Amendment) Act VIII of 1915.[59] By 1930, labour recruitment for the tea gardens of Assam was exclusively carried on by garden *sirdars*, who worked under licensed local agents appointed by the Tea Districts Labour Association and individual employers enjoying concessions granted under Act VI of 1901.[60] The repeal of this Act did not affect the Association's monopoly over recruitment, as is evident from Chart 4.5 (and Appendix Table 4.2) – the majority of migrants were recruited by *sirdars* working directly under TDLA.

The most important feature of the Amendment Act was the government's direct participation, as a form of more effective assistance, in the process of labour recruitment. Under this Amendment Act, the Government of India constituted the Assam Labour Board for the supervision of local agents, and of recruitment, engagement and emigration of labourers to labour districts in Assam. The labour district provisions of Act VI of 1901 were withdrawn from the Upper Assam districts with effect from 1 July 1915. Major W.M. Kennedy was appointed Chairman of the Assam Labour Board.[61] However, the Board was dominated by the tea industry: out of sixteen members, fifteen were drawn from the industry and only the Chairman of the Board was to be appointed by the Governor General in Council. The fifteen members representing the tea industry were to be elected from the following bodies: eight from the Indian Tea Association, Calcutta and London; four and three, respectively, from the Assam and Surma Valley branches of the ITA.[62]

The Royal Commission admitted that the monopoly of the Tea District Labour Association was fostered by the legal support given to it by the Assam Labour Board. They also admitted that this Board, except for its Chairman, was 'nothing more than a committee of the ITA, and the Tea District Labour Association is practically with the ITA and may be correctly regarded as the recruitment department of the ITA'.[63] Almost every new labour law and amendment, claimed the government, was meant to reform the existing system and remove 'abuses' from the recruitment system. Accordingly, local governments were empowered to cancel the recruiting licenses of local agents or prohibit recruitment from their respective areas in case of abuses. However, in spite of the above amendments in the labour laws and the founding of the Assam Labour Board to remove abuses from the recruitment system, the Bombay government reported cases of 'misrepresentation, false promises and use of force' in recruiting labourers by agents of the Assam tea plantations.[64] In 1925, district officials of the Bihar and Orissa government complained of illegal recruitment being carried on in Ranchi through the agency of the Roman Catholic Mission, in 'contravention of the Assam Labour and Emigration Act, 1901'.[65] No action was taken against them.

There were other instances where no government action was taken against the violation of labour laws by the planters. One of the conditions for the special facilities given under the Amendment Act of 1908 to *sirdars* working under the TDLSA was that no person engaged by them was to be put under a local contract. But the planters increasingly placed all such recruits under the Workman's Breach of Contract Act XIII of 1859 immediately after their arrival in the gardens, which provided them with extra-legal authority over them. Highlighting the oppressive features of the labour system in the tea gardens, the newspaper *Bengalee* carried a special editorial on 4 March 1901 in which Act XIII was decried as the most objectionable law in operation. The editorial argued that the planters were increasingly using this Act because it rendered verbal contracts valid and imposed more onerous obligations on the labourers than the other laws. On the other hand, it imposed no corresponding obligations on the planters.[66]

The Bengal government too had complaints against this, but no action was taken by the Government of India.[67] In fact, if recruitment in certain areas was adversely affected by the provision of certain labour laws, the Government of India showed willingness to repeal those provisions or even the Act itself. For example, Section 3 of Act VI of 1901 had vested the local governments of the recruiting provinces with the power to prohibit recruitment absolutely by means of a notification.[68] This provision, meant to check abuses in the recruiting districts, was exercised by the Government of the United Provinces in five divisions and two districts.[69] However the Government of India did not view the restrictions imposed by the provincial government with favour.

Accordingly, the Royal Commission recommended that the 'power to prohibit recruitment should be withdrawn immediately, and that no barriers should be put that would prevent the normal play of social and economic forces in attracting labour from one part of India to another'.[70] The Commission went so far as to recommend the repeal of Act VI of 1901 because 'several of its important provisions' have become inoperative by notification.[71] With the repeal of penal provisions from the above Act as well as the repeal of Act XIII of 1859 in 1926, the existing legislation was considered redundant and also restrictive of the 'flow of labour to Assam'.[72] The Government of Assam suggested to the Government of India that 'existing restrictions on recruitment should be relaxed in the interests of the tea industry'.[73]

Stripped of its penal provisions, the labour law appeared to the tea industry as an 'undemocratic anomaly'.[74] Therefore the ITA asked the Government of India to replace Act VI of 1901 with a new one.[75] Following the recommendations of the Royal Commission and the ITA's demand, the Government of India passed the Tea District Emigrant Labour Act (XXII of 1932), and repealed Act VI of 1901.[76] Under this new Act, the government appointed a Controller of Emigrant Labour whose main job was to supervise the recruitment and transportation of labourers to the Assam tea gardens according to the regulations of the Act.[77] It provided for repatriation of labourers on dismissal, and the Controller was given the power to enforce it. Moreover, every application for a license to recruit for the Assam tea gardens was to be certified by the Controller to ensure that the employers were complying with the regulations of the labour laws. The Controller was also given the power to inspect the forwarding depots, transit camps and trains carrying emigrants to Assam. However, he had no control over the living and working conditions of the labourers in the tea gardens. There were no provisions in the Act for regulating accommodation, sanitation, water supply, hours of work, educational facilities, etc., which had been, at least on paper, part of the earlier law. Even the provision of a minimum wage was dispensed with in the new Act because the tea industry opposed it, despite the fact that it was rarely enforced.[78] Moreover, since the new Act applied only to 'assisted emigrant' labourers, the vast majority of the labour force was not covered by its provisions.[79]

The Issue of Mortality and the Inspection System

One constant feature of labour life in the Assam tea plantations was sickness, undernourishment and a high rate of mortality, despite the provision of medical care, sanitary facilities and sickness allowance in the labour laws. Mortality rates in the tea gardens were invariably higher than the figures for the province as a whole. The incidence of mortality during the indenture period, which was appallingly high, was grudgingly acknowledged and 'lamented' in the official reports, and condemned by critics like Rev. Charles Dowding and the nationalist intelligentsia.[80] The most damaging revelations always appeared in the reports of the Sanitary Commissioners, which exposed the rationalizations and denials of high mortality in the immigration reports.[81] The picture in the post-indenture years may not have been as horrific, but whenever proper and serious investigations were conducted, as in 1920–21 and in the 1940s, high rates of sickness, undernourishment and mortality still remained important features of labour life in the Assam Valley tea gardens.[82]

One of the professed objectivess of labour laws with penal provisions was to 'protect' the ignorant and illiterate emigrant. Compliance of the protection provisions was to be ensured through regular inspections of the tea gardens by local officials. These inspections were expected to do the following: check the planters' books to see whether minimum wages stipulated by law were being paid; examine whether labourers were being provided with subsidized rations and with hygienic conditions in the 'coolie lines'; whether medical facilities for the sick were being provided; and so on. The inspecting officials were supposed to submit their reports to the Chief Commissioner's office after every visit.[83] But the inspections were often not carried out either with serious intent or with the regularity required under the law. With the rapid opening up of new tea gardens, the inspecting officials reported that they were not able to regularly visit the gardens for inspections as per the provisions of the laws. This was particularly the case in the Upper Assam districts. Confronted for this irregularity, the Chief Inspector, Dr Partridge, contended that it was impossible for him to visit the large number of gardens situated within his jurisdiction even once in the year.[84] Sections 111 and 112 of the Act I of 1882 required prior verification of labour contracts by the Inspectors. In reality, the contracts were verified many months or even a year after its signing, when the Inspector went to the garden on his official tour. In the meantime, the labourer could have been subjected to illegally imposed penal restrictions. Knox Wright, Deputy Commissioner of Sibsagar, summed up the reality of the inspection system as follows:

> it is not possible to verify all the contracts during the year. For instance the Inspector visits the garden in a certain month of the year, and he verifies all contracts registered before the visit is paid; in the succeeding months more contracts from the same garden are received and registered; but a year may lapse before the next visit is paid, and till then these must remain unverified. Besides, last year many tea gardens employing Act-labourers were not visited at all. It must be remembered that managers are very particular in taking contracts. They carefully avoid taking

TABLE 4.1
Inspections of the Tea Gardens held during 1889[86]

District	Total number of gardens	Number liable to inspection	Number of gardens inspected
Kamrup	61	16	5
Nowgong	56	48	7
Darrang	80	78	11
Sibsagar	178	172	25
Lakhimpur	140	136	19

a large number of contracts at one and the same time. . . . As gardens are visited only once a year, it follows that hundreds of contracts remain unverified for 9 or 10 or 11 months.[85]

Table 4.1 shows that a very small number of gardens were actually inspected, a clear indication of laxity in the implementation of the provisions of labour 'protection' in the labour legislation.

The district officials were fully aware of the inability of labourers to understand the nature and content of the contract forms which they signed without being able to read: 'There is not the smallest security that the coolie, when he is brought up to go through the form of touching the pen, in company of some dozens of others, at the garden, understands in the least what is signing to.' They also admitted the glaring omissions in the rule book: 'There is no provision that his agreement should be first explained to him, nor is it very likely that any objection he might make would be listen to. He is expected to sign with the rest.'[87] The Enquiry Committee of 1906 conceded that 'Government protection has not been very beneficial to the labourers'.[88] Even local officials admitted that inspections were often too infrequent, and that action in the case of unhealthy gardens was sometimes unduly delayed.[89] Chief Commissioner Bampfylde Fuller seems to have been rather sceptical of the 'effectiveness' of government supervision of labour welfare:

> The supervision which is exercised by Government ordinarily consists in brief – sometimes cursory – visit of inspection paid once a year, and often by an officer of very limited experience. It is true that when the death-rate on a garden exceeds 7 per cent a more detailed investigation is undertaken. But it must be remembered that the death-rates are taken as reported by the garden office, and on some estates great laxity notoriously prevails in the registration of infantile mortality. In truth, an inspecting officer's powers of interference on behalf of labourer are exceedingly limited.[90]

The findings of the Enquiry Committee of 1921–22 showed that ordinary

inspections of the tea gardens by junior and inexperienced government officials were not of much value, and that, as a rule, Deputy Commissioners
were unable to devote much time to inspection work. The members of the
Committee were 'struck with the meagerness of detail which is a characteristic
feature of ordinary inspection reports'.[91]

Act XXII of 1932 did not even prescribe inspections of labour conditions
on the gardens. In 1933, the Government of Assam issued executive instructions for regular inspections by the Deputy Commissioners and sub-divisional
officers.[92] These officials were required, primarily, to satisfy themselves that
the provisions of the new Act were understood and observed properly. Added
to this was the discretionary power to inspect medical arrangements, water
supply, level of wages in relation to the task, etc.[93] However, as late as 1946,
Rege observed that since there was no statutory authority for these inspections,
they had no binding force. He reported that all the inspecting officials hardly
ever interviewed labourers in private, and that they collected the necessary
information from the managers themselves.[94]

Yet another example of the official indifference was the lack of any organized system of checking the accuracy of records of wages submitted to the
government by the planters. According to the labour laws, the planters were
supposed to submit to the government the record of average monthly wages
earned by labourers in their gardens. They provided this information in an
arbitrary fashion. Often the figures submitted were inflated, showing higher
average earnings of labourers than the actual wages paid. Furthermore, the
planters always submitted records for only the last six months' wages. The
yearly averages of monthly wages published in the official reports were based
on these last six months' returns. These figures were misleading because the
last six months included the peak season, when the earnings of labourers were
generally higher than in the first six months of the year, which included the
slack period. However, the government never reprimanded the planters for
concealing the actual earnings of the labour force or for providing inflated
figures. Nor was any attempt made to establish a government agency to collect this information. The result was that labour was constantly underpaid
and the government officials, despite their awareness of this fact, remained
indifferent.[95]

Thus it appears that there was no communication between the labourers
and their 'protectors'. Labour was not allowed to move out of the gardens
freely, nor did they have access to any official organization to put forward their
complaints to the authorities and demand redress. Racial affinities between
the European planters and British officials created a further distance between
the 'protectors' and their subjects. The utter lack of any urban development in
the Assam Valley had helped to strengthen these social and racial ties through
the institution of exclusive clubs.[96] Many officials noticed the uselessness of

the government's avowed intention to protect labourers. As a senior official of the Government of India observed, 'there has been less strictness than has been desirable in the control exercised by government officers, and inspections have (I am aware) been far too much of the nature of a casual stroll around the garden after breakfast in the manager's bunglow'.[97] Another official statement came from Luttman Johnson, Commissioner for the Assam Valley districts, who after eleven years of service in the province said:

> The longer I live, the less I value protection from the labourers' point of view. No amount of inspection will improve wages. Some years of experience enabled me to become, or to think I became an efficient inspector when I had the time, but when are our officials to find time for efficient inspections.[98]

Contemporary accounts appearing in the nationalist press gave an unflattering view of the nature of inspections in the tea gardens by government officials. Most well known among these are the articles written by Dwarkanath Ganguli, assistant secretary in the Indian Association, which were published in the *Bengalee*.[99] 'When the inspectors visit the Gardens,' he wrote,

> they generally dine and peg with the planters, play and exchange with them the social amenities of life. This is the way in which they often perform the important duties of inspection. Whether a coolie has executed his contract, and if executed whether he has done so with a clear understanding, the inspector hardly ever cares to ascertain. The coolies are not often mustered before him, and if mustered they are made to stand in rows, those who have been won over by the promise of *sirdarship* or any other reward being allowed to occupy the front row and to answer for the whole lot any questions which may be asked. The rest remain absolutely ignorant of the fact as to why they are mustered there, and what they are required to do.[100]

Information about violation and non-implementation of the provisions of the labour laws, exercise of extra-legal powers and physical coercion of labour by planters, the discriminatory nature of court convictions involving planters and labourers, and abuses and malpractices in the recruitment system often reached the highest echelons of the colonial hierarchy, the Viceroy and the Secretary of State for India. The latter, in particular, would express serious concern, state his reservations and sometimes seek details on the nature of disciplinary actions. The Secretary of State expressed his discomfort at sanctioning 'the exceptional legislation', Act I of 1882, particularly the proposed extension of terms of labour contracts from three to five years, but gave his assent anyway. Being aware of the report of the Chotanagpur Commissioner about abuses and malpractices in the recruitment districts and high mortality in the tea gardens among the labour force, he directed the submission of a special report at the end of three years on the working of the new Act, in order to review and consider the possibility of 'abandoning' the 'exceptional legislation'.[101]

> While I have thought it my duty to make these observations on one particular portion of the Act which has received Your Lordship's assent, I readily allow that the measure contains many provisions likely to be beneficial to the native labourers as well as the planters, and I am unwilling to advise Her Majesty to disallow it. It will therefore be left to its operation.[102]

The two quarterly special reports on the working of Act I, submitted by the Government of Assam to the Secretary of State as per his instructions, revealed that the situation with regard to the high rate of mortality, abuses in the recruitment system, etc., had become far worse. But on both occasions the Assam government concluded that the time had not yet come when, in the interests either of the tea planters or of the labourers, it was possible to abandon exceptional legislation for emigration into Assam.[103] In their despatches to the Secretary of State, the Government of India often admitted that the working of the Act was less than satisfactory. It admitted that abuses existed in the system of recruiting, and that sanitary arrangements en route were defective. The Secretary of State was also aware that a memorandum submitted by the Indian Association to the Government of India had complained of the terrible conditions of labour life in the Assam gardens, the systematic violation of provisions of labour legislations, and the continued abuses in the recruitment system under the operations of Act I of 1882.[104] The Indian Association had made these charges on the basis of information published in the official reports. The Secretary of State still went ahead each time in concurring with the recommendations of the Government of Assam to continue with the Act.[105] His sanctioning, in 1891, of the continuation of Act I of 1882 was followed by the admission that there were

> two serious blots which accompany the working of the existing system – first, the excessive mortality, both on the way up to Assam and also on the gardens – a mortality which was not much less at the end of the last decade than it was, at the beginning; and secondly, the malpractices connected with the recruiting system in Bengal.[106]

He summed up his ambivalent attitude when he wrote to the Governor General:

> I concur with your views that emigration from the congested districts of Northern India to a province where there is an energetic demand, both on the tea gardens and on the virgin soil, for additional labour, is to be encouraged. I notice, however, the unanimity with which not only your government, but all the higher authorities

consulted, recognize that the special labour law of Assam, though necessary under existing conditions, is out of harmony with the civilized governments.[107]

A similar attitude was on display on the question of continuation of Act XIII of 1859 in the tea districts, as desired by the Government of India: 'There remain one or two points on which I can only accept your recommendations with some doubt.' Commenting that Act XIII of 1859 was objectionable in principle, the Secretary of State agreed to its continuation 'on the present occasion' but warned that 'its continued retention is not without serious prospective dangers'.[108]

Labour Protests and the Bureaucracy

The most glaring instances of official bias in the implementation of policy concerning labour could be found in the handling of cases arising out of confrontations between planters and labourers. In most such cases the labourers were awarded very harsh punishments even for minor offences, and sometimes even death sentences for violence against the planters. The planters, on the other hand, were mostly awarded small monetary fines or acquitted even when the charges were serious, as in some cases that involved the killing of labourers. Brutal violence by the planters against labourers often went unpunished or was treated with kid gloves by the colonial judiciary, but retaliatory responses by the labourers even of a very mild nature were punished very severely.[109]

The labour reports referred to a large number of such cases almost every year. One of the earliest cases reported was of the extremely brutal flogging of labourers by Richard Dunn, the assistant manager of Seerajuli tea garden of Assam Company in Tezpur district in 1866, resulting in the death of a young worker, Jhowree. The deceased, along with his father Seeboroth and other labourers, had run away from the garden because they were not getting enough food to eat. The District Commissioner, Captain T. Lamb, recorded in his Mofussil Diary on 12 March 1866, that they were caught and brought back to the garden, tied up and mercilessly beaten with a cane by Dunn, on orders from the manager of the garden.[110] Jhowree was subjected to a second round of beatings because he was unable to work as a result of the earlier punishment and consequently died the next day. Dunn was also accused of flogging other labourers including a woman named Beebeejan. As the details of this case reached the higher echelons of the colonial power hierarchy, it received attention, was well documented, and the conduct of the district officials came under scrutiny and censure. It is clear from the correspondence that Deputy Commissioner Lamb, despite expectation of stronger action from his superior officer, committed Dunn to trial under those sections of the Penal Code whereby the latter got away with light punishments in flogging cases – of small fines of Rs 10 and Rs 20. And in the case of the murder of the young labourer, he was only fined Rs 500 and sentenced to six months' imprisonment. The light conviction was facilitated by Major Bivar, Judicial Commissioner, who struck out the charge of murder at the outset of trial and appointed a jury consisting entirely of planters.[111] The manager, Donald, was not even considered for conviction as his complicity was not 'proven'. Lamb provided the following rationale for soft-pedalling Dunn's case: 'He is apparently an inexperienced young man, and his means are very limited, being only 80 rupees a month, and acting as he was under the instructions of the manager, I did not punish him so severely as otherwise I should have done.'[112] This despite the fact that, under the provisions of the existing labour law, he was supposed to 'protect' the interests of the 'ignorant' and 'hapless' labourers who had no one to argue their cases at the trial, and who earned no more than Rs 5 per month.

It is instructive to note that most district officials, despite their knowledge of the practice of flogging and its illegality as a form of disciplining the labour force by the planters, were often unwilling to admit or commit to this in their replies to enquiries from their seniors. Major Llyod, the Deputy Ccommissioner of Nowgong, in one such reply, mentioned 'rumours' regarding flogging, but assumed there was no truth in them in the absence of complaints from the labourers. Major Comber of Lakhimpur offered the same excuse of lack of complaints from the labourers as evidence that flogging was not practised, but quickly added that he had 'heard that some planters (especially those living at a distance) do occasionally take the law in their own hands, and administer perhaps a slight caning to refractory coolies'.[113] Captain Sconce, Deputy Commissioner of Sibsagar, was a little more circumspect:

> Although I cannot help thinking that coolies are too often beaten, it is exceedingly difficult to obtain legal proof. If the number of complaints were the criterion, one would say that assaults on coolies are very rare; but remoteness of many tea factories, and the inaccessibility of the two stations where magistrates are situated, could alone give great facility in the concealment of such offences.[114]

The geographical remoteness of the tea plantations from the magistrates' courts, and the environment of intimidation and close surveillance of the 'coolie lines' made it almost impossible for labourers to lodge complaints with the authorities. In the above-cited cases, the labourers told Lamb that they had wanted to lodge a complaint against the manager and assistant manager, but were not allowed to leave the garden.[115] The Indian Association complained to the Government of India that in cases between planters and labourers, the 'interest of justice' and the 'interests of the weaker party', were suffering in the judicial courts of Assam'. In its memorial, the Association reproduced cases reported in the official labour reports in support of their petition. In the Bawalia tea garden, in 1884, the manager was assaulted in retaliation for caning a boy in front of an assembly of labourers. Half a dozen labourers were sentenced to prison terms lasting from three days to one year, while the manager was only fined a sum of Rs 200. On appeal, the judge upheld the sentences on labourers but reduced the manager's fine to Rs 50. In another case, the assistant manager of the Chinkuri tea garden was besieged in his bungalow by labourers. The magistrate, despite finding no case of assault, sentenced some of the labourers to one month's imprisonment.[116] In the same year, the manager of Dygoroon tea garden was tried and acquitted by the court in the case of caning a woman labourer to death, despite the fact that the civil surgeon of Golaghat, Dr Conceicao, certified that the death was due to violence in his post-mortem report.[117]

The official information compiled, on Lord Curzon's insistence, on cases of assault in the Assam tea plantations during the last decade of the nineteenth century and early years of the twentieth century revealed several cases of such judicial discrimination. It is worth recounting some of them. In 1890, seven labourers of Balipara tea garden, Darrang district, were convicted and sentenced to one month's rigorous imprisonment for assaulting the manager who, they complained, had given them less than what they had earned. In the same year, fourteen labourers of Silghat tea garden, Sibsagar, were given a sentence of fifteen months' rigorous imprisonment for beating up the manager. They had complained that the manager had assaulted a woman labourer for disobeying his orders. On the other hand, a fine of Rs 100 was considered adequate punishment for a manager by the Sessions Court for causing the death of a labourer by brutal beating.[118] In 1891, at Borjuli tea garden, Darrang, a scuffle broke out when the assistant manager tried to force labourers out to work the day after a late night of cultural festivities and drinking to celebrate *Karmapuja*. They chased him up to his bungalow without resorting to any form of violence, but for this they were punished in a manner that was completely out of proportion to their 'crime': one labourer was sentenced to eighteen months and two others to one year of rigorous imprisonment.[119] There were a number of cases where the managers had beaten up female labourers because they refused to comply to sexual advances or disobeyed orders at work. In these cases, when the male labourers retaliated and assaulted the managers, they were sentenced to long-term rigorous imprisonment ranging from three to eight months. The managers got away with meagre fines of Rs 100 and Rs 50.[120] In 1900, an 'absconding' woman labourer was brought back to Phulbari tea garden after recapture and subjected to flogging in the 'most barbarous' manner on the orders of the manager. The court considered a fine of Rs 500 as adequate punishment for the manager.[121] In the same year, the assistant manager of Singrimari garden in Darrang district beat up a labourer with a cane. Thereupon, a group of his co-workers threatened to retaliate but no assault was actually committed. However, six of the labourers were prosecuted and sentenced to three months' rigorous imprisonment.

The attitude of the colonial bureaucracy in general towards cases of judicial discrimination was clearly reflected in the remarks of the Commissioner of Assam Valley, Melitus: 'As between man and man, I should consider the sentence excessive, but as between the manager of a garden and his coolies, I am not prepared to say that it is excessive.'[122] In another case in 1902, a couple of labourers were awarded three months' rigorous imprisonment simply for using abusive language against their manager.[123] The Chief Commissioner defended the harsh punishment meted out to the labourers on the ground that 'discipline must be maintained on tea gardens and unruliness which may lead to rioting must be strictly checked'.[124] Clearly, the onus of maintaining 'discipline' in the tea garden fell solely on the labourers, while the managers and assistant managers got away even with murder. Greig, superintendent of the Rajmai tea garden in Sibsagar district, had beaten one of his labourers to death, on suspicion of stealing some firewood in the lines. He was put to trial before the Sessions Judge on the charge of causing the death of a labourer. The jury unanimously returned a verdict of acquittal, which was accepted by the Sessions Judge.[125] In the case of the death of a boy labourer due to beating by the manager and his assistant, the Sessions Judge let them off with fines. No further action followed despite the case being raised in the British Parliament; the Governments of India and Assam managed to evade the Parliamentary concern citing the 'unreliable character of the evidence'.[126] Obviously, any evidence presented by the labourers against the planters was considered 'unreliable' to arrive at the 'truth'. However no such concern to arrive at 'truth' was displayed when the accused was a labourer. The Sessions Judge in the same district had no hesitation in ordering the hanging of a labourer who was accused of inflicting mortal wounds on the manager of the garden.[127] Such double standards of justice were seen in other cases as well. In Lakhimpur district, a colliery labourer was sentenced to death by the Sessions Judge on the charge of killing a European foreman. The enquiry into the case revealed that the deceased had treated the labourer harshly. The High Court later commuted the death sentence to transportation for life.[128]

Chief Commissioner Henry Cotton admitted that there was an undoubted tendency among magistrates in Assam to 'inflict severe sentences in cases in which coolies are charged with committing offences against their employers, and to impose light, and sometimes inadequate, punishment upon employers when they are convicted of offences against employers.'[129] He reported a number of cases where rigorous punishment was meted out to labourers by magistrates for minor offences, while a European planter was callously acquitted in a case involving the murder of a labourer.[130] That these observations were not purely the work of an overzealous Chief Commissioner or biased by his unpleasant relations with the planters was proved beyond doubt when the Viceroy, Lord Curzon, himself acknowledged their accuracy. Replying to Cotton's letters on behalf of the Viceroy, Sir John Hewett, Secretary, Home Department, wrote: 'with reference to the tendency . . . to pass excessive sentences when coolies are charged with committing offences against their employer, I am to say that his Excellency in Council considers that the inequality in the administration of justice thus indicated is an abuse'.[131] Despite the admission of such partiality, however, the government did nothing to prevent it. In his memoir, Bampfylde Fuller, Cotton's successor as Chief Commissioner, recounted the case of a young assistant manager, Bain, who was found guilty of killing a labourer by flogging with a stirrup leather and was sentenced to eighteen months of simple imprisonment. The planters' jury was expected to acquit him, but because of intervention by Lord Curzon, he had to undergo the imprisonment. Fuller felt 'very sorry for the youth. No doubt he had acted under the orders of his garden manager, and had refused to give him away – a married man with children to whom conviction would have been ruin'. Fuller arranged with the police officer who escorted Bain to prison to 'make things as smooth as possible' for him.'[132] Official bias against labourers was not confined to individual cases alone. Whenever the labourers offered collective resistance against ill-treatment, low wages and working conditions, the government always helped the planters suppress them. The annual labour reports regularly reported a number of cases of 'assaults', 'rioting', 'unlawful assemblies', etc., involving labourers which were suppressed by the police. Similarly, the upsurge of labourers in 1921–22 in the Assam tea gardens was suppressed by the police and paramilitary forces.[133] The Government of Assam called in ten-and-a-half platoons of the Assam Rifles to the 'disturbed' areas with a promise to the planters that they would remain there 'as long they were wanted for security'.[134] Throughout the 1930s, almost all the protests of the labourers were suppressed with the help of the police.[135]

None of the enquiry committees or commissions appointed by the government to look into the conditions of labour relations in the Assam tea gardens had any labour representatives. Most members of such committees/commissions were either representatives of the planters or government officials. For example, out of five members of the Enquiry Committee of 1906, two were representatives of the planters, and three were nominated by the Government of India, the Government of Bengal and the Government of Eastern Bengal and Assam respectively.[136] Similarly, the Enquiry Committee of 1921–22 consisted of five planters' representatives, one medical missionary and three officials.[137] In 1939, the Government of Assam, forced by the increasing number of labour strikes in the tea gardens, appointed a Tea Garden Labour Enquiry Committee consisting of government officials, ITA representatives and two Indian MLAs (Members of the Legislative Assembly).[138] However the enquiry committee never functioned because the ITA objected to the inclusion of the Indian MLAs on the ground that they were associated with the labour agitation, and withdrew its cooperation. Nothing more was heard of this committee after the ITA withdrew.[139] As to the impact on labour relations of the brutalities and ill-treatment inflicted on plantation labourers, the official perception and attitude was summed up by the Chief Commissioner of Assam, Sir Dennis Fitzpatrick:

> With about nine hundred gardens employing upwards of 323,000 hands, there must, of course, be a certain proportion of bad men, perhaps even of thoroughly depraved men, both among planters and coolies. There must be a certain amount of harshness and oppression, at times possibly even of downright cruelty, on the one side, and of turbulence, conspiracies, and maliciously concocted charges on the other; this, unfortunately, is human nature as displayed among all classes of men, and happily we have criminal courts strong enough to deal with it; but speaking generally, the relations between the employers and labourers seem to be fairly good.[140]

This was to become the general refrain of most of the official reporting by Assam civil servants with most officials of Assam affirming this perception.

It became usual practice in official reportage to mention cases of violence, physical coercion and the blatant use of extra-legal authority by planters, and at the same time to rationalize these as being aberrations or deny them altogether when confronted with non-official criticism. J.A. Craven, Deputy Collector and the head of the Santhali Deputation,[141] when confronted with highly unfavourable reporting by his fellow members, the Santhali tribal heads, dismissed their findings in his version of the report:

> It is a fallacy to suppose that the Assam coolie is hard-worked and [an] uncared for serf, earning a mere monthly pittance scarcely sufficient for the bare necessities of life. He is far better off on a tea garden than in his own country, and if industrious and careful, can easily earn from Rs 10 to Rs 15 a month, and it is to the planters' own interest to keep his coolie healthy and comfortable.[142]

Equally interesting were the official observations on the findings of the Santhali Deputation: 'The government has received the non-official view – not a pleasant one . . . it is a view of a free, high spirited and comparatively wild race, who cannot bear the thought of compulsion, or physical restraint or corporal punishment.' Further:

> As regards the real facts . . . there is no doubt that the deputation only repeat hearsay evidence, and a natural tendency to revel in gruesome stories. No one denies that there is a residuum of truth in these stories: instances have existed and have come to light of harsh treatment of sick coolies and of child bearing women, of

corporal punishment inflicted for short work or want of discipline, of heavy fines or by heavy tasks and by the impossibility of getting overtime pay, of difficulties placed in the way of the return of time-expired coolies, and so on.[143]

The official reasoning for condoning the exercise of such powers without explicit sanctions was based on the ground that the 'tea planter as a master of a large and irregular labour staff must enforce discipline by occasionally severe measures which need not be looked into too closely, because they are substantially just and for the good of the general body of coolies'.[144]

However, there were other civil servants whose perceptions and attitude differed from the general refrain of the colonial bureaucracy. Civil servants of Bengal like J. Ware Edgar and a few others who were appointed as members of the 1868 Commission by the Bengal government reported the incidence of high mortality, and inhuman treatment of migrant labourers on the plantation with candour and strong disapproval. Edgar was pained at the sufferings of the labourers during the 'tea mania' boom. He was very unhappy with his fellow civil servants for their negligence in protecting the emigrants within their jurisdiction:

> It is intensely unpleasant to have to write of these things, especially as in doing so I must reflect unfavourably upon past conduct of body of men . . . among whom are some intimate personal friends. . . . I should not be justified in letting my personal feelings keep me silent, however painful it may be for me to record my opinion.[145]

Similarly, DeRenzy, the Sanitary Commissioner of Assam, truthfully reported his findings on malnutrition, sickness and mortality due to insufficient incomes and unhygienic living conditions among tea garden labourers, in 1878.[146] His successors, Clark and Eteson, followed his tradition of truthful reporting during the course of their tenures in the early 1880s. Eteson was very critical of the adverse conditions of emigrant labourers after their arrivals in the tea gardens. He reported their 'injudicious care', lack of 'dietetic and carefully cooked food', 'inadequate lodging' and 'privations of climate.' The work assigned to the emigrant, he argued, 'exposes him to all weathers, and often to dangerous diseases'.[147]

> It is no wonder, therefore, that the ratio of sickness and mortality among the tea-garden labourers as a class has been always very great; that in many gardens it is above what is counted epidemic in civilised countries; and that the subject has been an unceasing anxiety to the Government of the Province.'[148]

Many of the civil servants posted in the recruiting districts were extremely critical of the coercive system of recruitment for the Assam plantations, and held low wages as the main cause for the unpopularity of the plantations as a destination for employment. Sir Alexander Mackenzie, Lieutenant Governor of Bengal, accepted the findings of the Bengal Labour Enquiry Commission without hesitation and recommended the abolition of the 'so-called free recruitment' for Assam from the recruitment districts, as well as a raise in the minimum wage to Rs 6 and Rs 5 from the prevailing rates of Rs 5 and Rs 4 for men and women respectively. The Enquiry Commission found that the wages 'are kept too low in Assam'.[149] However, these officials' efforts and exposures did not invoke any positive response from the Government of India.

Cotton Controversy

The sharpest and most complex contrast in the attitudes and perceptions of colonial civil servants towards the Assam indenture regime was reflected in Chief Commissioner Henry Cotton's Annual Report in 1900 on immigrant labour in the Assam tea plantations. This provoked a major controversy between him and the planters. In some ways this report was very different from earlier ones. The general impression that most previous reports gave about labour in Assam could be summarized in the following terms: labourers were well-fed and living in comfort; they were provided with proper medical and sanitary facilities, and subsidized rations; they earned adequate wages; and as a result, there was no tension between the employers and the labourers. Cotton's report of 1900, based on inspections carried out by local officials, presented an altogether different picture of labour life and labourers' relations with the planters. It showed that the mortality rate among Assam tea garden labourers in that year was much higher than in the previous two years. This was attributed to the effect of scarcity of resources because of low wages among immigrants, as a result of which they were vulnerable to disease.[150] The report showed that wages paid to the labourers were even below the statutory minimum rates of Rs 5 and Rs 4 for men and women.[151] The Chief Commissioner had come across numerous cases in which labourers in the fourth year of their agreement were not paid the higher wage to which they were entitled. He also noted cases where rice had not been provided at the statutory rate and subsistence allowance had not been paid to sick labourers.[152] His report regarded the relations between the employer and the labourer as being far from cordial; in fact the tension was clearly growing. Ten cases of 'riots' had been reported in that year alone.[153]

Cotton's report received a hostile reception from the planters. They accused him of distortion and exaggeration. A number of extracts from various previous reports concerning wages, labour relations, etc., were cited by the Indian Tea Association in an effort to show that Cotton's report was biased and 'fallacious'.[154] Cotton conceded that his report was different from the previous ones, but he denied that he was guilty of any bias. 'I came to this province five years ago,' he replied to the planters' charges, 'a great advocate and supporter of tea industry, and, as is well known, am identified with many active measures to promote its interests. My public utterances and official reports are proof of this.'[155] He reminded them of his cordial relationship with the planting community during the past four years of his stay in the province and stated that towards the end of his tenure, he was keen to 'say and do nothing to disturb the existing harmony'. He admitted that his earlier reports had been written in the 'easy-going and optimistic vein which has been the general characteristic of the Provincial labour reports'.[156] He was struck by the 'apologetic current' that ran through the reports written during the past twenty years in the province. He stated that the current change in his perceptions came as an outcome of enquiries and investigations he had initiated after the Government of Bengal, following the report of the Labour Commission of 1896, had recommended a raise in wages. These inspections had revealed many things of which 'a Chief Commissioner may remain, and often has remained, in ignorance. I was distressed beyond measure at the tale of suffering which came to my notice, and I felt it my duty not to conceal the truth. I reported on the facts.'[157] Among the many distressing facts mentioned in his report were the flogging of women labourers for attempting and helping to 'abscond'; violation of provisions of statutory minimum wages; and 'illegal debiting' of subsistence allowances, sick diets and even the reward paid for the arrest of deserters by the planters. Thereby the labourers were 'bound hand and foot to the garden service'.[158] These cases were not reported from some 'bad gardens' alone, but from gardens which yielded good dividends and were under 'respectable boards of management'.[159] These and the other 'objectionable' contents of his report, he pointed out, were based on the inspections carried out by his district officials.[160]

Cotton added fuel to the fire by proposing the recommendation of the Lieutenant Governor of Bengal, of an increase in the statutory minimum wages of labourers, in the Central Legislative Assembly through the Assam Labour and Emigration Bill. He proposed that the wages of labourers should be increased to a flat rate of Rs 6 per man and Rs 5 per woman for all five years of the contract period, instead of the existing graduated rates of Rs 5 per man and Rs 4 per woman for the first three years, and Rs 6 and Rs 5 respectively in the last two years. He pointed out that the wages of tea garden labourers, fixed in 1865, had remained stagnant, while the cost of living in Assam had risen considerably.[161] Secondly, even the statutory minimum wages were not fully paid to the labourers, the averages of previous years being much below the minimum wages fixed. He supported this second argument by providing the figures of average wages paid to the labourers in the last seventeen years, which never exceeded Rs 4.78 for a man and Rs 3.97 for a woman.[162] Third, the wages of unskilled labour in the province had gone up by 44 per cent between 1874–75 and 1898–99, and hence, there was sufficient justification for an increase in the wages of plantation labour. Finally, wages in other provinces where new industries were emerging (such as jute, sugar, railway construction and mines) had gone up, creating tough competition for the Assam tea gardens in recruitment of labourers.[163]

The matter was referred to a Select Committee of the Council, which, although appreciative of Cotton's arguments, reduced the proposed increase of wages to Rs 5 per man and Rs 4 per woman for the first year, Rs 5.50 and Rs 4.50 for the second and third years, and Rs 6 and Rs 5 for the last two years. In other words, the proposed increase in the average rate of wages amounted to only 6 annas. Cotton regarded the increase 'in all conscience a mild and moderate proposal'.[164] Even the Viceroy described it a 'very moderate increase'.[165] However Cotton felt unhappy when in the Council, Lord Curzon, 'in a moment of inconceivable weakness', announced the postponement of this graduated rate for two years 'owing to the depression in the market for tea', a euphemism for placating the enraged planters.[166] In the Legislative Council, the representatives of the tea industry put up a strong opposition even to the modified proposals of the Select Committee. Buckingham, a planters' representative, repeated the arguments already elaborated by the ITA, and claimed that the family earnings of the labourers were more than enough to keep them in 'comfort' and to save. He questioned Cotton's findings regarding the prices of food articles in the province.[167] I have examined below the validity of these claims made by the planters in opposition to the proposed wage increase.[168] Suffice it to point out here that their arguments did not impress even the official members of the Council.

The public response of the planter community against the wage increase recommended by Cotton was one of complete outrage and condemnation. The General Committee of the ITA unanimously protested against the recommendation of the Select Committee.[169] They organized a protest meeting which was held at the premises of the Bengal Chamber of Commerce. The meeting was attended mostly by agents, shareholders, managers and proprietors of tea concerns. The chairman of the ITA, H.G. Begg, made it clear that his organization would oppose only those provisions of the Bill which recommended enhancement of wages. 'While we are all of us opposed to this particular provision, I should like it to be understood that in other respects the Bill is by no means antagonistic to our interests, but, on the contrary, in my humble opinion, it is calculated to confer considerable benefits on the industry.'[170] Editorials and letters published in *The Englishman* were highly critical of the proposed enhancement of wages. It was argued that the industry was facing a crisis at that time and that if the proposal was accepted, it would adversely effect the entire industry: 'dividends will vanish and ultimately the industry will be destroyed and ruined'.[171] *The Englishman* lamented that '80 per cent of the gardens are being worked at a loss' and that the burden of increase will ruin the tea industry, which was solely responsible for bringing 'civilization and prosperity' to the province. The implications of this will be disastrous, it warned: 'The Province of Assam is what it is owing to the tea industry. Remove that and it will lapse into jungles inhabited by head-hunters.'[172]

The Indian Tea Association, both in India and England, sent protest memorials to the Viceroy and the Secretary of State for India.[173] The ITA claimed that labourers in the tea gardens earned extra income from overtime work, and received other benefits like housing, medical facilities and subsidized rations. Further, labourers had sufficient savings in the form of carts, cattle, goats and poultry. These facts, the ITA argued, were 'cogent evidence that labourers imported into Assam do not need the protection of the legislature to increase their minimum rates of wages'.[174] Moreover, any increase in wages was considered by the ITA as an encouragement to idleness among the labourers: 'We feel strongly that to be compelled by legislature to pay an increased minimum wages would be in effect to offer encouragement to the idle and slothful amongst our imported labourers.'[175] The ITA concluded that an increase of 8 annas per labourer per month would prove 'so heavy an additional burden' that it would 'undoubtedly mean ruin to a large number of tea concerns'.[176] The ITA wielded huge political clout both within the provincial and central governments in India, and in London.[177] They organized protest meetings, and mounted pressure on the colonial and home governments through memorials and deputations to the Secretary of State for India and the Viceroy.[178] The entire Anglo-Indian press in India and *The Times* in London started a powerful campaign in support of the industry, and launched a blistering attack on Cotton.[179] These attacks became even more vitriolic and acquired a personalized tone when the nationalist press came out in support of Cotton. Cotton recalled with bitterness: 'I was assailed with extra-ordinary virulence. I was charged with malignity, inveracity, and dishonesty, my motives were impugned in the most shameful manner, and one journal loudly called for my dismissal from the public service.'[180]

Cotton's proposed increase in the wages of tea garden labourers was actively supported by the nationalist press.[181] Among the Calcutta nationalist newspapers, *The Hindoo Patriot* wrote:

> The proposal is consistence with justice and equity. The coolie's wage was fixed thirty years ago. . . . The Government is responsible for his welfare. The Government affords great facilities to the planters in the matter of importation of coolie labour. The Government, therefore, is bound to see that justice is done to the coolie.[182]

The *Bengalee* supported Cotton and launched a counter-campaign against the pro-planter press:

> The *Englishman* is the Accredited organ of the planting interests of these provinces

and it is, therefore, scarcely surprising that Mr Cotton's unanswerable Minute of Dissent on the Assam Labour and Emigration Bill should have produced the same effect upon Hare Street journal, as a chilly inserted into the proboscis is found to have upon certain constitutions.

The Bengalee consistently championed the cause of plantation labourers and applauded Henry Cotton.[183] However the Chief Commissioner's recommendations were accepted only in a modified form in the final Act VI of 1901. As a further concession to the planters, as pointed out earlier, Lord Curzon announced in the Imperial Council that the enhancement in wages was to come in force not before two years of the passing of the Act.[184] *The Bengalee* was very critical of this 'stultifying' decision:

> Lord Curzon's Government has taken away with one hand what it gave with the other. The nominal increase of coolie wages is, at best, a most inadequate installment of justice, but by deferring the grant of this increment for two years, an element of cruelty has been imported into its kindness.[185]

The organized campaign against Cotton both in England and in India succeeded in putting pressure on the Government of India. O.B. Fuller, Chief Secretary to the Government of India, while censuring Cotton, conceded that the conditions of labourers in the tea gardens were similar to slavery. However, for him and many other senior officials of the British government it was a necessary price the colonial subjects must pay for the prosperity of the industrial and commercial interests in the metropolitan country. 'The truth is of course', he wrote,

> that serious abuses must occur under a labour system which is something of the nature of slavery, for an employee who can be arrested and forcibly detailed by his master is more of a slave than a servant and that these abuses are the price which has to be paid for the great advantages which has resulted from the establishment and growth of the tea industry in Assam.[186]

At the same time, Cotton's concern for labour as shown in his report was considered as an 'anti-planter manifesto which would do more harm than good'. Fuller rebuked Cotton's public criticism of the planters on the labour question because, 'by exciting class feelings, they alienate from us the leaders of the community whose assistance is of inestimable value in maintaining a proper standard of morality'.[187] He in fact wanted the position of managers to be protected and further strengthened: 'instances of organized rebellion and of attack on the managers are sufficiently numerous to indicate that the managers' authority is none too secure'.[188] It is interesting to note that the same Fuller considered Cotton's reports of labour–employer tension as highly exaggerated. This summed up the state's dilemma. It was committed to serve the interests of the planters; but it also had to *appear* as a 'protector' of labourers.

The most interesting aspect of the Cotton episode was the attitude and actions of Lord Curzon, the Viceroy. Curzon's official communications through bureaucratic channels, and his private correspondence with Cotton and George Hamilton, Secretary of State for India, on this subject are instructive. These show that both were knowledgeable about the labour relations prevailing in the Assam tea plantations and the attitude of the state bureaucracy. Curzon informed Hamilton on 24 July 1901 that he had come across cases in which English magistrates,

> who are entirely in the hands of the tea-planters, [and] have given the most partial and unjust sentences in cases between the planters or managers of the tea gardens and their coolies. If a coolie threatens or commits a technical assault upon an Englishman, he is given a year's rigorous imprisonment. The Englishman may thrash a coolie almost to death, or may criminally assault his daughter or wife, and he only gets a fine of Rs 50.[189]

He had learnt that it was a 'fashion' for magistrates to have prior consultation with the planters before pronouncing judgements. On another occasion, Curzon enlightened Hamilton that such practices were not confined to the District and Sessions Courts only, but that it was equally true of cases 'even before the High Court, [where] there is one scale of justice for the planter and another for the coolie'.[190] Hamilton in turn concurred with the Viceroy and admitted:

> The miscarriage of justice in India in the High Courts, and the conduct of Magistrates, where coolies and Europeans come in collision, causes me great concern. It seems to me a very serious reflection upon the whole basis of our rule in India, which is to secure justice between man and man.[191]

To Cotton, Curzon expressed grave concern about several aspects of the indenture regime on the plantations, including low wages, and emphasized that he was particularly upset about the 'miscarriage of justice', alluding to the collusion between planters and judicial officers in Assam and the rising cases of collision between planters and labour. Cotton found the tone of Curzon's early official and private pronouncements supportive and encouraging: 'The utterances of Lord Curzon on this subject have been far stronger than my own. The time, in my judgment, had fully come when it was necessary that comments of this kind should be made publicly.'[192] In his private letter dated 22 July 1901, Curzon expressed 'distress' regarding cases of 'miscarriage of justice' that had come to his notice. In a strongly disapproving tone, he wrote: 'The sentence of 9 months upon the man Gajhadar who assaulted or threatened Mr Oliver was a savage & inequitable sentence and is in violent contrast to the grotesque & inadequate fine of 60 Rs upon Mr. Black.'[193] On the issue of judicial partiality, he was equally perturbed:

> I have only refrained from secrecy concerning Mr Skinner (whose name has now come up before me three times in a year for partial conduct as a magistrate) in deference to your d/o appeal to Hewett. But if this be an anti-planter judge, god defend me from a pro planter specimen of the magistrate class.

Curzon wanted Cotton to warn the judiciary:

> I wish however to say the Govt of India will say in their letter that if this reign of unjust and partial sentences is to continue – light measure for the white manager, cruel measure for the coolie – the Govt of India will most certainly intervene in some form magistrates will find themselves in a position which it is most desirable for their own careers that they should avoid. I think you might let it be privately known that there is much dissatisfaction at headquarters and that renewed delinquencies will not be lightly treated.

And, in the matter of Cotton initiating action against gardens on account of reported low wages, Curzon wrote: 'I quite agree with your action in the case of a very bad garden where you detected a most scandalous shortage of wages.'[194] Thanking Curzon for this communication, Cotton hinted at the planters' reactions to his labour report:

> I have gone at some length into particular cases of the year. I say nothing about the attitude of the planters themselves & I am sure you realise it as well as I do. Many a rotten garden will collapse but that the abolition of a penal contract will ultimately be to the benefit of the province and of the industry generally I have little doubt.[195]

In reply, Curzon assured Cotton that 'planters will behave all right at the proposed decision and that any conflicting sections will be kept under proper restraint'.[196]

However, in the face of the pressure mounted by the powerful tea lobby through an organized and sustained campaign, supported by the colonial bureaucracy, Lord Curzon changed his tune. He informed the Secretary of State that the 'conflict between Cotton and the Assam Planters has reached a point at which the whole of Province seems to be up in Arms against the CC, while the Calcutta Press, which is largely inspired by the planters, is clamouring for his recall'.[197] The wide and loud public support from nationalist quarters for Cotton on this issue further hardened Curzon's stance. He now informed Cotton that the publication of his labour report was 'interpreted' as 'declaration of war against planters', and accused him of being biased against the planters. He advised caution and 'self restraint in his own interest' and to 'go slow'.[198] To the Secretary of State, Curzon admitted as true what Cotton has been reporting: 'I believe it to be true that on many plantations harsh and cruel and abominable things go on, and that the coolies get nothing like the wage which is stipulated for by the law.' He also confessed that

> in his endeavour to remedy both these scandals, I have earnestly backed up Cotton, in as much as I feel them not less acutely than he can do. But when, to use a vulgar metaphor, he goes bald headed for the planting community at large, and presents them as a lot of inhuman monster who are capable of any crime, he is going too far.[199]

For Curzon, turning against 'one of their own' was not due to any special regard for or personal affinity with the planters. He was not particularly enamoured of the planters as a community. He considered them as the 'most inferior class of Englishmen and Scotsmen' who were 'guilty of serious acts of lust and oppression',[200] a sharp contrast from the manager 'drawn from better class of society' image depicted by Griffiths.

Both of them were fully aware of the difficulties in persuading the judicial and civil officers in the state to comply with the provisions of the labour laws, and to act impartially vis-à-vis planters and labourers. Planters and civil servants had strong community ties and racial affinities. Hetherington's diary recorded a very active social life amongst the small European community of planters and colonial officials. His entry of 4 June 1907 noted that Gordon, the new Deputy Superintendent of Police, came and stayed overnight at his bungalow.[201] He also gave a graphic account of attending Light Horse Camp at Dibrugarh for a week, where he was in the company of other Europeans, civilians, fellow planters and army men. The camp was both a military training exercise and a social get-together.[202] Cotton summed it up well:

> I was never oblivious of the peculiar difficulty which besets a Magistrate, a member of a small European community in a distant land, who may be playing polo or bridge or billiards with a planter one month, or who may be serving under him as a trooper in the Light Horse, and who in the next month may be called on to try and punish him for cruelty to a contract labourer.[203]

Curzon shared similar views in his private communication with Cotton.[204] Cotton was aware that it was impossible for the European government officials to be altogether uninfluenced by 'their environment and their natural feelings towards their fellow-countrymen who are employed in the development of an important industry'.[205] That it was impossible to be impartial without being harmed, he learned from bitter personal experience. Cotton was sacked. His experience also served as a warning to others who might entertain any such ideas.

Cotton's 'crime' was joining forces with the nationalists against the planters, and becoming an 'agitator'. 'I do not think that outside the Bengali Press, he has anywhere found an advocate. The fact is that Mr Cotton is not a man of sound or reliable judgment or temper.'[206] While discussing the issue of the future course of action for Cotton, Secretary of State Hamilton expressed the imperial attitude: 'I suppose Cotton must have his K.C.S.I. He is a clever fellow, but it is rather disheartening to note the immediate popularity any Indian Civilian gets who attacks his own countrymen.'[207] There was also a fear that these developments would further fuel the already worrisome problem of growing labour resistance on the plantations. Curzon was worried about the relations between tea planters and their labourers in Assam, 'which seems to me to be entering upon a more acute and dangerous phase. The coolies are learning to combine, and very often, upon any provocation, they are apt to gather together and assault the European manager of the plantation.'[208] Cotton felt betrayed by Curzon, who 'saved his own skin but deliberately flung me to the wolves' when the Anglo-Indian press opened 'floodgates of abuse' against him and let loose a virulent attack. With regard to the treatment of labourers, he was content to accept the opinions that had been held in the past to justify a conclusion favourable to the employers. 'In the face of [the] rising storm of unpopularity from his own countrymen, Lord Curzon quailed.'[209]

In this entire controversy, Cotton's concern for plantation labour stood out in marked contrast to the attitude of most of the officialdom. What explains Cotton's different attitude? The answer possibly lies in his adherence to positivism.[210] The influence of positivism turned his awareness of the conditions of labour in the tea gardens into sympathy for labour. Henry Cotton was a follower of Richard Congreve, the founder of London Positivist Society. The English positivists condemned the British imperialist policies of exploitation in India. In their writings, they condemned the British empire as immoral. Their anti-imperialist and anti-colonial ideas led them to show concern for the conditions of the oppressed people, and created a desire in them to improve the economic and educational levels of the latter. The other possible explanation could be that Henry Cotton, in his official capacity, was committed to solving the labour recruitment problem of the tea industry in Assam. He believed, and rightly, that the only way of attracting more labour was by providing them better working conditions and offering higher wages. He was not alone in this assessment. Most of the persons interviewed by the Enquiry Committee of 1906 in the recruiting districts expressed similar views on the subject.[211]

Other Forms of State Assistance to Tea Planters

State assistance to planters extended to the promotion of tea sales as well as scientific research to increase its productivity. Public revenues were utilized for this purpose without any corresponding contribution in return by the tea industry. In 1903, the ITA approached the Government of India and the

Government of Bengal for a grant of Rs 75,000 to participate in the World Fair Exhibition to be held in the USA the next year. The Government of India provided the amount out of the state exchequer, and the Government of Bengal granted Rs 10,000 out of its provincial revenues.[212] In 1899, the Government of Assam made an annual grant of Rs 2,500 for three years and the Government of Bengal granted Rs 5,000 per annum to the ITA, for the purpose of promoting scientific investigation concerning the cultivation and manufacturing of tea.[213] Later, these sums were raised to Rs 3,000 and Rs 7,000 per annum by the Governments of Assam and Bengal respectively.[214] In 1905, the planters persuaded the government to provide more financial help for the expansion of their scientific department. The Government of India agreed to contribute Rs 15,000 annually, while the Government of East Bengal and Assam and the Government of Bengal agreed to grant Rs 12,000 and Rs 4,000 per annum respectively for a period of five years.[215] In 1911, the Governments of Assam and Bengal contributed Rs 10,000 and Rs. 5,000 respectively for the establishment of a scientific research centre by the ITA at Tocklai in Jorhat. To cover the recurring costs, the central and provincial governments gave grants totalling Rs 31,000 annually for five years from April 1911.[216] This kind of financial assistance continued even after the scientific centre had been well established. In 1923, the Government of Assam further contributed Rs 10,000 for the purposes of improving scientific research on tea. This sum came out of the provincial revenues at the cost of other works of public welfare, though the tea industry had become prosperous enough to afford this expenditure.[217] One of the Indian members of the Assam Legislative Council complained against the expenditure: 'The Honourable Finance Member has been forced to reduce the grant for eradication of water hyacinth from Rs 20,000 to Rs 7,000 and has dispensed with the post of Agricultural Chemist. The Kala-azar doctors also, I find from the Budget figures, have been reduced in numbers.'[218]

Equally crucial for the tea industry was the building up of the necessary infrastructure by the state in the form of railways and road construction. With the construction of railways, the journey time for immigrant labourers was reduced substantially. At the same time, the transport of manufactured tea to the coastal areas was made more secure, cheaper and faster than the river routes. The Public Works Department started its road construction programme from the 1860s, and building of railways began in the 1880s. Of major significance was the magnitude of capital investment by the state and the utilization of state revenues for railway construction in Assam. For example, Jorhat Railway (2'0" gauge), originally known as the 'Kokila Mookh State Railways', was constructed using the provincial revenues of Assam for the convenience of the numerous tea gardens in the neighbourhood of Jorhat; it involved a public investment of nearly Rs 1 million and carried an accumulated loss of Rs 5 lakhs up to 1901.[219] Similarly, the Government of India incurred a loss of Rs 35.9 million by supporting the Assam Bengal Railway during the period 1895–1917, i.e. an average annual loss of Rs 3 million.[220] Another example of using local revenues for railway construction was the Tezpur-Balipara Light Railways, which was constructed at the expense of the Borjuli Tea Company in 1895, but the government supplied timber free of royalty for the sleepers and the Tezpur Local Board paid a total subsidy of Rs 1 lakh in twenty annual instalments up to the end of March 1914.[221]

In defence of the 'special treatment' policy towards planters by the provincial government, it was often argued that the tea industry was mainly responsible for the 'development' and 'prosperity' of Assam. On the contrary, however, it has been shown that the growth of the plantation sector imposed numerous constraints on the development of the traditional agrarian sector.[222] One of the reasons for this was the discriminatory land revenue policy followed by the state in favour of the plantations at the expense of the traditional sector. During the nineteenth century, for example, the maximum revenue payable by the planters under the various special Waste Land Rules was much lower than that imposed on traditional cultivation. Under the 99-year-long lease provision, the revenue on three-fourths of the grant in the last 75 years was only 6 annas per acre. This was between one-half and one-fourth the rates prevailing in the rice lands till 1868, and about one-fifth of the same from 1868 to 1893.[223] Moreover, under the 1838 Waste Land Settlement Rules, the land revenue of three-fourths of the grant was nil in the first five to first twenty years. No such concessions were granted to the native cultivators.

Such a discriminatory policy also resulted in substantial loss of potential land revenue to the government in the long run. In 1901–02, it was officially reported that tea gardens occupied 27.4 per cent of temporarily settled areas in

TABLE 4.2
Land Revenue on Fully Assessed Settlements (Khiraj) and Wasteland Grants in Lakhimpur, Sibsagar and Darrang Districts[224]

Year	Lakhimpur Average Revenue Rs per acre		Sibsagar Average Revenue Rs per acre		Darrang Average Revenue Rs per acre	
	Khiraj	Wasteland	Khiraj	Wasteland	Khiraj	Wasteland
	Rs	Rs	Rs	Rs	Rs	Rs
1901–02	2.44	0.22	2.63	0.30	2.52	0.32
1909–10	2.39	0.26	2.61	0.34	2.42	0.41
1919–20	2.46	0.37	2.52	0.44	2.29	0.48
1929–30	2.37	0.59	2.87	0.57	2.11	0.65
1934–35	2.73	0.85	2.84	0.62	2.40	0.84
1939–40	2.67	1.20	2.79	0.77	2.35	1.08

the Assam Valley. But it contributed only 9 per cent of the total land revenue to the government.[225] The gap between the average per acre revenue payable between the fully assessed areas (*khiraj*) for ordinary cultivation and waste-land grants (for the purposes of tea cultivation) was substantial (Table 4.2). Table 4.2 shows that revenue assessment on lands settled for ordinary cultivation (*khiraj*) was much higher, as compared to the assessment on wasteland settlements. The higher rate of increase in the assessment of the latter was due to the nature of the settlement, by which periodically the revenue was to increase from the earlier nil or nominal amount. This becomes clear from the conditions laid down under some of the settlements made in Darrang district in the twentieth century: (1) such land was to remain revenue-free for the first two years; (2) for the next four years, the assessment was three annas per acre per annum; (3) for four years following, the revenue was to be six annas per acre per annum; (4) for the ten years next following, it was increased to eight annas per acre per annum, and so on.[226]

From the discussion above of various aspects of state policy towards capital and labour in the tea industry, its priorities in favour of the former become very clear. Apart from providing land at extremely lucrative terms and building infrastructure to promote the interests of tea industry, the assistance of the colonial state was particularly important in the context of the mobilization and control of the labour force. Its legislative interventions were meant to 'protect' the interests of the 'ignorant' and 'illiterate' migrants, and, at the same time, to ensure compliance of the indenture contract by inserting penal provisions. Theoretically, the state passed labour laws with two ostensible objectives: to safeguard the interests of the employers by ensuring that the labourers fulfilled their obligations of the contract, as the former had incurred a lot of expenses in their recruitment and transportation; to protect the interests of the labour force during their journey and period of employment in the tea districts. The labourers required protection, it was argued, because they were ignorant and unorganized. The employers' interests were safeguarded in the law by providing penal provisions of imprisonment, fines and magisterial powers against the labourers. The provisions for labour welfare included payment of minimum wages, medical facilities, housing, drinking water and sanitary arrangements as obligatory for the employers. Similar facilities were supposed to be provided by the employers during the transit period when emigrant labourers were brought to the labour districts. The laws also provided that state was responsible for the implementation of the above provisions.[227] But in reality, the labour 'protection' provisions were rarely implemented. On the other hand, not only were the employers' interests primarily served, but in fact, through these laws, the state provided legitimacy to the planters' extra-economic and extra-legal coercion and control over their labour force. The state encouraged monopolistic control over labour recruitment for the Assam tea gardens in the hands of a few Calcutta-based managing agency houses.[228]

The labour laws gave rise to the indenture system in the labour districts of Assam Valley. The policy of the colonial state vis-á-vis planters and labourers in the Assam Valley tea gardens could appropriately be characterized as one of discriminatory protectionism. While the former was able to control and exploit labour for the maximization of profits, the latter was condemned to a life of misery and deprivation under the indenture system (which was modified from time to time even after its legal abolition), which was maintained and perpetuated by 'protection' afforded by the state. One possible explanation for such an attitude on the part of the state could be the increasing influence of the planters over its policy as they became a well-organized and powerful pressure group in the province. The planters as a pressure group had easy access to the highest levels of policy-making both in India and England. On the other hand, the labour force lacked any such opportunities in the absence of a counter-organization of their own. The situation was made worse for them by the cultural nexus between their employers and their 'protectors' (the bureaucracy). Such a cultural nexus evolved around the small European community of both bureaucrats and planters, who socialized exclusively among themselves. But the colonial bureaucracy was after all not a monolith: there were officials like Cotton who did raise the issue of inequities suffered by the labour. Ultimately, however, the interests of the industry and its trade were of such importance to the state that the brutalities of the indenture labour regime were overlooked, civil servants like Henry Cotton notwithstanding. For the development of the tea industry under the monopoly of European capital, the state utilized public revenues in order to construct necessary infrastructure like roads, railways, etc., and to promote the marketing of tea and scientific research. Equally important was the land revenue policy under which, compared to traditional agriculture, the tea planters were granted vast areas of land at extremely low or nominal prices and with no expectations of revenue for a very long period. The result of such a discriminatory policy was that while the tea plantations in Assam emerged as a profitable enclave economy, the traditional sector benefited little from the emergence of this new enterprise. The loss of a substantial amount of potential revenue due to this policy severely limited the development of social overheads in the long run, which in turn placed further constraints on traditional agriculture.

Notes and References

[1] Those among the state scientific establishments in India who were actively involved in the project of 'discovering' an alternate cite for tea cultivation in India included Dr Falconer, civil surgeon, in charge of the Botanical Garden at Saharanpur; Dr N. Wallich, head of the Botanical Garden, Calcutta; William Griffith, assistant surgeon, Madras Establishment; and assistant surgeon McClelland, a geologist. Parliamentary Papers, 1839. Also see chapter 1.

[2] For details, see chapter 1.

[3] Encroachment on their lands provoked the Singhphos rebellion in 1845. Manilal Bose, *British Policy in North East Frontier Agency*, New Delhi: 1979; Mohammad Abu Siddique, *Evolution of Land Grants and Labour Policy of Government: The Growth of the Tea Industry in Assam 1834–1940*, New Delhi: South Asian Publications, 1990.

[4] Siddique, *Evolution of Land Grants*, pp. 20–54.

[5] Assam Company Papers (ACP), Mss. 9925, Minutes of Proceedings in India, Calcutta Committee Minute Book, 1850, Vol. 5, pp. 83–98.

[6] ACP, Mss. 9925, pp. 232–38.

[7] Ibid., p. 287.

[8] Ibid., p. 328.

[9] Papers Relating to Tea Cultivation in Bengal, *Selections from the Records of the Government of Bengal*, No. XXXVII, Calcutta: Bengal Military Orphan Press, 1861, p. 24. (Hereafter Papers Relating to Tea.)

[10] Ibid., pp. 3–9.

[11] See chapter 1.

[12] Papers Regarding the Tea, 1874, Parliamentary Papers, Calcutta, p. 20.

[13] Department of Revenue and Agriculture, Government of India, Emigration A, Nos. 68–72, December 1880, p. 4.

[14] Papers Relating to Tea, 1861.

[15] Report of the Commissioners Appointed to Enquire into the State and Prospects of Tea Cultivation in Assam, Cachar and Sylhet, Calcutta, 1868, p. 25. (Hereafter Commissioners Report.) Also see chapter 1.

[16] Rana P. Behal and Prabhu P. Mohapatra, '"Tea and Money versus Human Life": The Rise and Fall of the Indenture System in the Assam Tea Plantations 1840–1908', in E. Valentine Daniel, Henry Bernstien and Tom Brass (eds), *Plantations, Proletarians and Peasants in Colonial Asia*, London: Frank Cass, 1992, pp. 142–43.

[17] E.A. Gait, *Assam Immigration Manual*, Calcutta, 1893, p. 2.

[18] Proceedings of the Central Legislative Council (PCLC), 1901, Vol. XL, Calcutta, p. 84.

[19] Report of the Assam Labour Enquiry Committee (RALEC), 1906, p. 8; Rajani Kanta Das, *Plantation Labour in India*, Calcutta: R. Chatterji, 1931, pp. 80–82.

[20] Commissioners Report, 1868; RALEC, 1906, Appendix A, p. 135.

[21] Assam labour report, 1883; Department of Revenue and Agriculture, Government of India, Emigration A, Nos. 1–5, July 1888; Special Report, Government of India, 1891, pp. 217–26. Also see chapter 5.

[22] RALEC, 1906, Appendix A, p. 139.

[23] Department of Revenue and Agriculture, Government of India, Emigration A, Nos. 68–72, December 1880, para 4.

[24] Department of Revenue and Agriculture, Government of India, Emigration A, No. 18, 1881, para 2.

[25] Department of Revenue and Agriculture, Government of India, Emigration A, Nos. 36–39, December 1888, p. 3.

[26] Special Report, Government of India, 1891, para 36.

[27] Ibid.

[28] Department of Revenue and Agriculture, Government of India, Emigration A, Nos. 4–5, October 1883, paras 1–8.

[29] Ibid., paras 9–11.

[30] Ibid., para. 13.

[31] Department of Revenue and Agriculture, Government of India, Emigration A, Nos. 15–17, August 1886, p. 935.

[32] Department of Revenue and Agriculture, Government of India, Emigration A, Nos. 4–5, October 1883.

[33] Ibid.

[34] Department of Revenue and Agriculture, Government of India, Emigration A, Nos. 8–10, November 1888.

[35] East India (Assam Coolies), Parliamentary Papers, 1889, p. 51.

[36] Ibid.

[37] Ibid.

[38] Ibid., pp. 53–54.

[39] Department of Revenue and Agriculture, Government of India, Emigration A, Nos. 3–4, June 1890, p. 1.

[40] Ibid., p. 2.

[41] Department of Revenue and Agriculture, Government of India, Emigration A, Nos. 8–13, 1892, p. 9.

[42] RALEC, 1906, p. 22.

[43] Confidential Note, Government of Assam, Revenue A, Nos. 77–117, August 1904.

[44] PCLC, 1901, p. 47.

[45] RALEC, 1906, p. IX.

[46] Assam Labour Report, 1907–08, p. 1.

[47] Ibid.; ITA Report, 1908, p. 6.

[48] For more details, see chapter 2.

[49] Department of Revenue and Agriculture, Government of India, Emigration A, Nos. 23–24, 1898, para 3.

[50] Ibid.

[51] Ibid.

[52] Ibid.

[53] Ibid.

[54] Percival Griffiths, *The History of the Indian Tea Industry*, London: Weidenfeld and Nicolson, 1967, p. 292.

[55] RALEC, 1906, Appendix A, p. 146; Das, *Plantation Labour*, pp. 75–76; Rajani Kanta Das, *History of Indian Labour Legislation*, Calcutta: University of Calcutta Press, 1941, pp. 23–24.

[56] Assam Labour Report, 1902–03, p. 3.

[57] Assam Labour Report, 1907–08, p. 2; Report of the Assam Labour Enquiry Committee, 1921–22, p. 102.

[58] Assam Labour Report, 1907–08, p. 2.

[59] Assam Labour Report, 1914–15, p. 1

[60] Written Evidence, Assam and Dooars, Vol. VI, Part 1, Report of the Royal Commission on Labour in India (hereafter Royal Commission), 1931, p. 4.

[61] Assam Labour Report, 1914–15, p. 1.

[62] The Bengal Inland Emigration Manual, 1927, p. 40.

[63] Written Evidence, Assam and Dooars, Vol. VI, Royal Commission, 1931, p. 58.

[64] Finance Department, Government of Assam, Emigration Branch B, Nos. 187–210, March 1926, p. 15.

[65] Confidential, Finance Department, Government of Assam, Emigration Branch B, Nos. 216 to 278, September 1925, pp. 10–11.

[66] *The Bengalee*, 4 March 1900, p. 4

[67] RALEC, 1921–22, p. 88.

[68] RALEC, 1906, Appendix A, p. 146.

[69] Ibid.

[70] Royal Commission, 1931, p. 364.

[71] Ibid.

[72] Ibid., p. 366.

[73] Written Evidence, Assam and Dooars, Vol. VI, Part I, Royal Commission, 1931, p. 5.

[74] ITA Report, 1926, p. x.

[75] Ibid., p. 129.

[76] Report TDLA (XXII of 1932), 1934, p. 1; Central Legislative Assembly Debates, Vol. III, No. 15, April 1932, pp. 2978–98, and Vol. V, No. 4, September 1932, pp. 1285–303.

[77] R. Mathrubuthan and R. Srinivasan, *The Indian Factories and Labour Manual*, second edn, Madras, 1952, p. 250.

[78] Royal Commission, 1931, p. 391.

[79] Dattaraya Varman Rege, *Report on an Enquiry into Conditions of Labour in Plantations in India*, 1946, pp. 31–3.

[80] See chapters 2 and 3.

[81] See details in chapter 2 and 5.

[82] See chapter 5 for details.

[83] RALEC, 1906.

[84] Department of Revenue and Agriculture, Government of India, Emigration A, Nos. 13–16, March 1878, para 18.

[85] Department of Revenue and Agriculture, Government of India, Emigration A, Nos. 10–17, July 1893.

[86] Special Report, Government of India, 1891, para 6.

[87] Department of Revenue and Agriculture, Government of India, Emigration A, Nos. 10–17, July 1893

[88] RALEC, 1906, pp. 94–96.

[89] Ibid., p. 95.

[90] Confidential Note by the Chief Commissioner of Assam, Department of Revenue, Government of Assam, A, Nos. 77–117, 1904.

[91] RALEC 1921–22, p. 105.

[92] Rege, *Report,* p. 30.

[93] Ibid.

[94] Ibid.

[95] See chapter 5.

[96] These racial and social ties can explain to a large extent the general lack of concern shown by British officials towards the appalling labour conditions in the tea gardens. In this context the planters feeling disturbed and enraged by Cotton's attitude was understandable. His attempts at strict inspection of the tea gardens and championing the cause of labour appeared to be an exception.

[97] Department of Revenue and Agriculture, Government of India, Emigration A, Nos. 6–8, 1901, p. 2.

[98] RALEC, 1906, p. 93.

[99] See chapter 1.

[100] *The Bengalee*, Vol. XXVII, No. 47, December 1886, p. 557, reproduced in Dwarkanath Ganguli, *Slavery in British Dominions*, Calcutta: Jijnasa, 1972, p. 33.

[101] Department of Revenue and Agriculture, Government of India, Emigration A, Nos. 19–20, May 1882.

[102] Ibid.

[103] Special Report, Government of India, 1891.

[104] Department of Revenue and Agriculture, Government of India, Emigration A, Nos. 2–9, February 1889.

[105] Special Report, Government of India, 1891.

[106] Department of Revenue and Agriculture, Government of India, Emigration A, Nos. 2–8, 1892.

[107] Ibid.

[108] Ibid.

[109] In her recent work, Elizabeth Kolsky has argued that the planters' brutal treatment of labour in the Assam plantations was a part of endemic violence by the whites against natives in British colonial India. See Elizabeth Kolsky, *Colonial Justice in British India*, Cambridge: Cambridge University Press, 2010.

[110] Extract from Captain Lamb's Diary, Coolie Trade, Parliamentary Papers, 1867, p. 3. Also see chapter 3.

[111] Parliamentary Papers, 1867, pp. 4–19; also see chapter 1.

[112] Parliamentary Papers, 1867, p. 4.

[113] Ibid., p. 21.

[114] Ibid., p. 20.

[115] Ibid., p. 4.

[116] East India (Assam Coolies), Parliamentary Papers, 1889, p. 73.

[117] Ibid., p. 75.

[118] List of Serious Cases of Assault on Tea Gardens, 1890, Department of Revenue, Government of Assam, A, Nos. 77–117, August 1904, p. 1.

[119] Ibid., p. 2.

[120] Ibid., pp. 4–5.

[121] Ibid., p.13.

[122] Assam Labour Report, 1900, p. 23.

[123] Assam Labour Report, 1902–03, p. 12.

[124] Ibid., p. 12

[125] Assam Labour Report, 1900, p. 23.

[126] Assam Labour Report, 1903–04, p. 10. Also see chapter 6.

[127] Assam Labour Report, 1908–09, p. 9.

[128] Assam Labour Report, 1903–04, p. 10.

[129] Henry Cotton, *Indian and Home Memories*, London: T. Fisher Unwin, 1911, p. 273.

[130] Assam Labour Report, 1900, pp. 22–24.

[131] Cited in Cotton, *Indian and Home Memories*, p. 272.

[132] Bampfylde Fuller, *Some Personal Experiences*, London: John Murray, 1930, p. 119.

[133] RALEC, 1921–22.

[134] Financial Department, Government of Assam, Immigration B, Nos. 20–112, March 1922, p. 105.

[135] For details on the labour protests and their suppression by government, see chapter 6.

[136] Proceedings of Assam Labour Enquiry Committee, 1906, p. X.

[137] RALEC, 1921–22.

[138] General and Judicial Department, Government of Assam, Immigration Branch B, File No. 118, GIM 49/47, 1939, p. 167.

[139] Letter of the Chairman, ITA dated 26 May1939 to the Chief Secretary, Government of Assam, ibid., p. 137; ITA Report, 1939, p. 28; *Amrita Bazar Patrika*, 29 May 1939.

[140] Annual Labour Report, 1887, para 5; Department of Revenue and Agriculture, Government of India, Emigration A, Nos. 36–39, December 1888; Cotton, *Indian and Home Memories*, p. 269.

[141] A group of Santhal tribal headmen from the recruitment districts had been taken on a tour of the Assam tea gardens in 1894 by the president of the Assam branch of the Indian Tea Association, J. Buckingham, for the purpose of creating a favourable impression amongst the Santhals and to encourage them to migrate to Assam.

142 Department of Revenue and Agriculture, Government of India, Emigration A, Nos. 1–3, September 1894. Also see chapter 2.

143 Ibid.

144 Department of Revenue and Agriculture, Government of India, Emigration B, Nos. 1–3, September 1893.

145 Papers Regarding the Tea, 1874, p. 21.

146 Department of Revenue and Agriculture, Government of India, Emigration A, Nos. 32–35, November 1880; Annual Sanitary Report of the Province of Assam for the year 1878. For more details, see chapter 2.

147 Annual Sanitary Report of the Province of Assam, 1884, paras 39–41.

148 Ibid., para 42.

149 Bengal Labour Enquiry Commission Report, 1895, pp. 11–19; Department of Revenue and Agriculture, Government of India, Emigration A, Nos. 9 and 10, File No. 1, April 1897.

150 Assam Labour Report, 1900, p. 3.

151 Ibid., p. 8; see chapter 2 for more details.

152 Assam Labour Report, 1900, p. 10.

153 Ibid., p. 22.

154 Department of Revenue and Agriculture, Government of India, Emigration A, No. 6, File No. 90 of 1901, pp. 125–34.

155 Department of Revenue and Agriculture, Government of India, Emigration A, No. 7, February 1902, para 3.

156 Ibid.

157 Cotton, *Indian and Home Memories*, p. 259; Department of Revenue and Agriculture, Government of India, Emigration A, No. 7, February 1902, para 5.

158 Ibid.

159 Ibid.

160 Department of Revenue and Agriculture, Government of India, Emigration A, No. 6, File No. 90 of 1901, p. 170.

161 He argued that despite the subsidized ration price of Rs 3 per maund of rice, the tea garden labourers were badly affected by fluctuations in prices. PCLC, Vol. XL, p. 98.

162 Ibid., p. 94; for more details, see chapter 5.

163 Ibid., pp. 89–112.

164 Cotton, *Indian and Home Memories*, p. 261.

165 PCLC, 1901, Vol. XL, p. 144.

166 Cotton, *Indian and Home Memories*, p. 261.

167 PCLC, 1901, Vol. XL, p. 51.

168 See chapter 5.

169 Reported in *The Englishman*, 23 February 1901, p. 8.

170 *The Englishman*, 19 February 1901; *Capital*, 21 February 1901, p. 272.

171 *The Englishman*, 11 February 1901, p. 5.

172 Ibid.

173 ITA Report, 1900, p. 6; *The Englishman*, 14 January 1901, p. 5.

174 ITA Report, 1900, pp. 129–30.

175 Ibid., p. 131.

176 Ibid., p. 6.

177 Rana P. Behal, 'Power Structure, Discipline and Labour in Assam Tea Plantations under Colonial Rule', in Rana P. Behal and Marcel van der Linden (eds), *India's Labouring Poor: Historical Studies c. 1600–2000*, Delhi: Foundation Books, 2007, pp. 145–55.

178 ITA Report, 1900, p. 6.

179 *The Englishman*, 14 January, 11 and 23 February, and 7 March 1901; *Capital*, 21 February 1901. *The Times* (London) brought out a series of articles on the subject in 1902.

[180] Cotton, *Indian and Home Memories*, p. 275.

[181] The nationalist newspapers like the *Amrita Bazar Patrika*, *The Hindoo Patriot*, *The Bengalee*, *Hitabadi*, *Sanjibani* and others strongly supported Cotton's proposed increase in wages. For a detailed study of the nationalist press's campaign supporting Cotton, see Bipan Chandra, *The Rise and Growth of Economic Nationalism in India*, New Delhi, 1966, pp. 372–75.

[182] *The Hindoo Patriot*, 27 February 1901.

[183] *The Bengalee*, 14 February and 4 March 1900, and 17, 23, 24, 28 February and 1, 2, 9, 10 March 1901.

[184] RALEC, 1906, Appendix A, p. 146; Henry Cotton, *Indian and Home Memories*, p. 261.

[185] *The Bengalee*, 10 March 1901.

[186] Department of Revenue and Agriculture, Government of India, Emigration A, Nos. 6–8, File No. 90 of 1901, p. 2.

[187] Ibid.

[188] Ibid. p. 6.

[189] Curzon's letter to Secretary of State, 24 July 1901, Letter No. 50, Curzon Papers, Microfilm, Acct. No. 1632, National Archives, India. Original Mss. Eur F. 111/161-IOL, British Library, London. (Hereafter Curzon Papers.)

[190] Letter dated 11 September 1901, No. 62, Curzon Papers.

[191] Secretary of State George Hamilton to Curzon, 15 August 1901, Letter No. 55, Curzon Papers.

[192] Cotton, *Indian and Home Memories*, p. 275.

[193] Curzon to Cotton, 22 July 1901, Private Papers of Sir Henry John Stedman Cotton (1845–1915), Mss. Eur D1202/2, Correspondence between Sir Henry Cotton and Lord Curzon, OIOC, British Library, London. (Hereafter Cotton Papers.)

[194] Curzon's letter to Cotton, 22 July 1901, Cotton Papers.

[195] Henry Cotton's letter to Lord Curzon, 2 August 1901, Cotton Papers.

[196] Curzon's letter to Cotton, 22 July 1901, Cotton Papers.

[197] Curzon to Secretary of State, 11 September 1901, Letter No. 62, Curzon Papers.

[198] Curzon's letter to Cotton, 10 September 1901, Cotton Papers.

[199] Curzon to Secretary of State, 11 September 1901, Letter No. 62, Curzon Papers.

[200] Curzon to Secretary of State, 5 August 1903, Letter No. 55, Curzon Papers.

[201] F.A. Hetherington, *The Diary of a Tea Planter, 14 July 1907*, Sussex: The Book Guild Ltd., 1994, p. 150.

[202] Ibid., pp. 144–46.

[203] Cotton, *Indian and Home Memories*, p. 273.

[204] Curzon's letter to Cotton, 22 July 1901, Cotton Papers.

[205] Cotton, *Indian and Home Memories*, p. 272.

[206] Curzon to Secretary of State, 18 February 1902, Letter No. 16, Curzon Papers.

[207] Secretary of State to Curzon, 29 May 1902, Letter No. 47, Curzon Papers, Acct. No. 1632.

[208] Curzon to Secretary of State, 5 August 1903, Letter No. 55, Curzon Papers, Acct. No. 1633.

[209] Cotton, *Indian and Home Memories*, p. 276.

[210] However, the anti-imperialist tone of positivism had its limitations. Positivism emphasized only 'Moral influence' for the working class as a means to accomplish social and economic change. It condemned communism and socialism for advocating among the working classes a change in the class structure and admitting violence as a legitimate tactics. Its refusal to give the proletariat any power beyond 'moral influence' reflects the essential conservatism of its thinking on class structures. These limitations were discernible in Cotton's activities too. He justified the penal laws. In spite of his sympathy for the labourers, there was nothing very radical in his advocacy of an increase in wages and his exposition of the ill-treatment of the labourers at the hands of the planters. He himself consistently maintained that he was merely pointing out that the planters had not conformed to the provisions of the legislation

regarding minimum wages, and that his criticism of the planters' attitude towards labourers was within the legitimate powers conferred upon him by the law. See Cotton's speech in PCLC, 1901. For further details, see Sabyasachi Bhattacharya, 'Positivism in 19th Century Bengal', in Ram Saran Sharma (ed.), *Indian Society: Historical Probings*, New Delhi: Indian Council of Historical Research, 1974, pp. 337–55; Geraldine Hancock Forbes, *Positivism in Bengal: A case study in the transmission and assimilation of an ideology*, Calcutta: Minerva Associates, 1975, Chapters I and II.

[211] Proceedings of the Assam Labour Enquiry Committee in the Recruiting and Labouring Districts, 1906, pp. 3–129.

[212] ITA Report, 1903, pp. 162–63.

[213] Department of Revenue, Government of Assam, B Proceedings, Nos. 404–13, July 1900, pp. 8–9.

[214] Griffiths, *The History*, p. 431.

[215] ITA Report, 1910, p. 6.

[216] Griffiths, *The History*, p. 437.

[217] Proceedings of the Assam Legislative Council (PALC), Vol. III, No. 5, April 1923, p. 463.

[218] Ibid., p. 464.

[219] History of Indian Railway, Constructed and Progress corrected up to 31st March, 1945, Government of India, p. 25; Amlendu Guha, 'Socio-Economic Changes in Agrarian Assam', in M.K. Chaudhury (ed.), *Trends in Socio-Economic Change in India 1871–1961*, Simla, 1967, p. 577.

[220] Guha, 'Socio-Economic Changes', p. 576.

[221] History of Indian Railway, p. 325.

[222] Keya Deb, 'Tea Plantations in Brahmaputra Valley 1859–1914: A Case Study in Colonial Set-up,' unpublished Ph.D. dissertation, Centre for Studies in Regional Development, School of Social Sciences, Jawaharlal Nehru University, New Delhi, 1979; Keya Deb, 'Impact of Plantations on the Agrarian Structure of the Brahmaputra Valley,' Occasional Paper No. 24, Centre for Studies in Social Sciences, Calcutta, April 1979.

[223] Deb, 'Impact of Plantations', p. 45.

[224] Report on the Administration of the Land Revenue in Assam, Appendix I, for respective years.

[225] Ibid., 1901–02, p. 6.

[226] Instrument of lease for special cultivation, December 1914, Assam Revenue Form No. 20 – Settlement Rules, Section I, Appendix B, District Record Room, Tezpur, Sunitpur District (Erstwhile Darrang District). A large number of such settlements for special cultivation were made with the planters in Darrang district, and their records are available in the District Record Room, Tezpur.

[227] The Bengal Inland Emigration Manual, 1912, pp. 1–53.

[228] Amiya Kumar Bagchi, *Private Investment in India 1900–1939*, London: Cambridge University Press, 1972, Chapter 5.

5

The Political Economy of Tea Plantations

The general impression of the material conditions of labour in the Assam tea plantations projected by the planters and the colonial state was one of 'comfort' and 'well-being'. This impression was reinforced by claims of labour being paid well enough not only to live in 'comfort' but even to save. For example, the Assam Labour Enquiry Committee in 1906 wrote: 'on the whole the wages paid to the labourers are sufficient to keep them in comfort, and even to enable them with the practice of a little thrift to save money'.[1] The picture painted of the permanently settled labourers was even rosier. It was claimed that the object of such emigrants was not, as a rule, to save money but rather to lead a 'pleasant' life. Emigrants of 'aboriginal' stock were specifically mentioned as belonging to this category.

> He works enough to provide himself with food and clothing and a few luxuries, and if he has any surplus cash, he spends a good deal of it in drinking, gambling, and cockfighting. The standard of living of the ordinary coolie is certainly much in advance of what it would be in his own country. . . . In addition to the ordinary supplies, fowls, ducks, and fish are largely bought, and there is a general air of prosperity about the holiday making crowd, which is convincing proof that the coolie is fairly well off in his new home.[2]

It was further pointed out that the cash wage did not represent the total earnings of the labourer, since it was supplemented by grants of cultivable land, either free or for nominal payment, as well as by provision of cheap subsidized rice during certain periods.[3] Buckingham, a planters' representative in the Central Legislative Council, provided a longer list of such supplementary sources of income by including in this category medical comforts, sickness allowance, free diet for the sick, free housing, firewood, etc.[4]

The idea of the Assam tea plantation labour force enjoying 'prosperous' and 'luxurious' living standards was asserted with the assumption of 'family wage' as a contributing factor. The planters and the colonial state sometimes insisted that the 'family wage' should be considered as a measure of income that was good enough to provide 'prosperity' and 'luxurious' living standards. It was asserted, by way of comparison, that the tea plantations, by employing men, women and children, afforded the labouring family a much higher 'family wage' than in other major industries in the organized sector.[5] In the plantations, therefore, there were 'comparatively few non-working dependents in a working class family. The effect of this on the standard of living is important, for, even with low individual earnings, the total family income is sufficiently high to prevent the worker from feeling the pinch of poverty.'[6] In addition to the 'concessions' and 'family wage', *ticca* earnings were considered to be another supplementary source of income in the gardens. *Ticca* earning was possible, it was said, because the standard daily wage, *hazira*, was fixed with regard to the daily task, *nirikh*, which could be completed within four to five hours.[7] After the completion of this daily task the labourer had the liberty to undertake *ticca* work.[8]

However, the interesting aspect of the indenture contract was that it was signed by individual labourers and not together as a family. Neither recruitment nor employment in the Assam Valley tea plantations was ever contemplated to be family-based; women and children were employed in large numbers but as individual labourers. Sir Charles Rivaz (member of the Governor General's Council, and chairman of the Select Committee for Assam Labour and Emigration Bill, constituted by Viceroy Curzon to go into the question of wages of tea garden labourers in Assam) clarified this point during the debate on the proposed legislation in March 1901. During the course of the debate, Buckingham, the planters' representative, argued that wages in the tea gardens had already exceeded the legal minimum rates, and he presented combined family earnings ('an able-bodied man, an able-bodied woman and an able-bodied child and a further quarter of an able-bodied child – a normal family') as proof. Rejecting this 'proof', Rivaz argued that on Buckingham's own showing, the wages of the individual man and woman were less than the prescribed minimum wage, and 'what we have to look at is the individual and not the family'.[9] Why then insist on the 'family wage' as the earning unit? Obviously, as we shall have occasion to show below, the cash wage earned by individual labourers in the tea plantations was not sufficient to provide bare subsistence, and therefore had to be supplemented in kind for survival and for performing labour. For survival, the entire family had to work.

To examine the validity of the assertions stated above, it is essential to analyse the features of the wage structure in the Assam Valley tea plantations. Foremost was the fact that the foundation of the wage structure was the indenture system. Under this system, labour was bound to the gardens for a period of three to five years on the basis of fixed but differential payment rates of Rs 5 for men, Rs 4 for women and Rs 3 for children per month. This arrangement, with modifications occasioned by the exigencies of emerging situations, continued well after even the official termination of the indenture penal contract. Following the abolition of Act XIII of 1859 in 1926, the Indian Tea Association (ITA) enforced what came to be known as the 'wage agreement' (an agreement between the employers themselves), which functioned as an effective constraint on labour mobility and the emergence of a labour market in the plantation areas. Under the provisions of this 'wage agreement', every employer agreed not to pay labourers wages higher than that paid by his neighbours. At the same time, the planters' ability to control the mobility of labour, both within and outside the gardens, prevented the formation of any labour organization till well into 1940s. This put labourers in a truly helpless position vis-à-vis their employers in the tea gardens. Even the Royal Commission, though not objecting to the 'wage agreement', pointed out that 'workers suffer owing to the absence of any organization on their side to counteract the powerful combination of their employers'.[10]

Another important feature of the wage structure was that wage payments were made under two distinct systems: (1) the *hazira* and *ticca* system, and (2) the unit system, *nirikh*. The wages of tea garden labourers were generally piecework earnings depending upon the quantity and quality of work, and turned over. Whether expressed in terms of a daily or a monthly wage, they were contingent upon the execution of a standard daily task or *nirikh*, the payment for which was known as *hazira*. A labourer who completed the full *nirikh* on each working day of the month was entitled to receive the monthly wage.[11] Only after completing the daily task was a labourer entitled to earn *ticca* money. However, contrary to the claims of the industry, the labourers did not earn a significant amount through *ticca* earnings. The Assam Enquiry Committee of 1921–22 expressed its doubts in this regard: 'There are obvious limitations to the possibilities of *ticca* earnings. The rule of the maximum efficiency at the minimum cost holds good in tea gardens as in other industries.'[12] In 1946, Rege reported that '*ticca* earnings constitute a very small proportion of the total cash earnings of workers. It was found that such earnings were more in Indian-owned gardens which are generally short of labour and therefore offer more *ticca* to their labourers.'[13] The unit system, a modified version of the *hazira* and *ticca* system, was a later innovation. Under this system payment was made for each unit of work done, which, for example, in the case of hoeing and pruning, the Enquiry Committee of 1921–22 found, was based on the one-anna unit and, in the case of plucking, on the one-piece unit.[14]

One major flaw in both these modes of wage payment was the fact that while the daily task was linked with the fixed minimum statutory wage, the volume of work per unit or per *nirikh* was decided by the managers. This was conceded by Sir Charles Rivaz in the Central Legislative Council when he pointed out that the 'system of minimum wage-rate was contingent upon the condition of a daily task, the regulation of which is practically in the hands of the employer'.[15] The inability of labour to bargain was compounded by the complete absence of even a nominal legislative check on the regulation of the daily task. This gave the employers a free hand to use the *hazira* and *nirikh* system for extracting maximum work for a fixed minimum wage. In the absence of any regulatory device, the managers sometime assigned heavier tasks that the labourers often could not complete in a day's work. During the course of inspection of a tea garden in December 1900, the Deputy Commissioner of Sibsagar reported:

> From the nature of the work . . . coolies, especially women, would have to work very hard to earn a full *haziri,* and a glance at the *haziri* books will show that it seems almost impossible for a great number of men and women to be able to earn anything like a full day's pay. The numbers of fractional *haziris* far exceed the full one.[16]

This system was further loaded against labourers by the fact that it was the managers who determined whether they had completed the full day's task. The civil surgeon of Sibsagar district, while inspecting the garden books in 1899, 'noticed that a system of quarter *haziris* seems to have been started. This means that because the manager decides that only a quarter has been done, only a quarter of a full day's salary is to be paid.' He reported that 'fractional *haziris* preponderate in this month and not a single full wage has been earned by men and only one by a woman.'[17] He found that very few labourers earned their full *haziri*. Charles Rivaz, after examining some of the garden books, found that 'the practice of strictly enforcing the daily task and of keeping down the labour bill by method of fractional *haziri*, that is, of paying half or three quarters wages for short tasks, has grown of late years.'[18] Clearly, the daily task fixed by the managers was excessive, and this was one of the major complaints of labourers and a reason for their strikes in the late 1930s.[19]

The wage data published in the annual official reports do not reflect any significant wage differentiation in terms of skill variation, etc. A major reason for this was the statutory minimum fixed wage rates under the indenture system. In the post-indenture period the situation remained the same as a consequence of the employers' 'wage agreement' and 'labour rules'. The Royal Commission termed its effects as 'standardization': 'Each planter fixes his own piece rates, but in so doing, regard is paid to the agreement arrived at by the Committee in order that the wages of his employees may not be appreciably higher than the agreed level.'[20] And finally, the labour-intensive tea industry utilizing only limited technology did not generate a wide range of specialization that would require diverse work skills, which in turn could have created differential wages. Nevertheless, within this 'standardized' or 'uniform' framework there were variations, though limited, in wage figures between Act and non-Act labourers, and between men, women and children. In the case of Act and Non-Act labourers, the officially published statistics showed relatively higher figures for the latter.[21] The official explanations for this were the following: (i) non-Act labour was free labour, i.e. they were earlier working as Act labourers and, after expiry of their contract, they re-employed themselves as non-Act labourers; (ii) since these labourers were experienced and acclimatized to the conditions on the plantations they were able to earn more; and (iii) being 'free labourers', non-Act workers received a 'bonus' of Rs 12 in the case of men and Rs 10 for women for each year of engagement.[22] This 'bonus' in the form of an advance was a device for contracting time-expired labourers under the Workman's Breach of Contract Act XIII of 1859.

R.K. Das, in his pioneering work, seems to have accepted some of these explanations uncritically, particularly on the issue of 'bonus'.[23] It implied that the wages and living conditions of non-Act labour in the Assam Valley tea plantations were better than those of Act labour. This could be cited as an explanation for the increase in employment of non-Act labour and the decline of Act labour. However, while non-Act labourers were not under the indenture contract, the assertion that they were free labour is unfounded. Official reports on immigration clearly mentioned that the majority of time-expired or non-Act labourers were contracted under Act XIII of 1859, which provided no provisions, even nominal, for any kind of labour 'welfare' or 'protection'. They were bonded to the gardens for long periods and controlled by penal laws, just as was the case with Act labour. It could be argued that being experienced, many such labourers were employed in the tea factories where jobs paid more than work in the field. There is no evidence to confirm such an assertion, however. Tea factories used barely 10 per cent of the total labour force employed in a standard size tea garden.[24] Here it is worth mentioning again that the employment of non-Act labour increased very fast while that of Act labour declined rapidly after penal provisions were removed from the indenture Act in 1908. Act labour virtually disappeared after 1919 because without the penal provisions, it was no longer useful to the planters.

The variations in wages between men, women and children were totally arbitrary. Women and children were paid less than men, but the reasons for this were never given. The hours of work for women and children were the same as those for men. Women, moreover, performed most types of work done by men, like hoeing, pruning, etc. In fact women performed work that was described as highly specialized, i.e. plucking, and proportionately their number was very significant in the labour force. In peak season, it was estimated that nearly 60 per cent of the labourers were women who were engaged in

Women workers waiting to get their baskets of tea leaves weighed
(Samuel Cleland Davidson, personal collection)

plucking.[25] Nor was there any reporting of women performing less or inferior work as compared to men. Since the techniques and modes of production in the tea plantations did not undergo any radical change, and there was hardly any differentiation of skills which could explain the variations between male and female labour, they all performed similar tasks and for the same number of hours. The productivity per unit of male and female labourers did not differ significantly either. Therefore, it is clear that the variation between male and female wages was purely on the basis of the conventional norms of sexual discrimination. Besides, the lower wages for women and children served to further depress the overall wage bill. The lower wages for women and children based on such discrimination was certainly of significant magnitude, considering that their combined employment was equal to or higher than that of men. Women and children combined constituted more than 50 per cent of the total labour force employed in the Assam Valley tea plantations.[26]

A grant of land made by managers to the labourers for private cultivation was considered an important 'concession' to supplement their earnings.[27] Most of the labour reports remarked that gardens with plenty of cultivable land were popular with labour. The Royal Commission supported this view by asserting that, 'the garden worker is essentially an agriculturist, and his desire for the possession of a holding which he can cultivate with the help of the members of his family it great'.[28] These grants, however, were not rent-free and carried conditions: the labourer had no occupancy right over such land and could hold it only for so long as he was employed in the tea garden.[29] The land could be taken back on 'disciplinary' grounds. Besides, not all labourers received land for private cultivation.[30] Whether cultivation of such lands significantly contributed towards the extra earnings of labourers has to be critically examined. The size of such land-holdings was very small. For example in the Lakhimpur, Sibsagar and Darrang districts, it worked out to an average of one-third, less than one-fourth and one-half of an acre respectively per adult labourer (see Appendix Table 5).

From the limited evidence available, we have tried to work out the approximate money value of the total produce from such holdings. The Enquiry Committee of 1921–22 estimated that between 15 and 20 *maunds* (1 maund = 37 kilograms) of paddy per acre may be taken as a fair amount of the crop in a normal year.[31] For our purposes, we shall take both the highest and the lowest figure. The market price of unhusked rice for the year 1921–22 was on average quoted at Rs 2.69 per *maund*.[32] The total annual value of crop per acre then works out to Rs 53.80 (for 20 *maunds*) and Rs 45.35 (for 15 *maunds*). In that year it was reported that the labourers as tenants of the tea estates held 35.4 thousand acres of land in Lakhimpur, 18 thousand acres in Sibsagar and 9 thousand acre in Darrang.[33] There were 127 thousand, 128 thousand and 66 thousand permanent adult labourers employed in Lakhimpur, Sibsagar and Darrang respectively, in the same year.[34] The average holding, therefore, comes to less than one-third of an acre in Lakhimpur, little more than one-seventh of an acre in Sibsagar and about one-eighth of an acre in Darrang. The combined average for the three districts works out to be approximately one-fifth of an acre per labourer in 1921–22. After deducting the yearly rent (at the rate of Rs 1.58 per acre), the approximate money value of paddy comes to Rs 10.44 (for the highest figure) and Rs 7.80 (for the lowest figure) per labourer during the corresponding year.[35] Calculated in yearly average, it represented about 12.7 per cent (for the highest figures) and 9.46 per cent (for the lowest figures) of the annual income of an adult labourer in 1921–22 (this average represents all three districts).

However, even these figures may not be accepted at their face value as representing real extra income, for the following reasons. First, the labourers received no wages while engaged in their own cultivation because the concept of leave with pay (even on Sundays) did not exist in the gardens. Therefore, the wages foregone ought to be deducted. Secondly, deduction of the cost of seeds will further lower the figure. The Enquiry Committee of 1921–22 did not accept the argument that the cash value of crops so raised should be considered as a 'concession'.[36] Though private cultivation did not contribute significantly towards the total earnings of the labour force in the face of constantly declining real wages, their dependence on such land for reasons of survival increased. The colonial officials believed that the gardens with plenty of cultivable land were popular among labourers. The total number of land grants given by the planters to their labourers for private cultivation increased over the years (Appendix Table 5). Rege reported that in 1944, about 165,000 acres of land were held by workers as tenants of the Assam tea gardens.[37] For the planters, the grant of land for private cultivation became another instrument of control over labourers and their mobility through the conditionality of continuing employment attached with such grants. The Royal Commission, while referring to this, pointed out that 'ambition for private land, if satisfied, would remove desire for garden work, and in the allotment of garden land for private cultivation, the planter has therefore, to study his own interests as well as of the workers'.[38]

The role of other 'concessions' like 'bonus', sick diet and subsidized rations in supplementing earnings needs critical examination. The 'bonus' given to labourers contracting under Act XIII was an advance to be later deducted from their wages. The system of advances, however, was not confined to Act XIII labourers alone. In reality, the 'bonus' became a mechanism of indebting the labourers to their employers. Generally, the 'advances' were given to the labourers when they fell sick or when they joined the gardens. These 'advances' served two purposes. First, they kept labourers alive so that they remained capable of work in the gardens. Second, they put the labourers under a debt obligation, thereby binding them to the garden for a much longer period than the contract stipulated. Cotton reported that advances were often illegally debited against labourers on account of subsistence allowance or sick diet, as well as on account of rewards paid for the arrests of deserters, and labourers were thus 'bound hand and foot to the garden service'.[39] Often only a meagre amount was paid as wages to the labourers because 'the managers deemed that they were justified in making deductions right and left so long as they kept their labourers in good condition like their horses and their cattle'.[40]

These aspects were well brought out in the inspection reports of the local officials in 1901, which also revealed grave abuses in the management of some of the tea gardens. In September 1901, Captain Cole, Deputy Commissioner of Darrang, reported his findings to the Commissioner of Assam Valley after an inspection of a few gardens:

> Although the labour force appeared on the whole well nourished, it is clear that a very large proportion of them are unable to earn a living wage, and that they would inevitably starve if the management did not provide sufficient rations and enter the cost of the same as an advance against the coolie.[41]

He supported his statement with figures of earnings of some of the labourers collected from the garden books. These showed that during a period of sixteen months (January 1900 to June 1901), these labourers could not even complete the daily task, *hazira*, and hence were unable to earn even the statutory minimum wage. The result was an increase in the outstanding advances. Captain Cole also complained about the difficulties in inspecting the garden because the registers were not properly maintained.[42] While endorsing the above findings of the district official, the Chief Commissioner of Assam reported to the Government of India that the 'labourers are hopelessly involved under the garden advances, and although . . . the coolies appear to be fairly well nourished, their condition can only be described as unsatisfactory in the extreme, and in no appreciable degree distinguishable from servitude'.[43]

The Sibsagar district civil surgeon, Captain Asher Leventon, inspected the Latabari tea estate and reported that a very small number of labourers received a full month's 'haziri' wage. In other words, the majority could not earn a full wage. The result was a large number of outstanding 'advances' against the labourers. The manager of the estate attributed this to the 'laziness' of the labourers who were getting enough food to live and were therefore satisfied.[44] The inspecting official, however, did not feel satisfied with this explanation and he remarked, 'I do not think the class of coolies on the garden a lazy type . . . it is impossible to believe that the whole labour force is so lazy that only a few were willing to work a full month's *haziri*.'[45] He reproduced the figures, collected from the garden books during his inspection, of the amount of 'advances' outstanding. On the basis of the figures, Captain Leventon remarked that women labourers were unable to earn even the cost of their maintenance: 'a debt against a certain number or class of coolies steadily increasing month by month is a suspicious circumstance. It would not matter so much if they received good sums after deducting their rice amounts. The sums they get at the end of the month are very small indeed.'[46]

These ill-paid labourers got further indebted in cases of sickness. The manager of Latabari tea estate claimed that sick labourers were provided subsistence in the form of 'sick-diet' rations, etc. The inspecting official, while refuting this claim reported:

> I felt compelled to refuse to accept the statement that 'sick receive diet', except in the case of indoor patients; even those cases are open to doubt, for in the *haziri* books may be found numerous cases where people who have been sick for a good part of the month, or even the full month, have the cost of the rice they drew charged against them. . . . I have traced a good number of cases who have 'S' (sick) marked a few or many times in the month, and find they owe much more at the end of the month then at the beginning, that is, if they get rice they were charged for it. The cases of those who did not work on account of sickness and who did not get deeper into debt are very few.[47]

J.C. Arbuthnott, Deputy Commissioner of Sibsagar, while describing the conditions of the labourers in the above garden as 'legalized slavery', recommended strong action to be taken against the employers.[48] He remarked that the wages were 'scandalously low':

> Comfort is hardly compatible with a starvation wage, and the condition of the labourers, which is practically that of slaves, can hardly be satisfying, except to the owners, who naturally in their own interest supply them with food while gradually increasing the debt against them, in order that the period of bondage may be interminable.[49]

Thus a system of forced indebtedness by maintaining the wages below the subsistence level was imposed upon labourers by the planters in order to bind them to the gardens for an indefinite period. There is some evidence to show that very often, sick diet and subsidized rations did not function as concessions but as tools of indebtedness of the labourers. A number of cases were reported by the district officials where the subsidized rations given to the labourers were entered as outstanding advances against them. The cases of sick diet were no different. Complaining against the Nagora Tea Estate in Sibsagar district, the Commissioner of Assam Valley wrote:

> provision S.112 of the Assam Labour and Emigration Act, that requires that subsistence allowance as sick diet shall be given to sick labourers, have been ignored by the management and that sums have been illegally debited against the coolies on this account, as well as on account of rewards paid for the arrest of labourers.[50]

An important piece of information that we may add here is that the officially published wage statistics clearly mentioned that the value of such concessions were included in the wage figures. After the passing of the Tea District Emigrant Labour Act (XXII of 1932) many of these 'concessions' were no longer obligatory, and the annual reports of the Controller of Emigrant Labour pointed out that the majority of the gardens did not supply either rice or paddy at subsidized rates.[51] However the statements of wage figures in these reports continued to include the value of 'diet, rations and subsistence allowance' in the published wage figures.[52]

The planters and their apologists, whenever the issue of wage increase was raised, complained that labour in the tea gardens did not respond favourably to higher wages. We have earlier quoted quite a few such complaints. These complaints were lodged in defence of their opposition to any demand or suggestion for wage increases. Buckingham, the representative of tea interests in the Central Legislative Council, opposed the proposal by Henry Cotton, Chief Commissioner of Assam, for an increase in wages on the following grounds: 'An increased rate of payment leads to a lesser task instead of an augmented task, the coolies taking out the balance, so to speak, in the only form of luxury which appeals to an Asiatic viz., the luxury of sitting still and doing nothing.'[53] He contested Cotton's argument that wages had stagnated and not kept up with the rising cost of living by presenting the views of another colonial official, R.N. Campbell, civil surgeon of Shillong. The latter had argued that the cost of food had become cheaper in 1899 compared to twenty years ago because of improved communications: 'I think the labourer is well off, nay, better, than twenty years ago, though his minimum wage has remained the same.' In the same document, however, Campbell referred to the growing labour costs on account of increasing prices.[54]

There is enough evidence, as pointed out earlier, to contest these assertions and complaints of the employers. The findings of the Enquiry Committee, 1906 clearly established that the complaints were without any basis. The Committee members toured most of the recruiting and tea districts, and examined scores of witnesses. Among their witnesses in the recruiting districts were the managers of collieries, local labour agents, Christian missionaries, local officials, merchants and free contractors. Most of them were of the view that wages paid in the Assam tea plantations were inadequate and not competitive in the labour market. F.J. Agabeg, the manager of Messrs ApCar and Company's Collieries and Zamindaries in the Burdwan district, claimed that labourers in mines earned from Rs 15 to Rs 20 a month and were provided free housing and land for cultivation, and that because of increasing competition for labour, they had to increase the wages.[55] A second witness, Babu A.N. Sen, a labour agent in Raniganj, said that the long duration of contract and controlled mobility under special Acts were the major reasons for the unwillingness of labourers to go to the Assam tea gardens.[56] Another witness, a free contractor in Raniganj, suggested that a higher wage offer, between Rs 5 to Rs 8 per month, would be more attractive for labourers to go to the Assam tea gardens.[57] Two of the Christian missionaries pointed out that abuses like false promises of high wages but actually lower earnings, and wrong persuasive methods of recruitment were deterrents in mobilizing labour for the Assam Valley tea plantations.[58] T.C. Macpherson, Joint Magistrate of Ranchi, reported that local labour was increasingly attracted to places of employment where they got better treatment and higher wages. According to him, a great many of the labourers who were taken to Assam had been deceived. Many of them were given the impression that they were being taken to Duars. On arrival at Raniganj, however, they realized the truth and wanted to go back, but were threatened by the contractor's touts and forced to go to Assam.[59] The Deputy Commissioner of Manbhum too thought the wages offered in Assam were insufficient to attract people from here.[60]

In this context, the findings of the Enquiry Committee of 1906 were revealing.[61] The Committee found that:

people could not regard Assam, and they still do not regard it, as a desirable place for the emigrant, when the methods so long resorted to for procuring him were such as to create feeling of revulsion in the mind of every right-thinking man. It is impossible to expect that public opinion regarding the country should change merely with the passing of a new Act, more especially when in the course of legislation that took place much was said to confirm the belief in the undesirability of Assam. That the opposition of the tea industry to the rise in wages which had been proposed in 1901, told strongly against Assam in recruiting districts, can be gathered from the prevalence of the opinion that the tea garden wage is too low. This belief is shared by officials and non-officials alike.[62]

The Royal Commission on Labour also did not fully agree with the assertion that workers were not responsive to the offer of higher wages to improve their standard of living, or that they were content to work less just to earn bare subsistence.[63] The employers in the tea industry put forward a theory of what would today be called a 'backward bending supply curve of labour' for the sole reason that it was not the wage incentive that they used to maintain (or increase) productivity of labour, but compulsions and restraints of various kinds, including physical coercion. This is a factor to be borne in mind in considering the wage question in the Indian tea industry.

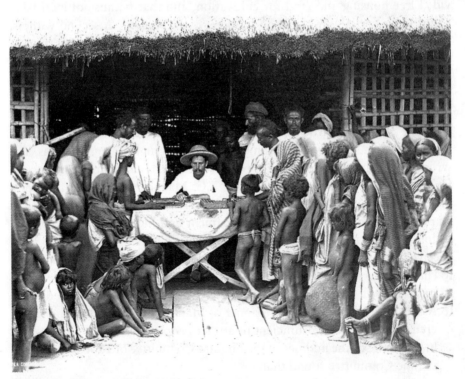

Tea garden labourers being paid their wages
(Samuel Cleland Davidson, personal collection)

Wage Structure

Before we go into the details of wages and wage data for Act and non-Act labourers, I would like to present a brief genealogy of official wage formation and the publication of data in the official reports on emigrant labour in the Assam Valley tea plantations. The indenture contract, formally introduced by Act VI of 1865, fixed the amount of minimum monthly wage at Rs 5 for men and Rs 4 for women and five years as the period of contract. The contract period was reduced to three years by Act II of 1870 but was again increased to five years under Act I of 1882. The minimum wage was to remain the same for the first three years, and then increased to Rs 6 for a man and Rs 5 for a woman for the rest of the period of contract. The period of the contract was once again reduced to four years by Act VII of 1893, while the wage amount remained unchanged. And then, with the passing of Act VI of 1901, a modified wage system was introduced. The contract period remained four years and the wages were to be paid in the following manner: Rs 5 for men and Rs 4 for women during the first year; Rs 5.50 and Rs 4.50 for the second and third years; and Rs 6 and Rs 5 in the fourth year.[64] The wages for the non-Act labour category were not regulated but it was the general understanding that the same system of wages would be applicable. The colonial official reports included wage data on child labour in the published statistics of wages of men and women under the non-Act category.[65] No separate wage data for child labour were published for Act labour, implying that children were employed only under Act XIII. From the beginning of the twentieth century, the planters resorted to increasing use of Act XIII of 1859 for employing labour. By 1918–19, the contracts under Act VI of 1901 ceased to exist. And finally, with the repeal of Act XIII of 1859 in 1925 and Act VI of 1901 in 1932, the above two categories also disappeared. The new legislation, called the Tea District Emigrant Labour Act (XXII of 1932), which came into effect in October 1933, replaced Act VI of 1901. The post of Controller of Emigrant Labour was created to regulate the process of labour migration. The annual reports on the working of this Act now began to publish wage statistics along with various other aspects of tea industry. From 1934 onwards, the wage figures were published under two different categories, viz. settled labour, and *faltu* or *basti* labour.[66] Under these categories, the average monthly wage figures for men, women and children were published separately for each district every year. *Faltu* or *basti* labour referred to ex-tea garden labourers who had settled down in *bastis* outside the plantations. Separate publication of wage figures for this category of labour signified the increasing use of temporary labour from the emerging surplus labour pool around the tea plantations by the 1930s. Planters began to increasingly hire *faltu* labour from this pool at even lower wages.

We shall now critically survey the sources, and the methodology of collection and compilation of quantitative data on wages in the Assam Valley tea gardens. The most important source was the annual reports on emigrant labour published by the Government of Assam from the mid-1870s till 1932, and from 1934 onwards by the office of the Controller of Emigrant Labour. These reports published figures of average monthly earnings of different categories of labourers in the tea districts for each year. The wage data published in the annual labour reports during the last two decades of the nineteenth century were prepared from information collected during inspections of the gardens by the district officials. The inspecting officials were required to ascertain the wages paid in the month preceding their visit. They then worked out the yearly average of monthly wages from the information on annual expenditure provided by the managers of the tea gardens during the inspections.[67] After a couple of years of this exercise, the Commissioner of Assam Valley started to suspect that the information given by the garden management included the wages of servants and skilled mechanics, whose higher pay inflated the wage figures. Doubting the accuracy of the information, he directed the inspecting officials to prepare the averages on the basis of the wages for two months, i.e. the cold month and rainy month, on the assumption that these two seasons represented lower and higher earning respectively.[68] These instructions, however, remained on paper and the existing practice continued – apparently with the belief that the inspections gave a 'fair idea of the actual money payments in the way of wages'.[69]

From 1901, a new practice of wage data publication was introduced based on figures which were to be submitted by the managers for the last six months of the year. The planters were not too pleased with this 'cumbersome' practice. The Indian Tea Association protested against the requirement of submission of monthly returns by the garden managers. As a result the practice was discontinued and from 1904–05, the planters submitted wage returns for two months (March and September) only, with the expectation of 'simplifying the return and of increasing its accuracy'.[70] A significant addition from this year onwards in the published statement was that the figures of cash wages now included the value of allowances paid under Sections 126(1) and 130(1), value of diet in lieu of such allowances and rations provided under Section 134(a), and *ticca* earnings. This practice of including the value of various concessions in the published wage figures was followed in the case of non-Act labourers too.[71]

However the issue of accuracy of statistical information submitted by the employers remained an unresolved one. The colonial bureaucracy was not too concerned if the figures represented the actual earnings of the labour force. While occasionally bemoaning the receipt of incomplete or 'faulty' statistical information, the officials generally ignored non-compliance of labour laws by the employers. Henry Cotton paid a huge price for trying to enforce compliance of the labour law on the planters. A closer scrutiny of the methods of collection and compilation of the wage statistics shows major flaws, making the accuracy of wage returns highly suspect. The district officials compiled a yearly average of monthly wages out of the statistical returns submitted by the planters without any system of ascertaining their accuracy.[72] A similar situation prevailed with regard to the data on vital statistics of tea garden labour in the province. The planters submitted statistical data regarding the births and deaths of labourers in their respective estates. This information was accepted and reproduced officially despite doubts about its accuracy because, as the Controller of Emigrant Labour admitted, there was no government agency for the registration of births and deaths in tea gardens.[73] The planters submitted the returns in an arbitrary manner. For example, between 1901 and 1904–05, wage returns were submitted for the last six months of the year. Therefore, the yearly average of the monthly earnings was calculated not on the basis of twelve months.[74] This was especially misleading because the last six months of the year included the peak season of work, during which the earnings of labourers were high as compared to the slack period in the first six months of the year.

From 1904–05 onwards, as pointed out earlier, the yearly average of monthly earnings was worked out on the basis of figures for two months, i.e. March and September, representing the slack and peak periods respectively. This again was an arbitrary method. While it is true that these two months fell in the slack and peak periods, it did not necessarily follow that the earnings of the labourers during these two months were also the lowest and highest in the year. Moreover, the original records of the wage returns data were not preserved. As a matter of policy, these documents were destroyed after the compilation of the yearly average of monthly wages was completed.[75] Thus any possibility of cross-checking of officially published time-series was eliminated.

There is another problem with regard to the publication of the wage statistics. The planters and sometimes even the officials asserted that there was supplementary income in addition to cash earnings for the labourers, through *ticca* work and other forms of concession provided under the labour laws.[76] This implies that the wage figures published in the Assam labour reports did not represent the actual earnings but only the cash earnings, excluding the supplementary income. However, the labour reports from 1901 onwards clearly mentioned that the wage figures represented 'average monthly cash wages including subsistence allowances paid under Section 128(i) and 130(i), value of diet in lieu of such allowances and rations provided under Section 134(a) and also including *ticca* earnings' of Act and non-Act labourers.[77] Thus it was made clear that these average monthly wage figures represented more than just the cash earnings. Then there was the matter of higher wage figures published for non-Act male labourers as compared to Act male labourers. The explanation for this was that the labourers engaged as non-Act labour were more experienced and, therefore, employed in better paid jobs in the plantations, as *sirdars, chowkidars*, etc.[78] This was a lame explanation since, given the increasing number of non-Act labourers, these so-called better paid jobs were few and far between.

Yet another problem related to the accuracy of the wage statistics arises from the two different sets of figures published under the heading of 'monthly average earnings' in the Assam labour reports. Both sets of figures were published under further sub-headings: calculated on the basis of total number of labourers in the garden's books; calculated on the basis of daily working strength.[79] The former figures were calculated by dividing the total wage payment by the total number of labourers on the books, and the latter by dividing the total wage payment by the daily working strength of the labour force during the same two months in each year. The former figures showed lower earnings compared to the latter. But the reports did not make it clear as to which ones represented the actual earnings of the labour force. And then, from 1927 onwards, the reports published wage figures based on daily working strength only. Given the fact that the Assam Valley tea plantations experienced an average rate of nearly 25 per cent of absenteeism, the wage earnings on the basis of daily working strength cannot be taken as representing the actual earnings of the entire labour force living in the tea gardens.[80] These figures simply represented what a labourer would have earned if he or she worked on all working days.

In 1933, serious objection was raised against this erroneous practice by Lee, the newly appointed Controller of Emigrant Labour. In a confidential report to the Government of India, he pointed out that the wage statistics recently published in the annual reports by the Government of Assam were misleading. In his opinion, the wage figures based on total number of labourers in the books as published earlier represented more accurately the earnings of the labourers.[81] Clow, a senior official in the Department of Industry and Labour, Government of India, agreed with the Controller of Emigrant Labour: 'the present method of calculating the average monthly cash earnings is open to serious objection as the figures do not represent what they purport to represent and are definitely misleading'.[82] However, the government no longer favoured publishing wage figures calculated on the basis of total number of labourers in the garden books. There was a note of caution that this could result in a big drop in the figures of average earnings, which 'might be misinterpreted by the public'. Instead it was suggested that the present figures should be substituted by the average amount earned by a labourer in a day's work. This could be worked out by dividing the total wage payment by the number of working days. It was hoped that 'this will not lend itself to misleading comparisons, and it would give a figure representing something real, whereas the present figures represent something that borders on the imaginary'.[83] The labour reports from 1934 onwards, however, again resorted to the practice of publishing wage data calculated both on the basis of the number of labourers on the books and daily working strength.[84]

Most other sources that published wage data basically reproduced figures from the official labour reports. For example, the Annual Reports on Tea Culture in Assam (1900–26) and the Indian Tea Statistics (1930–46) reproduced the provincial averages of monthly earnings which were originally published in the labour reports. In September 1943 a Tripartite Labour Conference took place in Delhi, and on its recommendation, the D.V. Rege Committee was appointed by Government of India to investigate questions of wages, employment, housing and social conditions of plantation workers.[85] The ITA, however, opposed detailed field investigations by the Rege Committee on the ground that it would unsettle the labour force in an area which was by now a war zone. As a result, Rege had to rely on his own efforts, without the aid of field staff, for the inquiry. He visited thirty-nine tea gardens, out of which twenty-nine were European and ten Indian owned.[86] Most of the data used by Rege in support of his field report were collected from Indian Tea Statistics and the labour reports. The same practice was repeated in the Indian Labour Year Books.

The outcome of another Tripartite Conference held in New Delhi in 1947 was the appointment of yet another Committee under S.R. Deshpande, to enquire into the cost and standard of living of plantation workers in Assam and Bengal. Deshpande followed a sampling method which covered sixteen European and four Indian tea gardens, in consultation with the Indian Tea Association.[87] Deshpande's report (1948), however, adopted the 'family budget' concept for calculating (based on data collected through the sample survey) the weekly average earnings and expenses of tea garden labour in Assam. It also assumed, erroneously, that recruitment and employment in the Assam tea plantations was family-based.[88] In Assam Valley, 560 family budgets of labourers out of twenty gardens were selected for tabulation.[89] The average size of the family was taken at 4.15 persons, including 2.44 earning members and 1.71 non-earning members (men, women and children) as dependents.[90] While calculating the weekly family income of tea garden labourers, Deshpande included wages, *ticca* earnings, dearness allowance, bonus, and the money value of concessions and incomes from other sources like land, etc.[91] He also assumed that all labourers were recipients of all the concessions. Using this method, he calculated the income earned by 2.44 persons (of an average family of 4.15 persons) as Rs 10.82 per week.[92] It is interesting that the concept of 'family wage' was officially used by Deshpande alone among all the official reports on wages in the tea plantations. None of the earlier official reports used this formally. The planters often referred to this to buttress their argument of higher earnings of labourers. In comparison with Deshpande's estimates of family wage figures, an alternative unofficial academic finding, also based on field investigations, by Radhakamal Mukherjee in 1945, showed only Rs 5.44 as the weekly earning of a labour family consisting of one adult male, two adult women and one male child in the Assam tea gardens.[93] Even the officially published wage data, which were on the higher side, showed a much lower figure compared to Deshpande's estimates. The average earnings of two adults (man and woman) and a child worker worked out to Rs 8.42 per week in 1947 for the Assam Valley tea plantations. This figure also included the value of concessions and *ticca* earnings, and represented the averages of daily working strength (which were higher than those based on total number of labourers on the garden books).[94] Thus Deshpande's estimated figure was 22 per cent higher than the figure published in the official time-series.

Two factors were responsible for this: first, the inclusion of money value of concessions; and second, the inclusion of dearness allowance by Deshpande. The assumption behind the first seems to have been that all labourers received full concessions. This was not entirely correct, as we have shown above. It was clear from the inspection reports of the district officials that 'sickness allowance', 'subsistence rations' and 'bonus' did not always represent as concessions. Secondly, although dearness allowance was officially introduced in February 1947,[95] from past experience of the antipathy and non-compliance of planters towards provisions regarding labour welfare in the law, it would be too optimistic to expect them to have implemented the dearness allowance clause immediately. The fact that the official annual report of the Controller of Emigrant Labour did not include this in its published wage figures for 1947 strengthens our argument. The official annual labour report of 1947 did not mention dearness allowance payment to labourers in the Assam tea gardens. Moreover, dearness allowance and the money value of concessions constituted nearly 41 per cent of the total weekly earnings of a labour family in Deshpande's calculations.[96] This appears too high a figure to lend credibility to its accuracy. For the same reasons, therefore, it cannot be used as a fair basis of comparison with the official time-series.

There is another set of wage figures available of average monthly earnings of the labour force which may be considered relatively more accurate. However these are only for two years, 1900 and 1901 and were reported by the district officials in the unpublished inspection reports of two tea districts in Assam Valley.[97] These figures were collected and compiled by the inspecting officials from the books maintained in the tea garden offices. These and the provincial average figures from the annual labour reports were cited by Henry Cotton in the Governor General's Council in 1901 in support of his proposal for wage increase. He argued that his predecessors had ignored the fact of non-compliance of minimum statutory payment of wages by planters: 'The accuracy of the statements of figures given in the Provincial Immigration Annual Reports, obtained from the employers' accounts, is perhaps open to question, and there is reason to believe that the averages returned in recent years are in excess of the wages actually paid.'[98]

The figures of monthly wages collected from garden books by the district officials during inspections in the years 1900 and 1901 were even lower than the published figures in the annual labour reports for the corresponding and earlier years. Captain Leventon, civil surgeon of Sibsagar District, collected wage data during his inspection visit for Act labourers in Latabari Tea garden in Sibsagar, for January to December 1900. He reported that the yearly average (based on the wage figures for twelve months in the garden books) of monthly earnings of men and women Act labourers were Rs 3.48 and Rs 2.74 respectively, which were considerably lower than the figures published in the annual labour report for Sibsagar district for the same year (Appendix Table 5.2).[99] Similarly, in Darrang district, Captain H.W. Cole, Deputy Commissioner, reported his findings during the inspection visit to Sadhrugops, Shakamato and Aberdeen tea gardens. He reported the yearly average of monthly earnings (based on the figures of January and June) of non-Act labourers during 1901 as Rs 3.54, Rs 1.98 and Rs 1.30 for men, women and children respectively. These figures too were much lower than the figures published in annual labour report for the same year (see Appendix Table 5.3).[100] Cotton also reproduced the wage figures of provincial averages from the annual labour reports for the last sixteen years of the nineteenth century to support his assertion of non-compliance by the planters of the statutory minimum wage payment, i.e. the wages earned were below the minimum Rs 5 and Rs 4 for men and women respectively (see Chart 5.1 and

CHART 5.1
Annual Averages of Monthly Wages of Act Labour in Assam, 1883–99

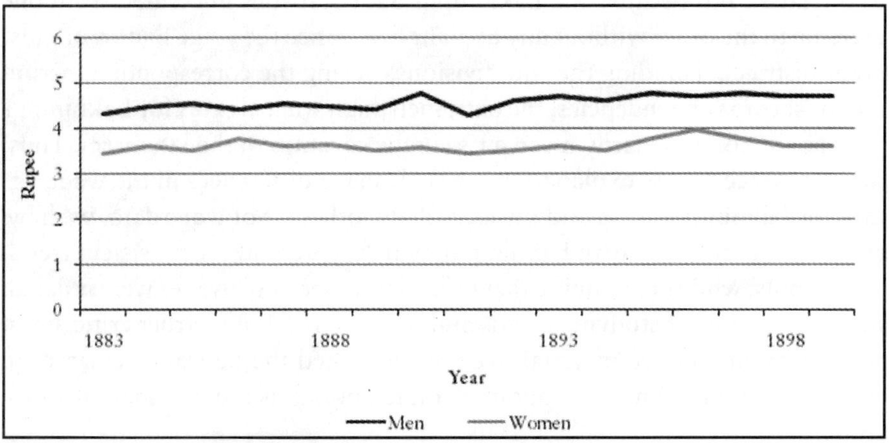

Appendix Table 5.1).[101] We have not come across any other report based on actual inspections for either before or after these years. Cotton's fate may have acted as a deterrent to subsequent fair-minded colonial civil servants to push that far in their official duties.

The bitter public controversy that took place between Cotton and the planters over the question of wages during his tenure as Chief Commissioner of Assam made the planters somewhat cautious. The increasing assertion through acts of resistance against ill treatment and low wages by labourers was seriously noted and concern was expressed by the Viceroy, Lord Curzon. Hence the necessity to produce wage figures for publication which would seemingly conformed to the statutory minimum rates, to placate such official concern. This was successfully achieved by adopting arbitrary methods of collection and compilation of wage returns instead of actually paying higher wages. The actual wages paid continued to be miserly and often at par with or below subsistence, as we shall show below. This could not have happened without the complicity and support of the colonial bureaucracy.

Wage Trends

In this section, we analyse the wage trends of different categories of labourers in the Assam Valley districts of Lakhimpur, Sibsagar, Darrang, Nowgong and Kamrup from 1883 (after the passing of Act I of 1882; wage data began to be published regularly in the annual reports on emigrant labour from this year onwards) till 1947. Statements of wages were published separately for the sub-divisions of the districts. We have taken the figures for the district head-quarters of Sibsagar, Darrang, Nowgong and Kamrup as fairly representative of the entire district. However, in the case of Lakhimpur we have preferred the figures for North Lakhimpur to those of Lakhimpur Sadr. The reason for this is not because the figures in the case of the former are lower compared to the latter, but because the Lakhimpur Sadr statistics fluctuated from one extreme to the other without any explanation. Since the wage figures of most other districts, including the sub-divisions, during the corresponding period do not show such tendencies, the extremely high wage figures for Lakhimpur Sadr might not necessarily mean a rise in the earnings of the labourers. Thus, in the absence of any explanation for such sharp differences in the wage figures for Lakhimpur Sadr, and the lack of any other set of wage data, we have taken the figures for North Lakhimpur, which represented a consistent trend.

Secondly, while maintaining that official time-series on wages were inflated, for the purposes of studying trends and in the light of our earlier criticism of wage data and source material, we have accepted the figures calculated on the basis of total number of labourers on the books as the nominal earnings.

Nominal Wages of Act Labour

As pointed out earlier, Act labourers worked for a minimum period of four years, and were subject to criminal proceedings for violation of terms of contract under penal laws. The majority of them were re-employed as non-Act labour under Act XIII of 1859 at the expiry of their contract. We therefore took the prescribed period of four years and fixed minimum wage as our base, which works out to be an average minimum Rs 5.50 for a man and Rs 4.50 for a woman. Charts 5.2 to 5.6 (and Appendix Table 5.2) show the yearly averages of monthly wages for men and women Act labourers in Lakhimpur, Sibsagar, Darrang, Nowgong and Kamrup districts in Assam Valley between 1883 and 1918–19.[102] There were no Act labourers after 1918–19. In all the five districts the nominal wages in the long run (with the exception of women's

CHART 5.2
Wages of Act Labour, Lakhimpur

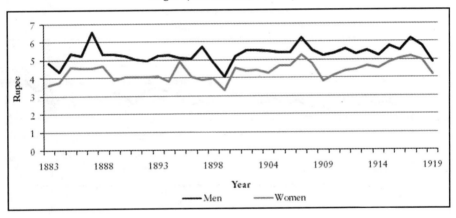

CHART 5.3
Wages of Act Labour, Sibsagar

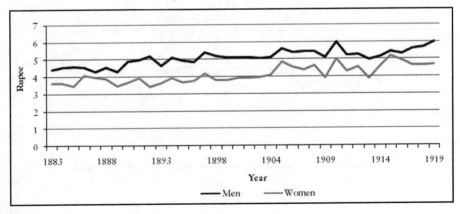

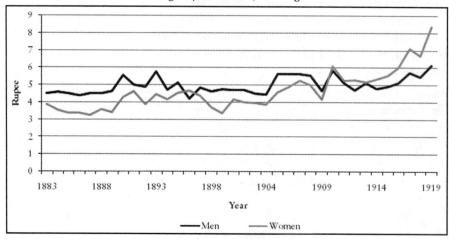

CHART 5.4
Wages of Act Labour, Darrang

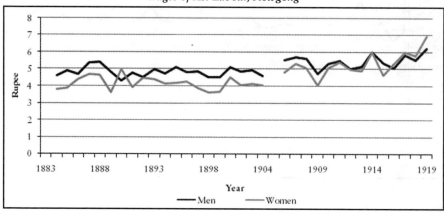

CHART 5.5
Wages of Act Labour, Nowgong

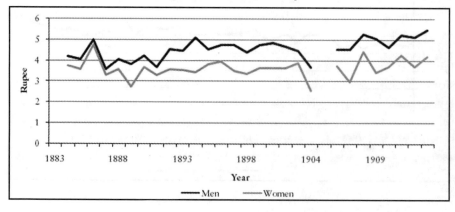

CHART 5.6
Wages of Act Labour, Kamrup

wages in Darrang) remained stagnant with sometimes declining tendencies and often below the statutory minimum wage during 1883–1900. The wage figures for the period 1901–19 again showed earnings below the statutory minimum in a large number of cases in all the districts. The long-term trends showed stagnation and lower than statutory wage figures in most of the districts with a few exceptions. In Kamrup the wage figures did not conform to the statutory minimum even for a single year throughout the period of Act labour employment (Appendix Table 5.2). The overall increase was very insignificant. Moreover these figures represented more than the cash earnings as the value of 'concessions' and *ticca* earnings were also included.

Nominal Wages of Non-Act Labour

We shall now examine the wage data (official time-series) of non-Act labour. One of the features of the data is that the wage figures of non-Act labourers are slightly higher compared to those of Act labourers. To lure time-expired labourers under Act XIII of 1859, cash advances were supposedly offered as 'bonuses'. The illiteracy of the labourers was cleverly exploited in this case. It seems the labourers were given cash advances as 'bonus' but on the contract document (written in English), it was mentioned as advanced money to be deducted later. The Enquiry Committee of 1921–22 reproduced some of these contract documents in which the labourers bound themselves under Act XIII of 1859 by declaring the following:

> The amount of any advance made to me, by the manager in cash or otherwise and the price of rice, or any other food I may receive from the garden godown shall be deducted from my monthly wages and I shall only be entitled to receive the balance of my wages after such deductions have been made.[103]

In none of the documents was there any mention of any bonus payment. Thus it appears that the average amount of these advances might have been added to the average cash wage of non-Act labourers, which obviously inflated the figures of their earnings. Unlike Act labourers, there was no provision of fixed minimum wage in the case of non-Act labourers. Nor were the employers bound to provide 'concessions'. Nevertheless, non-Act labourers were also contracted on a long-term basis and controlled by equally repressive penal laws. Besides, the official reports continued to include the value of 'concessions' (as in the case of Act labourers) in the figures of cash wages of non-Act labourers. Therefore, we take the same average prescribed minimum wages for non-Act labour also (Rs 5.50 for men and Rs 4.50 for women) as our base for the purpose of analysing the wage data of non-Act labour. The minimum average monthly wage figure for child labour, we assume as Rs 3.50.

The nominal wage trend of non-Act labour in all the districts showed variations and the wage figures were relatively higher than that of Act labour.

Lakhimpur wage figures, particularly for men, were much higher compared to all the other tea districts. The occasional official explanation for this was the remoteness of Lakhimpur and lesser availability of land there for cultivation by the labour force – thus providing them the opportunity to concentrate on garden work and earn extra wages. Appendix Table 5.3 shows the wage figures of non-Act labourers (calculated on the basis of number of labourers on the books) in Lakhimpur, Sibsagar, Darrang, Nowgong and Kamrup districts between 1900 and 1932. These figures are visually projected in Charts 5.7, 5.8 and 5.9, 5.10 and 5.11, for North Lakhimpur, Sibsagar and Darrang, Nowgong and Kamrup, respectively. The long-term trends show stagnation or very marginal increase of nominal wages till the beginning of World War I in all the districts. In most cases, except Lakhimpur, the non-Act wage figures were below Rs 5.50 for men, Rs 4.50 for women and Rs 4 (the average statutory minimum for Act labour) for children. Child labourers in most cases were the worst sufferers, followed by women, for not earning even the equivalent of the average minimum figure.

The nominal wages of non-Act labour showed upward movement in the post-World War I period. The combined wages of men, women and children increased by 44, 29, 24, 31 and 41 per cent in Lakhimpur, Sibsagar, Darrang, Nowgong and Kamrup districts respectively, between 1921 and 1930. However after reaching a peak in the late 1920s, the nominal wage figures registered a sharp decline of 18, 6, 21, 16 and 60 per cent in Lakhimpur, Sibsagar, Darrang, Nowgong and Kamrup respectively, between 1930 and 1932 (Appendix Table 5.3, and Charts 5.7, 5.8, 5.9, 5.10 and 5.11).

The newly passed labour legislation, the Tea District Emigrant Labour Act XXII of 1932, which came into force in October 1933, was mainly concerned with the process of labour recruitment and their journey up to the tea districts. There were no provisions in the new law to deal with living conditions or wages in the tea districts. 'Concessions' were no longer a statutory obligation of the employers. Thus, apart from the decrease in wages, the labour force was also deprived of statutory 'protection' with the final repeal of Act VI of 1901. However, the annual reports on emigrant labour published by the Controller of Emigrant Labour created confusion by their contradictory reporting. In some years the reports mentioned that the value of 'concessions' was included in the figures of cash wages, while in others it was pointed out that apart from cash wages labour supplemented its income out of various 'concessions' offered in the tea districts. However, despite this confusion, it was clearly stated that the practice of giving subsidized rations in the form of rice at concessional prices had been done away with because the labourers did not 'appreciate' it.[104] Secondly, it was also acknowledged that the wages were decreasing mainly because of fine plucking and economy on the part of the employers.[105] In the case of *ticca* earnings, Rege confirmed in 1946 that

CHART 5.7
Wages of Non-Act Labour in Lakhimpur, 1883–1932

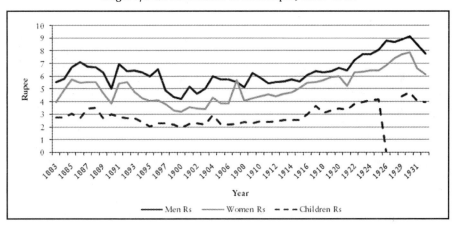

CHART 5.8
Wages of Non-Act Labour in Sibsagar, 1883–1932

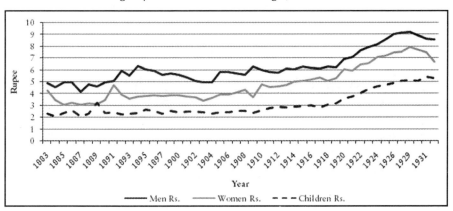

CHART 5.9
Wages of Non-Act Labour in Darrang, 1883–1932

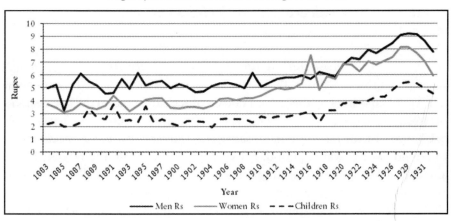

CHART 5.10
Wages of Non-Act Labour in Nowgong, 1883–1932

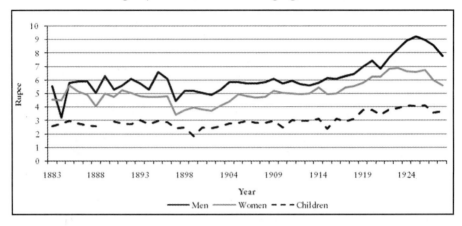

CHART 5.11
Wages of Non-Act Labour in Kamrup, 1883–1932

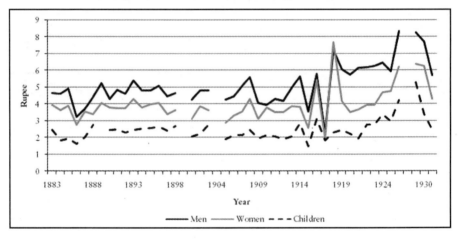

its value had been included in the wage figures given in the annual official reports.[106]

Nominal Wages of Settled Labour

Appendix Table 5.4 shows the wage figures (calculated on the basis of total number of labourers on the garden books) of settled labour in the five districts between 1934 and 1945. These figures are visually projected on Charts 5.12, 5.13 and 5.14 for Lakhimpur, Sibsagar and Darrang districts respectively.[107] In the pre-World War II period, between 1934 and 1938, the wages of men and children remained stagnant with a tendency to decline in all the districts. Women's wages remained stagnant in Sibsagar and Darrang, though there was slight increase in Lakhimpur. The World War II years experienced fluctuating tendencies which varied from district to district. The overall increase in the nominal wages between 1934–38 and 1941–45[108] for men was 14 per cent, 33 per cent and 24 per cent, for women it was 26 per cent, 22 per cent and 28 per cent, and for children it was 27 per cent, 33 per cent and 41 per cent, in Lakhimpur, Sibsagar and Darrang, respectively (Appendix Table 5.4).[109]

The year 1947 showed a massive jump in the wage figures for all categories of labour in all three districts. The labour report for that year offers no explanation for this sudden and unusually high rate of increase in wages. Deshpande asserted in his report in 1948 that because of a very high increase in prices of foodstuff and other necessities, the Indian Tea Association issued heavily subsidized rations and other necessities to the labour force from October 1946 onwards. He presented an estimate which showed that 27 per cent of a labour family's income in Assam Valley accrued from the difference between prices charged for commodities sold by the employers and the prices the workers would have to pay in the open market.[110] Deshpande's estimate of a labour family's earnings, as pointed out earlier, are debatable.

Nominal Wages of 'Basti'/'Faltu' Labour

In a new development from 1934 onwards, the Controller of Emigrant Labour reported the employment of *basti* or *faltu* labour in significant numbers, in addition to settled labour, in the Assam Valley tea plantations, and statements of their wages were published separately. More than seven decades of continuous recruitment of migrant labour, sponsored by the tea industry, had created an extra labour pool of ex-tea garden labourers. Many of them had left their employment in the tea gardens and settled on government and private lands in the vicinity of the plantations. Though their employment as *faltu/basti* labour was officially acknowledged from 1934, the official production and labour reports had been referring to them as temporary labour from the last decade of the nineteenth century. Their numbers were not insignificant either, often amounting to 15 per cent of the permanent labour force (Appendix Tables 5.5 and 5.18). The temporary category also included the local Kacharis who were employed in the tea gardens. But the Kacharis began to move away from temporary employment in the plantations and took up jute cultivation near their homes from the beginning of the twentieth century.[111] The numbers of temporarily employed were perhaps greater than the published official figures, as the planters did not show the employment of *basti* labour and underaged children in their returns.[112] That may have been why they were not enumerated as *faltu/basti* labour in the official reports till 1934, nor statements of their wages reported (Appendix Table 5.5).

Settling former tea garden labourers on government lands was a part of the colonization policy of the Government of Assam. The area granted to the ex-tea garden labourers as tenants of the government in the vicinity of

CHART 5.12
Yearly Averages of Monthly Wages of Settled Labour in Lakhimpur Tea Plantations, 1934–47

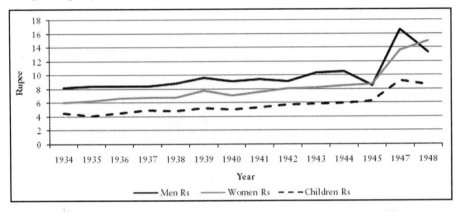

CHART 5.13
Yearly Averages of Monthly Wages of Settled Labour in Sibsagar Tea Plantations, 1934–47

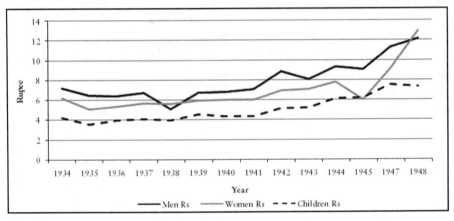

CHART 5.14
Yearly Averages of Monthly Wages of Settled Labour in Darrang Tea Plantations, 1934–47

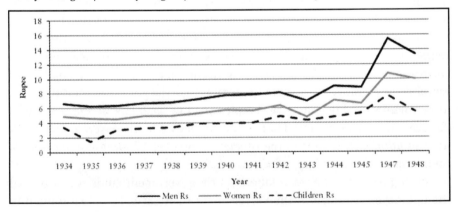

the plantations increased by 192 per cent during the early two decades of the twentieth century.[113] The bulk of these settlements were in the tea districts of the Assam Valley. Many of them took up employment for short periods in the tea gardens and were enumerated as *basti* or *faltu* labour. They were mostly employed in the peak seasons, particularly during plucking time. The wages paid to *faltu* or *basti* labourers were lower than that of settled labourers. Appendix Table 5.6 shows the average monthly earnings of *faltu* labour in Lakhimpur, Sibsagar and Darrang districts. The official explanation for their lower earnings was the absence of *ticca* work for *faltu* labourers.[114] They performed the same amount of work as regular labourers without receiving the benefit of 'concessions'. The growing surplus labour force in and around the tea gardens and, at the same time, the lack of any other avenue of livelihood might have created serious competition among them for seasonal employment in the plantations at lower wages. There was a significant gap between the numbers of the total labour force on the garden books and the numbers actually employed on a daily basis in the Assam Valley tea gardens (Appendix Table 5.16). This gap was increasingly filled by the availability of a large reserve army of unemployed labourers which could be exploited to keep the terms of employment within the control of employers. Moreover, given the subsistence level of agriculture in the province, casual employment in the gardens as a supplementary source of income became crucial.[115] This explains the willingness of such labourers to accept lower wages even during the peak season. And this helped the industry to keep down its wage bill.

From the above analysis of wage data, the following broad trends emerge. Between 1883 and 1900, the nominal wages of all categories of labourers often did not conform to the statutory minimum wage in Assam Valley. The nominal wages of Act labour remained stagnant and the overall increase, even in exceptional cases, was very insignificant. Similarly, the wages of non-Act labourers, though slightly higher than that of Act labourers, remained stagnant up to the period of World War I. There was an upward movement in the post-World War I period. The third decade of the twentieth century experienced a steady increase and nominal wages reached their highest in most cases by the end of that decade. However there was a sharp decline in nominal wages of non-Act labour from 1930 onwards. One possible reason for this decline was the worldwide depression of the early 1930s when employers cut down wages. The decline was further accentuated by the International Tea Control agreement among tea-producing countries which came into operation in 1933–34. The control restricted production, which in turn resulted in the reduction of work and consequently the earnings of labourers.[116] The planters further depressed wages by increasing employment of *faltu/basti* (temporary) labour during the 1930s and 1940s. The wages of temporary labourers were not published till 1934, but there is no reason to assume that they were higher than that of the permanent labour force. The wages paid to *faltu/basti* labour were lower compared to the average earnings of settled labour. This helped depress the overall wages of labour and keep the wage bill low for the industry as a whole. The wage trends showed recovery by the beginning of World War II and followed an upward movement but subject to fluctuations. However, the massive jump in the figures from 1945 to 1947 is a baffling feature of the wage increase that took place during and after World War II. Besides, at this juncture it seems appropriate to ask whether the periodical upward trend in nominal wages represented an increase in the real wages of the labour force in the Assam Valley tea gardens. We look for answers below by studying the level and cost of the standard of living of the labour force during the corresponding period, a task not as simple given the severe constraints of data.

Before we set about formulating the cost of living index of tea garden labourers, a comparison between plantation labour wages with those of agricultural labourers in the province would be instructive. The evidence on this is very limited and there is no way of examining its accuracy. Moreover we do not know whether the figures available represent lean or peak seasons. A comparison of two sets of wage figures of agricultural labourers in the province with wage figures of tea garden labourers shows higher earnings in former case. The first set of these figures for agricultural labour were published in the Prices and Wages in India series between 1900 and 1911. These figures were compiled by the district officials and they represented the average of the preceding six months' wages.[117] This set of figures, compared to the nominal wages of tea garden labourers (Appendix Table 5.7, Chart 5.15), shows that the wages of agricultural labourers outside the plantations were much higher. The second set of wage data on agricultural labour reported by Rege in 1944

CHART 5.15
*Yearly Averages of Monthly Earnings of Agricultural Labour
and Plantation Labour in Lakhimpur*

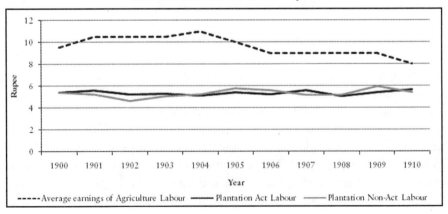

showed that the daily wages of agricultural labourers ranged between Rs 1.50 to Rs 2 in Lakhimpur, and Re 0.75 to Rs 1.25 in Sibsagar.[118]

Cost and Standard of Living

As late as 1946, Rege reported that there was no official cost of living index for the province of Assam. Around that time attempts were made to start family budget enquiries by the Director of Cost of Living Index Scheme in some districts of the province. However in the plantation areas even this type of enquiry was not undertaken. Rege observed that 'the absence of an authoritative cost of living index in Assam makes it difficult to assess accurately the fall in real wages of the plantation workers'.[119] The earliest attempt to properly conduct such an enquiry was made only in 1947, by S.R. Deshpande of the Labour Bureau of the Government of India. The official reports on emigrant labour in Assam, while publishing the figures of earnings of labourers in the tea gardens, never bothered to evaluate whether these earnings were good enough to meet the basic cost of living. Such apathy was perhaps due to the prevailing practice in the tea gardens of wages being partly paid in kind. That the practice of wages in kind had official sanction is clear from the provision for subsistence rations in the labour laws. And hence the assumption among the official circles that the tea garden labourers were being 'well-fed' by their employers, even though many of them were aware that the wages paid were below even the statutory minimum.

Harold Mann, the scientist official at Tocklai Tea Research Centre in Jorhat, was the first person to make an effort to work out the cost of the diet of tea garden labourers in Assam in 1906. Mann's data was extremely limited. It was not based on any proper or even general survey of consumption levels among the garden labourers. Instead he obtained the data on the basis of what was referred to as a 'hotel' diet in two gardens.[120] This 'hotel' diet included only limited items of simple food, like rice, *dal*, salt, spices, mustard oil, potatoes and onions. He did not include items of industrial consumption like clothing and expenditure on fuel in his estimates. Nevertheless, in the absence of any other source of information, Mann's estimates of the cost of a simple or subsistence diet for a labour family in tea gardens are very useful. The first formal official effort in this direction, to investigate the basic level of consumption, and the individual and family budgets of tea garden labourers, was made by the Enquiry Committee of 1921–22. These budgets showing the level and cost of consumption of a labour family or individual labourers were then compared with their levels of income. But most of these budgets were prepared either by local bureaucrats or by the planters themselves, who used very arbitrary methods to show compatibility between the expenditure and earnings of an individual labourer or a labour family. Even the Royal

Commission on Labour in India did not seriously enquire into the question of what constituted a fair living wage in the Assam tea gardens. A comparison of Mann's estimates with some of the moderate estimates of the Enquiry Committee of 1921–22 will be useful in analysing the extent of increase in the cost of subsistence and diet of tea garden labourers in Assam Valley.

Harold Mann estimated the cost of the 'hotel' diet of an adult labourer to be Rs 3.04 per month (taking the price of rice at Rs 3.00 per *maund*, equivalent to 37 kilograms). The diet consisted of rice, *dal*, salt, spices, mustard oil, potatoes and onion.[121] The Enquiry Committee in 1922 calculated the cost of exactly the same diet at Rs 5.49 per month for an adult labourer.[122] This represented an 81 per cent increase in the cost of monthly diet per adult labourer in the Assam Valley tea gardens between 1906 and 1922. As per the estimates of the Enquiry Committee of 1921–22, the cost of living of the tea garden labourers had increased by 44.4 per cent in Jorhat (Sibsagar), 50 per cent in Doom Dooma (Lakhimpur), and 50 to 75 per cent in Tezpur (Darrang) between the years 1913 and 1920.[123] The European accountant of the Empire of India Company in Tezpur had calculated the difference in the cost of living in 1920 as compared to 1913 at 100 per cent, taking the price of rice at current market rates. The Deputy Commissioner of Darrang thought that 75 per cent was a fairer figure.[124] The Enquiry Committee quoted the price of common rice (reported in Assam Gazette) for the years 1912–21, according to which the price of common rice increased by 91 per cent in Tezpur Sadr, 111 per cent in Mangaldai (Darrang), 96 per cent in Dibrugarh, 59 per cent in North Lakhimpur, 71 per cent in Sibsagar and 92 per cent in Jorhat (Sibsagar).[125] During the corresponding period, the combined nominal wages of non-Act labourers (men, women and children together) increased by 21, 26, 33, 7 and 18 per cent per cent in Lakhimpur, Sibsagar, Darrang, Nowgong and Kamrup, respectively (Appendix Table 5.3).

We have pointed out earlier that Assam lacked an authentic price index for the period under study. Data with regular survey-based prices of consumer goods, which could help in arriving at reasonable estimate of real wages, do not exist in Assam for the period under study. However, data on prices of foodgrain are available from diverse sources for different years. The major limitations of these data are: (i) no single source covers the entire period under study; and (ii) the data are restricted to the prices of rice and sugar (*gur*) only. Moreover, the categories of rice differ in different sources. For example, between 1900 and 1920, the annual reports on Prices and Wages in India published the retail and wholesale prices of rice (common), wheat, gram and salt in the district of Lakhimpur, and the average for the Brahmaputra Valley as a whole, separately. The data on prices of foodgrain in these reports were compiled from half-monthly statements from the districts, which were regularly published in the Gazette of India.[126] Sometimes, they were compiled from the fortnightly returns of selected markets in the province, furnished by local authorities and market reports published by Chambers of Commerce.[127] The second source of information on prices of the above-mentioned goods is the annual reports on the Administration of Land Revenue in Assam. These reports published the average prices for each district and sub-divisional headquarters separately. However, the figures were not published consistently or provided only a brief commentary on the prices of foodgrains in Assam Valley. And then we have K.L. Datta's report on the Enquiry into the Rise of Prices in India, 1914, which provided annual retail and wholesale prices of foodgrains and other articles of consumption in Assam. This report published figures up to 1912 for the prices of two categories of rice – ordinary and good rice.[128] The Enquiry Committee of 1921–22 published the annual averages of prices of common rice for the period 1912–21. These figures covered the districts and sub-divisional headquarters, and were calculated on the basis of average prices in the last fortnights of the months of January, April, July and October of each year provided in the Assam Gazette.[129] From post-World War I to 1947, our main source of prices of foodgrains is the officially published Agricultural Statistics of British India, but essentially for rice and raw sugar (*gur*) only. There are variations within this source: while for most of the years the figures quoted are average wholesale market prices during harvest time, in some years the prices quoted are based on 'median' average of harvest time. Secondly, harvest prices may not necessarily represent a fair average of the whole year. However, since the prices for the entire period are quoted on the basis of the harvest season, they may be taken as a fair indicator of general long-term trends. Thirdly, the price data were provided as provincial averages for 1917–18 and 1929–30, except in 1920–21 when separate figures for Lakhimpur were also given. The price of rice was reported under two categories, viz. 'winter rice cleared' and 'winter rice unhusked'. Acknowledging these constraints, we shall use these data to study the long-run trends in prices in Lakhimpur, one of the most important tea districts in Assam Valley, and the province as a whole.

Before we resume our analysis of the data on prices, it is important to ask whether a comparison of wage figures with the cost of foodgrains alone would be a fair indication of either decline or increase in real wages. Here two factors have to be taken into account. First, our evidence on the level and cost of consumption of goods other than foodgrains is superficial and scanty. Secondly, all the family or individual budgets reported by the 1921–22 Enquiry Committee and Deshpande's report uniformly demonstrate that a major portion of the total expenditure of a labour family was spent on the consumption of food. For example, in an annual budget of a labour family of five members (three adults, two children) in Suntak Tee garden in Sibsagar district, the cost of food consumption (rice, salt, oil, spices, fish, vegetables and milk) was as much as 78 per cent of the total expenditure. More significantly, out of this total expenditure on food, 94 per cent was on rice alone (Appendix Table 5.8). Similarly, a male and a female labourer in a Lakhimpur district tea garden spent 86 per cent and 74 per cent respectively on food (rice, mustard oil, *dal*, salt, spices and onion) out of their total annual expenditure.[130] A quarter of a century later, Deshpande's enquiry into the cost of living of Assam Valley's tea garden labourers revealed that food was still the major expense of a labour family consisting of 4.15 persons: 71.55 per cent of the total weekly expenditure.[131] In most of the budgets prepared by the Enquiry Committee of 1921–22, the expenditure on rice alone constituted 74 to 90 per cent of total food expenditure. In Deshpande's report, the cost of rice accounted for 64 per cent of the total food expenditure.[132]

Going back to the nineteenth century, the 1868 Commissioners had reported that rice was the dominant item of consumption in the labour diet of tea gardens. 'In very many gardens . . . coolies have been insufficiently nourished, not because the supply was scant or bad, but because it was not properly varied. Rice, to which their diet has been confined, however abundantly eaten, cannot support a human being in health for any length of time.'[133] They went on to emphasize that other basic food items like *dal*, oil, *ghee*, fish, etc., were beyond their means. A decade later, Dr DeRenzy and his successor Dr J.J. Clark, Sanitary Commissioners of Assam, were equally critical of the predominance of rice in the food intake of tea garden labourers because of their low earnings.[134] Clark minced no wards when he remarked: 'Rice is a poor food. A purely rice diet means, ill-health and a high death-rate, it means the loss of flesh and the loss of physical power, it means diarrhea, dysentery, scurvy, dropsy, inanition, failing powers and death.'[135] Thus, the cost of food remained the major expense of tea garden labourers in Assam Valley, which in itself was insufficient to maintain them in good health. Hence the validity of comparison between food prices and wages as a fair indication of an increase or decline in real wages.

We shall begin with an analysis of the data on prices of foodgrains given in the Prices and Wages series for the period 1900–20. Appendix Table 5.9 shows annual average retail prices of rice (common), wheat, gram and salt in the district of Lakhimpur and the averages for the Brahmaputra Valley (Assam Valley).[136] Charts 5.16 and 5.17 show the trends for Lakhimpur and Brahmaputra Valley respectively.

In Lakhimpur, the prices of rice, wheat and gram showed fluctuating tendencies throughout the period. The price of rice increased by 40 per cent during the first ten years (1900–09). Prices fell sharply in 1910 and 1911, followed by an upward movement from 1912 onwards. Though the upward movement of prices was not smooth, the increase between 1911 and 1920 was 106 per cent. During the first decade of the twentieth century, the price

CHART 5.16
Foodgrain Prices in Lakhimpur, 1900–20

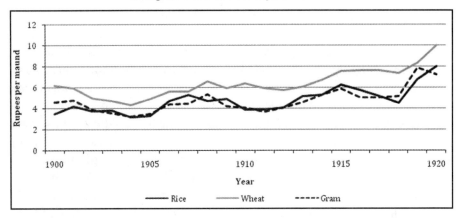

CHART 5.17
Foodgrain Prices in Assam Valley, 1900–20

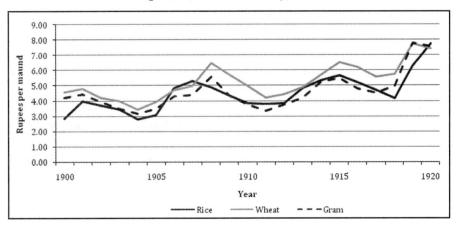

of wheat fluctuated with a tendency to decline. From 1911 onwards, it registered a constant upward movement, and increased by 98 per cent between 1911 and 1920. Similar tendencies were noticed in the case of gram. After a fluctuating first decade, its price increased by 88 per cent between 1911 and 1920. The prices of salt registered a downward trend right up to the outbreak of World War I. But during the war years salt prices increased and came up to the level of the early period. The overall increase was the highest in the case of rice, amounting to 128 per cent between 1900 and 1920. This represented an annual increase of 6.4 per cent. It was followed by a 62 per cent and 56 per cent increase in the prices of wheat and gram respectively during the corresponding period. This works out to an annual increase of 3.1 per cent in the case of wheat and 2.9 per cent for gram (Charts 5.16 and 5.17, and Appendix Table 5.9). The price movement of the above articles for the Assam Valley showed trends similar to those in Lakhimpur district.[137] But the percentage of increase in the former case was much higher in the case of rice, wheat and gram prices during the first decade.[138] The overall increase in Assam Valley prices between 1900 and 1920 was 169 per cent, 62 per cent and 72 per cent for rice, wheat and gram respectively (Appendix Table 5.9).

The above analysis of the price data shows two important trends. First, the percentage of increase in the prices of rice, wheat and gram was much higher during the second decade compared to the first decade. Secondly, the cost of these articles (the actual figures) was also the highest during the second decade. Another important feature was the fact that the increase in prices of rice was the highest among all the food items, while the price of salt declined during the first decade and then rose to its earlier level during the World War I years. Here, two crucial factors need to be noted. First, as pointed out earlier, expenditure on rice formed the major portion of the total value of food consumption, and the cost of food formed the bulk of the total expenditure of a labourer or labour family. Therefore, the extent of increase in the price of rice was the most important factor in determining the increase in the cost of living. Secondly, expenditure on salt accounted for only about 2 per cent of the total cost of food consumption, and therefore any increase or decrease in its cost was insignificant in determining the trend in the cost of living of a labour family in the Assam Valley tea gardens.[139]

A comparison of the movements in the prices of rice, wheat and gram with the movements of nominal wages of different categories of labourers shows that real wages declined in the Assam Valley tea plantations between 1900 and 1920. The overall wages of Act labourers (men and women combined) in Lakhimpur, Sibsagar and Darrang increased between 1900 and 1904–05, 1915–16 and 1919–20, by 11 per cent, 6 per cent and 25 per cent respectively, and of non-Act labourers (men, women and children combined) by 41 per cent, 30 per cent and 43 per cent respectively (Appendix Table 5.2 and Appendix Table 5.3). Compared to this, the combined increase in the prices of the above-mentioned articles between 1900–04 and 1916–20 was 57 per cent in Lakhimpur district and 59 per cent on average for the Brahmaputra Valley (Appendix Table 5.9). Even more interesting is the comparison between the two movements during the second decade, the period of World War I, when the tea industry was prospering. While the combined increase in nominal wages of non-Act labourers between 1910–14 end 1916–20 (men, women and children together) was only 20, 9 and 12 per cent in North Lakhimpur, Sibsagar and Darrang (Appendix Table 5.3) respectively, the combined increase in prices (rice, wheat and gram together) was 43 per cent in Lakhimpur and 44 per cent average in Assam Valley (Appendix Table 5.9).[140] Thus, while the nominal wages registered an upward movement, the real wages actually declined between 1900 and 1920. That the real wages in the tea gardens

TABLE 5.1
Nominal and Real Wages in Assam Tea Plantations[142]

Year	1895	1900	1905	1910	1912
Nominal	106	103	106	117	120
Real	101	96	90	98	95

declined during the early two decades of the twentieth century is also evident from other sources. For instance, K.L. Datta in 1914 reported a 5 per cent decline in real wages of tea garden labourers in Assam between 1900 and 1912 (Table 5.1). After comparing wages in different industries, Datta came to the conclusion that 'the coolies in tea gardens appear to be in the worst position'.[141]

Our only source of information for post-1920 price data is the Agricultural Statistics of British India. The price data from this source for the period 1920–30 are limited. Only the provincial averages of harvest prices are available for this period, and that too only for winter rice (both cleaned and unhusked) and raw sugar (*gur*). From 1930 onwards, however, the harvest prices of winter and autumn rice and raw sugar are quoted separately for two districts (Lakhimpur and Goalpara), and the averages for the province as a whole. Between 1921–22 and 1927–28, the prices of winter rice (unhusked) increased by 53 per cent and of winter rice (cleaned) by 33 per cent in Assam. The price of raw sugar, however, registered a decline of 22 per cent during the corresponding period (see Appendix Table 5.10).[143] The combined nominal wages of non-Act labourers (men, women and children together), on the other hand, increased only by 34, 29 and 26 per cent in North Lakhimpur, Sibsagar and Darrang respectively, in the corresponding period (Appendix

CHART 5.18
Harvest Prices of Winter Rice and Gur in Assam, 1921–22 to 1929–30

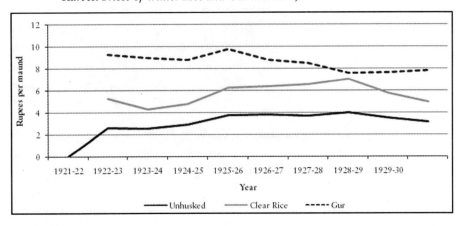

Table 5.3). In other words, despite an increase in nominal wages, real wages continued to decline in the early 1920s. But the decline in real wages was not as sharp as was the case in the second decade. Chart 5.18 (Appendix Table 5.10) shows the upward trends in price of rice (of both categories) up to 1927–28 and then the decline in the next two years. The price of unhusked rice declined by 27 per cent and of clear rice by 41 per cent, but the raw sugar price increased by 3 per cent between 1927–28 and 1929–30. During corresponding years, the combined nominal wages of non-Act labourers (men, women and children) registered a marginal increase of 3 per cent in Lakhimpur, but remained stagnant in Sibsagar and declined by 2 per cent in Darrang (Appendix Table 5.3). The prices of rice and wheat were generally higher in Lakhimpur compared to the provincial figures which would have nulified this marginal increase (Appendix Tables 5.9, 5.10 and 5.11), but the higher percentage of price decline does indicate a marginal increase in real wages. However the trend reversed quickly as the combined nominal wages of non-Act labourers (men, women and children) declined by 21 per cent, 6 per cent and 21 per cent in Lakhimpur, Sibsagar and Darrang respectively, between 1930 and 1932 (Appendix Table 5.3).

During and after the depression years, there was a general tendency of decline and stagnation in both prices of foodgrain and wages in the Assam Valley, right up to the beginning of World War II (Charts 5.19 and 5.20, and Appendix Table 5.11).[144] The wages were further depressed by the increasing employment of *basti/faltu* labour at still lower wages by the planters. From the beginning of World War II, prices of almost all varieties of rice and raw sugar showed a very sharp and secular upward movement. The price increase was massive: winter and autumn rice jumped by 369 and 213 per cent respectively in Lakhimpur district, and by 286 and 312 per cent respectively in Assam

CHART 5.19
Harvest Prices of Winter, Autumn Rice and Gur in Lakhimpur, 1931–47

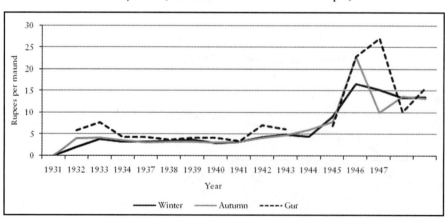

CHART 5.20
Harvest Prices of Winter, Autumn Rice and Gur in Assam Valley, 1931–47

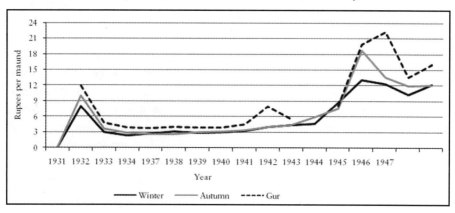

Valley between 1939 and 1945. The price of *gur* went up by 617 and 382 per cent in Lakhimpur and Assam Valley respectively during the corresponding period (Appendix Table 5.11; Charts 5.19 and 5.20). In comparison, the combined nominal wages of men, women and children who were settled labourers increased by 4, 23 and 24 per cent in Lakhimpur, Sibsagar and Darrang districts respectively, between 1939 and 1945 (Appendix Table 5.4; Charts 5.12, 5.13 and 5.14).[145]

Rege reported that the Government of India had conducted family budget enquiries through the office of the Director of the Cost of Living Index Scheme in Silchar, Gauhati and Tinsukia (some of the important towns in the vicinity of plantations in Assam) during 1939–45. The purpose behind this enquiry was to compile cost of living index numbers for the three centres. As per the findings of this enquiry, the cost of rice, *dal*, vegetables and mustard oil increased by 337, 367, 300 and 371 per cent respectively in Gauhati, and 356, 333, 538 and 371 per cent respectively in Tinsukia.[146] Similar trends of prices prevailed in the plantation areas too.[147] Rege estimated that the cost of living of Assam tea garden labourers had gone up by at least 200 per cent between 1939 and 1945. On the other hand, their earnings (including cash value of concessions in foodstuffs and cloth) had increased by only 82 per cent in the corresponding period.[148]

From the above analysis of movements of wages and prices in the Assam Valley tea plantations during colonial rule, the following conclusions emerge. During the first decade, wages remained more or less stagnant, while the prices of food articles showed a slight increase. In the second decade, nominal wages showed an upward movement but could not keep up with the increase in prices. Therefore, the first two decades experienced a decline in the real wages of the labourers. The decline in real wages was sharper during the second decade despite a high rate of increase in the nominal wages during and after

World War I. During the third decade, real wages continued to decline till 1926–27. Prices declined in the next two years while nominal wages continued to rise. In other words, for the first time, the increase in nominal wages actually represented an increase in real wages. The depression of the 1930s affected both prices and wages, and there was a sharp decline in both. The decline in prices was slightly high compared to that of wages in the 1930s. However, the possibility of even slight benefits was neutralized by the increasing employment of *faltu* or *basti* labourers, whose wages were much lower compared to those of settled labourers – which further depressed the overall wages. World War II created a boom for the tea industry and nominal wages also experienced a constant upward movement, reaching the highest figures of all time in 1947. But the war also created inflationary tendencies in prices and the price increase was massive. As a result, real wages declined very sharply.

Living Conditions of Labourers

An obvious result of the constant decline in real wages of the tea garden labourers in Assam Valley was their appallingly low standard of living. The employment of a large number of children is a clear indication that the earnings of adult workers were not enough even for the subsistence of a labour family. During the early decades of the opening up of tea plantations and till the end of the nineteenth century the mortality rates among labourers was appallingly high in Assam.[149] The district officials' lamentation and expression of serious concern failed to change the situation. The last three decades of the nineteenth century witnessed a frenetic expansion of acreage under tea, clearing up of vast areas of jungle, and intensification of labour for increasing production through a labour force subjected to an extremely precarious existence – low earnings and consequently poor nourishment took a heavy toll of human lives. Hard labour, imbalanced diets, and unsanitary and poor living conditions made them increasingly vulnerable to diseases. The worst affected were the new arrivals in the tea gardens, as per the official reports. The official reports on immigration published statistical information on mortality and desertions in the tea gardens. The cautionary notes of the district officials in these reports clearly reflected their scepticism about the accuracy of the statistics of mortality and desertions as provided by the planters under the labour laws. They suspected under-reporting by the planters, and reported instances of planters fudging the figures in order to avoid detection of irregularities committed under the labour laws. The Chief Commissioner of Assam reported:

> It is a well known fact that on some gardens where it is considered that the mortality among Act labourers is too high, i.e., where through the high death-rate it is

feared that a committee may be assembled or some disagreeable result may ensue, a number of healthy free labourers are put under the Act, solely for the purpose of increasing the number of Act labourers and thereby decreasing the percentage of mortality among them.[150]

Shlomowitz and Brennan's detailed quantitative study of the vital statistics of emigrant labourers in the Assam tea gardens give primacy to epidemiological factors for the high mortality. They have shown, on the basis of official data, that after a very heavy death toll during the 1860s, mortality rates declined in the subsequent years. They attribute this decline to the 'seasoning' process in building immunity and resistance among the immigrants to diseases, and improvement in transport facilities, administrative and health reforms in the gardens by the colonial state and the employers.[151] This explanation is based on uncritical acceptance of the official assertions of these claims despite suspecting the accuracy of the official data. Evidence from other official sources challenges these claims; evidence that they overlooked in their study.

In her perceptive study of colonial Punjab, Sheila Zurbrigg has raised issue with epidemiological factors as the cause of high mortality. She has shown that lack of a balanced diet due to high prices of foodgrain and consequent undernourishment made the marginalized poor more susceptible to high mortality by malaria. In support of her thesis, she cites contemporary official sanitation reports attributing poor health and high mortality to high foodgrain prices. She points out that undernutrition compromises the effectiveness of the body's immune system, an effect which heightens mortality for a number of infectious diseases.[152] Similarly, in Assam, Sanitary Commissioners like Dr DeRenzy and some of his successors, during the 1870s and early 1880s, clearly established the connection between imbalanced diets and malnutrition, and low income among tea garden labourers.[153] With the persistence of low incomes which prevented access to quality food and dependence on rice as the dominant intake in their daily diet, undernourishment remained a generational health feature of tea garden labourers in Assam. The observations on the health status of Assam tea garden labourers by medical and other official experts during the 1930s and 1940s point to the persistence of malnutrition. In contrast to the stereotype of 'well-fed' labour presented by the planters and various official reports, Rege's observations in as late as 1946 revealed a stark picture of their lives:

> The standard of living of tea garden labourers in Assam is appallingly low. They merely exist. They have hardly any belongings except a few clothes (mostly tattered) and a few pots (mostly earthen). Their womenfolk have no jewelry except German silver bangles in a few cases. Their houses presented a picture of stark poverty.'[154]

Subsequently even Deshpande, whose report was generally appreciated by the

Indian Tea Association, presented a similar picture: 'Speaking generally, the workers on the Assam tea plantations are very scantily clothed and children generally go about naked. Most of the workers and their families walk about bare-footed.'[155]

The annual official reports on emigrant labour in Assam published vital statistics every year. The information on vital statistics of labourers, like wage returns, was provided by the planters and reproduced in the official reports without any scrutiny regarding their accuracy. This practice continued throughout the period of our study. It took a long time before someone in the bureaucracy raised issue on this practice by dispatching a confidential letter to the Government of India. He pointed to the absence of any government agency for the registration of births and deaths in the tea gardens, and the total dependence on planters for this information.[156] We have presented the official time-series about mortality rates among tea garden labourers in the Assam Valley districts in Appendix Tables 5.12, 5.13 and 5.14. Appendix Table 5.12 covers adult labour for the period between 1882 and 1899, and Appendix Table 5.13 covers Act and non-Act adult labourers for the period 1900 to 1932, while Appendix Table 5.14 covers settled labourers for the years 1934–47. The data in Appendix 5.12 cover adult labour in general, and not Act and Non-Act labour separately, because official reports published the statistics inconsistently for those years. Compared to the figures of the 1860s, these figures certainly showed a decline in mortality, but even this rate of mortality was unacceptably high and the officials often lamented this fact. This is not surprising considering the frenetic pace of expansion and increase in production through labour-intensive strategies, and below-subsistence wages, particularly during the last two decades of the nineteenth century. The official data show that mortality among non-Act labourers was lower than among Act labourers, and a declining trend in the twentieth century. However there are sporadic sets of figures, also officially published, which show higher mortality. For example, official statistics for some of the tea gardens for the years 1919–20 and 1920–21 (based on field surveys) showed that the mortality figures in the regular time-series were much lower (Table 5.2 and Table 5.4). The year 1918–19 witnessed a phenomenal increase in the rate of mortality, which was attributed to the outbreak of cholera and influenza in the tea districts by the Chief Commissioner of Assam and later by the Labour Enquiry Committee of 1921–22.[157] While the official time-series showed declining mortality among tea garden labourers, it was still high compared to the trend in the general population living outside the gardens in the province (Table 5.3).

Besides, the qualitative evidence points to a glaring picture of the health and living conditions of labourers on the gardens. The Royal Commission reported persistence of infections playing an important part in lowering the standards of health and physique, and in causing most of the sickness in Assam's plantation areas. A large number of tea garden labourers were infected with hookworm because of highly inadequate arrangements for latrines.[160] Official supervision of the health and welfare of plantation labourers hardly existed. The Royal Commission noted that 'In Assam, the Director of Public Health has apparently little or no contact with the plantations, as he is neither an official inspector of factories, nor has the right to inspect plantations'.[161] The incidence of malnutrition and consequent deterioration in health were particularly high during the years of the two World Wars because of the extremely high cost of living and low wages. Rege reported that between 1941 and 1944, the death rate increased while the birth rate declined among the tea garden population.[162] Reports based on proper medical investigation were brought out only from the late 1930s onwards. In one of these reports Dr Lappying stated that malnutrition was widespread in the tea districts of Assam Valley. He attributed this to the economic inability of the labourers to purchase food rather than to any real shortage. In December 1943, K.C. Dutta, Assistant Commissioner of Labour, Assam, surveyed nearly 73 gardens in both Valleys, and reported that there was malnutrition amongst labourers in most of the tea estates, and that this was due to high prices and scarcity of the articles of food containing fats and vitamins.[163] However, this was not a war-time phenomenon only. In 1938 and 1939, the All India Institute of Public Health and Hygiene had carried out diet and physique surveys among Assam's tea labourers and cultivators in certain areas of Bengal. The surveys showed that the diet of Assam tea labourers was deficient both in quantity

TABLE 5.2

Statement Showing the Death Rate in some of the Tea Estates in Darrang District for 1919–20 and 1920–21[158]

Year	Name of Garden	Ratio per mills
1919–20	Dhekiajuli Tea Estate	99.18
	Shamuguri Tea Estate	193.35
	Panchnoi Tea Estate	131.96
	Dalhousie Tea Eatate	113.44
	Dufflagur Tea Estate	94.97
	Hirajuli Anuja Tea Estate	79.36
	Kherkheria Tea Estate	138.00
1920–21	Tarajuli Tea Estate	84.39
	Dhekiajuli Tea Estate	80.32
	Dalhousie Tea Estate	133.75
	Bermajan Tea Estate	165.93
	Groanland Tea Estate	127.89
	Kabira Tea Estate	101.01

TABLE 5.3
Comparison of Death Rate among Tea Garden Labourers and General Population
in the Province of Assam[159]

(per thousand population)

Year	Tea Gardens	Province
1939	21.79	19.25
1940	20.94	17.20
1941	18.72	16.75
1942	19.21	15.42
1943	25.42	16.24
1944	28.27	16.87

TABLE 5.4
Vital Statistics of 17 European-Owned Tea Estates Surveyed in Assam[168]

Live birth rate per 1000	Infantile mortality per 1000 live births	Maternal mortality per 1000
28.8	189.1	38.3
31.6	37.33	58.3
29.9	216.2	50.0
38.1	106.0	35.3
24.4	125.5	18.4
32.2	193.4	58.4
32.1	156.1	54.2
34.0	127.2	27.5
36.4	148.1	17.2
31.2	202.5	24.8
28.4	231.0	22.8
22.6	166.5	34.1
21.5	189.0	40.1
28.3	206.2	32.4
32.8	297.0	46.3
34.7	158.4	22.1
31.2	147.3	18.2
Total 514.2	Total 3,196.8	Total 598.4
Average: 30.2	Average: 188.0	Average: 35.2

and quality, and the nutrition and development of the children lower than that of other classes. The daily calorie intake of an Assam boy labourer of seven years was 1,090, as against the recommended 1,600 to 2,100 calories.[164]

Even more damaging was the information collected by E. Llyod Jones, the Deputy Director General, Indian Medical Services, in his report on the standard of medical care in tea plantations in India. Undernourishment and general weakness were evident among the people working in the gardens or walking along the roads. 'There seemed a general lack of vitality. Children were rarely seen running about or playing. They ambled along like old men.' Lloyd-Jones observed that the vast majority of patients attending outside treatment were undernourished and anemic.[165] Statistics obtained from seventeen European-owned gardens in Assam by Lloyd Jones showed that the infant mortality rate in 1946 was 168.8 per 1,000 births, and maternal mortality 26.8 per 1,000 live births (Table 5.4).[166] Among the causes listed by him for all this were malaria, bad water supply, lack of proper conservancy methods, poor housing and poor standard of nutrition of the labourers.[167]

The Enquiry Committee of 1921–22 had cautioned that the vital statistics for the tea gardens must be accepted with considerable reservation. The explanation for this caution was that the reporting agency for areas outside the municipalities was undoubtedly defective and unreliable. It was pointed out that despite the efforts to improve, 'there are instances in which figures reported are incredibly low, notably in the case of deaths of children'.[169] However such complaints fell on deaf ears, and deaths among tea garden labourers in the province continued to be under-reported. This is borne out by the fact that even as late as 1946, Llyod Jones' survey reported that many of the doctors were not familiar with the commonly accepted methods of maintaining vital statistics. For example, the figures supplied on infantile mortality represented the number of infant deaths per thousand of population instead of the number of infant deaths per thousand live births, which was the accepted definition of infantile mortality rate.[170] It was pointed out that figures collected through the survey (Table 5.4) were confirmed by reference to the daily attendance sheets, and the births and deaths registers, and therefore may be accepted as reasonably accurate.

Thus, to sum up, the picture that emerged from the above study was not one of a 'comfortable' and 'well-fed' labour force in the Assam Valley tea gardens. Their health status as reported by official medical and other experts are not compatible with the declining mortality figures published in the official time-series. Though nominal wages increased over time, real wages actually declined.[171] Through mechanisms of 'wage agreement', 'labour-rules', 'standardization', etc., the labourers were regularly underpaid. This created a situation of undernourishment and malnutrition, which in turn led to increasing sickness and disease heightening mortality. The situation became worse during periods of extremely high prices. However, to keep the labour force alive and working, the systems of advances and 'concessions' (subsidized rations, land for private cultivation) proved useful to the employers. Instead of paying a viable market wage it was the practice of wages in kind that appeared to be the major feature of capital–labour relations in the Assam Valley tea gardens. And this in an industry which, barring a few hiccoughs, had achieved spectacular growth and profitability, as we shall see below.

Indices of Growth of Tea Plantations

Assam Valley tea plantations recovered from the collapse of the 'tea mania' boom in the 1870s and grew spectacularly during the last two decades of the nineteenth century, and continued to expand steadily till well into the 1940s. Being predominantly an export-oriented enterprise, the Indian tea industry as a whole had to constantly face the challenges of fluctuating fortunes in the international market. However it survived and thrived despite severe price fluctuations caused by periodic global depressions and the two World Wars. In this section, we analyse various indices of growth of Assam Valley's tea plantations, including trends in acreage expansion, labour employment and production. The land grants and expansion of tea plantation in the early decades have already been discussed in chapter 1. From the latter half of the 1870s, official publication of statistical information on acreage, labour immigration and employment, production, export, prices, etc. acquired regularity and consistency, though the problem of accuracy remained a concern. From the mid-1880s district-wise data were published in the annual reports on production of tea and labour reports by the Government of Assam.

Acreage Expansion

The generous terms of the land grants offered by the colonial state encouraged the tea industry to garner a vast expanse of wastelands for its future growth. J. Edgar estimated in 1872 that the Indian tea industry was already in control of 804,582 acres of wasteland in the tea-producing areas, out of which only approximately 70,341 acres were actually under cultivation – less than 10 per cent of the total area held. He reported the area under tea cultivation in the districts of Assam Valley as follows: 3,943 acres in Lakhimpur, 12,980 acres in Sibsagar, 6,095 acres in Darrang, 2,154 acres in Nowgong and 1,498 acres in Kamrup. He estimated that tea plantations in the Assam Valley controlled a total acreage of 364,990 wastelands, out of which only 26,853 acres were under cultivation – about 8 per cent of the total area. However his estimates differed from another report of 1873–74, partly because he did not receive all the information from the planters.[172] After 1874 we do not have the district-wise data on acreage and production for the next decade and more. Appendix Table 5.15 and Chart 5.21 show the area under tea cultivation in the Assam Valley, and in Lakhimpur, Sibsagar, Darrang, Nowgong and Kamrup districts between 1872 and 1947.

The most important characteristic features of tea acreage growth in the Assam Valley districts between 1872 and 1947 were as follows: (i) the bulk of acreage expansion took place during the last three decades of the nineteenth century; (ii) the acreage under tea cultivation did not exceed more than 15 to 35 per cent of the total area in the possession of planters (Appendix Table

CHART 5.21
Acreage under Tea Cultivation in Assam Valley Districts, 1872–1947

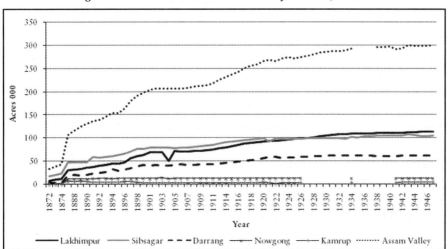

4.1). Large areas of forest and wastelands remained under the control of the planters throughout the period of our study. The expansion in the next over four decades was comparatively modest. In Lakhimpur, the acreage expanded by 1327.8 per cent at an annual rate of 17.7 per cent between 1872 and 1947. Most of this growth, 702 per cent, took place between 1872 and 1899, at an annual rate of 24 per cent. The increase between 1901 and 1947 was 64 per cent at an annual rate of 1.4 per cent. In Sibsagar, the acreage expanded by 501 per cent during 1872–1947, at an annual rate of 6.7 per cent. The major part of this expansion, 353 per cent, took place between 1872 and 1899, at an annual rate of 12.2 per cent. The area expansion in this district between 1901 and 1947 was 32.7 per cent, at an annual rate of 0.7 per cent only. In Darrang, the acreage growth was 1703 per cent at an annual rate of 38.6 per cent between 1872 and 1947. Here too, the bulk of the area expansion, 1120.6 per cent, was between 1871 and 1899, at an annual rate of 38.6 per cent. The acreage expansion was only 51.7 per cent between 1901 and 1947, at a modest annual rate of 1.1 percent.

Tea plantations were not a dominant enterprise in Nowgong and Kamrup districts of Assam Valley compared to the above three districts. In Nowgong, the acreage expanded by 430.4 per cent at an annual rate of 5.7 per cent between 1872 and 1947. The expansion percentage, 460 per cent, was even higher during 1872–99 at an annual rate of 15.9 per cent. However this expansion was mostly in the earlier period. There was stagnation with declining trends in acreage expansion between 1901 and 1947. In Kamrup, the acreage expanded by 114.2 per cent between 1872 and 1947 at an annual rate of 1.52 per cent. The bulk of this expansion, 81 per cent, took place during 1872 and 1899 at an annual rate of 2.3 per cent. The acreage expansion was 19 per cent only, at a very modest annual rate of 0.4 per cent, between 1901 and 1947.

Overall acreage in the Assam Valley expanded by 804.2 per cent between 1872 and 1947, at an annual rate of 10.7 per cent. The acreage increase between 1872 and 1899 was 496.4 per cent at an annual rate of 17.11 per cent; and 46.7 per cent between 1901 and 1947, at an annual rate of 1 per cent only (Appendix Table 5.15 and Chart 5.21).

Labour Employment

The trends in the rate of labour employment, compared to that of production and acreage expansion, were for more complex. Among the notable features was large-scale employment of women and children as labourers in the Assam Valley tea plantations. They formed almost 50 per cent of the labour force. Women labourers were paid less than men, and children were paid less than women. This structure of wages and employment had been statutorily legalized by the colonial state at the very inception of the tea industry. Secondly, there are two sets of data published in the official reports. The provincial labour immigration reports published data on importation and total number of labourers employed on the gardens from the mid-1870s. The tea production reports, on the other hand, published data on employment of 'permanent' and 'temporary' labour on the tea gardens from 1891 onwards. While the immigration reports provided detailed information on labour relations, wages, vital statistics and other aspects of plantation employment, the production reports barely gave any explanation for the variations in the quantitative data on labour employment, acreage and production. For example, no information was given about the composition of 'temporary' labour, their wages and terms of employment. In 1918, the Indian Tea Association added further confusion and classified the labour force into three categories: (1) Garden Labour (Permanent), i.e. those working and living on the gardens; (2) Garden Labour (Temporary), i.e. those working regularly on the garden but living outside it; (3) Outside Labour (Temporary), i.e. all those not falling under (1) and (2).[173] This classification found its way into the official reports from 1919 onwards without any explanation except to state 'revision of form for showing number of garden labourers and methods of calculating that number'.[174] Another important feature of labour employment was the constant import of fresh immigrant labourers. Regular employment of temporary/*basti* labour indicated the emergence of a surplus labour force in and around the plantations. However, the planters continued to import fresh labour every year right through the period of our study and even afterwards.[175]

The reports from the early 1870s show sizeable employment of local labourers along with immigrants in the Assam Valley tea gardens. In 1873, the number of immigrant and local labourers employed was reported as 7,215 and 2,779 respectively in Lakhimpur, 15,234 and 11,341 in Sibsagar, 1,911 and 3,165 in Darrang. In 1874, the number of immigrant and local labourers employed increased to 7,936 and 2,676 in Lakhimpur, 17,788 and 5,608 in Sibsagar, and 2,571 and 2,419 in Darrang respectively.[176] However, since then references to local labour disappeared from official reportage. From 1891 the annual production reports published figures for two categories of labour employment: 'permanent' and 'temporary'. These figures were lower than those published in the provincial immigration reports, which were calculated on the basis of numbers in the garden books. The Chief Commissioner's office did not consider these figures trustworthy since they did not reconcile with those published in the provincial immigration reports, and suggested that the latter figures should be accepted as more accurate.[177] The confusion got cleared only when, from 1903 onwards, it was mentioned in the statements that these figures represented the daily average strength of the labour force on tea gardens and not the total numbers on the garden books.[178] From 1934 the Controller of Emigrant Labour began to publish both sets of detailed figures separately in the same statement, which allow us to make a comparison of the proportionate strengths (Appendix Table 5.16). What is interesting to note is the disappearance of the category of temporary from the official statements. Now, temporary labour appeared in a new incarnation of *basti/faltu* labour, and their wages began to be published separately. It indicated the larger-scale employment of the reserve labour force settled around the plantations as temporary hands at lower wages and with no employment benefits. From Appendix Table 5.16 it appears that the there was a gap ranging from 8 per cent to 30 per cent between the total number of labourers on the books and the daily average strength of the labour force in Assam Valley plantations.

Appendix Table 5.17 and Chart 5.22 show the total numbers of the labour force, both working and non-working, and including children, in the Assam Valley, and in Lakhimpur, Sibsagar, Darrang, Nowgong and Kamrup districts, between 1877 and 1947. The long-term increase in the labour force main-tained a secular upward trend between 1877 and 1947 in all the districts of Assam Valley. In Lakhimpur it was 1150.7 per cent between 1877 and 1947 at an annual rate of 16.4 per cent; the increase during 1877 and 1899 was 399 per cent at an annual rate of 17.4 per cent; the increase during 1901 and 1947 was 210 per cent at an annual rate of 4.4 per cent. In Sibsagar, the long-term increase between 1877 and 1947 was 649 per cent at an annual rate of 9.2 per cent; the increase between 1877 and 1899 was 258 per cent at an annual rate of 11.22 per cent; during the course of 1901–47 the labour force increased by 126 per cent at an annual rate of 2.7 per cent. The overall increase in Darrang was 1737 per cent between 1877 and 1947, the highest among all the districts, and at an annual rate of 24.8 per cent. A major part of this increase took place between 1877 and 1899, 684 per cent, at an annual rate of 30 per cent. The increase during 1901–47 was less spectacular, 134 per

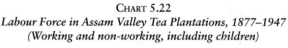

CHART 5.22
Labour Force in Assam Valley Tea Plantations, 1877–1947
(Working and non-working, including children)

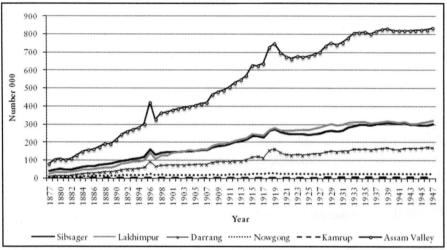

cent, at an annual rate of 2.9 percent. In Nowgong, the long-term increase in the labour force during 1877–1947 was 843 per cent, at an annual rate of 12 per cent. Here too the increase was very impressive between 1877 and 1899, 592 per cent at an annual rate of 25.8 per cent. The increase between 1901 and 1947 was modest, 46 per cent, at an annual rate of 1 per cent. The long-term increase in the labour force in Kamrup was 750 per cent during 1877–1947. The major part of this increase, 325 per cent, took place during 1877–99 at an annual rate of 14.1 per cent. By comparison, the increase during 1901–47 of 112.5 per cent was modest, at an annual rate of 2.55 per cent only. And finally, the long-term increase in the labour force in the Assam Valley as a whole was 959.2 per cent between 1877 and 1947, at an annual rate of 13.7 per cent. Following the general trends in the districts, the increase between 1877 and 1899 was 365.7 per cent at an annual rate of 15.9 per cent. The increase during 1901–47 was 119.9 per cent at an annual rate of 2.55 per cent (Appendix Table 5.17 and Chart No 5.22).

The data on labour employment presented and analysed above show the following trends. First, labour employment increased progressively and reached the highest numbers during the 1940s. Second, the percentage of increase in labour employment was fairly consistent with that of production and acreage expansion in the corresponding periods. The rate of labour employment was in sync with the massive expansion of acreage and increase in production during the last three decades of the nineteenth century. Like in acreage and production, the percentage of increase was the highest during these years. The twentieth century witnessed a steady but comparatively modest increase in labour employment. As to the repeated complaints of shortage of labour supply, enough evidence has been presented above to show that it had no basis. It is true that at the early stage the tea industry faced a problem of procuring adequate labour locally. This necessitated recruitment of labour from other areas, which started the process of immigration. However, by the early twentieth century, as a result of continuous, uninterrupted sponsored immigration of labour into Assam, supported by the colonial policy of the Government of Assam, the tea industry had surplus labour available for employment.[179]

Production

Remarkable growth of production was the most striking aspect of the history of the tea industry in the Assam Valley. District-wise production figures began to be published after the mid-1880s. We have district figures for a few years in the early 1870s. In 1872, an estimated 1.5, 3.8, 1, 0.32 and 0.03 million lbs of tea were produced in Lakhimpur, Sibsagar, Darrang, Nowgong and Kamrup, respectively. Assam Valley as a whole produced approximately 7 million lbs of tea.[180] Appendix Table 5.18 shows the growth of tea production in Assam Valley districts and the province as a whole between 1872 and 1947. Chart 5.23 shows the same for Assam Valley, and Lakhimpur, Sibsagar, Darrang, Nowgong and Kamrup districts. The figures also show that the growth of tea production far exceeded the increase in acreage and labour employment in all the districts of Assam Valley.

The long-term growth of production of tea was spectacular and the maximum increase took place during the last three decades of the nineteenth century. In Lakhimpur, production increased by 7200 per cent between 1872 and 1947 at an annual rate of 96 per cent. The increase between 1872 and 1900

CHART 5.23
Production of Tea in Assam Valley, 1872–1947

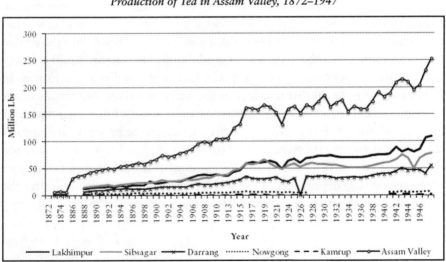

was the highest for the entire period – 1420 per cent at an annual rate of 50.7 per cent. Between 1901 and 1947 the rate of increase was 311.3 per cent at an annual rate of 20 per cent. Sibsagar experienced 1514 per cent production growth between 1872 and 1947, at an annual rate of 20 per cent. Between 1872 and 1900 production increased by 663 percent at an annual rate of 23.7 per cent. Between 1901 and 1947 there was a steady increase of 190 per cent at an annual rate of 4 per cent. In Darrang, the long-term increase was 3410 per cent, achieved at an annual rate of 45 per cent between 1872 and 1947. The production increase was 1410 per cent during 1872–1900 at an annual rate of 51 per cent, and 129 per cent at an annual rate of 2.8 per cent between 1901 and 1947. In Nowgong, the overall increase between 1872 and 1947 was 1933 per cent at an annual rate of 34.7 per cent. Most of this growth, 1332 per cent, took place between 1872 and 1900 at an annual rate of 47.6 per cent. Production increased by 80 per cent between 1901 and 1947 at an annual rate of 1.7 per cent. In Kamrup, the increase between 1872 and 1947 amounted to 800 per cent at an annual rate of 10.6 per cent. Between 1872 and 1900 there was 156.6 per cent increase at an annual rate of 5.6 per cent. In this case the major increase, 328 per cent, took place between 1901 and 1947 at an annual rate of 7 per cent. And finally, the Assam Valley as a whole experienced 3574 per cent increase in production between 1872 and 1947 at an annual rate of 47.6 per cent. The increase amounted to 991.3 per cent during 1872–1900 at an annual rate of 35.4 per cent. The increase between 1901 and 1947 amounted to 250 per cent at an annual rate of 5.3 per cent (Appendix Table 5.18 and Chart 5.23).

The production figures in Appendix Table 5.18 for the years between 1872 and 1947 show fluctuations for certain years (Chart 5.23). The production reports do not mention any specific reasons for these fluctuations. Minor fluctuations could be explained in terms of fine plucking which improved the quality of tea but restricted production in some years. The demand generated by the outbreak of World War I expanded production.[181] Soon after the war, in 1920–22, there was a sharp decline in production. Two factors could possibly explain this: (i) post-war depression which also affected other industries in India, and (ii) political disturbances in the wake of strikes and mass exodus of labour from the Assam tea gardens, in protest against low wages and poor living conditions.[182] From 1922 onwards once again the production figures of tea followed an upward trend. The second instance of decline in production was during the early 1930s. The sole cause of this decline was the impact of the worldwide depression of the 1930s. The situation improved after the mid-1930s and from then on, production rose constantly.

Fluctuations in Tea Prices

The massive growth of tea acreage, production and labour employment in the Assam Valley took place in the face of constant fluctuation of tea prices (Appendix Table 5.19 and Chart 5.24). Being predominantly an export-oriented enterprise, the Indian tea industry had to constantly grapple with these phenomena which were beyond its control. The highest percentage of increase in production and acreage expansion during the last three decades of the nineteenth century took place, as pointed out earlier, against the backdrop of declining prices of tea in the international market. In the face of this decline, the planters pushed for massive production by intensifying labour. It was also during this period that Indian tea exports to Britain overtook China.[183]

Official reports, our main source of quantitative information, do not offer much by way of explanation. On the other hand an analysis of the price movement of Indian tea sold at Calcutta auctions is helpful since the fluctuations in production and acreage trends were very much interlinked with the movement of prices. Throughout its history, the prices of Indian tea experienced a series of instabilities. There were periods of very high prices followed by decline and sometimes slumps. Appendix 5.19 and Chart 5.24 show the average prices of Indian tea sold at Calcutta auctions, and the index variation between 1900 and 1947. The years immediately after World War I and during the Great Depression of the early 1930s were two situations when a slump followed a period of high prices. Similar situations had occurred on at least three occasions earlier in the nineteenth century, in 1866, 1879 and 1896.[185] Excess supply caused by overproduction was widely believed to be the major cause in most cases.[186] Thus it will appear that the prices of tea were determined by the supply factor. However, at the same time, the

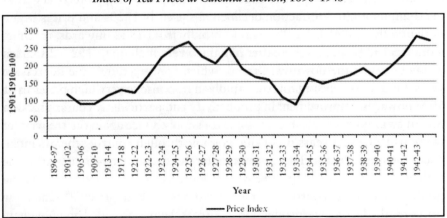

CHART 5.24
Index of Tea Prices at Calcutta Auction, 1896–1943[184]

evidence shows that at least on two occasions, demand fluctuations played the determining rule. The high prices of Indian tea in the World War I and II years were largely due to the bulk purchase policy introduced by the Government of the United Kingdom. During World War I the British Ministry of Food entered into contracts with tea producers (both in India and Ceylon) for buying the bulk of their tea. The prices were fixed on the basis of averages of two pre-war years and the increase in the average cost was added to it. Similar arrangements were made during World War II.[187] The immediate result was an increase in production in response to the high prices. This was achieved through expansion in acreage and increased productivity. Thus the high rate of increase in tea production and acreage under tea during the World War I years is explained by an increase in prices following growing demand. Extension of acreage and rise in productivity in response to high prices, over a long period, led to overproduction. The expansion in acreage during such periods of high prices created problems of excess capacity once the increased supply appeared on the market after a normal gestation period of six to seven years. Soon after World War I such a situation arose and it was made worse when, in the spring of 1919, the British government decontrolled tea and released its stocks into the market. Stocks began to accumulate both at the producing points as well as in London. Besides, shipping difficulties and the loss of some markets due to the war added to the problems. Stocks in London jumped from 145 million lbs in November 1919 to 213 million lbs in December 1919. By 1920 the prices of tea fell sharply, in both the Calcutta and London auctions (Chart 5.24).[188]

The failure of demand to rise sufficiently to absorb the extra production in the immediate post-World War I period necessitated control over supply in order to keep prices remunerative. This control was exercised not by regulating the volume of export alone but by restricting production as well. The emphasis now was more on controlling the plucking operations in order to regulate output rather than acreage alone. This policy helped recovery from the slump of 1920. Production declined in the early 1920s and prices began to rise by the end of 1921. Prices rose rapidly from 1922 onwards, reaching a peak in 1924–25, and thereafter remained very high up to 1927–28. From 1928–29 began the downward trend, which continued into the depression years. Production once again rose rapidly in response to very high prices from 1923 onwards. Improvement in productivity and particularly coarse plucking played an important role in creating extra supply. Once again the recovery of the post-depression years was made possible through control schemes introduced by the industry. This also explains the decline in production in the early half of the 1930s. The inter-war period was characterized by increasing production through control schemes in response to high prices.[189] When low prices resulted from overproduction, control schemes provided an immediate solution, thereby encouraging a further increase in production. This in turn caused yet another period of downward movement of prices. These cyclical movements, given the constraints of demand, could not be smoothened except through greater and longer-term control over supply, something the industry found difficult to achieve.

Output per Acre per Labour

From our analysis of the production, acreage and labour employment data of the tea industry, it is clear that production growth far exceeded the other two. Two important features of this growth were a significant increase in per acre and per labour productivity. Appendix Tables 5.20 and 5.21, and Charts 5.25 and 5.26, provide figures of quinquennial averages of per acre and per labour output of tea in the Assam Valley between 1890 and 1947. The per acre out-turn of tea increased by 129, 124, 106 and 116 per cent respectively in Lakhimpur, Sibsagar, Darrang and Assam Valley, between 1890–94 and 1945–47. Increase in per labourer out-turn of tea was even more impressive. It was 268, 127, 183 and 187 per cent respectively in Lakhimpur, Sibsagar, Darrang and Assam Valley during the same period. While the overall per capita acre and labour productivity maintained a upward secular trend, there were periods of fluctuations which in turn were linked with the production cycle. The decline during 1920–24 was due to post-war depression and political disturbances of 1920–22 which affected production, while the acreage under cultivation remained unaffected. The figures for the next quinquennial show an improvement in per acre out-turn. But once again the average per acre production was adversely affected with the worldwide depression of the 1930s. To solve the problem of overproduction caused by a decrease in demand in the international market, the Indian Tea Association advised its members to restrict production in the 1930s. The voluntary crop restriction scheme, despite some violations of the 'gentleman's agreement', brought down production in the early 1930s.[190] From 1935 onwards, the per acre out-turn of tea increased progressively and by the end of our period, in 1947, it had more than doubled (Appendix Table 5.20 and Chart 5.25).

The per capita labour out-turn follwed a similar trajectory. Just as in the case of per acre out-turn, the figures show a progressively upward trend till about 1919 and then a decline till the mid-1920s. Post-World War I and early 1920s political developments in the plantations were important factors behind this. Then the depression years brought stagnation and decline, but from the mid-1930s it recovered fast and there was an impressive increase in per labour out-turn of tea in the 1940s reaching the highest figures in the last five years of that decade. On the whole, in spite of the decline during the immediate post-war years and the 1930s, the overall trend was an impressive increase in

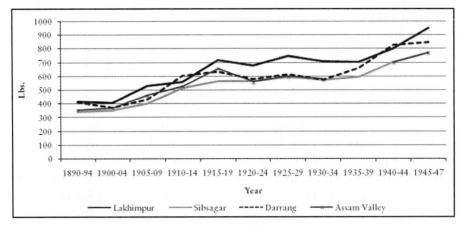

CHART 5.25
Quinquennial Averages of per Acre Out-turn of Tea in Assam Valley, 1890–1947

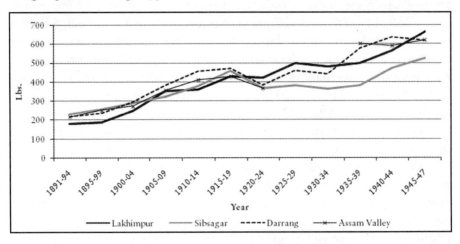

CHART 5.26
Quinquennial Averages of per Labour Out-turn of Tea in Assam Valley, 1891–1947

the out-turn of tea per labourer in the Assam Valley plantations (Appendix Table 5.21 and Chart 5.26). This was achieved by increasing labour productivity through labour intensification. The rationalization of inputs as a result of scientific research in methods of cultivation further strengthened efforts to improve the productivity of land. In fact, with the increasing sophistication of such scientific inputs, labour employment per acre was reduced, while production per acre and per capita of labour increased.

Technology and Output

Here we turn to the role of scientific research and technological improvements in raising per capita output of tea. Data on these aspects are however scarce. Among the sources available are the official history of the Indian tea industry which provides useful information. Similarly an article written by the British agricultural scientist Harold Mann, in 1931, gives an account of the development of scientific research for the improvement of production of tea in India.[191] Finally, the India Tea Association's scientific department brought out a quarterly journal which provided information about work done by their scientists. Apart from these, there are a few books whose authors were connected with scientific research on tea. Harler's *Culture and Marketing of Tea* and Bald's *Indian Tea* are important works which go into the details of the process of tea cultivation and manufacturing. Information gathered from all these sources helps to form some idea of the nature of scientific research carried out and its benefits to the tea industry during the late nineteenth and twentieth centuries. It is, however, pertinent here to point out that tea, being an agricultural industry, did not go through the same pattern of technical change as in the organized modern industries in India. Most of the efforts at rationalization of production techniques were in the nature of improving the productivity of land and field work. While manufacturing techniques and the mechanization process improved over the years in the tea factories, the agricultural process underwent little fundamental change from the end of the nineteenth century onwards.[192] Attempts to introduce machinery as a substitute for labour were unsuccessful.[193] This was largely because of the availability of cheap and abundant labour. Hence labour remained a major factor in the process of tea production.

During the nineteenth century, when the tea industry started to expand rapidly, individual planters, beginning with A.C. Bruce, brought about innovations in the process of tea cultivation and manufacturing. These innovations were based mostly on the personal experience and initiative of the planters. By the end of the nineteenth century the industry felt the need for systematic scientific research to improve tea production. From the very beginning the industry was fortunate in having acquired the services of experienced agricultural scientists like Harold Mann and George Watt. In 1904, with substantial financial help from the central and state governments, the tea industry started a scientific research centre at Heeleeka near Mariani, in Sibsagar district. The successful operation of this centre led to the establishment of a bigger one at Tocklai at Jorhat in 1911. These scientific centres carried out experiments on manure requirements, methods of pruning, variations in plucking, use of shaded trees, improvements in methods of weeding and hoeing, application of fertilizers, establishment of nurseries, use of vegetative propagation, quality of seeds, and treatment of blights and pests. Extensive surveys were carried out of work on the field. After World War I, in 1928, a small factory was established within the Tocklai centre.[194] The scientific officer of the ITA reported that systematic manure supply increased the crop by 40 per cent.[195]

Mann was the first to point out that scientific research had resulted in an increase of per acre yield of tea in Assam. He, however, did not estimate the specific contribution of scientific inputs to the profits. It was H.R. Cooper, an official of the scientific department of ITA, who estimated the cost of production per acre and per lb of tea inclusive of the cost of scientific input. He pointed out that in 1929, Upper Assam produced 333 kg of tea per acre at an average cost of about Rs 450 or 10 annas per lb, often more. The use of an additional 40 lbs of nitrogen per acre increased the output to 407 kg at a cost of Rs 513.50 per acre. Therefore, he concluded, additional manure and other scientific inputs increased profits on both per acre and per lb of tea produced.[196] Cooper would have been doubly gratified if he had seen the annual reporting on the financial health of the tea companies, which we point to below.

Capital and Profits

A constant refrain and lament of the planters and their representatives was the recurring trade depression and the financial problems faced by the tea industry due to high labour costs, government taxation, etc. The data on declared dividends by the tea companies, however, present a different picture altogether – one of prosperity and a high rate of profitability (Appendix Table 5.22). It is possible to argue that dividends may not be an indication of a high rate of profits. This argument may be valid for the short term where the companies sometimes declare dividends in spite of setbacks in order to maintain the confidence of the shareholders and the market. However in the long run it is not possible to declare dividends consistently unless there are real profits. It is clear from Appendix Table 5.22 that between 1904 and 1947, the majority of the tea companies consistently declared handsome dividends on a major part of their aggregate capital, except during the early 1930s – the years of the Great Depression. The percentage of dividends maintained a secular upward trend, except during the slump in the depression years. The years of the two world wars, in particular, were a bonanza for the tea industry, with most of the tea companies declaring handsome dividends ranging from 15 to 34 per cent. It is interesting to note that even politically disturbed conditions in the tea plantations did not impact the declaration and rate of dividends. For example, at the height of the 1921–22 labour revolt, out of 132 registered tea companies with paid-up capital of Rs 447 lakhs, 88 declared 33.2 per cent dividend on their aggregate capital of Rs 319 lakhs.

From the above discussion certain important features characteristic of the Assam Valley tea plantations are discernible. The industry experienced a very high rate of growth over a period of three-quarters of a century, beginning from the 1870s. The expansion was spectacular during the last three decades of the nineteenth century, and for the rest of the period at a relatively modest pace. The increase in production far exceeded the increase in acreage and labour employment. This was achieved by raising per acre and per labour out-turn of tea through labour-intensive methods and scientific inputs. The most interesting aspect of this impressive growth is that it took place in the face of price instability. Tea prices declined sharply during the last two decades of the nineteenth century and constantly fluctuated over the next four decades. But despite highly unstable international tea prices, the industry in India grew financially with a very high rate of profitablity. A significant feature of the tea plantation was its ability to keep wages very low and yet maintain a stable labour supply over a long period of time. Regularly sponsored mobilization and the creation of a surplus labour force ensured this. Abundant and cheap supply of labour was the mainstay of the plantation system. For sustaining the profitability of the industry, it was imperative to keep labour costs as low as possible. This was achieved through a complex system of gender-differential wages in cash and kind, dependence on land grants, and a system of advances that was evolved during the late nineteenth and early twentieth centuries.

Notes and References

[1] Report of the Assam Labour Enquiry Committee (RALEC), 1906, p. 71.

[2] Ibid., p. 3.

[3] Griffiths, Percival, *The History of the Indian Tea Industry*, London: Weidenfeld and Nicolson, 1967, p. 297.

[4] Proceedings of the Central Legislative Council (PCLC), 1901, Vol. XL, p. 51. Also see Indian Tea Association Report (heraefter ITA Report), 1900, pp. 129–30. Another spokesman of the industry provided even a longer list of 'concessions', which included 'free housing, sanitation, water supply, medical attendance, fixed wages, security against famine, and subsistence when sick.' *The Times* (London), 4 April 1902, p. 6.

[5] PCLC, 1901, Vol. XL, p. 52: Report of the Royal Commission on Labour in India (hereafter Royal Commission), 1931, p. 385; Griffiths, *The History*, p. 297.

[6] Royal Commission, 1931, p. 385.

[7] Ibid., p. 383; Griffiths, *The History*, p. 299.

[8] Griffiths, *The History*, p. 299.

[9] PCLC, 1901, Vol. XL, p. 71.

[10] Royal Commission, 1931, p. 386.

[11] RALEC, 1921–22, p. 31; Royal Commission, 1931, p. 383.

[12] RALEC, 1921–22, p. 31.

[13] Dattaraya Varman Rege, *Report on An Enquriy into Conditions of Plantation Labour in India*, 1946, p. 46.

[14] RALEC, 1921–22, p. 31; *Royal Commission*, 1931, pp. 384–93.

[15] PCLC, 1901, p. 72.

[16] Ibid., p. 110.

[17] Ibid., p. 110.

[18] Ibid., p. 73.

[19] For details, see chapter 6.

[20] Royal Commission, 1931, p. 386.

[21] See below.

[22] Assam Labour Report, 1902–03, p. 8.

[23] Rajani Kanta Das, *Plantation Labour in India*, Calcutta: R. Chatterji, 1931, pp. 140–62.

[24] C.R. Harler, *The Culture and Marketing of Tea*, Oxford University Press, 1956, second edn, p. 64.

[25] Ibid., p. 65.

[26] Assam Labour Reports, 1875–1932; Annual Reports on the Working of the Tea District Emigrant Labour Act (XXII of 1932), 1834–1947 (hereafter RTDEL Act XII of 1932); RALEC, 1921–22, p. 24.

[27] Griffiths, *The History*, p. 302; Royal Commission, 1931, p. 384.

[28] Royal Commission, 1931, p. 384.

[29] RTDL Act XXII of 1932 for the year 1937.

[30] RALEC, 1921–22, p. 24.

[31] Ibid., p. 23.

[32] *The Agriculture Statistics of British India*, 1921–22, Vol. I. This figure represented the provincial average.

[33] RALEC, 1921–22, p. 23. These figures also include the acreage held in the sub-divisions of each district.

[34] Report on Tea Culture in Assam, 1922 (hereafter Production Report).

[35] The Enquiry Committee of 1921–22 reported that generally a notional rent was charged but economic rents up to Rs 6 an acre were not unknown. The Committee estimated that an average rent of Rs 1.58 per acre (provincial average) was paid by the labourers. RALEC, 1921–22, pp. 23–24.

[36] Ibid., p. 24.

[37] Rege, *Report*, p. 48.

[38] Royal Commission, 1931, p. 384.

[39] Henry Cotton, *Indian and Home Memories*, London: T. Fisher Unwin, 1911, p. 266.

[40] Ibid.

[41] Department of Revenue and Agriculture, Government of India, Emigration A, No. 6, File No. 87, November 1901, p. 941.

[42] Ibid., p. 946.

[43] Ibid., p. 939.

[44] Department of Revenue and Agriculture, Government of India, Emigration A, Nos. 6–8, File No. 90 of 1901, p. 145.

[45] Ibid.

[46] Ibid.

[47] Ibid., p. 146.

[48] Ibid., p. 147.

[49] Ibid., p. 145.

[50] Ibid.

[51] RTDEL Act XXII of 1932, 1938, p. 9.

[52] Ibid.

[53] PCLC, 1901, p. 63.

[54] Ibid., p. 56.

[55] Proceedings of the Assam Labour Enquiry Committee (PALEC), 1906, p. 3.

[56] Ibid.

[57] A similar opinion was expressed by a merchant and banker of Raniganj who added that if the period of contract was reduced to one year, it would attract more labour for the tea gardens in Assam. Ibid., p. 7.

[58] Ibid., pp. 12–13.

[59] Ibid., p. 16.

[60] Ibid., p. 25. For a detailed analysis, see Nitin Varma, 'Unpopular Assam: Notions of Migrating and Working in Tea Gardens', in Sabyasachi Bhattacharya (ed.), *Towards a New History of Work*, New Delhi: Tulika Books, 2014, pp. 227–44.

[61] RALEC, 1906, pp. 16–33.

[62] Ibid., p. 32.

[63] Royal Commission, 1931, p. 388.

[64] RALEC. 1906, p. 146; PCLC, 1901, Vol. XL, p. 144.

[65] All those labourers who were not contracted under Act VI of 1901 or were time-expired labourers who did not renew their contract were mostly referred to as non-Act labour. Most of this category of labour was employed under the Workman's Breach of Contract Act XIII of 1859.

[66] The term 'settled' referred to permanently employed labourers and *faltu* to the temporary labour force.

[67] Assam Labour Report, 1884, p. 5.

[68] Assam Labour Report, 1886, p. 4.

[69] Assam Labour Report, 1895, p. 40.

[70] Assam Labour Report, 1904–05, p. 4.

[71] Assam Labour Report, 1901, p. 6.

[72] Production Report, 1902, 9. 1.

[73] General and Judicial Department, Government of Assam, Immigration Branch B, Nos. 127–35, September 1934, p. 20

[74] Assam Labour Report, 1901, p. 6.

[75] Department of Commerce and Industry, Government of Eastern Bengal and Assam, B Proceedings, Nos. 356/360, May 1905, p. 9.

[76] Griffiths, *The History*; Production Reports; Royal Commission, 1931.

[77] Assam Labour Reports, 1900, 1900–05.

[78] Assam Labour Report, 1902–03, p. 8.

[79] The yearly average of monthly earnings in both sets of figures were calculated on the basis of earnings during two typical months, i.e. March and September, in each year.

[80] Royal Commission, 1931, p. 387.

[81] Lee's letter dated 21 November 1933, marked Confidential, to Mr A.J. Clow of the Department of Industry and Labour, Government of India. See General and Judicial Department, Government of Assam, Immigration Branch B, Nos. 127–35, September 1934, p. 20.

[82] A.J. Clow's letter to Lee dated 6 December 1933, ibid., p. 21.

[83] Ibid.

[84] RTDEA XXII of 1932 for 1934–47.

[85] Rege, *Report*, preface.

[86] Ibid., p. 11.

[87] Shantaram Ramkrishna Deshpande, *Report on an Enquiry into the Cost and Standard of Living of Plantation Workers in Assam and Bengal*, Labour Bureau, Ministry of Labour, Government of India, 1948, p. 1.

[88] Ibid., p. 8.

[89] Ibid., p. 2.

[90] Ibid., Table XI, p. 24 and p. 22.

[91] 'The money value of concessions was evaluated by taking into account the difference between the market prices of the selected commodities and the concession rates at which they were supplied to the workers by the management.' Ibid., p. 5.

[92] Ibid., Tables XIII and XIV, pp. 27 and 28 respectively.

[93] Radhakamal Mukherjee, *The Indian Working Class*, Bombay: Hind Kitab Ltd. Publishers, 1945, p. 107.

[94] RTDEA XXII of 1932, 1947.

[95] Deshpande, *Enquiry Report*, p. 6.

[96] Ibid., Table XIV, p. 28.

[97] Assam Labour Reports, 1900 and 1901.

[98] PCLC, 1901, Vol. XL, p. 93.

[99] Department of Revenue and Agriculture, Government of India, Emigration A, Nos. 6 to 8, File No. 90 of 1901, p. 153; Assam Labour Report, 1900, p. 10.

[100] Department of Revenue and Agriculture, Government of India, Emigration A, No. 6, File No. 87, November 1901, pp. 944 and 947; Assam Labour Report, 1901.

[101] PCLC, 1901, Vol. XL, p. 94.

[102] Assam Labour Reports for respective years. These figures include the value of allowances paid under Sections (128(1) and 130(1), value of diet in lieu of such allowances and rations provided under Section 134(A), and also including *ticca* earning and 'bonus' (calculated on the basis of number of labourers in the garden books).

[103] RALEC, 1921–22, Appendix XIII, p. 140.

[104] RTDELA (XII of 1932), 1934, p. 12 and 1938, p. 9.

[105] RTDELA (XXII of 1932), 1935, p. 15.

[106] Rege, *Report*, p. 46.

[107] Because of incomplete data, the figures for Nowgong and Kamrup are not visually projected.

[108] Here too, as earlier, the quinquennial averages are used for working out the percentage of increase. 1947 being an extreme year has been excluded, and figures for 1946 are not available.

[109] For the purpose of comparison, five-yearly averages from both ends have been used as the basis.

[110] Deshpande, *Enquiry Report*, p. 29.

[111] Production Report, 1907, p. 1.

[112] Production Report, 1909, p. 1.

[113] Assam Labour Reports for respective years.

[114] RTDEA (XXII of 1932), 1935, p. 5.

[115] For details about the agrarian economy of Assam, see Amalendu Guha, 'Socio-Economic Changes in Agrarian Assam', in M.K. Chaudhury (ed.), *Trends in Socio-Economic Change in India 1871–1961*, Simla, 1967.

[116] Rege, *Report*, p. 44.

[117] *Prices and Wages in India*, 1910, p. 175.

[118] Rege, *Report*, p. 56.

[119] Ibid., p. 54.

[120] According to Mann, these gardens had an arrangement to feed weak or sick labourers before going to work in the morning and after returning from work in the evening. The idea was to improve their health so that they could work properly in the gardens. The place at which the labourers were provided food was referred to as 'hotel', and hence the term 'hotel diet'. For further details, see Harold H. Mann, 'Note on the Diet of Tea Garden Coolies in Upper Assam and its Nutritive Value', in Daniel Thorner (ed.), *Social Framework of Agriculture*, Bombay, 1967, pp. 65–72.

[121] Ibid., p. 72.

[122] RALEC, 1921–22, p. 69

[123] Ibid., p. 35.

[124] Ibid., p. 36.

[125] Ibid., p. 38, Appendix Table IX.

[126] *Prices and Wages in India*, 1902, Preface.

[127] Ibid., p. 2.

[128] K.L. Datta, *Report on the Enquiry into the Rise of Prices in India, 1914*, Vol. III, pp. 382–83.

[129] RALEC, 1921–22, p. 38.

[130] RALEC, 1921–22, Appendices (d) and (e), pp. 34–55. Appendix VII (A), p. 123 of this Report shows another annual budget of a labour family consisted of one man, two women (all working) and 2 children (1 working). The expenses on food consumption of this family were nearly 70 per cent of the total annual expenditure. The other budgets reported revealed a similar trend.

[131] Deshpande, *Enquiry* Report, Appendix XV, pp. 98–101.

[132] RALEC, 1921–22, Appendices (d) and (e), pp. 34–35.

[133] Report of the Commissioners Appointed to Enquire into the State and Prospects of Tea Cultivation in Assam, Cachar and Sylhet, Calcutta, 1868, p. 60. (Hereafter Commissioners, 1868.)

[134] Assam Sanitary Reports, 1878–80.

[135] Assam Sanitary Report, 1880, para 171.

[136] *Prices and Wages in India*, 1900–20.

[137] The Assam Valley is also referred to as Brahmaputra Valley.

[138] But in most cases the figures of prices are higher in the district. In other words, prices at the Valley level presented a conservative average compared to the average in the district.

[139] For the same reason we shall exclude salt prices from our analysis when we compare the price trends with the wage trends.

[140] For the purposes of comparison between prices of foodstuff and wages, we have used five-yearly averages on either ends as the basis for both.

[141] Datta, *Report on the Enquiry into the Rise of Prices in India, 1914*, Vol. I, p. 171.

[142] Ibid.

[143] *Agricultural Statistics of British India*, respective years. Raw sugar constituted an extremely small proportion of the total food consumption. Deshpande's estimate of a labour family budget shows that sugar consumption constituted only 2.6 per cent of the total food expenditure. Therefore 5 per cent decrease in its prices during the periods 1921–22 and 1925–26 would not have significantly reduced the total expenditure on food. Deshpande, *Enquiry Report*, Appendix XV, pp. 98–101.

[144] *Agricultural Statistics of India*, Vol. I, for respective years.

[145] The figures of wages for 1946 were not available; figures for the year 1947 were unusually high compared to the previous years and no creditable explanation was offered either in the Indian Tea Association papers or in the annual Assam Labour Reports. Hence we take 1945 as the point of comparison.

[146] Rege, *Report*, p. 55.

[147] Ibid.; P.P. Pillai (ed.), *Labour in South East Asia: A Symposium*, New Delhi, 1947, p. 18.

[148] Rege, *Report*, p. 56.

[149] See chapters 1 and 2.

[150] Under the rules a garden could be declared unhealthy and subject to official sanctions if the mortality rate exceeded 7 percent. Assam Labour Reports, 1989, p. 25 and 1900, p. 12; Special Report, Government of India, 1891.

[151] Ralph Shlomowitz and Lance Brennan, 'Mortality and migrant labour in Assam 1865–1921', *Indian Economic and Social History Review*, Vol. 27, No. 1, 1990, pp. 85–110.

[152] Sheila Zurbrigg, 'Hunger and Epidemic Malaria in Punjab, 1868–1940', *Economic and Political Weekly of India*, Vol. 27, No. 4, 25 January 1992, p. PE-17.

[153] Assam Sanitary Reports, 1878–84; for more details, see chapter 2.

[154] Rege, *Report*, p. 55.

[155] Deshpande, *Enquiry Report*, p. 33.

[156] General and Judicial Department, Government of Assam, Immigration B, Nos. 127–35, September 1934, p. 20.

[157] Assam Labour Report, 1918–19, p. 4; RALEC 1921–22, p. 94.

[158] Finance Department, Government of Assam, Immigration Branch, Progs. B, Nos. 8–29, June 1922, p. 39

[159] Rege, *Report*, p. 60.

[160] Royal Commission, pp. 406 and 409–10.

[161] Ibid., p. 417.

[162] Rege, *Report*, p. 60.

[163] Cited in ibid.

[164] Dr Wilson and Dr Mitra, 'A Diet and Physique Survey in Assam Rural Bengal and Calcutta, a survey conducted for the All-India Institute of Hygiene and Public Health, Calcutta', *Indian Journal of Medical Research*, Vol. XXVII, pp. 131–54.

[165] Lloyd Jones, *Standards of Medical Care for Tea Plantations in India*, 1946, p. 70.

[166] Ibid.

[167] Ibid.

[168] Ibid., Appendix III, p.70.

[169] RALEC, 1921–22, p. 95.

[170] Lloyd Jones, *Standards,* Appendix III, p. 70.

[171] Chapter 3.

[172] Report on Tea Operations in the Province of Assam 1873–74, Shillong, pp. 13–15.

[173] ITA Report, 1918, p. 22. From 1920 onwards the number of labourers working in the tea gardens was shown under this classification in the Assam labour reports.

[174] Production Report, 1919, p. 1.

[175] For more details on this, see chapter 6.

[176] Report on Tea Operations in the Province of Assam, 1873–74.

[177] Production Reports, 1892, p. 2, 1893, para 5, and 1894, p. 2.

[178] Production Reports, 1903–04.

[179] See chapter 6 for more details.

[180] Report on Tea Operations in the Province of Assam, 1873–74, p. 13.

[181] This was acknowledged by the official historian when he stated that World War I was a time of prosperity for the Indian tea industry. Griffiths, *History of Tea*, p. 170.

[182] RALEC, 1921–22, pp. 6–20. Also see chapter 6.

[183] See chapter 2.

[184] Indian Tea Statistics, 1930, 1934, 1940–47.

[185] Himansu Roy, *Tea Price Stabilization: The Indian Case*, Calcutta: World Press, 1968, p. 5.

[186] Ibid., p. 3; Griffiths, *History of Tea*, pp. 106, 178, 191.

[187] Roy, *Tea Price*, p. 8; Griffiths, *History of Tea*, pp. 171, 201; Bishnupriya Gupta, 'Stabilization of Prices in Plantation Economics: A Comparative Study of the Tea Industry in India and the Coffee Industry in Brazil', unpublished M.Phil. dissertation, Centre for Historical Studies, School of Social Sciences, Jawaharlal Nehru University, New Delhi, 1981, p. 20.

[188] Roy, *Tea Price*, p. 6.

[189] During the inter-war years a number of control schemes were started by the tea industry. The first control scheme was imposed by the Indian Tea Association (London) in 1920, by which all members were asked to restrict production to 90 per cent of the overall average or, alternatively, stop plucking in that season. The second control scheme was a joint effort of the tea interests in India, Ceylon and Indonesia. In this scheme the production of common tea was sought to be restricted. The third control scheme, known as the International Tea Agreement, was again a joint effort of the above three countries. An International Tea Committee was set up to coordinate the production restriction scheme. The Indian Tea Association approached the Government of India to provide statutory status to the above scheme but without success. See Detailed Reports of the General Committee of Indian Tea

Association, 1934, p. 12 and 1935, p. V; Gupta, 'Stabilization of Prices', pp. 27–30; Griffiths, *History of Tea*, pp. 190–91.

[190] ITA Report, 1935, p. vi.

[191] Harold H. Mann, 'The Indian Tea Industry in its Scientific Aspects', in Daniel Thorner (ed.) *Social Framework of Agriculture*, Bombay, 1967, pp. 437–55.

[192] Griffiths, *History of Tea*, p. 487.

[193] Claud Bald, *Indian Tea*, Calcutta: Thacker, Spink & Co., 1922, fourth edn, pp. 17 and 218.

[194] Griffiths, *History of Tea*, pp. 413–43; ITA Reports, Scientific Department, 1907, pp. 3–4, and 1908, p. 3. The process of tea manufacturing after the leaves are brought to the factory involves withering, fermenting, rolling, firing or drying, and sorting. These aspects were the subject of many experiments, and in the third decade of the nineteenth century, a good deal of new knowledge about methods of manufacturing was obtained. Also see chapter 2.

[195] ITA Report, 1928, p. XIII.

[196] Quarterly Journal, Scientific Department, ITA, 1931, pp. 10–11.

6

Labour Life and Labour Resistance to the Plantation Regime

The large-scale recruitment and transportation of migrant labourers to the Assam Valley from the 1860s onwards initiated a process that transformed more than 2 million peasants of Chotanagpur, Bihar, Bengal, Orissa and Upper India into tea plantation 'coolies' for over three-quarters of a century.[1] The transformation began the day they were recruited and set on their journey towards Assam. The individual identities of these labour communities were subsumed into anonymous 'gangs' and 'muster rolls', to be confined in 'depots' during the journey and 'coolie lines' upon arrival in the plantations. Like many of their counterparts, they have been relegated to the category of a 'people without history'.[2] They were described and treated as a 'mass' or 'mob' of nameless multitudes. The indenture regime in Assam identified labourers only using numbers and cancelled their names. Thus their identities disappeared from the plantation and colonial records. Even in the information about migrant labour meticulously maintained by the colonial bureaucracy, there is no trace of contract documents, nor details such as names and thumb impressions of the labourers, which were supposed to have been a part of the contracts according to the labour laws. There is no information as to whether records of contracts existed at all in the business archives of tea companies in the UK. Most of the archives and holdings of the British tea companies and the Indian Tea Association did not keep records of their contracts with the labour force. This is incredible, and bewildering, considering the fact that over a million migrants were recruited to the Assam tea plantations and made to 'sign' indenture contract forms during the last thirty-five years of the nineteenth century.

The daily lives of the labourers remained confined within the socially and culturally insulated world of the 'coolie lines', of which they themselves left no record. Denied even a semblance of education for generations and, as a result, remaining illiterate, the labourers produced no written records. The colonial state, which facilitated the mobilization of tens of thousands of labourers every year to become 'coolies' in the tea plantations, simply enumerated them under elaborate administrative norms framed for this purpose. Skimming through thousands of colonial documents, very rarely does one come across a glimpse of the labourers being acknowledged as human beings – and the few references that do exist are most often couched in overtly negative terms, relating to violent incidents, drinking 'problems' or conviction by the court.[3] It took nearly three quarters of a century after the organized system of recruitment for the Royal Commission on Labour in India to feel obliged to hold personal interviews with some of the labourers. These interviews, which took place in 1930, were of a perfunctory nature however, based mainly on one-line questions and answers. That was the first glimpse of the voice of labour, albeit a very faint one. The short conversations the labourers had with the members of the Royal Commission, mostly through interpreters, hardly made any impact on the general perception of them.

The report of the Royal Commission on Labour in 1931 reinforced the stereotypical perception of emigrant labourers in the Assam tea plantations, which had acquired almost a 'folklorist' status among members of the colonial bureaucracy:

> The imported labour is almost entirely illiterate and composed of men and women with a low standard of living, conservative by nature, suspicious of change, and excitable. In dealing with such people caution is necessary. They are not intelligent body of men who desire to raise their own standard of living and can appreciate and make good use of any improvement introduced for their benefit. On the contrary, the tendency of this labour force too often is to treat with suspicion and resent any change that is introduced, however, well intentioned and their resentment is quickly fanned into violence. A large proportion of this labour force has little or no ambition to improve its standard of living. It is content with little and does not want to do any more than is necessary to secure that little. Any large increase in the wage rates would often mean less work or a dissipation of the additional earnings. Changes introduced by the employers, which were directed to raise the labourers' standard of life, would often be suspected and resented.[4]

Although members of the colonial bureaucracy were prolific 'ethnographers' and 'anthropologists' of tribal communities of North East India, the negative portrayals of the labouring community may have prevented them from recording information about the lives of labourers in Assam's tea plantations. Given the severe limitations of colonial documentary sources, how does one recover the 'voice' of the labourers, and construct the stories of their social, cultural and personal lives spent working and living in the isolated tea plantations of Assam? We will make an attempt to tell the story of their lives based on snippets of information gleaned from the same colonial documents from which we have built the descriptions of the labour force, planters and plantations.

Who were these agrarian communities and from where were they recruited and brought to the Assam Valley tea plantations to work as labourers? The official labour reports and the Census of 1911 and 1921 provide us with data about their places of origin and social background. There was organized and uninterrupted sponsored recruitment and transportation of tens of thousands of tribal, peasant and aboriginal peoples to the Assam Valley for over a century from the 1860s, until the post-colonial decades of the 1950s and 1960s. Appendix Table 6.1 and Chart 6.1 provide detailed information on the import of labour into the Assam Valley districts between 1873 and 1947. These figures show that there was no uniformity in the number of immigrant labourers imported every year into the province. An unusually large number of immigrants were imported during certain years. One of the reasons for this was a bad harvest and consequent scarcity in the recruiting districts, which created a situation of cheap and abundant labour.[5] Sometimes the abnormal increase in immigration was necessitated by a sudden spurt in the demand for labour, due to the following factors. First, a boom in the tea industry in certain years created demand for a large number of labourers – for example, the World War I years which witnessed very rapid expansion of acreage and a tremendous increase in the production of tea. In the 1940s the diversion of labour towards defence projects in the region raised demand, which was responsible for the unusual increase in labour immigration in those years. The second factor was a very high rate of mortality among the labourers, caused by malnutrition, unhealthy living conditions and epidemics.[6] Even in normal years mortality rates were often high in the tea gardens, certainly higher than for the population in the province as a whole. This continually depleted the

CHART 6.1
Labour Import into Assam Valley Tea Districts, 1873–1947
(including women and children)[7]

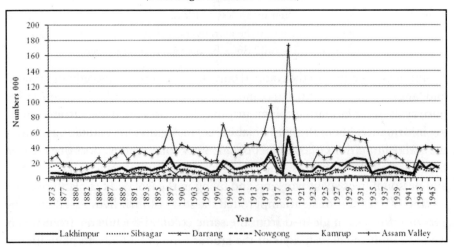

labour force, hence the need for large-scale recruitment of migrant labour. The increasing tendency among ex-tea garden labourers to settle as tenant cultivators on government land also necessitated constant recruitment of fresh labour. Moreover, the cost of recruitment per head, which was estimated to be between Rs 100 and Rs 150 at the beginning of the twentieth century, considerably reduced over the years.

At this juncture it is important to examine a much-debated issue in tea industry circles, i.e. the shortage of labour in the Assam tea gardens. The planters often complained of scarcity or shortage of labour.[8] This outcry on their part was necessary to justify the regular recruitment of immigrant labour under the complete monopoly of the Tea District Labour Association. The data on the labour force shows the existence of surplus labour from the 1890s, which was a result of the regular and uninterrupted process of sponsored immigration of labour into Assam for nearly a hundred years. The planters continued to import fresh labour every year despite the emergence of surplus labour (due to settlement of ex-tea garden labourers) and the availability of the local Kachari community for plantation work. The planters regularly employed this local labour force as temporary/*faltu* labour from as early as the 1890s.[9] In the last three decades of the nineteenth century, the increasing demand for labour in the tea gardens was due to the expansion of acreage under tea, and to replace those who had either died or deserted in large numbers. The second cause for the increased demand was the low rates of natural reproduction of labourers in the coolie lines. In later years the pace of growth slackened but the intensity of cultivation continued with more labour employed per acre.

The increasing demand for labour was not determined by variations in acreage alone and the fluctuations in supply were relatively independent of it too. Planters could expand acreage with a higher supply of labour. Thus the planter's ability to expand acreage remained dependent on the amount of labour brought in annually, while the actual amount of labour supply was relatively independent of this need for labour.[10] The high demand for labour was not related to variations in wage rates either, which were very low and mostly stagnant throughout the period of our study. The wage rates were further depressed by the import and employment of a large number of women, (nearly 45 per cent) and children who were paid less than the men. Official explanations for the fluctuation in the labour supply were related to the cyclical famines and depressed agricultural conditions in the recruitment areas.[11]

Social Origins of the Labouring Communities

The vast majority of the labour force was recruited from Chotanagpur, Santhal Parganas, Bihar, Bengal, Orissa, Central Provinces and Madras Presidency

(Appendix Table 6.2). The majority of the aboriginals and tribals came from Chotanagpur and Santhal Parganas, followed by those from Orissa, Central Provinces and the Madras Presidency district of Palamau in Bihar.[12] Labourers from Chotanagpur and Santhal Parganas alone constituted 59 per cent of the men and 50 per cent of the women in 1878, 48 per cent of men and 48 per cent of women in 1891, 44 per cent men and 44 per cent women in 1901, 38 per cent men and 39 per cent women in 1910, 38 per cent men and 39 per cent women in 1921, and 34 per cent men and 39 per cent women in 1931 (Appendix Table 6.2). It is interesting to note that the proportions of women migrants was almost equal to men. A large section of labourers were drawn from social communities officially ranked as aboriginal tribal groups: Mundas, Oraons, Kharias, Kols or Hos, Bhumij and Santhals, Kurmis and Murasis. The second most important group of migrants came from semi-aboriginal castes like the Ghasis and Goraits, Bauris, and Turi. A smaller number was drawn from low-caste Hindu communities like the Bhogtas, Rautias, Chamars and Dasadhs.

The aboriginals and tribals, often referred to by the planters and colonial officials as 'junglees', represented economically and socially the most marginalized strata of the society in the recruiting regions. Numerically they formed the largest group among the tea garden labour force in Assam Valley. The bulk of these groups was mobilized under two recruitment methods: through the agency of licensed private contractors, and by *sirdars* who were plantation employees and sent to the labour districts by garden managers for this purpose. In the 1860s the planters sent out labourers from their gardens to recruit in their home districts; this came to be known as the garden *sirdari* system. Categorized as aboriginals and tribals, these labour communities in the Assam Valley tea plantations (Appendix Table 6.3) were described by colonial Census officials as of Dravidian origin, many of them 'still in a primitive stage of Hinduism and consume fowls and liquor'.[13] The largest group among tea garden labourers in the Assam Valley, they constituted 61, 49 and 58 per cent in 1911, and 60, 45 and 59 per cent in 1921, of the total plantation labour population in the districts of Lakhimpur, Sibsagar and Darrang, respectively (Appendix Table 6.3).

The lower-caste labour communities (other than aboriginals and tribals) in Appendix Table 6.4, who occupied the lowest position in the Hindu caste hierarchy, were described as cultivating or fishing or menial castes of non-Aryan or Dravidian or 'degraded Aryan' or 'refined Dravidian' origins; their social status was low because they ate beef, fowl, pork, etc.[14] Together they formed the second largest group among the labouring population of the tea gardens, constituting 27, 35 and 30 per cent in 1911, and 28, 39 and 32 par cent in 1921, in the districts of Lakhimpur, Sibsagar and Darrang, respectively (Appendix Table 6.4).

Appendix Table 6.5 shows labourers from castes whose status was considered higher than those in Appendix Tables 6.3 and 6.4. Some of these, even if of non-Aryan origin, were described as ranking sufficiently high for Brahmins to accept water from their hands. Some of them were described as cultivating castes or metal working castes of Bihar and Bengal.[15] Together these castes (other than aboriginals, tribals and low castes) constituted 12, 16 and 12 per cent in 1911, and 12, 16 and 9 per cent in 1921, of the total labouring population in the districts of Lakhimpur, Sibsagar and Darrang, respectively.

The above analysis of census data on the social composition of labourers in the tea gardens shows that aboriginals, tribals and other lower-caste communities together accounted for nearly 88, 84 and 88 per cent in 1911, and 88, 84 and 69 per cent in 1921, of the total labour population in the districts of Lakhimpur, Sibsagar and Darrang, respectively. That the employers showed a special preference for these specific social groups is also quite clear from the census and other government reports. The 1911 Census reported that the great majority of these immigrants were welcomed in the Assam Valley 'on account of their capability of withstanding hard work in the jungle and the effects of the climate'.[16] Similar sentiments were expressed by the Superintendent of Census operations in Assam in 1921, G.L. Lloyd, about the planters' preference for migrant labourers from Chotanagpur, Orissa and Central Provinces. The 'Jungly Coolies' of Chotanagpur and Central Provinces were considered the best for tea garden work.[17] The Royal Commission on Labour in India also observed that aboriginal communities from Chotanagpur and Santhal Parganas were preferred in the Assam tea gardens, and that substantial numbers were also brought from Bihar, Orissa, Bengal and Central Provinces.[18]

The aboriginal and tribal *junglis* and *dhangars* were at one time autonomous and proud forest and hill communities of the Chotanagpur region. They were subdued through pacification campaigns launched by the British army and then alienated from their lands through colonial revenue policies. Kaushik Ghosh has argued that the colonial state introduced alien land tenures and in the process dispossessed many hill villagers, nobles, chiefs and headmen. It also encouraged a rapid growth in the market for land and the extensive moneylending business. 'Alien traders, landlords and administrators at the forefront of frontier colonial capitalism increasingly controlled the resources, and managed to get the Chotanagpur peasant into enormous debts.'[19] They were, in the process, alienated from their lands in a big way. Such distress conditions provided fertile hunting ground for the *arakatis* and *sirdars* to recruit and transport these communities to Assam Valley's tea plantations.

Everyday Labour Life on the Plantations

The life-cycle of plantation labourers was impacted by the work experience and the nature of servitude under the indenture and post-indenture labour regimes in Assam, over a period spanning more than a century of what in practice became generational employment. The daily lives of the labourers were shaped and constrained by the plantation regime, which controlled their mobility, placed their working and living spaces under constant surveillance, and used coercion to discipline them. Fuller, retired Chief Commissioner of Assam, in his memoir stated that 'coolies were virtually prisoners, being . . . under guard the whole night. I came across notices at river ferries and railway stations describing runaway coolies, and offering rewards for their apprehension, that reminded one of *Uncle Tom's Cabin*.'[20] Several tea garden labourers told the Whitley Commission in 1931 about the midnight visitation of the garden *chowkidars* for this purpose. Kadamoni, a woman labourer of Cinanamara tea garden, said that the *chowkidar* 'comes around at night to see if we are at home. He flings the door open even if we are not properly dressed. I am even made to work when I am ill.'[21] Chuttan, a male labourer from the same garden, complained: 'Even when I go for a call of nature the *chowkidar* keeps an eye upon me in case I run away.'[22] Ramaswami, a male labourer of Baloma tea garden, similarly deposed that they were 'kept here by the *chowkidar* and sometimes beaten, and the *chowkidar* goes around at night with a lamp, and even opens the door to see if we are there.'[23]

The relentless push for increase in tea production over the last three decades of the nineteenth century involved a combination of new planting as well as production from already mature acreage. This was achieved by intensifying the cultivation process through manual labour while organizing the rhythm of work in the manner of industrial supervision, and, at the same time, mechanizing the process of manufacture. For the sustenance of this production organization, it was imperative that labour was available at all times and during all seasons. This could only be ensured through residential compulsion of labourers in clusters called 'coolie lines' within the plantations, from where they could be easily mobilized to labour from sunrise to sunset every day. The sun rose earlier in the north east of the Indian subcontinent and to extract maximum labour, the planters devised a method of utilizing maximum hours of sunlight for work: the garden clock was advanced by one hour ahead of the rest of India's subcontinental time-zone. Everyday life and work on the plantations was scheduled on 'garden time'.[24]

To extract maximum work, the daily life of the labourers was disciplined, controlled and organized to the hourly efficiency of the garden clock. A gong at 5 o'clock to wake up and a gong at 6 o'clock to go to the field, *kamjarrie* – under the close supervision of a hierarchy of *sirdars*, *muhurrirs* and young assistant managers (*chhota sahibs*), and the overall charge of the manager or *burra sahib*. The gong at 6 in the evening announced the end of the work-day when labourers could return to the coolie lines.[25] Work had to be carried on till sunset with short breaks for drinking water and lunch on the field itself. Negligence and slackness in the performance of tasks could invite severe reprimand and punishment. This mode of extracting maximum labour became a distinguishing feature of colonial plantations producing for global markets during the nineteenth and twentieth centuries. Tamil migrant labourers in the rubber plantations in colonial Malay were subjected to a similar rhythm of life: 'with clockwork regularity' their working day began with roll-call before 6 in the morning, proceeded to the mid-day break, and then continued till sunset. This was recounted by generations of Tamil labourers in their folk songs.[26] The intensification drive certainly increased the quantity of tasks demanded of labour. Crole observed:

> In Upper Assam, at any rate, coolies accomplish much more work now than they did twenty or thirty years ago. The daily task ('nirikh') for such work as hoeing, for instance, has increased from twenty five to thirty per cent, more than what used to be demanded of coolies. This has been brought about by more efficient supervision.[27]

The work schedule in the plantations were designed to extract maximum labour at minimum cost – low wages and long hours of work.

Women and Reproduction: Perpetuation of Generational Servitude

A characteristic feature of the labour force employed in the Assam plantations was the large number of women and children. In fact the combined strength of women and children outstripped the ratio of men (Appendix Table 6.6). Both women and children received lower wages than men despite performing the same amount and number of hours of work.[28] It was a successful strategy adopted by the tea industry to keep the overall wage bill low throughout the period under study. Women labourers experienced far worse treatment in their everyday life than their male counterparts. Apart from ill-treatment at the hands of the supervisory staff at the workplace, there was often a strong element of sexual exploitation that they had to face at the hands of the managers and assistant managers. The indenture laws and law enforcement authorities rarely offered any protection against this.

Women, in many ways, had to live a life of greater hardship both at the workplace and at home. A new rhythm of daily work was created for them by the very nature of the work process specifically assigned to them – plucking, plucking and plucking. They were woken up by the 'gong' at 5 am to prepare the family meals and perform other household chores before the next 'gong' at 6 pushed them out of the home to the field to perform the day's labour. The 6 pm 'gong' brought them home, after a back-breaking day's work in the field, to perform, still more family chores till they fell asleep of exhaustion.

A recurring experience of life on the Assam tea plantations for labour families was to live with pain, grief and sadness at losing loved ones to death and desertion at regular intervals. No description of such experiences was ever found to be worth recording by the colonial bureaucracy or the 'prolific' autobiographer planters. But given the large-scale desertions and deaths reported in the annual labour reports, it is not inconceivable to imagine that an all-pervading atmosphere of gloom and sadness prevailed in the 'coolie lines' every time someone died or deserted, which was a frequent occurrence. Death and grief are normal experiences of human life. For the plantation labour communities, however, its visitations were frequent, and caused by a very high degree of undernourishment, malnutrition and sickness. Overwork and undernourishment remained the most common causes of sickness and death. And they experienced pain and suffering constantly from personal and family sicknesses. The everyday life of women labourers was harder still because they had to cope with having to provide basic food and amenities for the family in the face of perpetual pain and suffering, and poverty, alongside performing back-breaking labour for long hours. They were discriminated in the form of lower wages than men despite performing specialized tasks. Women also had to bear the burden of reproduction of labour from their undernourished bodies. Confronted with the harsh realities of everyday life – of hard work, low wages, malnutrition and impoverishment – many of them chose to defy the burden of reproduction, as is evident from the reported termination of pregnancies. There is evidence that women labourers defied the logic and expectations of reproduction of the labour force for the plantations. Many of them chose to not let children be born in an environment of sub-human existence by aborting pregnancies. The low birth rate during the last two decades of the nineteenth century was attributed by medical opinion to the widespread practice of abortion among women labourers.[29]

For children, their labouring life as 'coolies' began at the tender age of between five and six years. They were supposed to supplement the 'family' income and were paid the least wage: Rs 3 per month, as compared to Rs 5 and Rs 4 for men and women respectively. Beginning with assisting their mothers in plucking and other odd jobs in the tea factories, they were then enrolled in gangs that worked in 'withering chungs' and graduated to work the rolling machines. By age sixteen, those who had survived the 'climate', sickness and rigours of plantation work were alleviated to the status of adult labourers.[30] They were then made to work for the rest of their lives – until they died or managed to leave the garden on account of 'old age', as there was no concept of retirement age for labourers in the Assam tea plantations till well into the post-independence era.

Another significant feature of labour life in the Assam Valley tea planta-tion was the almost universal illiteracy among labouring children, despite the fact that the employers had the statutory obligation to provide schooling to the children of their employees. Not only were they were forced to live in isolation over a long period from the world outside the plantations, but even elementary education was denied to their children. After 80 years since its inception and nearly 55 years after the introduction of labour laws[31] in the Assam tea industry, the Census of Assam in 1921 reported only 0.25, 0.39 and 0.36 per cent rates of literacy among tea garden labourers in the districts of Lakhimpur, Sibsagar and Darrang, respectively.[32] In the province as a whole, only 0.64 per cent of the entire tea garden labour force was reported to be literate.[33] The Superintendent of the Assam Census of 1911 offered the following explanations for this situation. Some of the managers were enthusiastic about running schools for the children of tea garden labourers, but the latter were allegedly averse to the scheme. Most of the other manag-ers were either indifferent or hostile towards the scheme because education could cause a distaste for manual labour when the children grew up.[34] As a result, as late as 1948, it was reported that most plantations in Assam had no facilities for the education of children above the age of twelve. On this basis, therefore, it was suggested that employment of children above twelve years should not be prohibited in the tea gardens.[35] The employers' lack of interest in educating tea garden labourers and their children was explained by the Royal Commission in terms of fear of upsetting the labour force rather than any antagonism to the principle of the scheme. And because labour supply was 'scarce', it would have been too much to expect employers to risk the loss of labour by any attempt to insist on educating the children. Therefore there could be little improvement in literacy among labourers until the supply of labour increased.[36]

As far as the labourers' apathy towards education was concerned, it was asserted that they did not appreciate the 'ultimate advantages' their children would derive from education. It was argued that the loss of additional income to the family if the children went to school instead of working in the garden had condemned the education scheme in the eyes of the labourers. It was this economic compulsion that accounted for labourers' 'apathy' towards their children's education. The Royal Commission advanced this thesis of labour-ers' 'laziness', claiming that they pushed their children into employment to supplement family earnings instead of sending them to school.[37]

Contrasting Lifestyles on the Plantations:
Planters and Labourers

Lives of Planters

The Assam tea plantations witnessed hugely contrasting lifestyles of its inhabitants, determined by their differential status, incomes and perks. The European managers drew a monthly salary between Rs 800 and 1,000, plus 5 per cent commission on net profits, as compared to the monthly wages earned by labourers – Rs 5 for men and Rs 4 for women – at the turn of the twentieth century.[38] Along with their cash salaries, the planters enjoyed perks and privileges that could have been the envy of even the better paid civil servants. They earned additional income through commissions and bonuses on production and profits. By the 1880s, the managers' bungalows 'were like palaces, compared to those in the dark old days', well furnished and insect-free.[39] The 'coolies' also provided domestic labour for the planters. Retired planter Barker recounted the members of his bungalow staff:

> Kitmutgar [khitmadgar – one who serves] or waiter/butler; bearer to look after the bedroom; khansama [cook] and his assistant, two or three paniwallahs [water carriers], the mater (mehtara – sweeper), two chowkidars [watchmen], punkah-wallahs [fan pullers], sysces, malee [gardener], moorgie-wallah [to look after the chickens], gorukhiya [cowherd], and a few others.[40]

The seclusion and social isolation of the 'pioneering' days had given way to a very comfortable and luxurious social and sporting life. Young planter Hetherington's diary is full of entries depicting a life of high pleasure, entertainment and socialising among the planters – with constant rounds of visits to each other's bungalows. They describe dinners, drinking and dance parties, church services, social gatherings of planters and colonial officials at the planters' club in the evenings, hunting in the surrounding forests and other sports. The list of favourite sports enjoyed by the planters included polo, bridge, cricket, billiards, angling and hunting. Again unlike the 'pioneering' days of the European planters' lives when families were not on the scene, white women were no longer scarce. Planters were staying longer periods on their jobs, and bringing their wives with them or getting married once their contracts were renewed.[41] The European assistant managers lived in slightly smaller and a little less luxurious bungalows, and drew smaller salaries and perks compared to the managers. However their bungalows and lifestyle were far superior in comparison to the 'coolie lines' and even the living quarters of the native clerical staff.

The managers and their assistants supervised the entire production process on the tea garden personally, with the help of native staff of muharrirs, jamadars and sirdars both in the field and factory. The planter in this regime

Planter's bungalow (Samuel Cleland Davidson, personal collection)

was no mere employer of wage labour. He occupied a pivotal position around which revolved the lives of the entire plantation communities of assistants, supervisory staff including clerks, *sirdars, muharrirs, jamadars* and labourers.[42] The manager of a tea plantation in Assam often exercised extra-legal powers with the air of a little ruler of his domain. Behind the assertion of such authority over their labourers was the assumption of the inherent inferiority of the labouring classes as sub-human beings. At worst they could be compared to animals, as T. Kinny, a planter, did in his description: 'Assam imports . . . a number of curious and expensive animals known as Act I coolies.'[43] The planter acquired the traits of an omniscient and supreme authority in the plantation, and became a 'coolie-driver'. The fact that on the basis of net profits a bonus in addition to the salary was awarded by the management to the planters in the tea gardens meant that extraction of maximum output from the labourers was of immediate personal gain for them, and was not just a matter of performing their duties.

Lives of Labourers

In contrast, the labourers lived with their families in small huts in the 'coolie lines' with minimum basic requirements of daily life. Many of them also performed labour at the residences of the planters. Their low-income status reflected in the sparseness of their household possessions. Their sustenance,

'Coolie lines' (Samuel Cleland Davidson, personal collection)

in the face of low wages, was possible only if most members of the family worked. And despite 'family incomes', their standard of living was very low and sparse. Crole enumerated the possessions of a labourer's household:

> couple of wooden bed-frames with rope netting stretched across, a few brass 'lotas' for cooking in . . . a flat bamboo scoop, or 'jarru' in which they toss and sort the 'dahn' preparatory to their staple food, a native mortar and pestle, a basket or two for storing things in, some blankets . . . and occasionally a hideous idol, and there I think the average inventory would end.[44]

Their living and working spaces were constantly under surveillance by *chowk-idars* (guards) appointed by their employers.[45] Low wages, intensive labour, physical coercion, high mortality and low rate of reproduction were the main features of labour life in the Assam tea plantations.

How did the labouring communities of the tea gardens respond to this transformation process that plantation employment foisted upon them? Equally significant are questions of their character and sensibility, about which images were projected through the employer's lens. Were they truly an ignorant, unintelligent body of men and women who resisted change, prone to violence and immune to economic incentives, as alleged by their employers, the colonial bureaucracy and its institutions? Did they allow themselves to be tamed, disciplined and controlled by their employers without resistance, and become docile, passive and mute sufferers in the face of physical coercion, economic and sexual exploitation? We will look for answers below.

Awareness of Rights and Solidarity

Contrary to the stereotype of their being 'ignorant' and 'helpless', the labourers often showed a great deal of awareness of their rights when, on many occasions though often unsuccessfully, they went to the offices of Deputy Commissioners *en masse* to register their complaints against maltreatment and extraction of excess work by the manager, and demanded redress of their grievances, sometime even threatening action. As early as 1866, in a case of flogging of labourers on the charge of desertion at Serajoolee tea garden of Assam Company in Darrang, Captain Lamb, the Deputy Commissioner, reported that the labourers were prevented from coming to his office for complaining against the manager and assistant manager.[46] In 1888, when some female labourers were flogged in Mesaijan tea garden, a large group of labourers left the garden and went to the office of the Deputy Commissioner of Lakhimpur office to complain about ill-treatment at the hands of the manager and his assistant.[47] They persuaded him to order an enquiry. The enquiry by the District Superintendent of Police and the Deputy Commissioner himself found that the women labourers Panu, Khumti and Sukhi had been flogged for desertion and short work. They were tied to a post in the porch of the manager's house, their clothes lifted up to their waists, and beaten on the bare buttocks with a stirrup leather on the orders of the assistant manager. This was a rare case where the labourers succeeded in getting the assistant manager, Anding, convicted by the court to ten months' rigorous imprisonment and a fine of Rs 450.[48]

The Deputy Commissioner of Lakhimpur reported in 1892 that 'The tendency for coolies to come in numbers to complain in court appears to be increasing, and employers urge with justice that there should be a penalty for coolies leaving the garden when the procedure of section 134 has been complied with.'[49] This observation was recorded when the Rewa labourers of Khobang tea garden struck work and went *en masse* to his office to complain against the extraction of excess work by the manager and lack of sufficient food. Many of them did not want to renew their contract either. He had 'persuaded' them to go back instead of taking action against the errant manager. He was soon informed of 'riots' in the garden. The labourers assaulted not only the manager but also others from lower ranks of the hierarchy, like the *hazira muhrriri*, holding him responsible for payment of short wages. Eight labourers were sentenced to three months' rigorous imprisonment in this case.

Many district officials began to acknowledge growing awareness of their rights and familiarity with the provisions of the labour laws among the labour force in the tea plantations. The Labour Immigration Resolution of 1902–03 observed: 'The coolies are aware that the conditions of their employment are regulated by rules, not by the bargaining of the market; the rules are unfavourable to them in some respects but favourable to them in others, and they resent any attempt to exact more labour than the rules warrant.'[50] P.J. Melitus, Commissioner of Assam Valley districts, did not think that labourers were knowledgeable about the rules. However he was aware that over the years and through experience, 'round the rule certain local practices, or *dusturs*' had grown in the tea gardens. The labour force had developed a sense of what was beyond the norms of the rules and any 'departure from *dusturs* in a direction unfavourable to them which they really resent'.[51] The Deputy Commissioner of Lakhimpur, Major H.W. Cole, also observed that over the past ten years there was an increasing tendency among labourers of 'unlawful assembly' and that the 'attitude of coolie towards his employer has deteriorated'. Among the various causes for this tendency among labourers that he enumerated was 'a fair knowledge of the labour laws, gained by experience', and 'the publicity and importance attaching to cases between employers and employed, the frequent discussion in the press – European and Native – have not been without their result on the mind and attitude of the coolies'. Major Cole added a cautionary note, borne out of his stereotypical perception of the labourers: that while 'no one wish to curtail a coolie's knowledge of the law under which he labours, nor his power to resist *bona-fide* oppression, but the danger lies in the coolie being an unthinking individual, easily led, especially in his cups, ready to resort to violence on insufficient provocation'.[52] D.H. Lees, Deputy Commissioner of Darrang, was another observer of deterioration of relations between the employers and their labourers. He attributed this to stricter discipline being enforced on many gardens where 'in order to secure economy', excessive work is extracted:

> Work on tea gardens has therefore become more irksome, and coolies, being now better acquainted with their rights, are more and more disinclined to endure the strict discipline under which they are kept. The growing dislike to work on tea gardens is shown by the increasing number of coolies who leave the gardens.[53]

He blamed the Calcutta agents and their intervention in the working of the gardens for the managers' compulsion to extract excessive work.[54]

Nature and Forms of Resistance

For any act of defiance, punitive measures such as flogging and confinement became a normal practice in the tea estates. The labouring tribals and semi-aboriginals were perceived as inherently inferior humans by the planters. This attitude was akin to that of the white masters towards their black slave labour in the antebellum era in Southern America. The British tea planters established an omnipotent, super-authority over their labour force, within what has been termed a 'paternalistic' framework.[55] The planters considered intervention in the social and personal lives of labourers a part of their 'paternalist' obligations.[56]

The empowerment of planters with the right to private arrest of labour under the penal system became an important tool in containing labour mobility. This practice originated under Section 33 of the Act of 1865, and remained in force till 1908 under Act I of 1882 as well as Act VI of 1901. Wielding this power, captured runaways and recalcitrant labour were arrested and held within the *phatak*, a private 'prison', erected in the plantation.[57] For the labourers, the *phatak* was a symbol of the indenture regime based on penal provisions. The formal dismantling of indenture did not lead to any major relief from the dependency relationship for the labourers, as the planters adopted alternate strategies to maintain control in the post-indenture period.[58] Physical coercion, confinement, disease, malnutrition, low reproduction and a high rate of mortality were the harsh realities of plantation life for the labourers. Wages below subsistence level, even when supplemented by wages in kind, were the main features of the wage structure in the Assam Valley tea plantations.[59] These and other features mentioned above were specific to the organizational structure of plantations that operated in contrast to a viable free labour market. For those who were living and working under this plantation regime, what was the quality of everyday life, and what kind of resistance was offered and what were the struggles waged by them? We have attempted to provide some answers, albeit briefly given the constraints of data, in this chapter. We also discuss the shifting trajectory of workers' protests in the Assam Valley tea plantations over time during colonial rule.

While presenting the dominant patterns of protest by workers against planters' control in different time-periods, we will attempt to juxtapose it with the evolving power structure in the plantations. This will help understand not just why the workers protested and why this protest took certain forms, but also the limits of such protests and the forms they took at certain historical conjunctures. Standard histories of workers' protests in India have often framed these protests within a teleology of gradually ascending forms of resistance and working-class consciousness.[60] Alternatively, workers' protests have been analysed in terms of the cultural or sociological characteristics of the labour force, namely their tribal, rural or pre-capitalist cultural heritage.[61] My argument here eschews both economic and cultural determinism, and instead seeks to locate the shifting character of workers' protests in their historical context as well as in the changing power structure of the plantations. The characteristic features of the plantation regime described above may have imposed constraints on the growth of an early and organized labour movement in the Assam tea plantations, but resistance by labourers in various forms was far from absent. An analysis of these forms dispels notions of their utter passivity and submissiveness.

The earliest resistance offered by labour surfaced in the form of 'absconding', 'desertions' and even strikes in the Assam Company's tea estates. It is interesting to note that while in the period prior to the indenture legislations, the Assam Company's official correspondence described collective actions of labourers as strikes, the term strike disappeared from the colonial records after the indenture legislations came into operation – and resurfaced only in the early 1920s, after the official dismantling of the indenture regime.

The opening up of new plantations in remote and isolated locations in Upper Assam caused a great deal of hardship in the daily lives of labourers including for obtaining provisions, which was made worse by low and often delayed wage payments. These experiences built up discontent among the local Kachari labourers who had been employed for this purpose. Matters were made worse with growing arrears of wages due to delayed remittances from Calcutta, resulting in the 'absconding' of many Kachari labourers in 1845.[62] What may be considered as the first recorded strike of tea garden labour occurred in 1848: on 22 March that year, Stephen Mornay, the Superintendent of Assam Company's gardens, informed the Calcutta Board that Kachari labourers had struck work, created disturbance and crowded around the Company's office. They were however 'persuaded' to return to work on the promise that in future their pay would not be held up for more than one month.[63] The Kachari labourers put up continuous resistance against efforts to increase the work load or reduce wages by the Company's garden management.[64] Moreover, the increasing competition for labour in the province during this period put pressure on the Company's Superintendent to offer concessions to the Kacharis to prevent them from leaving the garden.[65] There were constant complains of Kachari labourers absconding by the Superintendent to the Local Board.[66]

Equally troublesome to the management were the newly brought 'Bengal coolies' from the neighbouring Bengal districts, many of whom deserted either en route or after arrival in Assam. Faced with problems of acclimatization, low wages (compounded further by reductions), excessive work and high mortality, they deserted. The monthly wages offered in the Assam Company's gardens were Rs 3.5 for men, Rs 2 for women, Rs 1.5 for boys and for girls, Re 1 and 4 annas per month.[67] The emergence of alternate sources of employment at higher wages in infrastructural work of the Public Works Department offered incentives to desert.[68] The garden management complained of 'severe shortage of coolies as many of them are going to work at the building of Roads, Public Works started by the Government'.[69] These were years when the tea industry had still not stabilized and was financially insecure, and therefore the management was wary of desertions as they affected production. There were reports of production being 'clipped' in gardens for want of labourers because of '250 Kacharies having absconded at different time.'[70] A note of caution was issued by the Assam Company to the Superintendents of gardens about extraction of excessive work and coercive supervision of labour force, to prevent desertions.[71] The Board's Secretary, on being informed of desertions by Bengali labourers, wrote that 'he had heard rumours that the increased amount of work now required from the coolies at the plantations is more than they can perform'. Further,

> if the Superintendent in his zeal for the company's interest is urging the labourers to hoe an equal quantity of land in the still soil of Assam as is performed in Bengal, it is more than they can do, and suggests that in such case some relaxation in this respect would be politic.[72]

In 1859 serious trouble started again when Kachari labourers who had been recruited from Darrang district demanded an increase in wages, failing which they demanded that they be allowed to leave the Company's service and refused to serve the period of their contract. The Company sought and received military help to control the situation. Henry de Mornay and McIntosh, the Superintendents, suppressed the strike with the help of Captain Holroyd, the Magistrate, by arresting twenty-two 'ringleaders' who were sentenced to imprisonment for one year, while twenty others were dismissed. The difficulty in controlling and disciplining the Kachari labour pushed the issue of bringing migrant labour from other places to the forefront, forcing the Company to consider procuring labour from the northern and eastern districts of Bengal – Santhal Parganas, Chotanagpur and Ranchi.[73]

The Indentured Regime and Desertion

The term desertion as an act of labour resistance acquired a different connotation and meaning during the period of the 'tea mania' and the indentured regime, from 1860 onwards. The frenetic pace of acreage expansion, and the clearing of vast tracts of forest land for opening up a large number of new tea plantations, generated a large-scale demand for labour in the Assam Valley. Large numbers of migrants were recruited from among the tribal, aboriginal and lower-caste communities of the agrarian districts of Bengal – Chotanagpur, Santhal Parganas and Ranchi – through private professional recruiters called *arakatis*, and shipped to Assam to work in the tea plantations.[74] Confronted with the harshness of their travel experience, disease and high mortality, and the brutalities of daily life on the tea gardens, these migrants found desertion to be the only means of escaping the plantation regime. Reporting the increasing incidents of desertion, Edgar remarked: 'it is not surprising that during these evil times the idea of escaping was always present to the coolies' minds, and it was equally natural that the planters should do all in their power to prevent it'.[75] Ashley Eden, Secretary, Government of Bengal, while forwarding the report of the Commissioner of Assam, informed the Government of India on 5 September 1864 that the 'breaches of contract by the labourers were almost daily occurrence' in the tea districts, and that as a result, relations between planters and their imported labourers were on 'most unsatisfactory footing'. He strongly recommended government intervention because 'a serious and growing evil has sprung up which must be dealt with vigorously and promptly'.[76] He was acutely aware at the same time that the wages paid to the migrant labourers in the plantations were 'considerably lower than those current in the immediate neighbourhood of their homes', and therefore their response was 'careless indifference to the interests of the master, sullen idleness and apathy, constant attempts to abscond, and sometimes even violence to the employer'.[77] That desertion was becoming a serious problem is clear from the fact that Assam Company especially employed *chupprassies* and *barkandauzes* to apprehend deserting coolies.[78]

Desertion symbolized rejection of the relationship of servitude that the emigrants were coerced into under the indentured regime in the Assam Valley's tea plantations. It was both an individual and, sometimes, a collective act of resistance, comparable to what Peter Wood described as an act of 'stealing themselves' by slaves in the eighteenth-century South Carolina colony in America.[79] The effort, courage and risk involved in this act reflected the intense desire of the runaways to reject their life of subordination under indenture in the tea plantations. The planters referred to deserting as 'absconding', and it was declared a criminal offence under the existing labour laws. Prior to 1865 a deserter from the tea gardens, if caught, was punished under Section 492 of the Indian Penal Code, which provided for one month's imprisonment.[80] The newly enacted Act VI of 1865 empowered employers to arrest runaways without a warrant. The main provision of the Act lay in sanctions for breach of contract by labourers: planters were given powers to arrest labourers who 'absconded' without warrant, and imprisonment was the penalty for refusal to work. While this provision was applied to the newly arrived labour, time-expired labour was increasingly engaged under the Workman's Breach of Contract Act XIII of 1859 with inbuilt provisions restraining the mobility of labour. The indenture system was further modified and strengthened with the passing of Act I of 1882, which was designed to serve the need of planters to regulate and control an expanding labour force.[81]

The act of desertion was not an easy one either. It was extremely difficult to succeed in running away for serious efforts were made to prevent desertions. Describing the nature of surveillance mounted by the planters to prevent desertion, Edgar mentioned the posting of *chowkidars* at every possible outlet in the 'coolie lines' from where the labourers were not allowed to leave at night. 'The savage hill men were in special request to track out fugitives, and I have even heard of one planter who had dogs trained for the purpose.'[82] The use of dogs for tracking runaways is reminiscent of slaves tracked down by dogs in British-owned plantations in Jamaica during the seventeenth century.[83] Hill men were specially employed in Assam to track down 'absconders' with a promise of a reward of Rs 5 per head. In the tradition of the slave owners of South Carolina, the Assam tea planters put in place an organized system of recovering deserters through advertisements in posters and newspapers.[84] For example, a notice was issued in Dibrugarh town on 12 April 1912, which mentioned that 'a gang of 30 absconders was captured on last Tuesday noon. Gardens concerned enquire immediately at the *Times of Assam* office with usual reward, feeding and advertisement charges. Feeding charges – 4s a day, per head.'[85] In 1902–03 the Deputy Commissioner reported that the Steamer Agent's staff was instructed to report and to prevent runaways from leaving by boats.[86] Babu Bhod Ram Baruah, the clerk of Steamer Agent Wolforston, during his cross-examination in a case tried by Krishna Chandra Chowdhary, Extra Assistant Commissioner, Tezpur, disclosed that his employer was also the agent for Monabari tea estate and on instruction would prevent runaway labourers from leaving by denying them tickets to travel by steamers, and inform the managers.

We get reward for every such coolie, if he is received by the managers. The garden manager sends us letters, sometimes giving names and sometimes the number of the run-away coolies from his garden, and on such information we do not issue tickets, but give intimation to managers detaining the coolies at the ghat. We do not issue tickets to coolies even if they come to complain against managers. This has been our practice for a long time. If a coolie happens to come to ghat and states that he is going to make a complaint against his manager, we detain even him and inform the manager. The latter then takes him back by sending a *sirdar*.[87]

That was not all. The labourers, after being caught, were punished either by imprisonment or fines or both. Fines ranged between Rs 20 to Rs 100, and imprisonments between one month and six months. The percentage of convictions for desertions was 13.2 in 1886, 15.9 in 1887 and 18.2 in 1888; and the percentage of arrests for desertions, 14.1 in 1886, 17.7 in 1887 and 20.9 in 1888. A large proportion of the runaways were arrested in the jungle tracts of Brahmaputra Valley and convicted for desertion. In 1885, out of 558 labourers arrested on charges of desertion, 482 were convicted; and in 1892, out of 1,055 arrested, 992 were convicted.[88] There was also an elaborate and cruel system of deterrent punishment. If the absconder was caught he was tied up and flogged, and the reward paid to his capturer was deducted by way of fine from the absconder's future earnings. But severe flogging often meant no future earnings: 'often runaways enfeebled by their sufferings in the jungles, died under or from the effect of the floggings they received when caught'.[89] However not all cases of desertion were reported. The official labour reports published only cases about which information was sent by the planters. There was no official agency that could independently collect the necessary information about such cases. Finally, even if the labourers succeeded in running away without being caught, there was always the possibility of them being killed by the local tribals or the jungle beast.

The severity of the law and other hardships did not substantially deter deserters or diminish the scale of desertions, as is clear from the official reports. The Enquiry Commission of 1868 (though it did not provide figures) reported a very large number of desertions.[90] In 1875 the Darrang Deputy Commissioner reported 6.22 per cent desertion rate among tea garden labourers. In 1876 the deserters numbered 5,821 at a rate of 6.16 per cent, and in 1877 the number of desertions reported was 4,724 at a rate of 4.48 per cent.[91] In the succeeding years, increasing desertions by labourers continued to be reported: 9,855 in 1884, 6,432 in 1897 and 10,244 in 1900.[92] Rev. Dowding, an ardent critic of the tea planters, used the figures published in the official immigration reports to present the following conclusions:

> In 1892 . . . from the mean force of, say, 457,700 souls, 354,700 of whom were in healthy gardens, and 103,000 recorded living in unhealthy gardens, there were 17,263 desertions; 12,568 from healthy gardens, 4,695 from unhealthy ones, producing a desertion-rate of 35.3 per mille from healthy gardens, and 45.4 per mille from unhealthy ones, a mean rate, over the whole force, of 37.6 per mille. As however, the force contained some 173,900 children, and children could scarcely be counted amongst the deserters, we should deduct them; and calculating the desertion rate on the 283,800 adults, we find it 60.8 per mille.[93]

There were references even to children deserting. In 1884, as many as 1,179 desertions reported were of children.[94] Actual desertions were, however, much more numerous than reported. Many deserters were caught in the immediate vicinity of the gardens while attempting to escape. Some of the captured labourers were not taken to police stations by their employers, as required under the law, and hence were not reported as deserters. Chief Commissioner Henry Cotton reported in 1900 that in all the districts, imported labour had deserted in large numbers. He also pointed out that the figures provided in the half-yearly returns considerably understated the facts, as cases of desertions were not entered very often as the deserters had been apprehended before the close of the half year in which they absconded.[95] And even after withdrawal of the penal provisions of the labour laws in 1908, desertions remained an important item of official reporting well up to 1920.

District officials occasionally recorded their diagnosis of the causes of desertion. One explanation offered was that the labourers were finding life in the labour districts not quite as pleasant as was depicted to them by the designated recruiters, and therefore became dissatisfied with their lot.[96] The Chief Commissioner of Assam offered his opinion that 'desertions are often mainly owing to desire for change, and home sickness, which are naturally engendered by the isolated position of most tea-gardens'.[97] They believed that it was mostly new and unsettled labourers who deserted. Their general diagnosis of the causes of desertion included low wages, the unhealthiness of the gardens, high mortality, discipline and strict supervision at work and living quarters. Some district officials observed that the newly arrived labourers deserted because they were disgusted with the coercive imposition of discipline, supervision and confinement, which they were not used to.[98] Desertion sometimes meant a transfer of labour power from a particularly unhealthy, low-wage or highly undermanned garden to a more favourable one. One of the reasons given for the high rate of desertions among labourers was the 'bonus system', and the readiness with which some of the planters enlisted all comers without any attempt to ascertain whether they were already under engagement elsewhere. 'It has transpired that in a certain garden a bonus of Rs 25 is offered to ask coolies who take a local agreement for one year. Such a state of things the planters themselves alone can remedy.'[99]

'Shirking', 'Cheating' and 'Laziness'

Those who could not 'steal themselves' away adopted other strategies of resistance against the coercive day-to-day chores of plantation work, which included shirking and sabotaging the work process and schedule. They found ways of subverting the work process or getting their earnings with 'short' work, which in turn got them branded as 'shirkers', 'lazy' and 'cheaters' by their employers. Since these strategies of resistance were not overt, the official reportage refrained from commenting on them. Our sources of these stories come from the planters themselves, whose published memoirs and other writings give glimpses, though unintendedly, of such acts of labour resistance. Barker, for example, bitterly recorded the 'shirking' efforts of his labour during work in the field and that even severe punishment was no deterrent. This is worth quoting in length:

> The deep hoeing nerrick averages about two-thirds of the light; and here occurs an opportunity for the coolie to shirk his work and get the better of his employer, for it is impossible, as the coolie well knows, to go over a large extent of ground and distinguish, by merely looking at it, which has been double hoed: a walking-stick plunged into the earth is about the handiest and the most effective test. By dexterous manipulations the coolie cuts the top earth in such a way as to present

the appearance of a good deep cut, and so saves that additional chop which he is supposed to have made. This artifice is most easily overlooked, and very hard to detect; but when found out, that coolies' next ten minutes are passed in a way not to be envied. Various forms of punishment – from a good thrashing to making him do two or three times the amount over again – are inflicted, but always with the same after-result, that if an opportunity presents itself he will invariably adopt all the devices of which he is master (and they are many) to shirk his work; as a result, I regret to say, that is not entirely confined to the black labourer.[100]

He also wrote about subversion of the quality of work by labourers even when they were under the watchful gaze of *sirdars* who supervised work in the field. The *sirdars* were assigned supervision of a number of men and women labourers to do hoeing and plucking work during the high season. Barker complained that his *sirdars'* charges were 'occasionally very willful, and pluck according to their own inclinations, instead of carrying out instructions, bringing in coarser leaf when fine only is required, and doing anything to fill their basket and save a little trouble'.[101] For labourers who were found out for feigning illness in order to escape hard work, 'the wrath of the sahib when he places his hand on the cool unfevered wrist of an impostor is justifiable, and the judicious application of the cane quickly convinces the coolie that he has made a mistake in imagining that there could be anything the matter with him'.[102]

Reminiscing about his days in the plantations, another planter, W.M. Fraser, recalled his experience in the 1890s of a senior manager chastising women labourers for faulty leaf-plucking: 'The ground become strewn with bad leaf, while from one woman to the other went the admonishing Thomson, his tongue and hands fully employed.'[103] In another instance Hetherington, a young assistant manager, recorded the punishment he inflicted on women labourers for plucking bad leaf on 1 August 1901: 'Went round the new lines plucking and nearly caused a riot by clouting three women. . . . They were plucking into *kapre*, which was strictly forbidden.'[104]

Crole tried to decipher the 'cheating' methods of female labourers in plucking work.

> The wily Hindoo of the female persuasion is by no means above trying on various dodges to make her basket of leaf register more weight on the scales than it would do without any artful and adventitious aid. Thus she often immerses her basket of leaf bodily in a pool of water, or puts a soaking cloth, or even sheets of lead foil (purloined from the packing-room of the factory) into the bottom of her basket, sometimes hiding it with a cunningly-devised false bottom, is only to prevent the leaf from falling through the interstices of the wicker-work at the bottom.

He was both amused and unhappy that these women were trying even 'cruder' methods of 'surreptitious introduction amongst the leaf of heavy materials, such as bricks'.[105] Punishment for such chicanery in the form of fine of a day's wage and, more often, through the *sahib*'s forcible venting of public expression in '*coolie baat*', functioned only as temporary deterrents.[106]

Maurice Hanly, a planter in the Laojan tea estate in Assam who wrote a fictionalized account of his experiences as a planter, produced an imagined 'coolie song' about the 'brick trick':

> Oh it's plucking time, my lassie,
> And your baskets are full,
> There is a brick below
> If only you could see,
> But the Sahib he does not look there,
> And he'll never find that brick there,
> So just come along,
> Pluck the leaf with me.
> The Sahib persists in working,
> And talking too of work,
> We feel quite limp when
> He goes on that way,
> For we cannot stand the bridle,
> We prefer to sit and idle'
> And for doing nothing,
> Still to draw big pay.
> Oh it's plucking time, my lassie,
> And the money is coming in,
> An extra brick will make
> You draw more pay;
> And we'll teach you how to cheat,
> We can do it quite a treat,
> So just listen sisters all to what I say. [107]

Cultural Traditions as Means of Resistance

The migrant labour communities never allowed the memories of their social cultural traditions and practices to be marginalized or erased. While they grieved for their dead and deserted ones, they also celebrated festivals, marriage and childbirth ceremonies in their traditional cultural and social forms – dancing, drinking and music being an integral part of these. By keeping these memories alive, the diverse labour communities managed to cope with their everyday lives of grief and wretchedness. Both Barker and Crole, in their own cynical and convoluted ways, gave graphic accounts of cultural celebrations among the labourers on the occasions of marriages and festivals. Barker mentioned that on the three or four successive days given off work to the labourers between the expiry of their old contract and the signing of a new contract, they were given to 'certain amount of debauchery'. On every native holiday, and on Sunday, when all work ceased, the labourers went for weekly purchases to the *haat*. After the purchasing was done, the remainder of the day was given over to 'nautches and carousing'. Very often Mondays or days after festivals were 'bad' days for work – the effects of drinking and celebration were very visible in large-scale absences from work. Referring to their celebration of festivals, marriage or childbirth, Barker commented

> the din is terrific, five or six tum-tums all along at once, mixed a varied assortment of discordant wails and the perpetual monotony of the curious droning noise, that forms the basis of all native minstrelsy. This *hullabaloo* (I know no other more appropriate term), kept up without a lull until two or three in the morning, forms a charming accompaniment to a restless night. Continual tum-tumming in the lines is at first, to the uninitiated, a source of maddening annoyance; I cannot imagine any more exasperating noise to a musical man. . . . A nautch is impossible of description, no pen describe the weird, wild, creepy sensation that steals over a European watching for the first time these strange people, twisting, writhing, wriggling about, to the sound of the most unearthly music, the tum-tum always the chief offender.[108]

While these dance forms, music and songs may have been exasperating, and appeared wild, weird and even creepy to the alien European planters, these forms of folk traditions carried and reflected the migrants' painful experiences of their recruitment and harsh lives on the plantations – descriptions of exploitation, love, grief, protest, etc. Among the most popular forms that are still regularly performed are the *Jhumar* folk songs and dances. They relate to *Karma Puja* and occupy a very prominent place in the cultural life of the tea garden labourers of Assam Valley. *Karma Puja* was, and still is, celebrated in the festive season, in the months of August–September, followed by the *Vijaya* festival in November–December every year. Every *Karma Puja* is accompanied by the *Jhumar* folk dance.[109] According to Mahato, male and female dancers perform this dance accompanied by *Dhol* and *Mandal* at every fair and festival, presenting a colourful picture of social cohesiveness among social clusters of migrants. *Jhumur* is a collective and composite tune, and revolves around love songs based on Radha and Krishna; but the vitality of *Jhumur* opens up other dimensions also.[110] Recently put together and translated by Indian scholars, some of these *Jhumar* songs are self-explanatory. In *Jhumur* there is description of the day-to-day lives of labouring communities in the tea gardens. One of the famous *Jhumur* composers of Jharkhand, Uday Karmakar, from erstwhile Manbhum, composed a song in the last part of the nineteenth century, which is still prevalent among the labour communities:

Paka Khatai lekhaeli nam
Re Lampatiya Shyam
Phanki diye bandu chalali Assam
Depughare maritari
Uthailele terrene kori
Hoogli sahare dekholi Akash
Mane kari Assam Jabo
Jora Pankha tanabo
Sahab dilo Kodaleri Kam
Dina Udaya bhane
Akale peter tane
Tipki tipki pareh gham

(Our names were written in the permanent book. The recruiter Shyam deceived us and sent us to Assam. We were beaten in the depot-ghar [godown where labourers were kept during transit]. We first saw the sky in Hoogly town. We thought we would be engaged to draw fans in Assam but the Sahibs gave us spades. We sweat while working.)[111]

The following *Karma-Jhumur* is still very popular in almost all the tea gardens:

Sardar bole kam kam
Babu bole dhari an
Saheb bole libo pither cham
Re Jaduram,
Phanki diye bandu pathali Assam

(The Sardar asks for more work. The Babu abuses and the Sahib threatens to peel the skin of the back. Alas Jahuram, you sent me to Assam by deceiving me.)[112]

It has been pointed out that *Jhumar* songs and dances convey the aesthetic sensibility of the people. They communicate the life, joys and sorrows of the community. The authorship of the songs is not known as they are preserved by oral tradition. The language of the folksongs and folklore provide an insider's view of typical ways of life.[113]

One of the most interesting features of labour life in the Assam tea plantations was the distinctive caste, ethnic and community identities of the labourers. Despite living together in the vicinity of 'coolie lines' for over a century, they maintained their distinctive ethnic and caste identities as Santhalis, Mundas, Gonds, Kandhs, Oraons, etc. During a recent field trip to one of the tea labour *bastis* in a tea plantation near Kaziranga National Park in Assam, I learnt that inter-caste and inter-ethnic marriages are still discouraged among the tea labour communities. However, such considerations and strict maintenance of caste and ethnicity were often overlooked while resisting or retaliating against acts of coercion perpetrated by the planters. In the report of the enquiry (specially ordered by the Viceroy, Lord Curzon) into the causes of friction between the planters and the labour force in Assam's tea plantations, several cases of collective resistance and retaliation against physical coercion or in support of economic grievances were mentioned.[114] Even though organized labour trade unions did not emerge till well into the 1930s and 1940s in the Assam tea plantations, colonial reports from as early as the 1880s and 1890s recorded several cases of collective resistance where they acted as labourers, and not just Santhalis, Oraons or Mundas.[115] They retaliated collectively against planters' acts of sexual coercion of women labourers. The threat of severe punishment for standing up in support of their fellow-labourers did not act as deterrent. Through the preservation and celebration of their cultural and social traditions, and acts of collective resistance, the labourers resisted being transformed into 'docile' and 'disciplined' 'coolies'.

Labour Protest and 'Crime'

Very often incidents of protests and resistance in the tea gardens were deliberately suppressed or underplayed in official reporting so as to present a picture of well-being and harmony, and official reports often invoked the low level of prosecution under the penal laws as a sign of good relations prevailing on the plantations. The cases of resistance which did get reported were interpreted as illegal, and invariably described as 'assault', 'unlawfull assembly', 'mobbing' and 'rioting' because the provisions of the labour legislations considered these as criminal actions. The projection of harmonious labour relations by the provincial bureaucracy was done to buttress the case for perpetuating indenture legislation. While advocating the continuation of Act I of 1882 with the Secretary of State for India, the Chief Commissioner of Assam in 1891 presented sanitized reports by his subordinates about labour relations in the plantations:

> Planters as a whole are well disposed towards their labourers and treat them fairly. If there is ever any dissatisfaction in a garden, it is usually due to some act of native officials, it may be their own *sirdars* or *duffadars*, and not to any harshness or ill-treatment on the part of the employers.

'Vast improvement in the relations between employers and labourers, a great improvement over the past year' was a general refrain of the district officials.[116]

However, despite these efforts, the growing number of incidents of rioting, mobbing, assaults and unlawful assembly pointed to a different reality. The very next year, 1892, the Chief Commissioner reported an increase in 'criminality' in several tea districts: 'rioting' cases increased from 65 to 106, 'assault' from 55 to 66 cases, 'contempt of lawful authority' from 2 to 15, and 'theft' from 118 to 160 cases.[117] The intensification of the labour process which was contested by the labourers is also clear from the increase in cases of rioting and unlawful assembly, reaching 272 prosecutions per year by the end of the century, and the corresponding increase in the number of prosecutions.[118]

In sharp contrast to the official projection of harmony, the detailed report on the relations between planters and labourers in the tea gardens during the past fifteen years submitted by the Government of Assam to the Government of India in 1904, as per the instructions of Viceroy Curzon, showed continuous friction between the labourers and planters in the tea gardens. The details given in this report provide us with a range of causes that provoked action on the part of labour, and the nature and extent of the punishment meted out to them. A closer scrutiny of the report reveals certain interesting features regarding the nature and forms of labour resistance. The involvement of labourers in acts of violence, both minor and serious, against managers and assistant managers was mostly retaliatory in nature. Most of the acts of resistance were collective in nature, and often in solidarity with fellow labourers who were subjected to public indignity and physical coercion by the planters.[119] In several cases, the issues were economic – for example, low wages, denial of rice as a part of wage in kind, extraction of excessive work, etc. In other cases, it was anger against the physical coercion, confinement and indignities heaped upon the labourers – like insults and beatings, public caning of male and female labourers and sometime even children, causing injury and occasional death.[120] There were also cases of violence against managers and assistant managers in retaliation for sexual harassment of women labourers and in response to severe chastisement for drunkenness. Several other factors like refusal of leave, coercion to work at the end of festival periods, ill treatment, punishment for unsatisfactory or inadequate work and drunken behaviour, physical confinement, etc., were also reported as reasons for the increasing collision between planters and labourers in the tea gardens.[121]

One of the most important issues on which labourers were provoked to violent action was the indignities perpetrated on them and their womenfolk by the garden managers and their assistants. In 1890, a gang of forty labourers of Silghat tea garden in Nowgong district assaulted the manager because he had beaten a woman labourer allegedly for disobeying orders. While the manager was acquitted of the charge, fourteen labourers were sentenced to nine months' rigorous imprisonment. In 1892, labourers assaulted the manager of Maduri tea garden, Sibsagar, because of sexual harassment and ill-treatment of a labour girl. In this case the manager was convicted of wrongful restraint and simple assault, and sentenced to a week's imprisonment and a fine of Rs 100. In 1893, the labourers of Boekl tea garden, Lakhimpur, attacked the manager and assistant manager with sticks and bricks for public caning of a labourer. One labourer was sentenced to rigorous imprisonment for six months and five others for five months. In Darrang district, labourers 'assaulted' the managers of Kalakuchi and Ghoiralla tea estates. The reason for the 'assault' in one of these cases was that the manager had abused and assaulted the wife of a labourer. The husband was sentenced to five years' rigorous imprisonment, one labourer to rigorous imprisonment for six months and five others to five months.[122]

Sometimes denial of leave or coercion to work in the immediate aftermath of social cultural festivities was resented by the labourers and led to confrontations. In 1890, six labourers were sentenced to three weeks' rigorous imprisonment for simply threatening violence against the manager of Daklingia tea garden, Sibsagar, because they were denied leave. In 1891, the assistant manager of Barjuli tea garden, Darrang, went around the lines to make reluctant labourers turn out to work after a night of drinking and festivities of *Karam Puja*. This led to confrontation between the *sirdar* and other labourers. The assistant manager was then assaulted by several labourers who pursued him as far as his bungalow. One labourer was sentenced to eighteen months' rigorous punishment in this case, two labourers to one year each, and five others to five months.[123] In 1898, the manager and assistant managers of Kellydon tea garden in Nowgong were attacked by a number of labourers with sticks and hoes; the reluctant labourers were being 'persuaded' to work after three days of absence on account of the *Holi* festival, and were provoked into violent action when a woman labourer was being physically coerced to work. Eight of the 'ringleaders' were given rigorous imprisonment terms from three months to two years for their 'crime'.

The labourers sometimes contested and defied the management's strict implementation of tasks. For example, in 1892, the women labourers of Sapakati tea garden, Sibsagar, did not show up on time for plucking and as punishment the manager ordered them to be put on hoeing work. The order led to a confrontation in which other labourers joined and beat up the manager so severely that he fell unconscious. Three of them were sentenced to rigorous imprisonment for eight months, and five for three months each, and all of them were fined Rs 10 each. In 1896, the labourers of Joyhing tea garden in Lakhimpur were provoked to rioting because they were asked to work on a Sunday. Several of them were sentenced to long terms of rigorous imprisonment. In 1899, some of the labourers of Tiphuk tea garden in Sibsagar simply refused to work and defied all efforts at 'persuasion' by the manager, which caused serious trouble. Those who threatened to attack the manager at his home were sentenced to rigorous terms of imprisonment varying from four to nine months.

Equally important were wage-related issues on which the labourers contested and challenged the managers and their subordinates. In 1890, six cases were listed in the Assam Valley districts involving managers and labourers – in one case seven labourers were convicted and sentenced to one month's rigorous imprisonment on a charge of simple assault on the manager of Balipara tea garden in Darrang. Their complaint was regarding short payment for a full month's work. In 1894, several labourers of Towkok tea garden in Sibsager collectively went to the manager and demanded rice from the godown. Their request was refused as it was not the day for issue of rice. The refusal led to confrontation and the manager was struck by one labourer with an umbrella and by two others with sticks. A head constable enquired into the case, arrested five persons and took them to the police station, where a group of labourers surrounded him and released the five men by force. Six of them were convicted for rioting. One was rigorously imprisoned for eight months, and four for six months. In 1897 at the Adabari tea garden in Darrang several women labourers attacked the assistant manager with their umbrellas and threw him into a ditch. They were angry regarding a dispute about their *ticca* earnings and for being ordered to work for a full day on a Sunday. Many of them were sentenced to six months' rigorous imprisonment. In 1899, the change of the payment system at Naharajan tea garden created a great deal of discontent among the Kachari labourers. Their discontent turned into a violent attack on the manager in retaliation for the beating of an elderly labourer. The punishment was swift and very harsh. Forty of them were sentenced to rigorous jail terms of one year, twenty-five to nine months, and thirteen to six months.[124] In the Hukanpukuri tea garden in Lakhimpur district, on pay day, the assistant manager, Hennessy, struck a labourer for objecting to inadequate wages. This action aroused the anger of the other labourers who had assembled to receive their pay in front of the manager's bungalow. And despite the attempts of the senior manager to pacify their anger, the labourers, including women, attacked the bungalow of the assistant manager. The Europeans and their Indian staff escaped unhurt through the bathroom. But fourteen labourers, including two women, were sentenced to terms of rigorous imprisonment varying from six months to five years.[125] Most cases reported were similar in nature.

Provocation to violence often followed incidents of humiliation, of being flogged, caned and insulted in front of fellow labourers in public by the managers and their assistants. While in most of these cases the labourers acted in groups, there were also occasions when they adopted individual forms of defiance and sabotage. A case was reported of a labourer who cut down 200 tea bushes in the Nahartali tea garden. He was allegedly under the influence of *ganja*. He was imprisoned for twenty-one days for his misdeed. Another labourer of Kellang tea garden was punished with six months' imprisonment because he had 'maliciously' wounded a pony of the manager with a pruning knife. He was angry because he had been dismissed from the position of a syce.[126]

Chief Commissioner Henry Cotton's annual labour report, which was strongly contested by tea planters, published information on the growing number of cases of conflict and tensions between employers and labourers in the tea gardens. There were 1,024 complaints filed by managers of absence or desertion of labourers under Act XIII of 1859 or Act I of 1882. There was a considerable increase in the number of cases in which labourers were brought to trial for unlawful assembly, rioting, assault on or insult to the planters, or complaints made by them against garden managers, charging them with the use of force or intimidation in order to procure renewal of contracts.[127] Cotton also reported the increasing number of convictions and punishment of labour with varying terms of imprisonment by courts in response to the filing of complaints by managers. In 1901 the Chief Commissioner observed that there was a considerable increase in 'general criminality' amongst tea garden labourers. In Darrang, serious riots occurred in April 1901 in the Bindukuri and Balipara tea gardens, where *haats* were looted by tea garden labourers and others because of the high prices of paddy demanded by the traders. The disturbances at these two *haats* alone produced five cases of rioting with twenty-four persons convicted, and fourteen cases of theft with twenty-eight persons convicted. Sixty complaints were made by labourers against garden managers, charging them with use of force or intimidation in order to procure the renewal of contracts.[128]

There were two other very serious cases of assault on managers by labourers in Darrang district. The manager of the Kolakuchi tea garden was attacked and received serious blow on the head from a labourer, from whom he was trying to protect a *sirdar* of the garden. The labourer was sentenced to eighteen months' rigorous imprisonment, and another labourer who assisted him was awarded six months' rigorous imprisonment. The manager of Ghoirally tea garden in the same district received very serious injuries at the hands of five labourers whom he had abused and assaulted the wife of one of them. The husband was sentenced to one year's rigorous imprisonment, two others received six months, and the rest two to three months' rigorous imprisonment.[129]

There were also cases when the labourers did not merely react to the planters' acts of violence, but acted in demand of certain social and cultural rights. In Halimguri tea estate in Sibsagar district, it was reported that some Santhal labourers attacked the manager, James Begg, on *Kali Puja* day. They had demanded a holiday, and the manager not only refused it but tried to force them to work. Although the manager was not hurt, the court sentenced one labourer to rigorous imprisonment for six months, two to five months, and seventeen to shorter terms.[130]

By 1903, instances of serious conflict between European planters and the labour force were numerous enough to merit the attention of the Viceroy,

Lord Curzon, who wrote about the deterioration of labour relations in the tea gardens of Assam, and sought details from the Home Department about cases of collision between the managers and labourers. Expressing his concern, he wrote on 7 June 1903: 'My own impression is that their number is steadily increasing, and that the relations between masters and coolies on many of the plantations are becoming a public danger.'[131] On Curzon's insistence, a detailed report on the relations between employers and labourers was prepared and submitted. He was not satisfied with the responses of some of the officials like H.H. Risley, who denied that there was any appreciable increase. He wrote a reminder to them on 1 August 1903:

> I remember that in September or October 1900 there was a violent assault upon a coolie by an Englishman on one of the plantations. He was fined Rs 50/- by the District Magistrate and Sir Cotton was so angry that the he took the case on a motion for enhancement to the High Court, who straightaway rejected the appeal. Again in early part of 1901 there was a Mr Black who was fined only Rs 60/- for a very gross assault. I do not find either of these cases in the synopsis, and I am under the impression that some others have also been omitted.[132]

Curzon was convinced of the growing tension in the Assam tea plantations:

> My own impression is that, if the collisions are not more frequent (and I think that they are), the tempers of both sides are more inflamed, and that more violent incidents occur, arising sometimes from the increasing license of the natives, at others from the lack of self-control of a low class of Europeans.

He also shared Chief Commissioner Fuller's belief that 'if there was no penal contract, there would be tendency in time for them to disappear'.[133]

In 1901, ten cases of 'rioting' reported to the Chief Commissioner by the district officers were marked as 'serious'. It must be noted at this point, as also suspected by Curzon, that the number of cases reported were clearly underestimates. The planters themselves were not interested in publicizing such cases, preferring to treat them as insignificant local outbursts. Cases which could not be ignored were presented as 'criminal' and the law took its course. Quite naturally, the planters did not wish to allow such cases to have any spread effect among the plantation labourers.[134] In most of these cases, like on many earlier occasions, the labourers acted in groups, rarely alone. Officials investigating cases of rioting repeatedly pointed to their retaliatory nature, often in response to assaults by the European staff. The Deputy Commissioner of Lakhimpur reported in 1900: 'Blows given by managers, or more commonly by assistant managers, to coolies, either for bad work or refusal to work, were the immediate cause of most of the rioting cases which occurred during the year.'[135] Referring to the reaction of the labourers, it was observed that the 'coolies have generally come up prepared to risk and sometimes go to the length of tempting the manager to strike them'.[136] In the cases reported up to 1920, there were many instances of labourers resorting to violence against managers for similar reasons.[137] The district officials reported the use of firearms by managers against labour.[138] In 1902–03, out of fifteen serious cases of 'violence' and 'intimidation', in four cases managers or their assistants were seriously beaten up, and in a fifth the manager saved himself by the use of a revolver.[139] About 90 labourers were convicted and sentenced to imprisonment upon charges of 'intimidation', 'assaults'or 'rioting'.[140] In 1903–04 one of the assistant managers, 'who seems to have been a new man and injudicious in his treatment of the coolies, was set upon and severely beaten by a mob of coolies, who left him unconscious'.[141] In 1904–05, an assistant manager in the Jorhat sub-division was attacked by some thirty labourers because he had very 'injudiciously taken a woman by the ear to force her to return to work'.[142]

The violent clash between labourers and the management of Rowmari garden in Lakhimpur district in 1903 was a typical example of overt conflict in the plantations. In July 1903, at the height of the plucking season, the labourers of the garden rose as a body and assaulted the European managers and their Indian underlings, causing grievous injuries (the manager had to return to England for treatment). The next day they all marched to the magistrate's court at Dibrugarh to complain about the management. They refused to resume work till their grievances were redressed. It amounted to a strike but was not recognized as such in the official reporting, which interpreted as an offence under the law. As a result forty-two labourers were prosecuted and many of them sentenced to long terms of imprisonment. The ostensible cause of violence was the garden management confiscating umbrellas which the labourers used while plucking tea leaves during the rains, and forcing them instead to wear *jhampi*, broad-rimmed hats. The ferocity of the assault for an apparently trivial reason surprised the investigating official, and initially it was ascribed to the labourers' natural 'excitability' and to a few 'malcontents' who made the reversion from the umbrella to a *jhampi* a matter of prestige. However, further investigation showed that the garden had been subject to a fairly strict work regimen: leave was not granted freely, and there was considerable resentment over production speed-ups. Unlike the broad-rimmed hat, which allowed both hands of the labourer to be used for plucking leaves, the umbrella had to be held with one hand, and this affected the efficiency of plucking. The use of the umbrella by the labourers was therefore a form of resistance to the speed-up of production demanded by the garden, and its deprivation acted as a flash-point for the built-up resentment against the drive for work intensification. The incident in Rowmari was not an isolated one: it was reported that in many gardens, the managers' attempt to enforce the use of the *jhampi* instead of an umbrella was met with stiff resistance. 'The coolies will use umbrellas and the managers have generally had to give in.'[143]

Labour resistance in these forms of day-to-day confrontations, and threats or actual violence against the planters at the workplace continued to be reported by the district officials even after the official dismantling of the penal system. In August 1909, W.K. Allies, the manager of Tilbhum tea garden, complained that his labourers had confronted him using abusive language, breaking his office windows. About 150 of them had come armed, threatening violence against him and the clerical staff because wages were not paid. The manager asserted that they had not performed their tasks. On the basis of his complaint, thirteen labourers were sentenced to one month's rigorous imprisonment and in addition made to pay a fine Rs 15 each. In another case, the manager of a Lahimpur tea garden, F.J. Tweedie, complained that his labourers were becoming violent and had attacked him on being reprimanded for disobedience. All the accused were sentenced to two months' rigorous imprisonment. The assistant manager of Hathigarh tea garden in Darrang, Noad, registered a complaint against Bidu, a labourer, who had hit him with the handle of the broom on his hand causing injury for reprimand on impertinent behaviour. Bidu was sentenced to six months' rigorous imprisonment.[144] On 1 July 1914, J.S. Saunders, the manager of Khowang tea garden, filed a complaint against Bhola and nine others under Section 147, Indian Penal Code. A female labourer, Durpati, had defied his instructions on plucking work and when reprimanded, she and others attacked him. All the accused held guilty were subjected to varying degrees of punishment. Drupati was sentenced to six months' rigorous imprisonment, one labourer for four months, six for one month each, and two others were sentenced to receive ten stripes each in lieu of rigorous imprisonment of one month. Similarly, a case was instituted by Manders, the manager of Hapjan tea garden in Lakhimpur, on 28 July 1914, against six of his labourers, claiming that they were planning to attack him in retaliation for a slap he had administered to one of them. They were further accused of attacking the manager with *lathis* (sticks). Invariably, as in earlier cases, all the accused were 'found' guilty and sentenced to varying terms of rigorous imprisonment – from one to nine months. On 24 August 1914, F.G. White, the manager of Sukerating tea garden in Lakhimpur, 'boxed' Mango Urang on his ears. He then went on to institute a criminal case against Mango Urang accusing him of retaliatory attack, for which the latter was awarded six months' vigorous imprisonment. On 15 October 1914, G.T.B. Baddley, assistant manager of Karunating tea garden in Sibsagar, accused Bandhua and sixteen others of forming an unlawful assembly and threatening to attack him. The accusation resulted in Bandhua and fourteen other labourers being sentenced to rigorous imprisonment for terms of three to six months.[145]

Judicial Discrimination and Labour Relations

From the above descriptions it is clear that in a majority of these cases the judicial measures, in the form of sentences and prosecution, were far more severe in the case of labourers as compared to punishments awarded to the planters – about which both Cotton and Curzon were very concerned.[146] While the labourers were awarded rigorous and long-term imprisonment even for very mild offences, the punishment given to the managers were scandalously mild even for charges of extreme violence. There were cases in which the managers of gardens who had brutally beaten labourers to death or inflicted severe punishments including illegal confinements were let off with small fines by the courts. In 1890, a labourer was beaten to death by the manager of a garden in North Lakhimpur but was let of with a fine of Rs 100 only by the Sessions Court.[147] In 1892, a labourer managed to escape and complained against his illegal confinement and flogging by the manager of Dhuli tea garden in Sibsagar because he refused to continue work in the garden. The manager received only a very light punishment of Rs 100 as fine. Even in extreme cases of violence by the managers, the sentences were scandalously mild. For example, in 1899, in Rangliting tea garden of Lakhimpur district, a boy labourer was severely beaten and whipped to death by the manager. The civil surgeon deposed that the whipping had nothing to do with the death. The manager got away with a fine of Rs 5 only. The Sessions Judge instituted proceedings with a view to moving the High Court for enhancement of the sentence. But he subsequently stopped the proceedings after hearing the accused, and gave the finding that he was not prepared to say that a nominal punishment did not meet the requirement of the case. This case created considerable excitement in the Bengali press.[148] There were similar cases reported in other tea gardens also.

Such cases of judicial discrimination were numerous and were known to the highest levels in the colonial official hierarchy. By the beginning of the twentieth century they were serious enough to draw the critical attention of the Viceroy, Lord Curzon, and the Secretary of State for India.[149] In his private communications to Henry Cotton and Hamilton, Secretary of State for India, Curzon expressed his 'distress' and described these as a 'miscarriage of justice'.[150] In May 1905, Thom and Reid, the manager and his assistant of Dhendai tea garden in Darrang, severely beat up a labour boy to death on a charge of theft in the manager's bungalow. The manager and assistant manager were charged with simple assault and fined Rs 150 and Rs 5 respectively by the Sessions Judge. The case was reported in the newspaper *Englishman* and Sir Brampton Gordon raised the issue in the British Parliament, prompting the Government of India to make enquiries of the state government. The state government washed its hands off the case in a perfunctory manner by simply asserting that 'in view of the wholly unreliable character of the evidence for the prosecution there appeared to be no case for an appeal against the Session Judge's decision'. Chief Commissioner Fuller, even while holding that the action of Reid and Thom in this case was exceedingly blameworthy, did not believe that 'they were actively or intentionally concerned in the murder of the boy'.[151]

The growing militancy among labourers had its impact. The arbitrary power of private arrest came under critical comments from Fuller, the Governor of Assam, and Lord Curzon too expressed his unhappiness.[152] The Government of Assam sought complete withdrawal of the provision of private arrest. These recommendations were reiterated by the Assam Labour Enquiry Committee of 1906, leading to the enactment of Act 1908 which struck a blow at the penal contract system in Assam. The legal basis of indenture system was dismantled. However, the actual operations of the indenture system survived as labourers continued to be engaged under Act XIII of 1859 for a couple of decades more. It received its death blow only after the major labour upsurge of 1920–22, which led to its abolition in 1926.[153]

The Revolts of 1920–22

During the years 1920–22, for the first time, the numbers and organization involved in labour resistance showed a greater effort on the part of labourers. The removal of penal provisions from the indenture system created the space for more organized and collective labour resistance in the Assam Valley tea gardens. The resistance during the events of 1920–22 achieved a larger scale and scope with greater emphasis on economic issues, and the numbers involved in the struggles surpassed all previous figures.[154] The intensity and seriousness of the revolt was sufficiently alarming for the government to appoint an Enquiry Committee to investigate into the events of 1920–22.[155] The qualitative difference between earlier instances of labour unrest and the phenomenon witnessed from 1920 onwards was recognized in the language of the bureaucracy. The official terminology broadened in order to record and classify the events of these years. Terms like strike, disturbance and exodus were added to the older repertoire of 'assault', 'unlawful assembly', 'riots', 'intimidation', etc. A detailed study of the incidents of strikes, disturbances and riots during this period helps to throw light on some of the new features of labour struggle.

Between September 1920 and January 1922, a number of strikes, disturbances and riots were reported from several tea districts in Assam.[156] It is interesting to note that the term strike appeared for the first time along with the term riot in the official reportage of the incidents of 1920–22, even though the penal clauses of the labour legislation had been withdrawn in 1908 and collective action could no longer be considered illegal. The first among a series of riots was reported to have occurred in September and October 1920 in the Doom Dooms group of tea gardens in Lakhimpur district. The names of the gardens involved were Hansara, Raidang and Sandang belonging to the Doom Dooma Tea Company; Dhoedaam tea garden owned by Pabhojan Tea Company; Hukanguri tea garden of Assam Frontier Company; and Daisiyan and Deamuli tea gardens.[157] In 1921 a series of incidents in Lakhimpur district were reported as strikes – in Kachrujan, Woodbine, Nahortoli, Babari, Dinjam, Muttak, Greenwood, Mokal-bari, Linglijan, Rangagora, Nadna, Rangliting, Gellapukhuri, Hatiali, Limunguri, Nakhroj and Hazebank tea gardens. These were followed by strikes in May 1921 at Ramai, Laukhasi, Sealkoti and Mathola tea gardens.[158] Similarly, in Darrang district, in October 1920, a number of strikes and riots were reported at Monabari and Katonibari tea gardens, while the Halem incidents of March 1921 were described as riots. The cases involving the Thakurpari, Sonaguli, Kacharigaon and Rupajuli tea gardens during September and October 1921 were termed as strikes.[159] Incidents in Dhendai and Bamgaon tea gardens in the Sadr sub-division in October 1921 and Khairabari tea garden in Mangaldai sub-division in January 1922 were reported to be riots.[160] So were the cases of resistance in Sibsagar district.[161]

The detailed information relating to the above incidents collected by the Enquiry Committee reveals interesting features of the prevailing labour exploitation on the plantations. Apart from the European planters (managers and assistant managers), there were others in the hierarchy (among their Indian staff: garden *babus* or clerks, *zamadars*, *chowkidars* and *muhurirs*, and the *kaya* or the Marwari shopkeeper within the vicinity of the gardens) who subjected the labour force to varying degrees of economic exploitation and physical coercion. The riots and strikes of 1920–22 showed increasing articulation by the labourers of their grievances and growing identification of this hierarchy of exploiters. For example, in a number of cases their targets of attack were not only the Europeans but also the Indian staff. There were cases of the *keya* trader shops and weekly bazaars being looted, and property (bungalows, etc.) being attacked.[162] According to the district officials, in the gardens where the most serious disturbances took place, complaints of extortion of money against the garden *babus* were 'bitter and insistent'.[163] There were complaints about short weight and poor quality of foodstuffs in the *kaya* shops in the vicinity of the gardens where most labourers purchased their daily requirements.[164] A.J. Lane, Deputy Commissioner of Tezpur, reported to the Enquiry Committee that the garden *babus* and *muhurrirs* 'squeezed the coolies unduly'. He mentioned cases of 'unreliable' recording of work by the garden *babus* who maintained schedules of the daily work done by labourers, and even extraction of bribes by the garden doctors from the labourers for sanction of sick leave. He considered such factors also as responsible for labour discontent.[165]

Among several issues around which labour resistance grew at this time, economic factors like wage levels and prices acquired new dimensions. There were many such cases earlier too where the labourers had protested against the inadequacy of wages and high prices. But now these were severe enough for the *London Times* to take notice. It reported serious outbreaks of riots on pay day in Doom Doma, Pabhojan and Deodham tea gardens, involving over 7,000 labourers in which five Europeans were seriously assaulted. The bungalow of Deodam manager was destroyed and police officers including Furze, the Superintendent of Police, who arrived from Dibrugarh, were 'severely beaten'. It further reported the looting of three Marwari dealers' shops and destruction of other buildings. The rioting lasted more than ten days and was ultimately suppressed by the arrival of the military under H.A. Colquhom, the Deputy Commissioner, with the arrest of fifty 'ringleaders'.[166] At Monabari and Katonibari tea gardens the labourers struck work, looted some shops and assaulted Indian members of the garden staff. The Deputy Commissioner observed that the causes of the outbreak were entirely economic.[167] During September and early October 1921, several minor strikes were reported in tea gardens in the Thakurbari area in Darrang district. The common feature of these strikes was a demand for higher pay – a minimum daily wage of 8 annas for men and 6 annas for women. The strikes spread to gardens lying to the north and assumed a more serious aspect. During the *Durga Puja* festival at Sonajuli on 9 October, labourers, allegedly under the influence of liquor, beat up the Superintendent of the Company and the manager. On being informed, the Deputy Commissioner arrived at the spot to make enquiries. The labourers complained of low rates of pay, excessive work and inadequate leave owing to reduction of the labour force, and the high price of food and clothing. In some instances they complained that their pay was withheld on the charge or suspicion that absconders had been assisted to leave the garden. The next day, on 10 October, a serious riot occurred at Kacharigaon where the manager and some of the Indian staff were seriously assaulted. Here the labourers complained that apart from excessive tasks, they were not given enough leave on market days and for paddy cultivation. During the previous month, they had had to work on three Sundays out of the four, and young children and persons in ill health were made to do heavy work. Many of these complaints were found to be true during investigations. The most serious outbreak took place at Dhendai on 14 October, where the Superintendent of Police was severely beaten and some members of the Indian garden staff injured.[168] Committee members who visited Dhendai and Sonajuli tea gardens found the complaints of excessive tasks to be true and that 'there was a tendency to overdrive the coolies'.[169] On 22 June 1921 it was reported that a large body of labourers of Assam Company's Suntok tea garden had beaten up the garden *sirdars* and damaged buildings in the *muharrirs'* lines. In this case their grievance was linked to the wage issue, of illegal deductions by garden clerks and other Indian staff.[170] The strike by labourers of Nahortoli tea garden in Dibrugrh in April 1921 was based on a demand for higher wages. The Deputy Commissioner informed the Committee that there were strikes demanding a higher wage in many neighbouring gardens and as a result the local planters, after holding a meeting, agreed to raise the wage by one rupee per month. The agents James Finlay and Company objected to the raise decided by local planters, on the ground that this would be considered as surrending to the strikers. However the increase of Re 1 was finally accepted when the police was unable to control the labourers even after three attempts.[171]

A serious riot was reported on 21 March 1921 at Halem tea garden. A large number of labourers assembled around the garden office and announced stoppage of work and putting down of their tools. The supervisory staff of *jamadars* and *muhhurrirs* were roughed up and beaten. The managers of Halem and a neighbouring garden were also attacked when they arrived on the scene. In this case the acts of violence were allegedly inspired by social and political propaganda.[172] The Indian Tea Association and others in tea industry circles in London were concerned about the safety of European planters in Assam tea gardens. Sir C. Yates questioned the Secretary of State for India in the House of Commons as to what steps were being taken up by the Assam government for 'protection from Gandhi volunteers, who are breaking up and looting market, and boycotting and intimidating the Government servants and tea garden employees'.[173]

The significant upsurge of labour unrest at this time needs to be explained. The planters and their spokesmen alleged that the ignorant and illiterate labourers were incited and influenced by outsiders who were part of the Gandhian non-cooperation movement. The ITA's Calcutta office informed the London headquarters that 'the suddenness of these outbreaks points out clearly to the facts that they have been organized and there does not appear to be any doubt that the non-cooperators are at the bottom of the trouble'.[174] E.J. Nicholas, manager, Dikorani Division of Bishnath Tea Company, while giving evidence before the Enquiry Committee, remarked, 'I think they have been the unfortunate dupes of non-cooperators.'[175] The majority of managers were convinced of this argument. As to the possibility of low wages as a cause of the labour unrest, the planters asserted that the 'earnings of the labourers, including concessions in the form of subsidized ration, housing, medical facilities, garden land, etc., are more than enough to maintain them in health and reasonable comfort'.[176] Therefore, according to them, the labourers did not have any reason to complain on economic grounds. Playfair, a representative of the industry who supported this view, even argued that wages were much higher in the disturbed gardens than in the quiet ones.[177] If the non-cooperators still succeeded in inciting the 'reasonably well off labourers it was because the coolies' religious feelings and superstitions have been wrought on!'.[178] The non-cooperators, according to Langford James, clearly failed to make much headway by talking about the dangers of alcoholism, but were enormously successful in pointing out 'that the British Raj is a thing of the past and that a Hindu Raj with Mahatma Gandhi as Maharaja has taken its place'.[179] Not everyone shared Langford James' paranoia. Congrave, the Deputy Commissioner of Lakhimpur, in discussing the reasons for strikes in his district, stated, 'there is little or no evidence to show that the strikes were due to the influence of Congress agitators. In my opinion the strikes were mainly due to economic causes, i.e. the high cost of living.'[180] The Enquiry Committee did not find evidence of any direct link between the non-cooperation movement and the strikes of the plantation labourers of Assam Valley.[181] Political influence may have percolated through the atmosphere created by the non-cooperation movement around this time, but this could hardly be regarded as critical or dominant.

Despite the planters' denials, the failure of wages to match the increasing cost of living was among the most important grievances that formed the basis of labour revolts during 1920–22. In the majority of strikes, assaults and unlawful assemblies, the almost universal complaint of the labourers was about low wages. In many cases labourers complained that the rice sold to them at subsidized rates was inadequate and of very bad quality. In the case of the Monabari riots in Darrang district, the Deputy Commissioner observed that the causes were to be found in the rate of wages in force which had remained unchanged for a quarter a century. 'In view of the enormous increase in the cost of all foodstuff and of all articles of wearing apparel,' he observed,

> no further comment is necessary. Even when full allowance is made for *ticca* earnings, and for the fact that paddy rations are supplied at a rate considerably below cost price, the total pay earned by the labour force on this garden (as well as on some other gardens in this district) is not sufficient to enable the coolies (with their families and dependents) to live in decent comfort.[182]

Low wages and rising prices, combined with the extortions of shopkeepers and *babus*, pushed the labourers into direct action. The looting of *kaya* shops and the attacks on the Indian staff by labourers were a consequence of the exploitation and coercion practised by the former. The Enquiry Committee found evidence of doctor *babus,* shopkeepers and garden clerks extorting money from labourers in a number of gardens.[183] In the case of Monabari tea estate, the Committee found evidence to show that the doctor *babu* in the out garden had been exacting bribes from the labourers for granting sick leave.[184] Similarly, in Sonajuli,

Kacharigaon, Dhendai and other gardens in the Thakurbari area (Darrang district), complaints against garden *babus* were very bitter and insistent, and 'there was evidence that money had been extorted by them from the coolies under various pretexts'.[185] The Deputy Commissioner also reported that the complaints about the quantity and quality of foodstuff obtained at the shop of the garden *kaya* (Marwari traders) were well-founded. At Sonaguli tea estate complaints were made that the tasks were not reduced for fine plucking. At Kacharigaon tea estate it was admitted that pressure had been applied to force labourers into work. This was often done with the help of *chaukidars* and *sirdars*.[186] In the case of Suntok tea estate riots in Sibsagar district, the Deputy Commissioner reported that labourers' earnings had been regularly subjected to illegal deductions by the garden clerks who were singled out for attack.[187] The attacks on the police, as the chief instrument of suppression of their revolts, were often retaliatory.

A few more words about incitement from outside may be in order here. As pointed out earlier, paucity of evidence makes it difficult either to establish or deny a direct link with the non-cooperation movement as far as the Assam Valley is concerned. But indirectly the movement seems to have made an impact on the labour agitations. There are references to the non-cooperators holding meetings at the *haats* (weekly bazaars) near the tea gardens which were already discontented because of economic grievances. In one case a man named Chandra Nath Sarma was reported to have addressed a non-cooperation meeting at Gahigaonhat near Halem tea estate (already on strike) which was attended by a number of labourers. But district officials and the police could not find evidence of any of the non-cooperators directly inciting the labourers, though 'from the language used by the coolies in course of the riot it is evident that the general attitude has been affected by the prevalent social and political propaganda'.[188] It was reported by the Deputy Commissioner of Darrang that the labourers of Belsiri tea garden, who had come to Tezpur to file their complaint with the district authorities, also paid a visit to the local Congress camp. While not finding any evidence of political instigation by the Congress workers, the Deputy Commissioner reported that 'there is no doubt that the activities of volunteers in the villages created an atmosphere which was favourable to the occurrence of strikes and outbreaks among ignorant coolies'.[189]

The more famous case of the Chargola exodus and the Gurkha outrage against thousands of tea garden labourers at Chandpur in the Surma Valley of Assam province certainly had links with the non-cooperation movement. This incident attracted a lot of attention in the nationalist press in Calcutta and also from some of the important nationalist leaders. The case was well-publicized and became widely known, particularly after the sympathetic strike by workers of the Assam Bengal Railways in which C.R. Das was actively involved. In the Chargola exodus incident C. F. Andrews played an active role in championing the cause of the tea garden labourers.[190] But as compared to this, labour revolts in the Assam Valley tea gardens during the same period passed off virtually unnoticed by both the nationalist press and the leadership.

Apart from the non-cooperation movement, there were other external factors that seem to have had an indirect bearing on labour agitations. For example, there was a successful strike by the workers of the Dibru-Sadiya Railways that had preceded the Doom Dooma riots. The workers of Dibru-Sadiya Railways struck work in July 1920 demanding a 50 per cent increase in their wages. The ten-day-long strike was withdrawn only after the company agreed to an increase in wages by 30 to 35 per cent.[50] Many employees of the Dibru-Sadiya Railways had started life on the tea gardens and continued to have connections with the labourers in the estates. Moreover, the railway line ran through or near many of the tea gardens. Therefore it is likely that the success of the Dibru-Sadiya Railway strikers encouraged the tea garden labourers in their struggles. The Deputy Commissioner of Lakhimpur came to similar conclusions in his report on the incidents.[191]

The Halem tea garden riots were also reported to have been influenced by outside factors. On 21 March 1921, the labourers assembled in large numbers near the estate office and announced their intention of handing in their tools and ceasing work. This was followed by the usual story of attacks on the European and Indian staff on the garden. The information gathered by the Deputy Commissioner shows some interesting features which make it a special case among riots. A large number of labourers in this garden were Munda Christians from Ranchi district and there were three churches in the vicinity of the garden. One of these churches was of the Lutheran denomination, and until the war had been under the supervision of a German pastor. It was alleged that the teachings of this pastor had imbued the workers with a certain rebelliousness. The Commissioner claimed that there were links between the 'social and semi-political propaganda which appears to be now prevailing in the Munda Country' (i.e. Ranchi) and the labour unrest in Halem tea estate.[192] These linkages were possible owing to the fact that many of the Munda Christian labourers were literate, and their religious interests were looked after by pastors and *pundits* of their own caste. Some time before the riot the chief resident *pundit*, Christoson, obtained leave to go to his country – from where he returned shortly before the incident. During this period, it was reported, correspondence between the labourers and their country-folk had increased unusually, and a number of subscriptions had been sent by the Christian labourers towards the expense of the social and political propaganda that was being carried on in Ranchi. The visit of the *pundit* to his own locality 'appears to have increased his sympathy with the movement, and on his return there is no doubt that he and his friends have attempted to spread it in the garden'.[193] This is perhaps the only case of a direct political influence on tea labourers in the Assam Valley.

The labour revolts of 1920–22, despite their intensity and extent, did not succeed in forcing the employers to accede to the labourers' demands or having their grievances redressed. It is true that in some cases individual managers, under pressure of agitation, agreed to raise the rate of wages. But in almost every such case the manager's decision was vetoed by the higher authorities of the respective companies.[194] The main reason for this failure lay in the fact that these struggles remained isolated and no linkages emerged between them. Although they coincided with a general mass movement in the province (in the form of the non-cooperation movement), these revolts were barely affected by it. As a result no organized effort, from inside or outside the labour struggles, could be made to pressurize the employers to even consider their demands. On the other hand, the planters were highly organized and influential, and the most powerful commercial and industrial lobby in the province. The efficiency of their organization was demonstrated when the state assisted them in ruthless repression of the labourers' revolts. The Government of Assam, complying with the planters' request, detailed ten platoons of the Assam Rifles to the disturbed districts, with an assurance that they would remain there 'as long as they were wanted for security'.[195] Official circles openly admitted that the Assam Rifles rendered valuable assistance to the civil police in connection with a strike on the Dibru-Sadiya Railway, and strikes and rioting amongst tea garden labourers in the Assam Valley.[196] Further, most of the revolts were ruthlessly handled by the local police by punishing a large number of labourers, by court prosecutions, and by convictions of varying terms of rigorous imprisonment.[197] However, the labourers' struggles in 1920–22 certainly succeeded in giving a death blow to the notorious labour law. In 1926, the Workman's Breach of Contract Act XIII of 1859 was abolished on the recommendations of the Enquiry Committee despite tough opposition from the tea industry.[198]

Labour Unrest in the Aftermath of 1920–22

The official dismantling of the indenture regime opened up opportunities for more collective, organized, large-scale protests at the local level. However the planters now proceeded to work out their own internal system to maintain their control over labour mobility within the tea districts, through the adoption of 'labour rules' and 'wage agreements' which prevented an employer from employing labourers from other gardens.[199] No manager would generally employ a labourer from another garden without the permission of the previous employer. In 1939 an agreement known as the Brahmaputra and Surma Valley Local Recruitment Agreement was signed among the planters, which prohibited a manager from deliberately 'enticing' or recruiting labourers from another garden.[200]

Under such circumstances, the labourers evolved their own strategies and newer forms of protests while continuing with the older ones. Despite ruthless suppression by the state, labour resistance continued to be manifested in the form of riots, assaults and strikes. Between 1922–23 and 1924–25, a number of serious cases of assaults and rioting were reported in which labourers had attacked managers, assistant managers and police officials. A number of labourers were convicted and sentenced to varying terms of rigorous imprisonment.[201] The immigration labour reports of the succeeding years (1927–30) continued to report about strikes, 'unlawful assembly', 'disturbances' and even 'absconding', and most of these were suppressed with the help of the police. A new aspect that appeared during these years was the participation of a much larger number of labourers in some of the strikes. At Rajmai tea estate, for example, the entire labour force numbering about 2,000 went on a strike on 9 June 1927 against cruel methods of extracting work adopted by the management.[202] The Deputy Commissioner of Lakhimpur used the term 'strike epidemic' for the unrest spreading over eighteen gardens, while many incidents were still not brought to the notice of the officials.[203] Unfortunately no details of any of these cases are available. The next year, in 1928, again an 'epidemic' of strikes in the gardens of the Sadr sub-division of Lakhimpur was reported. Though there was no violence, the police was sent to control and suppress these strikes. The duration of most such strikes was short – sometimes lasting only one day.[204] A number of other strikes reported during these years involved between 200 to 350 labourers. Often there were complaints of managers or assistant managers being beaten up by labourers in retaliation for the physical coercion they were subjected to by the former.[205]

En Masse Exodus

The post-indenture period witnessed a new and novel form of labourers' resistance which was described in the official reports as exodus. While in the case of desertions the workers defied the indenture regime which defined their actions as a 'crime' under the penal system, exodus represented a collective expression of their unwillingness not only to work but an utter rejection of the rhythm of life in the plantation. Exodus in the Assam Valley tea plantations meant a mass of labourers in one or more gardens leaving work and walking away. Incidents where labourers walked off *en masse* from the tea garden had been reported earlier too. In the 1920s it assumed the form of an exodus. While exodus fell short of becoming an organized movement, it was an advance over desertion and distinctly political in nature.

The earliest case of exodus, of 139 *Madrassee* labourers from the Tiphuk tea garden in Dibrugarh, was reported on 7 July 1924. The labourers complained of ill-treatment.[206] They were joined by another 70 labourers from the Ethelwood tea garden. All of them left by road towards Sibsagar with the intention of returning to their homes. Unable to persuade them to go back to the gardens, the government had to repatriate them from Nazira railway station. The repatriation by the government was resented by the Tea District Labour Association and the Indian Tea Association, who sent protest telegrams. In another case, nearly 1,000 labourers left the Lukwa tea garden and went to Jorhat town. There were further reports of exodus from other tea gardens in Dibrugarh and Sibsagar, and also from Khumbri, Melong and Barbari tea gardens.[207] The Deputy Commissioner of Lakhimpur reported that forty labourers from Khumtai tea garden, within the jurisdiction of Sibsagar, arrived in Dibrugarh and were unwilling to go back. The Commissioner of Assam Valley Division reported that 148 'Madrasee' labourers were marching by road from Jorhat to Nowgong, and that another batch of 163 were walking out of Melang tea garden.[208] There were also reports of labourers marching out of Borbari and Rajabari tea gardens. They submitted a petition to the Deputy Commissioner of Lakhimpur complaining of excessive work and bad quality of rice supplied by the garden management.[209] There were more reports of labourers walking out of gardens in Dibrugarh and Sibsagar.

Looking at the immediate reasons for these incidents, it is interesting to note that not only the imposed rhythm of plantation life was rejected by labourers but that they also protested against the extra-economic methods of exploitation used by the employers. The Melang tea estate labourers complained that at the time of their recruitment they were promised a daily wage of Re 1 per male and 12 annas per female for light work. They were also promised that rice would be supplied at 16 seers per rupee. However the wages actually paid were much less than promised and rice was supplied at 4 seers per rupee. They therefore refused to work and preferred to return to their homes.[210] In Lakhimpur district labourers left the gardens complaining that they were subjected to excessive work and that they were unaccustomed to such labour especially at such low wages.[211] The Tea District Supply Association (the main labour-recruiting organization of the tea industry) and Indian Tea Association protested against the repatriation of such labourers by the government, and alleged that the exodus was due to the influence of non-cooperators.[212] However the Governor of Assam was not convinced; there was no evidence to show that political agitators had induced the labourers to leave their gardens.[213]

Exodus as a form of protest sometimes entailed great suffering for the labourers. Yet, in the face of the greater miseries and hardships of everyday life in the tea gardens, this appeared preferable to them. On 11 July 1939, Bombay labourers left the Tonganagaon tea estate and reached Dibrugarh, where they asked the Deputy Commissioner to repatriate them. The latter's attempts to induce them to return failed. They were joined by 54 more labourers of the same garden on the long march to Gauhati which took one-and-a-half months. Most of them were found to be sick and badly emaciated, and had to be hospitalized. However, fearing that the authorities would send them back to the garden, they walked out of the hospital before recovery. There were eighteen women and nineteen children among them, and none of them were traceable after that. The persistent attempts of the government officials to persuade them to return to the garden at various stages during their march failed. There were more cases of a similar nature.[214]

The Depression and Intensification of Wage Struggles: The 1930s

The Great Depression of 1930 caused a slump in the tea industry. Export of tea declined sharply as a result of fall in demand. The situation became worse with a decline in internal consumption of tea. Stocks of tea, both in London and Calcutta, piled up and prices fell. Consequently, profitability was adversely affected; none of the companies declared dividends in 1930 and 1931. To combat the effects of the depression, the tea industry resorted to measures which badly affected the earnings of labourers. One was direct wage cuts and the other, control of production. The labourers reacted sharply to wage cuts. The district officials reported more than twenty strikes in Assam Valley tea gardens specifically on the issue of wages in the year 1931 alone. These strikes, well spread all over the Assam tea gardens, involved large number of labourers and lasted for longer periods than was the case earlier.[215]

About 150 labourers went on a strike on 6 January 1931 at the Borbam tea estate. The report referred to a few '*badmashes*' (bad characters) who had been causing trouble and inciting others to demand higher wages. The strike lasted twenty-four hours and labourers were 'persuaded' to return to work. The manager agreed to pay one anna for pruning twenty plants instead of twenty-five plants as before.[216] The Police Superintendent in charge of CID, Darrang district, reported a strike by 350 labourers at Orang tea garden because they refused to accept wages at reduced rates. The planters in Darrang district had decided in March 1931 to reduce the daily wage rate from annas 8, 6 and 4 to annas 6, 5 and 3 for men, women and children, respectively. Armed police was sent to suppress the strike.[217] The same month, the Deputy Commissioner reported that about 90 labourers had violently threatened the manager of Borpatra tea estate, demanding either increase of wages or return fares to their country. The government sent two sections of armed police and after a week the sub-divisional officer reported suppression of the strike with six arrests.[218] About 250 labourers were repatriated and the rest had to accept the reduced wages.[219] At Borbari tea garden on 22 April, about 60 labourers went on a strike which lasted twenty-four hours. They complained that *hazira* had been reduced from 6 annas to 4 annas a day. They demanded the old rates and wanted weekly payments of wages instead of bi-weekly.[220] On 4 May, 167 Santhal labourers walked out of Ananda tea estate saying they were unwilling to work at the reduced rate of wages offered to them.[221] In May 1931, more than 800 labourers went on a strike at Sessa tea garden. In this case nearly 100 women workers had protested against low and further reduced wages. Men workers who also complained of excessive work joined them in the strike. The strike lasted four days and a number of labourers were arrested.[222] In the same month about 50 labourers of Ikrajan tea estate struck work because their wages were not paid regularly, and another group of thirty labourers of Halima tea garden refused to work and left the garden. In both cases the police 'persuaded' them to go back to work.[223] On 1 June, nearly 200 women labourers went on strike at Singlijan tea estate. They assaulted the manager and his brother-in-law for misbehaviour and also demanded higher wages. They were joined by 160 men labourers. The strike lasted three days. It was suppressed with the help of the police; six women were convicted and were asked to execute a bond of Rs 100 each with a surety of Rs 100 for one year.[224] About 1,000 labourers of Dhulapadung tea garden went on a strike on 19 June 1931 in protest against excessive work. The strike lasted one week and the labourers succeeded in forcing the management to reduce the tasks.[225] A day before that, the Special Superintendent of Police in charge of CID reported a strike involving 200 labourers of Jaipur tea garden which was suppressed by the armed police within two days.[226] Two weeks later, about 300 Munda labourers struck work demanding higher wages, particularly for hoeing work. The strike lasted for a week before it was suppressed by the police. Five labourers were sent to jail for one year.[227]

During August and September, labourers struck work and left the Lakhia tea garden protesting against inadequate wages.[228] On 14 August, about 400 labourers of Katong tea garden struck work and beat up the manager. The labourers complained that women were kept out longer-than-usual hours on an extremely hot day, and they were also unhappy about the method of plucking insisted upon by the management. The strike lasted two days, and then the 'appearance of the armed police in the garden had the effect of changing the attitude of man from one of threatening to conciliation'.[229] In October about 50 labourers went on a strike lasting two days at Hoolonguri tea estate because of low wages.[230] On 10 October there was an exodus of about 200 labourers from Monabari tea estate. The main grievances of the labourers were that they had long hours of work and that their pay was withheld.[231] And then there was the case of exodus of 95 labourers (including many women and children) from Gillapukri tea estate where the main complaint of the labourers was that the conditions in the garden were unhealthy.[232] Most of these strikes were suppressed by the planters with the help of the state.

Despite the repression the labourers continued to show their discontent through strikes and exodus during the years 1931–39.[233] In August 1933, 475 labourers of Mathola tea estate in Lakhimpur district went on a strike against the faulty weighing of green leaf by the management.[234] In March 1934, more than 700 labourers went on strike in Dhooria tea estate in Sibsagar district against the employers' refusal to give the bonus which had been promised.[235] The Controller of Emigrant Labour reported twenty-two strikes in Assam Valley tea gardens in the year 1935, mostly on the issue of wage reduction.[236] Out of these twenty-two strikes, nineteen took place in Assam Valley alone.[237] In 1936, more strikes were reported at Dholaguri, in the Dejoo and Gelapukhuri tea gardens, involving 370 and 400 labourers respectively. The main complaints were low rates for plucking and clearing jungle, and excessive work.[238] In 1937, a series of strikes were reported in Barbari, Desam and Diksam tea gardens in Lakhimpur district; Holungoorie and Mezengah tea gardens in Sibsagar district; and Harchurah, Sessa, Neharani tea gardens in Darrang district. In 1938, a number of strikes were reported in Mankhushi, Ledo, Keyhung, Baghjan and Panitola tea gardens of Lakhimpur district; Satai tea garden of Sibsagar district; and Berangajuli, Koloni, Seajuli tea gardens of Darrang district.[239] The official emigration report of 1938 mentioned seventeen complaints by labourers against managers and one complaint by a manager against labourers. It was reported that there were seventeen strikes in tea gardens by labourers demanding pay and less work.[240] Four of these were in Sibsagar district, where the demands were increase in *hazira* rates, correct estimation of the amount of work done, and provision of carts to carry the leaves plucked by women workers to the factory which was situated at a considerable distance.[241]

So, by the 1930s, we notice that strikes and exoduses subsumed the spontaneous 'unlawful assemblies', 'assaults' and 'riots' of the early years. There also emerged a clearer articulation of demands in which the issue of wages came to be the dominant one. Unfortunately little is known about the organization of these strikes. No details are available about the background and activities of the 'ring-leaders' so often mentioned in the criminal proceedings instituted against striking labourers. The Royal Commission on Labour, 1931, found no organization among labourers in the Assam Valley.[242] Strikes remained uncoordinated and isolated. Yet there is little doubt that protest and resistance were now of a more specific economic nature, more widespread and more prolonged.

The formation of trade unions was a relatively slower process. Only in the late 1930s do we notice the emergence of trade unions in their embryonic form. By 1938 it became clear that there would probably be attempts to form trade unions on the tea gardens, and a policy was evolved by the ITA defining its general attitude towards unions and providing recommendations for the line of action to be adopted by managers. The ITA sent out circulars.[243] In 1939 there did emerge a semblance of a trade union type organization. Strikes spread from the Swedish-owned Assam Match Company at Dhubri, the Assam Oil Company (a subsidiary of Burma Oil Company) in Digboi and the British-owned Assam Railways and Trading Company, to the tea gardens and government establishments.[244]

The Emergence of Labour Unions, 1939–47

The year 1939 witnessed a fierce outburst of labour struggles all over the province of Assam. The Controller of Emigrant Labour reported in 1939 that there were 'an unusually large number of strikes, viz. 17 and much unrest'.[245] This number was an underestimates, as Rege and the ITA reported many more strikes, viz. thirty-seven, that year.[246] The ITA's Assam branch compiled a list of gardens where labourers went on strike during 1939. Out of the total of thierty-seven strikes reported in the Assam Valley districts, twenty-one took place in Lakhimpur, eight in Sibsagar, three in Nowgong and five in Darrang (Table 6.1).

The ITA considered these strikes as 'deliberately engineered agitation'

TABLE 6.1
Labour Strikes in 1939 in Assam Valley Tea Gardens [247]

	Lakhimpur District	Sibsagar District	Darrang District	Nowgong District
1	Hansara	Towkok	Bagumari	Jiajuri
2	Samdang	Behnbor	Barpukhuri	Seconee
3	Ridang	Tyroon	Shakomoto	Sagmootea
4	Hapjan	Konikor	Sonabheel	
5	Longsol	Balijan	Dhekiajuli	
6	Ledo	Dhunseri		
7	Powai	Lattkoojan		
8	Margherita	Moheema		
9	Dirok			
10	Dehing			
11	Chubwa			
12	Hattiali			
13	Kharjan			
14	Rungagora			
15	Dikom			
16	Dhallajan			
17	Nahortoli			
18	Santi			
19	Namroop			
20	Pengaree			

from outside storm centres – from Digboi, Tinsukia and, to a minor extent, Dibrugarh. It was alleged that a special school for the training of agitators with special view to work on tea gardens had been instituted in Dibrugarh.[248] Fear of outside intervention on behalf of labour was one that always haunted the ITA. Before the troubles of 1939 started, garden managers were clearly informed that, in case of strikes or labour unrest, no negotiations of any sort were to be entertained either with the labourers, or with outsiders who professed to represent the labourers or to be interested in their welfare. Frequent attempts were made, particularly by Congress Party members, to intervene as mediators. In some cases they would have been quite prepared to advise the labourers to return to work without concessions, being content to derive no more than the prestige they would obtain from the fact that the management had accepted their mediation; in other cases they asked for small concessions for the labourers. In every case – except for one in 1938 when the management found it convenient to gain time, and one in 1939 – the offers of mediation were refused.[249]

The year 1939 also witnessed the formation of labour unions in many of the non-plantation industries and in some of the tea gardens. The Digboi oil workers had formed their union in February 1938 and were recognized by the Assam Oil Company in March 1939. In April 1939, the Assam Oil Company's workers went on a strike against low wages and victimization (the Company had dismissed more than 70 workers). This strike lasted for more than six months and it marked the most heroic period in the history of workers' struggle in Assam.[250] Similarly the workers of Assam Railways and Trading Company went on a general strike in the various establishments of the Company (tea gardens, Dibru-Sadiya Railways, saw mills, collieries, etc.) in Lakhimpur district.[251] The strikes in the tea gardens, to a large extent, seem to have been inspired by the general spirit of workers' struggles reflected in the Digboi strike and in other industrial establishments in the province.[252]

The major grievances of the striking labourers were essentially the same as during earlier strikes, viz. low wages, excessive work, incorrect estimates of the amount of work done, ill-treatment at the hands of management, etc. In Sibsagar, the labourers in one of the tea gardens went on a strike against the dismissal of two labourers.[253] The strike at the Oakland tea garden in Lakhimpur district was due to similar reasons. The manager, with the help of armed *chowkidars*, had forcibly dismissed two labourers on charges of bad work and indiscipline.[254] The Hapjan tea garden labourers' strike lasted three days. In Darrang, labourers of the Dhekiajuli tea garden went on a strike which also lasted for two days.[255] In January 1939, about 3,432 labourers of the Longsoal tea garden of Assam Frontier Tea Company in Lakhimpur district went on a strike demanding higher wages. Their other grievances were related to the allotment of tasks and the proposed removal of four labourers from their jobs on disciplinary grounds. The strike lasted three days.[256] The intensity of the labour unrest alarmed the government.

The Government of Assam expressed its anxiety over the 'frequency of strikes and disturbances on the tea gardens in several parts of the province'.[257] Even the Indian Tea Association seems to have been alarmed; it made anxious representations to the government and the attention of the ministry was drawn to the need for urgent action in order to maintain 'law and order'.[258] In response to the ITA's anxiety and the pressure of the tea lobby, the Government of Assam appointed a Tea Garden Labour Committee to investigate the causes of these recent strikes and disturbances.[259] The government warned against strikes and activities 'which might prejudice the results of the committee's efforts',[260] while the Deputy Commissioner of Lakhimpur sent a warning notice to persons suspected of organizing strikes.[261] However, before the Committee could make any headway the ITA objected to the appointment of some of its members on the ground that they had connections with the labour disturbances.[262] The ITA withdrew its cooperation, making the Committee defunct.[263]

In one important respect the events of 1939 represented a significant chapter in the history of tea garden labourers. For the first time we notice the emergence of labour organizations in Assam Valley. A confidential official document reported one Chota Nagpuri Association as early as April 1938. P.M. Sarwan was described as its moving spirit. The main object of the Association was amelioration of the welfare of tea garden labourers.[264] It seems that at an early stage some Christian missionaries were linked with this Association through a number of labourers from the Chotanagpur area who were Christians. But once the Association's activities assumed political overtones, the Bishop of Assam ordered the missionaries to disassociate from it.[265] Not much is known about the activities of the Chota Nagpuri Association except that it held one or two meetings in the gardens. It was reported that at one of these meetings a speaker told the labourers not to be misled into

TABLE 6.2
Plantation Labour Unions in Assam Valley, 1939[268]

Name	Headquarters	Date of Registration
1. Upper Assam Tea Co. Labour Union.	Dibrugarh	27th April, 1939
2. Rajmai Tea Co. Labour Union.	-do-	27th April, 1939
3. Greenwood Tea Co. Labour Union.	-do-	6th May, 1939
4. Maku (Assam) Tea Co. Labour Union.	Margherita	30th Way, 1939

strikes as they would eventually be the sufferers.[266] There is evidence of a few other labour unions formed in 1939 in the Assam Valley (Table 6.2). But the available evidence tells us very little about the activities of these unions. It is likely that they never really became very effective. One of the main reasons for this was the outbreak of World War II. The war gave an easy opportunity for the government to crush the newly formed labour unions by promulgating the Defence of India Rules.[267]

The early years of the 1940s were a setback to the labour struggles in the tea gardens, and in Assam as a whole. Rege reported that since 1941 there was a definite reduction in the number of strikes. The reason for this was the severe restrictions on political activities in the province during the war years, in order to secure stable conditions for the war efforts.[269] However, the sharp decline in real wages due to the huge increase in prices and the tea industry's efforts to extract excessive work in order to increase production were creating a lot of resentment and defiance among the labourers. Even at the height of political repression during the war years, a series of short-term strikes were reported in some of the tea gardens. On 31 May 1943, the entire labour force of Baghmari tea garden in Tezpur sub-division of Darrang district went on a two-day strike. The huge escalation in the prices of foodstuff during the war years was making it difficult for the workers even to survive on subsistence, and therefore their demand for increased quantity of rations even for those labourers who were absent from duty.[270] Rege reported that labourers in the gardens whom he had the opportunity to talk to particularly complained about the inadequacy of rations supplied by the garden management. Not only were the rations given not enough, rations were not always provided, or were reduced and cut for those who were absent.[271] There was a report that 362 workers of Mainajuli tea garden in Darrang went on a strike on 27 May 1944, demanding higher wages. Similarly, 338 workers of Dhendai tea garden in the same district struck work for three days on 3 October 1944, demanding a reduction in daily tasks. The district officials reported a strike by 681 workers of Bokial tea garden in Sibsagar on 25 August 1945. The workers here complained of shortage of foodstuff and also demanded the freedom to cut firewood from any part of the garden's jungle.[272]

Protest activities increased after the end of war in 1946. 'The economic conditions', it was reported, 'are producing signs of discontent, both among regular labour forces and in Defense projects'.[273] Moreover, the labour struggles outside the tea plantations were maturing into the formation of a provincial-level labour organization. The Assam branch of the All India Trade Union Congress (AITUC) – APTUC (Assam Provincial Trade Union Congress) – was formed in 1943, and became fairly active in the course of the next two years. The first conference of APTUC was held at Dibrugarh on 28 November 1943, where several issues conerning tea garden labour were raised. The conference pointed to the growing discontent among garden labourers, and their 'spontaneous strikes and other forms of Direct Action' against oppression, exploitation and inhuman living and working conditions imposed by the tea planters. It was very critical of the provincial government, led by the Congress Party, for its inability and failure to help improve the conditions of labour life in the tea gardens, and to bring about any change in the attitude of the bureaucracy towards the labourers.[274] The APTUC raised the following demands on behalf of the tea garden labourers at the conference: (i) minimum daily wage of Rs 1 irrespective of the sex of the workers; (ii) no increase in the *nirikh* while raising the wages; (iii) complete ban on child labour; (iv) adequate rations at concessional rates for labour families; (v) provision of cloth at concessional rates for workers; (vi) pucca quarters with latrines; (vii) free compulsory primary education under the direct control and supervision of the government; (viii) setting up of a tripartite committee with equal number of representatives from trade unions, employers and the government to consider the economic, social and political conditions of labour; (ix) grant of full civil liberties to workers with a right to hold meetings and demonstrations; and (x) supply of pure drinking water.[275] The communist workers of the APTUC made efforts to establish contacts with the tea garden labourers. Between 1943 and 1945, APTUC had increased its strength in Assam from 4,345 members belonging to ten affiliated and associated units, to about 16,000 members with forty-one affiliated and associated units.[276]

The influence of APTUC became increasingly important among tea garden labourers in the Assam Valley. This was demonstrated in the labourers' strike at Suntok tea estate, owned by Assam Company, in Sibsagar district, on 16 September 1946. Nearly 900 labourers struck work on the basis of the APTUC demands (mentioned above).[277] Warner, the manager, tried forcing the labourers to resume work with the help of garden *sirdars* but without much success for the next two days. He threatened to close the garden and the factory if work was not resumed. The situation developed into a confrontation on 18 September, when 500–600 labourers gathered outside the garden office complaining of bad working conditions, shortage of foodstuff and clothing, and demanding more supplies. It became explosive when Warner, the manager, fatally stabbed Bankuru Saura, one of the labourers, with a stick-sword.[278] The death of their colleague at the hands of the manager enraged the gathered labourers and they attacked the garden office. The manager fled from the scene and his assistant manager, Devendra Baruah, fired upon the agitated labourers, wounding many of them. The police was called in by the manager and about 50 labourers were arrested and others terrorized, while both the manager and assistant manager were let off.[279]

Gaurishankar Bhattacharya, the general secretary of APTUC, immediately took up the cause of the Santok tea estate labourers with the Government of

Assam. Letters of protest on behalf of APTUC were sent to the Prime Minister, Home Minister and the Labour Minister of Assam.[280] Jawaharlal Nehru,
upon receiving the information, asked the Assam government to investigate
and report.[281] The Assam Cha-Bagan Mazdoor Union (founded by communist activists) investigated into the incident, the details of which were sent
to the general secretary of AITUC. The incident was given publicity as well
as condemned by some of the nationalist newspapers.[282] Jadunath Bhuyan,
joint secretary of Assam Mazdoor Sangha, demanded an enquiry into the
Suntoak tea garden incident, and condemned the 'attempts to stem the tide
of rising labour movement in Assam as well as in India by means of guns
and daggers'.[283] The Bengal Assam Rail Road Workers' Union (Dibrugarh
Branch) held a meeting in sympathy with the Suntok tea garden labourers'
strike, and passed a resolution condemning the manager for killing a labourer.
They demanded from the government an immediate enquiry and punishment
of culprit, release of all the arrested workers, and withdrawal of police from
the garden.[284] This was the first instance when workers in other industries
and labourers in the tea gardens began to form some kind of a united front
against oppression and exploitation. Labour meetings were held in other tea
gardens like Myzon and Duklingia. The result of all these developments was
the formation of the Assam Cha-Bagan Mazdoor Union under the communists.
That the influence of communist activists had increased was confirmed by a
confidential report of the Controller of Emigrant Labour. He reported that
the communist workers had organized a union at Rajapul in Upper Assam,
and that they were becoming influential among the tea garden labourers.
Although not really convinced that the communists were directly linked with
the Suntok tea estate incident, he readily admitted that

> the wages in almost every industry and particularly in the tea industry have not
> kept pace with the rise in the cost of living. The necessities of life are scarce and
> low paid employees all over India are the hardest hit. . . . The agitation potential
> of the labour force is therefore extremely high at the moment and I have not the
> slightest doubt that communist workers have taken good deal of trouble to exploit
> this potential at Suntok.[285]

The communist-dominated APTUC's involvement in the tea gardens,
however, could not go beyond this and remained limited. While taking up
specific issues of the tea garden labourers, APTUC seems to have had its
priorities elsewhere, in the industrial sector. There is scant evidence of its
entrenchment in unionized form in the tea gardens. The relative ease with
which the Indian National Trade Union Congress (INTUC) could establish
itself in 1947 points to the limitation of the APTUC hold. However partly
this was due to the patronage given to the INTUC by the planters and the
suppression of the communist trade union by the new Congress government

in the period immediately after independence. The joint secretary of APTUC, M.N. Sarma, reported to their national organization that the work of the Provincial Committee has been limited in scope during 1947–48 because it had to face a great attack from the government and the government-sponsored INTUC patronized by the employers. Many of the Congress Ministers in the province and their departments were following a policy of hostility towards the AITUC. The government machinery of the Labour Department was freely used to build up INTUC and for the disruption of AITUC. A large number of communist trade unionists were put behind bars and a large number of them detained without trial by the new government.[286]

There were also individual efforts to organize unions. P.M. Sarwan, a Christian and an educated member of the depressed community of plantation labourers, seems to have remained active among tea garden labourers during the war years, and formed the Assam Tea Labourers' Association in 1943 at Jorhat. He forwarded the report of its 'General Meeting' held on 2 March 1943 in a representation to the Government of Assam on 11 March 1943, which requested that matters affecting the 'legitimate aspirations of the Tea Labour Community' be taken up. He demanded that the government improve primary education for labourers' children, reserve seats for the labour community in the Legislature, grant wastelands to the ex-tea garden labourers who were landless, increase the supply of rice at concessional rates and increase their wages.[287] In May 1945, five individual plantation unions and the Assam Tea Labourers' Federation affiliating them were formed in Sibsagar, largely through the efforts of Sarwan.[288]

However, despite the emergence of such unions and the existing potential of labour militancy, the tea garden labourers' struggles did not emerge into a united labour organization which could involve the entire labour force working in the Assam Valley tea plantations till the end of colonial rule. The significance of this cannot be overemphasized, particularly when it is clear that the entire labour force had common grievances and demands arising out of a standard built-in mechanism of exploitation and oppression. In the section below, we shall try to look into the reasons as to why the labourers' resistance and their struggles did not crystallize into a unified labour organization till the end of colonial rule.

We shall discuss some characteristic features of the Assam Valley tea plantation labour force to analyse the constraints on their solidarity and organizational unity. While, over the long period reviewed above, this solidarity did develop in the course of struggles against capital on the one hand, and against the colonial bureaucracy and its sanction system on the other, there were certain factors that inhibited the possibility of a wider and consolidated movement and organization. One of these was the labourers' enforced isolation from the world outside. The planters successfully achieved this by various means.[289] As we have shown earlier, the planters' strategy was to immobilize migrant labour within the plantations after their arrival from various other parts of the subcontinent. Labour mobility within the plantation areas was restricted by maintaining a strict physical control through supervision of the 'coolie lines' by watchmen during the night, and at the workplace by assistant managers, *sirdars*, *jamadars*, *muharrirs*, etc. The situation was well summarized in 1937 by Omeo Kumar Das when he tabled his 'Assam Tea Garden Labourers' Freedom of Movement Bill' in the Assam Legislative Assembly:

> The freedom of movement of tea garden labourers is limited in a manner unheard of in any other industry. They are not allowed to go out of the estate whenever they want to do so. It is a common practice to engage night chowkidars to keep watch over the lines and prevent labourers from leaving the estates. The impression had been created in the minds of the labourers that they have no right to go out of the gardens of their own will. This constant restraint on their right of free movement has reduced them to a state of slavery.[290]

Even after the official dismantling of the indenture system, labourers' mobility continued to be restricted through 'labour rules' and 'wage agreements' adopted by the planters, prevent an employer from employing labour from other gardens.[291]

Secondly, the planters succeeded in preventing most attempts from outside to contact labourers in the garden. They considered the entire area of the plantation as their private property and therefore anyone from outside who wished to go through the gardens had to seek prior permission of the manager.[292] The Royal Commission admitted this fact when it observed: 'We do not regard as satisfactory the existing position where workers are largely isolated from outside influence and any member of the public may be effectively prevented from approaching the workers' lines except with the manager's permission.'[293] The planters defended this practice openly on grounds that they wanted to keep away 'interested people attempting to make use of the illiterate and ignorant labour force in the tea gardens'.[294]

Here we should take note of the planters' reaction and attitude towards the issue of trade unions in their gardens. As pointed out earlier, as late as the 1930s, there were no trade unions in the Assam Valley gardens. Only in the late 1930s do we notice the emergence of trade unions in their embryonic form. At first the planters were outright in their opposition to the very idea of trade unions among their labour force. In 1937 the ITA's argument against the formation of trade unions was that conditions on the gardens were fundamentally different from those in industrial areas. The standard defence against setting up labour organizations was the often repeated argument of the 'primitive' nature of the labour force who were hence susceptible to 'outside influences', and if unions were started they would most probably be run by outsiders. 'In such cases the prevailing opinion is that they should be discouraged.'[295] The reaction of the planters to the large number of labour strikes in 1939 was an echo of their earlier stand of 1921–22. While the allegations of the economic and other grievances of the labourers were denied, the blame for the agitations was put on 'political agitators' from outside.[296] The chairman of ITA was emphatic that 'our labour is a contented and peace loving one and troubles as a rule only arise as the result of the activities of the professional agitators – particularly those having communistic tendencies'.[297]

However, once it became clear that despite the repression launched under the Defence of India Rules, trade unions in the tea gardens had come to stay, the ITA modified its attitude. Its new policy was not to show outright opposition to a trade union; it adopted strategies to deal with the new political realities, after the formation of a popular ministry in the province, and to keep undesirable 'outsiders' at bay from the labour force.[298] The planters were not yet willing to acknowledge the fundamental right of labour to form trade unions.[299] They would, however, recognize unions which were willing to accept their terms and conditions.[300] ITA remained hostile to the communist-dominated unions: 'with irresponsible and unrepresentative unions, organized by communist agitators, whose avowed aim is the expropriation of our estates, we have had and will have nothing whatever to do'.[301] In 1947, when INTUC emerged as a dominant substitute for the communist unions, the ITA established a working relationship with it – even encouraged its activities. Why was the ITA so willing to work with INTUC? The answer was provided by the ITA's General Committee itself:

> The outstanding development in labour organization during 1947 was undoubtedly the growth of the Indian National Trade Union Congress, formed in May by the Congress Party to counteract the disruptive influence of the communist dominated All-India Trade Union Congress. In contrast to the direct action policy of the latter body, the new organization purports to encourage the settlement of labour dispute through the medium of conciliation and arbitration machinery.[302]

Following an agreement with Robin Kakati of INTUC and Bordoloi, Assam's Chief Minister, the ITA allowed free access in the tea gardens to those INTUC organizers who were accredited by Kakati.[303] The INTUC on its part assured the ITA that its activists would conform to 'legitimate' trade union activity and would not upset the existing labour–management relations.[304]

While the planters were determined to keep 'outsiders' at bay from the labour force in the gardens, the outsiders themselves did not seem to be very enthusiastic about it. This reference to outsiders was obviously pointed at political activists in the province. As far as the planters were concerned, judging by the experiences of other industries in Bengal and Bombay Presidencies, their fears were not completely unfounded. In the case of Bombay, during the late nineteenth century, it was the outsiders – some of the liberals among nationalist leaders of middle-class origins like Lokhande and Bengalee – who tried to organize the workers.[305] In Calcutta, the *bhadralok* were actively involved in organizing the workers in jute mills, railways and other transport industries.[306] During the late nineteenth century, most of the Indian nationalist leadership adopted a sympathetic attitude towards the working class but primarily in European capitalist enterprises, while they opposed any proposed or actual labour legislations for the labour force in Indian-owned capitalist enterprises.[307] In the case of the Assam tea plantations, almost the entire nationalist leadership and the press all over India championed the cause of labour, and condemned their horrible and inhuman working conditions and ill-treatment at the hands of the employers.[308] In this respect, some of the younger Brahmo Samaj reformers and activists in Bengal, such as Dwarkanath Ganguly, played an important role in publicizing the cause of the Assam tea garden labourers through the English and vernacular press.[309]

Later on, at an individual level, N.M. Joshi, Diwan Chaman Lall and a few others took up the cause of Assam tea garden labourers. Joshi visited the tea gardens in Assam, and his experience of this visit was published in the form of an article in *Servant of India* in 1924. In this article he pointed out the inadequacy of the labour laws, the low wages and lack of freedom of movement of the labourers in the tea gardens. In the Legislative Assembly, he and some other Indian members (during the debate on the Tea District Emigrant Labour Bill, 1932) expressed their sympathy with the cause of the labourers, and recommended amendments favourable to labourers. Diwan Chaman Lall, a member of the Royal Commission on Labour in India, wrote a book on the conditions of labourers in Assam in which he condemned their exploitation and ill-treatment by the planters.[310] These efforts, however, remained confined to individuals and never really became a part of the programme of the nationalist movement. The early enthusiasm of the nationalists and their concern for the cause of Assam tea garden labour seem to have considerably declined in the period when the nationalist struggle became a mass movement. This was particularly true as far as labour in the Assam Valley gardens was concerned. During the 1920–22 labour struggles, while the nationalist leadership and newspapers from Bengal took a very keen and active interest in the Chandpur exodus case (Surma Valley), simultaneous strikes in the Assam Valley were not even noticed by them.[311] There was no effort to connect Gandhi with the labour communities in Assam Valley tea gardens at the height of their struggle in 1921, while he met the planters, at the suggestion of president of the Dibrugarh Congress Committee, at Dibrugarh District Club on 26 August 1921. Gandhi is supposed to have told the planters that he had not come to enquire into the conditions of labour in Assam tea gardens; nor was the non-cooperation movement a fight of labour against capital, or industrial concerns or industries such as tea.[312]

In contrast to the experience of Bombay and Bengal (during the nineteenth century), the Assamese middle-class nationalist leadership in Assam Valley showed an utter lack of concern for the problems of the tea garden labourers. Despite their genuinely nationalist sentiments, they were remarkably silent or casual in their attitude towards the helpless and brutally oppressed labourers in the European-owned tea gardens of Assam Valley.[313] Amalendu Guha has put forward two explanations for this apathy of the Assamese middle-class nationalists. First, several of the local Congress leaders were either planters themselves, or were socially and matrimonially related to planter families. The second explanation lies in the ideological reservations of the Congress organization as a whole towards working-class forms of struggle, i.e. strikes, which were not a part of the Congress agenda. It was *hartals*, according to Guha, not strikes that suited the Congress ideology and its organization best.[314] We may add a third factor to Guha's analysis, viz. the social and cultural distance of the Assamese middle class from the migrant labourers. They were outsiders of socially lower origins who, apart from working as labourers in the tea gardens, also performed menial labour for the middle classes. Most of the tea garden labourers, referred to as Deswalis by the Assamese middle class, were Hindi speakers from Bihar or aboriginals from Chotanagpur, Santhal Parganas and Orissa. If status was a barrier to sympathy, the language difference was a barrier to communication.

Summing up

From the 1860s onwards, Assam Valley witnessed the growth of a plantation structure which was woven around the obnoxious indenture system. The planters wielded extra-legal authority over their labour force which was comparable to that of white masters over their black slaves in the antebellum era in Southern USA. Within this structure, the workers were subjected to physical coercion and social control which severely restricted their mobility within and outside the plantations, and isolated them from the outside world. Within the boundaries erected over vast isolated spaces by the plantation regime to tame and discipline labour, the workers expressed their protest in different forms over time. During the indenture period, the acts of resistance included desertions and what the officials termed as cases of riots, assaults, intimidations and unlawful assemblies. There were cases of strikes also, but these were not recognized as such in official reporting. These acts of resistance were both individual and collective. While economic grievances were important factors provoking the workers' actions, there were other equally significant issues such as the demand for social and cultural rights. One common and persistent feature of these acts of resistance was the resort to violence by workers in retaliation against extreme forms of physical and economic coercion, indignities and sexual harassment of their women-folk by planters. Through the preservation and practice of their cultural and social traditions, the labour communities kept alive the memories of their experiences, which helped to cope with the everyday life of grief and wretchedness. Through celebration of their cultural and social forms, they resisted becoming disciplined 'coolies'.

The process of dismantling the indenture system as a consequence of increasing labour militancy provided opportunities for more organized forms of protest. The years between 1920 and 1922 witnessed increasing articulation of workers' grievances and intensity of protests in the form of strikes. One immediate consequence of the 1920–22 labour upsurge was the withdrawal of the final vestiges of the indenture system, with the abolition of the Workman's Breach of Contract Act of 1859 in 1926. Official withdrawal of the indenture system prompted the employers to work out their own internal mechanisms in the form of 'labour rules' and 'wage agreements', which effectively curbed labour mobility within the tea plantations. While this may have restrained the possibility of workers' struggles crystallizing into a unified and organized labour movement in the Assam Valley, the workers adopted new and novel forms of resistance including exodus. Exodus, like desertion, represented a political act of *en masse* rejection of the imposed rhythm of life in the plantation regime. The shifts in the character of protest do not represent any ascending order or teleological sequence. The shifts in the forms were often in response to the changing configurations of power and changing historical context. While new and more organized forms of resistance developed, older forms continued to persist. Overlapping forms like acts of desertion, 'unlawful assembly' and 'mobbing' persisted well up to 1920, when more organized, larger-scale forms of protest like strikes and exodus forced recognition in the official reporting. The increasing intensity of labour militancy during the 1930s in response to the sharp decline in wages during the depression paved the way for the emergence of trade unions in the Assam tea plantations. The imposition of the draconian Defence of India Rules by the colonial state at the onset of World War II constrained the activities of trade unions temporarily. However the resistance surfaced in a more organized form during the war years despite the imposition of the draconian law. An important feature of the war-time resistance was the growing influence of communist activities in the working-class circles of Assam, including the tea plantations in Assam Valley. The planters devised strategies of countering the growing communist influence on their labour force by forging alliances with the leadership of the newly formed Congress trade union who were backed by the newly formed Congress government in the province.

Notes and References

1 Jan Breman and E. Valentine Daniel, 'The Making of a Coolie', in E. Valentine Daniel, Henry Bernstein and Tom Brass (eds), *Plantations, Proletarians and Peasants in Colonial Asia*, London: Frank Cass, 1992, pp. 268–96.

2 Eric Robert Wolf, *Europe and the People Without History*, California: University of California Press, 2010.

3 Nitin Varma, 'For the Drink of the Nation: Drink, Labour and Plantation Capitalism in the Colonial Tea Gardens of Assam in the late nineteenth and early twentieth century', in Marcel van der Linden and Prabhu P. Mohapatra (eds), *Labour Matters: Towards Global Histories, Studies in Honour of Sabyasachi Bhattacharya*, New Delhi: Tulika Books, 2009, pp. 295–318.

4 Report of the Royal Commission on Labour in India, 1931 (hereafter Royal Commission), Written Evidence, Assam and Dooars, Vol. VI, Part I, p. 3. Such a perception provided the rationale for opposing any demand for wage increase. These were precisely the arguments put forward by the planters in their opposition to recommendation of a small wage enhancement by Henry Cotton, Chief Commissioner of Assam, at the turn of the twentieth century.

5 Assam Labour Report, 1900, p. 1; *RTDELA* (XXII of 1932), 1936, p. 5.

6 We have already cited the case of 1918 when cholera and influenza took a great toll on labour life.

7 Report on Tea Operations in the Province of Assam 1873–74; Assam Labour Reports 1877–1932; Report of the Tea Districts Emigrant Labour Act (XXII of 1932), 1934–47 (hereafter RTDELA XXII of 1932).

8 ITA Reports: 1924, pp. iii–iv; 1925, pp. iv–v.

9 See chapter 5.

10 For the supply side, see Prabhu P. Mohapatra, 'Coolies and Colliers: A Study of the Agrarian Context of Labour Migration from Chotanagpur, 1880–1920', *Studies in History*, Vol. 1, No. 2, 1985, pp. 247–303.

11 Assam Labour Reports, 1888–1897.

12 Census, 1911, Vol. III, Assam, Part I, Report and Part II, pp. 128–30.

13 Ibid.

14 Ibid., pp. 129–37.

15 Ibid.

16 Ibid., p. 129.

17 Census of India, 1921, Vol. III, Assam, Part I, p. 38.

18 Royal Commission, 1931, p. 359.

19 Kaushik Ghosh, 'A Market for Aboriginality: Primitivism and Race Classification in the Indentured Labour Market in Colonial India', in Gautam Bhadra, Gyan Prakash, Susie Tharu et al. (eds), *Subaltern Studies X: Writings on South Asian History and Society*, New Delhi: Oxford University Press, 1999, pp. 18–30.

20 Bempfydle Fuller, *Some Personal Experiences*, London: John Murray, 1930, p. 118.

21 Royal Commission, 1931, Written Evidence, Vol. VI, Assam and Dooars, Part II, pp. 114–15.

22 Ibid.

23 Ibid, p. 116.

24 The practice of 'garden time' was in vogue till the 1980s in Assam Valley tea plantations.

25 Special Report, Government of India, 1891, para 186; George Barker, *Tea Planter's Life in Assam*, Calcutta: Thacker, Spink & Co., 1884, p. 134; David Crole, *Tea: A Text Book of Tea Planting and Manufacture*, London: Crossby Lockwood and Son, 1897, p. 8.

26 Sunil S. Amrith, *Crossing the Bay of Bengal: The Furies of Nature and the Fortunes of Migrants*, Cambridge: Harvard University Press, 2013, p. 125.

27 Crole, *Tea*, p. 49.

[28] See chapter 5.

[29] Special Report, Government of India, 1891, para 186, pp. 273–4. Also see chapter 2.

[30] Crole, *Tea*, pp. 203–04.

[31] Under the provision of the various laws in force the employers were responsible for the education of the children of tea garden labourers.

[32] Census of India, 1921, Vol. III, Assam, Part II, p. 344.

[33] Ibid.

[34] Census of India, 1911,Vol. III, Assam, Part I, p. 108.

[35] Shantaram Ramkrishna Deshpande, *Report on an Enquiry into the Cost and Standard of Living of Plantation Workers in Assam and Bengal*, 1948, p. 65.

[36] Royal Commission, 1931, Written Evidence, Assam and Dooars, Vol. VI, p. 13.

[37] Ibid.

[38] *Capital* (Calcutta), 23 August 1900.

[39] John Weatherstone, *The Pioneers 1825–1900: The Early British Tea and Coffee Planters and Their Way of Life*, London: Quiller Press, 1986, p. 80.

[40] Barker, *Tea Planter's Life*, p. 104.

[41] F.A. Hetherington, *The Diary of a Tea Planter, 14 July 1907*, Sussex: The Book Guild Ltd., 1994, p. 24.

[42] They were the native field staff in the plantation social hierarchy who assisted the European planters. *Sirdars* were labourers who had risen in the hierarchy. The *sirdars* were supervised by Assamese *muhurrirs* (generally pronounced as *moories*) who acted under a head, or *'burra muhurrir'* who was answerable for the conduct of all outdoor work. Crole, *Tea*, p. 8.

[43] T. Kinney, *Old Times in Assam*, Calcutta: Star Press, 1896, p. 11.

[44] Crole, *Tea*, p. 198.

[45] Ibid., p. 49.

[46] Coolie Trade, Parliamentary Papers, 1867, p. 2.

[47] Government of Assam, Revenue A, Nos. 77–17, August 1904, p. 12.

[48] Assam Labour Report, 1888, p. 71.

[49] Department of Revenue and Agriculture, Government of India, Emigration A, Nos. 8–13, December 1892, p. 49.

[50] Government of Assam, Revenue A, Nos. 77–17, August 1904; Annexure B, p. 13.

[51] Ibid.

[52] Ibid., p. 16.

[53] Ibid., pp. 17–18.

[54] Ibid., p. 17

[55] Rana P. Behal, 'Coolie Drivers or Benevolent Paternalists? British Tea Planters in Assam and Indenture Labour System', *Modern Asian Studies*, 44, 1, 2010, pp. 29–51.

[56] Percival Griffiths, *The History of the Indian Tea Industry*, London: Weidenfeld and Nicolson, 1967, p. 376.

[57] For more details, see Chapter 2; Hetherington, *The Diary*, p. 77.

[58] Chapters 2 and 3.

[59] For details, see chapter 5; Rana P. Behal, 'Wage Structure and Labour: Assam Valley Tea Plantations, 1900–1947', NLI Research Studies Series, No. 043/2003, V.V. Giri National Labour Institute, NOIDA, 2003.

[60] Sukomal Sen, *Working Class of India: History of emergence and movement, 1830–1970*, Calcutta: K.P. Bagchi & Co., 1977; Ranajit Das Gupta, 'Poverty and Protest: A Study of Calcutta's Industrial Workers and Labouring Poor, 1875–1899', in Ranajit Das Gupta (ed.), *Labour and Working Class in India: Studies in Colonial History*, Calcutta: K.P. Bagchi & Co., 1994, pp. 315–405.

[61] Dipesh Chakravarty, *Rethinking Working-Class History: Bengal 1890–1940*, New Jersey: Princeton University Press, 1989, chapter 6.

[62] Assam Company Papers (ACP), Mss. 9925, Vol. 4, Calcutta Proceedings, 18 July and 31 October 1846.

[63] Ibid., 12 June 1848; H.A. Antrobus, A History of the Assam Company, Edinburgh: T. and A. Constable, 1957, p. 389.

[64] ACP, Mss. 9925, Vol. 4, Calcutta Proceedings; also see Kalyan K. Circar, 'Labour Management: First Twenty Years of Assam Company Limited (1839–59)', Economic and Political Weekly of India, Vol. XXI, No. 22, 31 May 1986, pp. M38–43.

[65] ACP, Mss. 9925, Vol. 6, Calcutta Proceedings, 12 May 1853.

[66] ACP, Mss. 9925, Vol. 7, Minutes of Proceedings in India, 4 January 1854.

[67] ACP, Mss. 9925, Vol. 4, Calcutta Proceedings, 13 July 1847.

[68] ACP, Mss. 9925, Vol. 6, Minutes of Proceedings in India, December 1853.

[69] ACP, Mss. 9925, Vol. 4, Calcutta Proceedings, 31 March 1847.

[70] Ibid., 18 July 1846.

[71] ACP, Mss. 9925, Vol. 5, Assam Company Minutes of Proceedings in India, Calcutta Committee Minute Book, 1851.

[72] Ibid.

[73] ACP, Mss. 9925/10, Calcutta Proceedings, October 1859; Antrobus, Assam Company, p. 98.

[74] See chapter 1.

[75] Papers Regarding the Tea, Calcutta, Parliamentary Papers, 1874, p. 23.

[76] Home Department Proceedings, Legislative, Government of India, November 1864, p. 679.

[77] Ibid.

[78] Ibid., p. 681.

[79] Peter H. Wood, Black Majority: Negroes in Colonial South Carolina from 1670 through the Stono Rebellion, New York: W.W. Norton & Company, 1974, p. 239. While the number and percentage of the blacks in the colony were growing, individual slaves were finding it increasingly difficult to exercise even the rudimentary aspects of independence and autonomy that had been possible during earlier decades. Personal and social initiatives among slaves were being checked by the evolving economic patterns and legal codes imposed by the European settlers. Changing circumstances prompted an increasing number of runaways. In a society where slaves were defined as property and where blacks were becoming artful in appropriating things they were denied, these were the people who, in a real sense, elected to 'steal themselves'.

[80] Home Department Proceedings, Legislative, Government of India, November 1864; Report of the Commissioners Appointed to Enquire into the State and Prospects of Tea Cultivation in Assam, Cachar and Sylhet (hereafter Commissioners Report), 1868, p. 50; S.M. Akhtar, Emigrant Labour for Assam Tea Gardens, Lahore, 1939, p. 42.

[81] Rana P. Behal and Prabhu P. Mohapatra, '"Tea and Money versus Human Life": The Rise and Fall of the Indenture System in the Assam Tea Plantations 1840–1908', in E. Valentine Daniel, Henry Bernstien and Tom Brass (eds), Plantations, Proletarians and Peasants in Colonial Asia, London: Frank Cass, 1992, pp. 146–47.

[82] Papers Regarding the Tea, 1874, p. 23.

[83] Richard Dunn, The Rise of the Planter Class in the English West Indies, 1624–1713, University of North Carolina Press, 1972, p. 248.

[84] Wood, Black Majority, pp. 239–41.

[85] Rev. Charles Dowding's letter to India Office, 3 June 1912, Judicial Department, Government of Assam, Immigration Branch, B Proceedings, Nos. 21–25, October 1912, p. 7.

[86] Department of Revenue, Government of Assam, A, Nos. 77–117, August 1904, pp. 1–2.

[87] Ibid., p. 2.

[88] Assam Labour Report, 1892, p. 25.

[89] Papers Regarding the Tea, 1874, p. xxi.

⁹⁰ Commissioners Report, 1868, p. 54.

⁹¹ Revenue and Agriculture Department, Government of India, Emigration A, Nos. 13–16, March 1878.

⁹² Assam Labour Reports for respective years; Report of the Assam Labour Enquiry Committee (hereafter RALEC), Calcutta, 1906, p. 81.

⁹³ Dowding, *Tea Garden Coolies*, p. vii.

⁹⁴ Assam Labour Report, 1884, p. 26.

⁹⁵ Department of Revenue and Agriculture, Government of India, Emigration Proceedings A, Nos. 6–8, February 1900, p. 74.

⁹⁶ Revenue and Agriculture Department, Government of India, Emigration A, Nos. 2–4, May 1877.

⁹⁷ Ibid.

⁹⁸ Special Report, Government of India, 1891, pp. 187–92.

⁹⁹ Revenue and Agriculture Department, Government of India, Emigration A, Nos. 13–16, March 1878.

¹⁰⁰ Barker, *Tea Planter's Life*, p. 130.

¹⁰¹ Ibid., p. 135.

¹⁰² Ibid., p. 267.

¹⁰³ Fraser, *The Recollections of a Tea Planter*, London: The Tea and Rubber Mail, 1935, p. 15.

¹⁰⁴ Hetherington, *The Diary*, p. 24.

¹⁰⁵ Crole, *Tea*, p. 55.

¹⁰⁶ Ibid.

¹⁰⁷ Maurice P. Hanley, *Tales and Songs from an Assam Tea Garden*, Calcutta: Thacker, Spink & Co, 1928, pp. 93–94.

¹⁰⁸ Barker, *Tea Planter's Life*, p. 176.

¹⁰⁹ Sarthak Sengupta and Jagadeeshwar Lall Sharma, 'Jhumar: Folksongs and Dances of Tea Garden Labourers of Assam', in Datta Ray and Sebastian Karotemprel (eds), *Tea Garden Labourers of North East India: A Multidimensional Study on the Adivasis of the Tea Gardens of North East India*, Shillong: Vendrame Institute, 1990, pp. 214–26.

¹¹⁰ Pashupati Prasad Mahato, 'World View of the Assam Tea Garden Labourers from Jharkhand', in Ray and Karotemprel, *Tea Garden Labourers*, pp. 131–42.

¹¹¹ Ibid., p. 140. For a detailed discussion, see Nitin Varma, 'Producing Tea Coolies?: Work, Life and Protest in Colonial Tea Plantations of Assam, 1830s–1920s', unpublished dissertation, Humboldt University, Berlin, Germany, 2011.

¹¹² Ibid., p. 141.

¹¹³ Sengupta and Sharma, 'Jhumar', p. 225.

¹¹⁴ Government of Assam, Revenue A, Nos. 77–117, August 1904.

¹¹⁵ It is important to note that trade unions emerged as legal entities only in 1926 in India.

¹¹⁶ Special Report, Government of India, 1891, p. 240.

¹¹⁷ Assam Labour Report, 1891, p. 23.

¹¹⁸ Assam Labour Report, 1896, p. 46

¹¹⁹ Elizabeth Kolsky, *Colonial Justice in British India*, Cambridge: Cambridge University Press, 2010.

¹²⁰ Department of Revenue, Government of Assam, A, Nos. 77–117, August 1904.

¹²¹ Ibid.

¹²² Assam Labour Report, 1901, p. 13

¹²³ Department of Revenue, Government of Assam, A, Nos. 77–17, August 1904, p. 4.

¹²⁴ Ibid.

¹²⁵ Assam Labour Report, 1900, p. 24.

¹²⁶ Department of Revenue, Government of Assam, A, Nos. 77–117, August 1904, p. 22.

¹²⁷ Assam Labour Report, 1900, p. 20.

[128] Assam Labour Report, 1901, p. 12.

[129] Ibid., p. 13.

[130] Assam Labour Report, 1900, p. 23.

[131] Department of Revenue and Agriculture, Government of India, Emigration A, No. 17 November,1903.

[132] Ibid.

[133] Department of Revenue and Agriculture, Government of India, Emigration A, No. 11, November 1903.

[134] Their preference to do so is understandable in the light of the tremendous labour militancy on display during these events. There were cases of violent outburst on the part of the labourers in response to the brutality and oppression by their employers, leading sometimes to the death of the managers or assistant managers. This could easily have been a cause of genuine fear among the planters considering they were vastly outnumbered by the labour force. Communication constrains in the plantation areas during those days made it difficult to quickly summon the police for help. This may explain the frequent use of firearms like revolvers by the planters against the labourers.

[135] Assam Labour Report, 1900, p. 22.

[136] Ibid.

[137] See the Assam Labour Reports for respective years.

[138] Assam Labour Report, 1903, p. 12.

[139] Another case of the use of a revolver by the manager against labourers was reported in 1906–09. Assam Labour Report, 1908–09, p. 9.

[140] Assam Labour Report, 1902–03, p. 12.

[141] Assam Labour Report, 1903–04, p. 10. In the same year sixteen other such cases of 'rioting', and 'violence' were reported.

[142] Assam Labour Report, 1904–05, p. 8; *Eastern Bengal and Assam Era*, 21 February 1906, p. 4.

[143] Department of Revenue and Agriculture, Government of India, Emigration A, No. 11, November 1903.

[144] Department of Commerce and Industry, Government of India, Emigration B, No. 32, January 1911.

[145] Assam Labour Report, 1915–16.

[146] See chapter 4; Kolsky, *Colonial Justice*.

[147] Government of Assam, Revenue A, Nos. 77–17, August 1904, p. 1.

[148] Assam Labour Report, 1900, p. 22.

[149] Behal, 'Coolie Drivers'.

[150] Chapter 4.

[151] Financial Department, Government of Eastern Bengal and Assam, Immigration Branch, B Proceedings, Nos. 52/73, December 1905, pp. 18–32.

[152] Department of Revenue and Agriculture, Government of India, Emigration A, No. 17, November 1903.

[153] Behal and Mohapatra, 'Tea and Money', pp. 167–68.

[154] The economic issue becoming a dominant factor during the 1920–22 events was a reflection of the sharp decline in real wages, causing tremendous hardship to the labourers. For details, see chapter 5.

[155] RALEC,1921–22, p. 1; *The Bengalee*, 29 June 1921.

[156] In the same period equally serious and better known cases of exodus and strikes occurred in the Surma Valley (the famous case of Chargola exodus, May 1921). For the Chargola episode, see Nitin Varma, 'Coolie Exodus in Chargola: Mobilization, Control and Collective Action in the Colonial Tea Plantations of Assam', unpublished M.Phil dissertation,

Jawaharlal Nehru University, New Delhi, 2003. We are concerned here with the incidents which occurred in the Assam Valley.

157 Assam Labour Report, 1920–21, p. 2; RALEC, 1921–22, pp. 6–7.
158 Evidence Recorded by the Assam Labour Enquiry Committee, 1921–22, p. 10.
159 RALEC, 1921–22, p. 15.
160 Assam Labour Report, 1921–22, p. 4.
161 The names of the gardens where cases of riots, unlawful assembly and disturbances reported were the following: Joboka, Suffry, Barkathani, Mathurapur, Amguri, Barsilla and Suntok tea gardens. Assam Labour Report, 1921–22, p. 4; RALEC, 1921–22, p. 17.
162 RALEC, 1921–22, pp. 6–7.
163 Ibid., p. 16.
164 Ibid.
165 Evidence Recorded by the Assam Labour Enquiry Committee, 1921–22, pp. 14–15.
166 *The Times* (London), 4 October 1920.
167 RALEC, 1921–22, pp. 6–7.
168 Ibid., pp. 15–16.
169 Ibid.
170 Ibid., p. 17.
171 Ibid.
172 Ibid., p. 9.
173 ITA Papers, Mss. EUR/F174/57, 28 April 1921.
174 ITA Papers, Mss. EUR/F174, Bay 1, April 1921.
175 Evidence, ALEC, 1921–22, p. 3.
176 Evidence, ALEC, 1921–22, p.3.
177 Financial Department, Government of Assam, Immigration Branch B, Nos. 20–112, March 1922, p. 108.
178 Langford James' article, 'The Tea Coolies', *The Englishman*, 13 July 1921, p. 10.
179 Ibid.
180 RALEC, 1921–22, p. 19.
181 Ibid., p. 6.
182 Ibid., p. 8.
183 Ibid., pp. 9–16.
184 Ibid., p. 9.
185 Ibid., p. 16.
186 Ibid.
187 Ibid., p. 17.
188 Ibid., p. 10.
189 Ibid., p. 16.
190 For more details, see Amalendu Guha, *Planter Raj to Swaraj: Freedom Struggle and Electoral Politics in Assam 1826–1947*, New Delhi: Indian Council of Historical Research, 1977; A.C. Bhuyan and S. De (eds), *Political History of Assam, 1920–1939*, Gauhati: Government of Assam, 1978, Vol. II, pp. 235–70; Nitin Varma, 'Coolie Exodus in Chargola'.
191 RALEC, 1921–22, pp. 6–7; Guha, *Planter Raj to Swaraj*, pp. 131–40; Bhuyan and De (eds), *Political History*,Vol. II, pp. 235–70.
192 RALEC, 1921–22, pp. 6–7.
193 Ibid., p. 9.
194 Ibid., pp. 7 and 17; Financial Department, Government of Assam, Immigration Branch B, Nos. 20–112, March 1922, p. 221; Proceedings of the Annual Meeting of General Committee of Assam Branch of India Tea Association, March 1920, p. 137.
195 Financial Department, Government of Assam, Immigration Branch B, Nos. 20–112, March 1922, pp. 105–07.

[196] Report on the Administration of Assam, 1920–21, p. 1.

[197] Assam Labour Report, 1920–21, pp. 2–5.

[198] Rana P. Behal, 'Power Structure, Discipline and Labour in Assam Tea Plantations under Colonial Rule', in Rana P. Behal and Marcel van der Linden (eds), *India's Labouring Poor: Historical Studies c. 1600–2000*, Delhi: Foundation Books, Delhi, 2007, p. 169.

[199] Royal Commission, 1931, p. 386.

[200] Dattaraya Varman Rege, *Report on An Enquiry into Conditions of Labour in Plantations in India*, 1946, p. 28. To enforce compliance of the agreement a financially punitive clause was inserted which stipulated that if a garden employed an assisted immigrant from another garden the former had to pay a transfer free of Rs 75 for the first year, Rs 50 for the second and Rs 25 for the third, to the estate from which he had moved.

[201] Assam Labour Reports, 1922–23, 1923–24 and 1924–25.

[202] Assam Labour Report, 1927, p. 3.

[203] Ibid.

[204] Assam Labour Report, 1928, p. 4.

[205] Assam Labour Reports, 1927, pp. 3–4; 1928, p. 3; 1929, p. 3; 1930, pp. 3–4.

[206] W.J. Reed's letter to the Member, Finance and Revenue, 24 October 1924, in Finance Department, Government of Assam, Immigration Branch B, Proceedings, Nos. 403–648, June 1925, pp. 7–9.

[207] Ibid.

[208] Finance Department, Government of Assam, Immigration Branch B Progs, Nos. 19–124, September 1925, pp. 1–13.

[209] Ibid., p. 15.

[210] Ibid., p. 11.

[211] Ibid., p. 15.

[212] Finance Department, Government of Assam, Immigration Branch, B Progs, Nos. 403–648, June 1925, p. 9.

[213] Ibid.

[214] ITA Report, 1931. At least two more cases of Sibsagar district were referred to in the ITA Report for the year 1931.

[215] General and Judicial Department, Government of Assam, Immigration Branch, B, Nos. 1–15, 1931; 41–50, 1931; 108–24, June and 71–64, September 1931; 16–26, December 1931. Also Assam Labour Report, 1931.

[216] General and Judicial Department, Government of Assam, Immigration Branch B, Nos. 19–22, March 1931, p. 2

[217] General and Judicial Department, Government of Assam, Immigration Branch B, Nos. 41–50, June 1931, pp. 4–10

[218] General and Judicial Department, Government of Assam, Immigration Branch B, Nos. 108–24, June 1931, pp. 8–10

[219] Assam Labour Report, 1931, p. 4.

[220] General and Judicial Department, Government of Assam, Immigration Branch B, Nos. 23–4, June 1931.

[221] ITA Report, 1931, p. 115.

[222] General and Judicial Department, Government of Assam, Immigration Branch B, Nos. 1–15, December 1931; Assam Labour Report, 1931, p. 4.

[223] General and Judicial Department, Government of Assam, Immigration Branch B, No. 25, June 1931, p. 2.

[224] General and Judicial Department, Government of Assam, Immigration Branch B, Nos. 13–33, September 1931, p.4

[225] Assam Labour Report, 1931, p. 4.

226 General and Judicial Department, Government of Assam, Immigration Branch B, Nos. 71–64, September 1931.

227 General and Judicial Department, Government of Assam, Immigration Branch B, Nos. 16–26, December 1931, pp. 5–16

228 General and Judicial Department, Government of Assam, Immigration Branch B, Nos. 47–8, December 1931, p. 2.

229 General and Judicial Department, Government of Assam, Immigration Branch B, Nos. 56–70, December 1931, pp. 5–12

230 General and Judicial Department, Government of Assam, Immigration Branch B, Nos. 71–64, December 1931.

231 General and Judicial Department, Government of Assam, Immigration Branch B, Nos. 77–81, December 1931.

232 General and Judicial Department, Government of Assam, Immigration Branch B, Nos. 138–46, December 1931.

233 General and Judicial Department, Government of Assam, Immigration Branch B, Nos. 6–16, June 1934, p. 5.

234 General and Judicial Department, Government of Assam, Immigration Branch B, Nos. 73–90, June 1934, p. 10.

235 General and Judicial Department, Government of Assam, Immigration Branch B, Nos. 6–16, June 1934, p. 5.

236 RTDEL XXII of 1932, 1935, p. 18.

237 Ibid.

238 General and Judicial Department, Government of Assam, Immigration Branch B, Nos. 14–7, March 1936, pp. 8–14. Similar trends of strikes continued in the next two years which were reported by the officials. See RTDELA XXII of 1932, for 1937 and 1938.

239 ITA Papers, Mss. EUR, F174/2070, Labour Matters, January 1940 to December 1941, pp. 27–28.

240 RTDELA XXII of 1932, 1938, p. 12.

241 Ibid., p. 15.

242 Royal Commission, 1931, p. 386

243 ITA Papers, Mss. EUR, F174/2070, 1938.

244 Fortnightly Reports, Assam, Home Political Department, 1939; Guha, *Planter Raj*, pp. 236–63.

245 RTDEL XXII of 1932, 1939, p. 386.

246 Report on Labour Troubles in Tea Gardens of Assam Valley, 1939, compiled by Secretary, Assam Branch, Indian Tea Association, ITA Papers, Mss. EUR, F174/2070, Labour Matters, January 1940 to December 1941; Rege, *Enquiry Report*, p. 72.

247 ITA Papers, Mss. EUR, F174/2070, 1940.

248 ITA Papers, Mss. EUR, F174/2070, Labour Matters, January 1940 to December 1941.

249 ITA Papers, Mss. EUR, F174/2070, 1940.

250 Assam Administrative Report, 1939–40, p. 1; Assam Legislative Council Proceedings, 1939; Guha, *Planter Raj*, pp. 238–41; Bhuyan and De (eds), *Political History*, Vol. II, pp. 263–70.

251 Guha, *Planter Raj*, p. 24; Bose, *Capital and Labour*; Assam Administrative Report, 1939–40, p. 1.

252 The Digboi oil workers' strike was preceded by a lightning strike (and lockout) of workers in the Swedish-owned Assam Match Company at Dhubri in 1936–37. The years 1938–39 also witnessed increasing unrest among workers of Assam Railways and Company. The spirit of militancy spread all over Assam and labourers in a number of Surma Valley gardens went on strike. Strikes in the transport industry and railways were also reported. For details, see Guha, *Planter Raj*, pp. 238–46.

253 RTDEL XXII of 1932, 1939, p. 15.

254 Government of Assam, Home Political, File No. 18/8/1939, Confidential Fortnightly Report, Later half of August, 1939, p. 3

255 Government of Assam, Home Political, File No. 18/7/1939, Fortnightly Report, Confidential. Second half of July, 1939, p. 3

256 Government of Assam, Home Political, File No. 12/1/1939, Poll., January, 1939, p. 28.

257 General and Judicial Department, Government of Assam, Immigration Branch B, File No. Imm 118, G.I.M. 49/47, 1939, p. 167.

258 ITA Report, 1939, p. 26

259 The Committee consisted of F.W. Hockenhull, MLA (ITA), Baidyanath Mukherjee, MLA (Indian Planters), A.K. Chanda, MLA, Debeswar Sarma, MLA, and K.C. Ghosh, ICS as its chairman. Following were the terms of reference to the Committee: (i) to determine what is the root cause of recent strikes and other manifestations of discontent on tea gardens in Assam, and particularly whether there are economic grievances either generally in the district concerned or in the affected estates; (ii) what measures are required in order to remove the root cause or causes or the said strikes; and (iii) whether and if so what forms of organization is desirable for enabling labourers on tea gardens to communicate their grievances to the management in such effective manner as will remove any doubt that their interests are secure, and to procure settlement of such grievances, if any, by negotiation. All India Congress Committee Papers, File No. P1-12, TL No. 1020, 1939, p. 3, Nehru Memorial Museum and Library, New Delhi; *Amrita Bazar Patrika*, 29 May 1939; General and Judicial Department, Government of Assam, Immigration Branch B, File No. Immigration 118, G.I.M. 49/47, 1939, p. 167.

260 General and Judicial Department, Government of Assam, Immigration Branch B, File No. Immigration 118, G.I.M. 49/47, 1939, p. 167.

261 Ibid., p. 161. The following persons were warned not to hold meetings in the tea gardens in view of the appointment of the above committee:
1. Babu Bideshi Ram Tanti, MLA
2. Shyam Chandra Chaudhuri
3. Sardar Gurudat Singh
4. Lilaram Kakuti
5. Bireson Saikia
6 Bangshidhar Dutta
7. Benoy Bhuahan Chakravarty
8. Sam Goala.
General and Judicial Department, Government of Assam, Immigration Branch B, File No. Immigration 118, G.I.M. 49/47, 1939, p. 161.

262 The members whose appointment on the Committee was objected to by ITA were Debeswar Sarma and A.K. Chanda.

263 ITA Report, 1939, p. 28; Government of Assam, Home Political, File No. 16/7/1939, Confidential Fortnightly Report, first half of July, 1939, p. 2.

264 Government of Assam, Home Political, File No. 18/4/1938, Poll., D.O. No. 260-C.B., Fortnightly report for Assam for the first half of April, 1938, p. 1.

265 Ibid.

266 D.O. Home Political, File No. 18/4/1938, Poll., D.O. No.304–C.B., Fortnightly report for Assam for the first half of April,1938.

267 Assam Administrative Report, 1939–40; Griffiths, *The History*, p. 384; Bhuyan and De (eds), *Political History of Assam*, Vol. II, p. 270.

268 Assam Legislative Assembly Proceedings, 1940, Vol. I, p. 1313; Guha, *Planter Raj*, p. 242; Bhuyan and De (eds), *Political History of Assam*, Vol. II, p. 252.

269 Rege, *Report*, p. 72; Griffiths, *The History*, p. 384.

[270] General and Judicial Department, Government of Assam, General Branch, File No. GIM 21/43, 1943.

[271] Rege, *Report*, p. 51.

[272] General and Judicial Department, Government of Assam, General Branch, File No. 8/45, 1945.

[273] Government of Assam, Home Political, File No. 18/3/1943, Fortnightly report, first half of June, 1943, p. 102.

[274] All India Trade Union Congress Papers, File No. 45, 1942–44, p. 25, Nehru Memorial Museum and Library, New Delhi (hereafter AITUC Papers); General and Judicial Department, Government of Assam, Immigration Branch, No. GIM 7, 1943.

[275] General and Judicial Department, Government of Assam, Immigration Branch, No. GIM 7, 1943.

[276] During this period the APTUC had also extended its activities to the oil industry at Digboi, transport – railways, steamers, motor and rickshaw, and other industries like coal, cement, match workers, electricity supply, rice mills, shops, bank employees, etc. Report of Secretary APTUC at its 3rd Annual Session held on 14 and 15 December 1945 at Dibrugarh, reproduced in General and Judicial Department, Government of Assam, File No. GIM 7, 1943–47.

[277] AITUC Papers, File No. 46, 1945–46, p. 18; General and Judicial Department, Government of Assam, General Branch, File No. GIM 17/46, 1946, p. 7.

[278] ACP, Ms. 11497, Vol. 4, 1946.

[279] General and Judicial Department, Government of Assam, General Branch, File No. GIM 17/46, 1946, p. 7; ACP, Ms. 11497, Vol. 4, 1946.

[280] General and Judicial Department, Government of Assam, General Branch, File No. GIM 17/46, 1946, p. 7.

[281] Ibid., p. 13; *Assam Tribune*, 20 November 1946.

[282] *The Nationalist*, 25 September 1946, reported the killing of the labourer by the manager of Suntok tea estate, and the statement of Ram Nath Das, Minister of Labour, in the Assam Legislative Assembly. *Hindustan Standard*, 25 September 1946, also reported the incident.

[283] *Hindustan Standard*, 25 September 1946.

[284] General and Judicial Department, Government of Assam, General Branch, File No. GIM 17/46, 1946, p. 12.

[285] Ibid., p. 13.

[286] AITUC Papers, File No. 47, T.L. No. 4, 1947–48, p. 31. For details of planters' patronage to INTUC, see chapter 4.

[287] General and Judicial Department, Government of Assam, File No. GIM-7, 1943.

[288] Guha, *Planter Raj*, p. 293; Rege, *Report*, pp. 71–72.

[289] For details, see chapters 2 and 3.

[290] The Bill, however, was withdrawn as the planters' representatives managed to convince the Congress Ministry that the grievances would be removed. Only after 1947 were rules framed under the plantation code to guarantee freedom of movement. General and Judicial Department, Government of Assam, Immigration B, Nos. 34–63, September 1939, p. 49; Assam Administrative Report, 1938–39, p. ii; Guha, *Planter Raj*, p. 243; Assam Legislative Assembly Debates, 1938, Vol. II, pp. 820–21.

[291] Royal Commission, 1931, p. 386.

[292] Assam Legislative Council Proceedings, 1927, Vol. VII, No. 5, pp. 40–103.

[293] Royal Commission, 1931, p. 378.

[294] Ibid. Planters in the Ceylon tea gardens adopted similar methods to isolate their labour force from the 'mainstream of political and trade-union developments in the rest of the country. A strict surveillance was maintained on plantations and trespass laws prevented "outside agitators" from having access to the labour force at its place of work.' And Jayawardene concludes from this that 'these restrictive features of plantation life inhibited the rise of trade

unions or any form of independent organizational activity among the workers.' Visakha Kumari Jayawardena, *The Rise of the Labor Movement in Ceylon*, North Carolina: Duke University Press, 1972, p. 22.

[295] ITA Report, 1937, p. 37.

[296] ITA Report, 1939, p. 25.

[297] ITA Report, 1940, p. VIII.

[298] ITA Report, 1945, p. 24. Also see chapter 3.

[299] This attitude was reflected in ITA's opposition to the India Trade Unions (Amendment) Bill, 1946, on the ground that the Bill provided for compulsory recognition of trade unions by employers. Once again the stereotype argument of 'outside agitators' exploiting illiterate labour for political reasons was put forward as the basis of their opposition. ITA Report, 1946, p. 84.

[300] Griffiths, *The History*, p. 391; Guha, *Planter Raj*, p. 293.

[301] ITA Report, 1946, p. XIV.

[302] ITA Report, 1947, p. 41.

[303] ITA Circular to Garden Managers, No. L.D. 600, dated Dibrugarh 21 July 1947, cited in Guha, *Planter Raj*, p. 297.

[304] Guha, *Planter Raj*, p. 298.

[305] L.A. Gordon, 'Social and Economic Conditions of Bombay Workers on the Eve of the 1908 Strike,' in I.M. Reisner and N.M. Goldberg (eds), *Tilak and Struggle for Indian Freedom*, New Delhi, 1966, pp. 532–35.

[306] Sumit Sarkar, *Swadeshi Movement in Bengal*, Calcutta, 1973; Dipesh Chakravarty, 'Sasipada Banerjee: A Study in the Nature of the First Contact of the Bengali Bhadralok with the Working Class in Bengal', Occasional Paper No. 4, Centre for Studies in Social Sciences, Calcutta.

[307] For further details, see Bipan Chandra, *The Rise and Growth of Economic Nationalism in India*, New Delhi, 1966, Chapter VIII.

[308] The indenture system was condemned as slavery by the Indian nationalist leaders and the press when the Plantation Labour and Inland Emigration Bill in 1882 and the Assam Labour and Emigration Bill in 1901 were being discussed in the Imperial Legislative Council. Most of them supported Henry Cotton, Chief Commissioner of Assam, who introduced the 1901 Bill with a provision to increase the wages in tea gardens. Ibid., pp. 360–75.

[309] Dwarkanath Ganguly, *Slavery in British Dominion*, edited by Sris Kumar Kunda, Calcutta: Jignasa, 1972: reprint of thirteen articles published in the newspaper *Bengalee* between September 1886 and April 1887.

[310] Central Legislative Assembly Debates, April 1932, Vol. III, pp. 2978–98; Diwan Chaman Lall, *The Coolie: The Story of Labour and Capital in India*, Lahore: Oriental Publishing House, 1932, Vol. II.

[311] C.F. Andrews, C.R. Das and others were very actively involved in the Chandpur case and the *Bengalee* and *Amrita Bazar Patrika* championed the cause of the oppressed labour in the Surma Valley tea gardens during 1920–22. A number of editorials and articles were devoted to the above issue.

[312] ITA Papers, Mss./F174, Bay 1, April 1921. The report of this meeting was prepared from memory after the end of the meeting. The proceedings of the meeting were not recorded and it was prepared from memory by members of the ITA general committee who were present. As per this report, Gandhi showed his awareness of the issues involved in the tea garden labourers' struggle, including the matter of sexual harassment of female labour by European planters and discriminatory differential wages on gender lines.

[313] Except for occasional reference, the Indian members of the Provincial Assembly and Council were remarkably silent on issues concerning labourers in Assam Valley tea gardens. Even during periods of intense labour unrest (1931, 1939, etc.), we do not come across any

meaningful discussion being raised by them in the provincial legislative bodies. It was only in the late 1930s and 1940s that we find some of the Assamese leaders like Omeo Kumar Das publicly taking up the question of freedom of movement of labourers in the gardens. However even they did not make serious efforts to organize the labourers into a trade union organization.

314 Guha, *Planter Raj*, p. 139.

Conclusion

The emergence of tea as a commodity of 'prodigious consumption' in British society and the addiction to opium among the Chinese populace during the eighteenth and nineteenth centuries had a direct bearing on the British 'discovery' of the utility of the tea plant in the forested areas of Upper Assam. A contraband beverage in the early half of the eighteenth century, it acquired the status of the 'national drink' of the United Kingdom in 1784.[1] Its import into the UK through the East India Company's monopoly over Chinese trade was hugely profitable to the Company and a lucrative source of revenues for the British government. The conquest of Bengal and other territories in the Indian subcontinent during the second half of the eighteenth century brought opium production under the monopolistic control of the East India Company who embarked upon opium smuggling into China. This new venture further boosted the Company's fortunes as its proceeds were utilized to finance its tea trade. In the early decades of the nineteenth century the supply of this lucrative trade and the widely consumed 'national drink' of the UK was threatened by the Chinese authorities demanding stoppage to the illegal opium trade by the EIC. The alarming threat prompted the British imperial and commercial establishments to launch campaigns to search for alternative sources of tea supply from within the empire. The discovery of the tea plant in the Singhpho country of Upper Assam, followed by successful state-sponsored experiments for the commercial production of tea, attracted private British capital. The incorporation of joint-stock companies, the Assam Company in London and the Bengal Association in Calcutta, in 1839, generated excitement among prospective investors towards the new venture of opening up tea plantations in Assam. This was facilitated by the annexation of Assam into British Indian territories after deposing its ruler Purandar Singh. Tea plantations in Assam became the first major venture of private British capitalist investment in colonial India.[2] Not all the investments were imported from the UK as several planters had earned their capital while working in India. With the exception of the Assam Company (Bengal Association had merged with it) which was a corporate entity, most of the plantation owners were individual investors during the early two decades. After the initial hiccups and financial uncertainties of the 1840s, the newly opened plantations survived and stabilized by the late 1850s.

A major push came in the 1860s when Lord Canning, Viceroy of British India, offered large tracts of wasteland at throwaway prices for opening new plantations in Assam. The generous offer stimulated a wild speculative boom, the 'tea mania', marked by the doubling of tea prices, soaring profits and the mushrooming of large number of new companies for producing tea. Prospects of quick fortunes attracted a large number of British investors to acquire large tracts of wastelands or existing plantations. Both existing owners and new ones turned into unscrupulous speculators. Large-scale cheating, fraud and deception were reported in the official enquiries during the 'mad rush' for opening new plantations. The boom period witnessed acreage expansion at a massive scale without any check or regulatory system in place. Wasteland acquisition in the Assam Valley alone grew from 59,049 acres in 1858–59 to 364,990 acres in 1872, most of it during the speculative boom years.[3]

The industry survived the 'tea mania' boom and, in the course of last three decades of the nineteenth century, grew spectacularly in the Assam Valley. Acreage expanded, production increased exponentially and to sustain this growth, an increasing number of labourers were imported to work in the plantations. By the late 1880s, Indian tea exports to the UK overtook China. The industry continued to grow, though less spectacularly, during the next fifty years. It was also marked by an upward secular trend in per labour and per acre productivity of tea. The increasing mechanization of factory production through technological innovations in the late nineteenth century, and scientific research into soil, disease and pest control from the beginning of the twentieth century, also contributed significantly towards the increase in productivity.

This growth was marked by several characteristic features. First, soon after the recovery from the speculative boom, the tea industry was quickly transformed into a well-organized corporate structure through rationalization. The management of tea plantations was transferred to the monopolistic control of British managing agency houses based in Calcutta with headquarters in the UK. The operations of the bigger companies stimulated the amalgamation of a number of smaller gardens into large-scale enterprises under these managing agencies. This led to an incredible transformation of the very landscape of the tea plantations in Assam. The plantations, increasingly referred to as estates or gardens, covered a vast, uniformly green, tailored and undiluted landscape. These large amalgamated 'estates' were converted into exclusive spaces – gated, isolated and protected from the 'outside' world with fencing and guards. This landscape was dotted with small numbers of big, luxurious and elegant bungalows of European managers and their assistants, relatively modest cottages of Indian office staff, and larger numbers of residential quarters of the lowest denomination, the 'coolie-lines' of the labourers. The managing agency houses appointed European managers and assistant managers to administer these 'estates'. The seasonal nature of the tea production process induced residential compulsion for labour, clerical and the managerial staff on the 'estate'. All residents of the 'estate' had to live and work under the omnipotent authority of the managers, the *burra sahibs*. As master of his domain, assisted by a hierarchy of junior managers, office staff and field supervisors, the manager was solely responsible for ensuring uninterrupted production of tea for a growing global market. This had an important bearing on the way in which plantation labour system evolved in the Assam Valley.

The second distinguishing feature was the formation of the industry's apex body, the Indian Tea Association, headquartered in London and with important branches in Calcutta and Assam during the 1880s. The ITA was manned by senior members of tea companies and retired British bureaucrats from Indian Civil Services. This combination made it a powerful organization representing and advocating the interests of the tea industry, both from inside the legislative bodies and outside, to the colonial state. The racial affinities of the British planters and company executives with the colonial bureaucracy were important for providing access to the official hierarchies in the provincial, central and home governments. The ITA successfully influenced government policies for building infrastructure required for scientific research, mobilization of labour from distant recruitment areas, and transportation of manufactured tea to Calcutta for export to the global market. Its political clout played a significant role in influencing, largely successfully, the labour policies of the provincial and central governments. It remained the most powerful and influential commercial organization of the tea planters and wielded significant political clout in Assam till the very end of colonial rule. The ITA used its political influence to prevent state intervention in support of plantation labour by the newly elected popular ministries in Assam during the late 1930s.

The third important feature was that this incredible expansion and growth took place while tea prices, unlike in the pre-1865 period, were falling in the international market. During the last two decades of the nineteenth century tea prices fell by half. During the next fifty years, international tea prices fluctuated constantly, subject to the ups and downs of international markets, and growing competition from other tea-producing countries like Ceylon and Dutch East Indies. It is remarkable that the tea industry, in the long run, despite constant fluctuations and downward trends in tea prices, remained financially profitable and declared handsome dividends for its shareholders in most years.

All these features were closely linked to the evolving labour regime, both in the indenture and post-indenture periods, and had an important bearing on the structure of labour recruitment and labour system in the Assam tea plantations. While the availability of land and capital presented no difficulty, the mobilization of labour for the growth of the tea industry was a critical problem. The adoption of labour-intensive processes of tea production by the early 'pioneers' generated a large demand for labour. A common refrain in the tea industry circles throughout its history was the shortage of labour. While the demographic situation of the province initially may have constrained adequate labour supply, the fact remains that the local Kachari community worked for the plantations from the very beginning till at least the end of the nineteenth century. They, however, were considered to be 'troublesome'. They refused to be tamed and tied down, demanded higher wages, and accepted only the task of clearing the forest and no regular employment. The Assamese peasant, on the other hand, found employment on the plantations unattractive both for social and economic reasons. They were stigmatized as naturally 'indolent', 'lazy', and largely addicted to the use of opium for their unwillingness to accept plantation employment at low wages.[4] The planters complained of the absence of a labour market and cited this as the reason for opting for long-distance recruiting. However, there is no doubt that reluctance to offer the higher wages demanded by local labourers was an important consideration for long-distance recruitment.

During the early two decades the planters looked for labour in neighbouring Bengal through private recruiters. However, unwilling to offer competitive wages for the extremely difficult working and living conditions in the plantations, the industry faced uncertainty and instability of labour supply. In addition, high costs of importing labour and large-scale desertions and mortality were serious concerns for both the individual and corporate owners. The situation became more exasperating in the 'tea mania' speculative boom period. A massive expansion of tea acreage in the course of just five years, 1860–65, generated a huge demand for labour. Existing arrangements of labour supply were far too inadequate to keep pace with this. Mobilization of labour was outsourced to Calcutta-based private contractors and recruiters by the planters. The recruiting areas' network of the newly launched 'coolie trade' expanded beyond Bengal into Bihar, Orissa and United Provinces for labour supply. Aboriginal and tribal communities of Santhal Parganas and Chotanagpur became favourite hunting grounds for the new recruitment drive. The lucrative business of labour supply for the Assam tea plantations acquired notoriety as 'coolie trade' for abusive recruitment practices, high rates of sickness, mortality and desertion of labourers during transit. Even before the speculative boom burst in 1865, the tales of emigrants suffering ill-treatment at the hands of planters and the extremely high mortality in the plantations began to surface, causing concern and state intervention.

State intervention in the form of labour legislations took place in the context of extremely high rates of sickness and mortality, both during transit and on arrival in the plantations, akin to the 'horrors of slave trade', as revealed by the official enquiry commissions of 1862, 1868 and 1874. The labour legislations (1863 and 1865) aimed at regulating the recruitment and transportation of migrant labourers and labour relations in the Assam tea plantations. These legislations laid the foundations of the obnoxious indenture system by sanctioning a penal contract system, initially for four to five years. In due course of time, however, the 'persuasive' and coercive strategies adopted by planters ensured that the labourers renewed their contracts, thereby perpetuating generational servitude. Re-engagement of time-expired labourers under Act XIII under a system of 'advances', land grants, debt and wages in kind were some of the methods. This marked the beginning of a dependent relationship which remained a dominant feature of labour relations in the Assam Valley tea plantations for the entire period under study.[5] Periodic modifications of the indenture law and its formal closure in 1926 did not alter the status of servitude of the labourers to any significant extent.[6] This experience was not exactly 'giving up much of their freedom for a period of years in hope thereby to amend their estate.'[7] Nor did it prove to be a rational and deliberate choice prompted by hopes of bettering their future, an 'escape hatch.'[8]

The recovery and stability of the tea industry after the disastrous speculative boom period was closely linked with the setting up of the indenture labour regime in the Assam plantations. The planters achieved this massive growth in the face of fluctuating and sharply declining tea prices by maximizing production through intensification of the labour process, and using industrial organization of time at lower wages. Two important developments followed as a consequence of this. Large-scale labour mobilization became imperative. The practice of sponsored recruitment and transportation of labour through the *sirdari* and *arakati* systems from distant labour districts for the Assam tea plantations was already in vogue from the pre-1865 years. The planters now complained about the existing labour law as a deterrent to mobilizing more and cheaper labour. They successfully lobbied with the colonial state to suitably modify the labour law in 1882, to remove 'cumbersome' provisions of state 'interference' for uninterrupted supply of 'free' and 'cheaper' labour. Tens of thousands of labourers were recruited and transported to the Assam tea plantations from the recruiting areas during the next two decades under Act I of 1882. By the end of the nineteenth century nearly 400,000 labourers along with their families were working and living in 'coolie lines' in the tea plantations in the Assam Valley.[9] This huge scale of mobilization was marked by increasing allegations and mounting official evidence of deception, abuse and fraudulent recruitment practices, and increasing costs in the recruitment of labour for the tea plantations.

Secondly, in the gardens, the planters, armed with penal sanctions and the right of private arrest of 'absconding' labourers under the indenture labour law, pushed very hard to extract maximum work from the labour force by adopting coercive strategies, including long hours of work by turning the clock into a special 'garden time'; immobilization through surveillance and confinement; and physical punishment aiming to tame, discipline and control. Constantly under pressure from the corporate expectations of high dividends, and incentives of higher commissions and bonus or insecurity of their jobs in the event of failure, the managers often pushed harder. In the process they were transformed from average British youngsters into 'coolie-drivers'. Their attitude and behaviour towards the labour force reflected a combination of racism and class prejudice. For many of them, inflicting brutal flogging upon 'troublesome' or 'absconding' labourers became a regular feature of their managerial persona. Physical and sexual coercion, an almost universal practice in most of the European capitalist plantations in their overseas colonies, became integral to the indenture regime in the Assam plantations, as a device to deter desertions and non-compliance to the contract. While the brutality of physical coercion failed to check desertions, low wages, ill-treatment, and harsh living and working conditions resulted in undernourishment, sickness, high rate of mortality and negative rate of reproduction of labour life in the plantations.

Low wages were an important link to sustain the profitability and financial health of the industry, on the one hand, and high rate of mortality and negative rate of reproduction, on the other. The planters paid wages below the statutory minimum to the labour force, whereas the industry achieved very high growth rates in the face of sharply declining tea prices during the last two decades of the nineteenth century. The provincial sanitary reports linked undernourishment and high mortality among the labour force in Assam's tea plantations to their low earnings. The death rate outstripped the birth rate among plantation labourers in the same period. The government medical officer reported deliberate abortions by women labourers due to harsh working conditions and low wages. Women were paid lower wages as compared to male labourers, which also helped to further depress the overall wage bill.[10] Similarly, real wages remained stagnant in the plantations, whereas the tea companies declared dividends regularly despite fluctuating downward trends in tea prices during the first half of the twentieth century. While the official time-series reported declining mortality during this period, the death rate remained higher than the birth rate. Besides, the death rate among tea labour was also higher compared to the population outside the plantations in the province.[11] The accuracy of official time-series seems highly suspect, looking at the higher mortality figures and incidence of undernourishment among labour in some plantations based on inspections reported by the Labour Enquiry Committee of 1921–22, and revealed by the official medical surveys in the late 1930s and early 1940s and by the Rege Committee in 1946.

The important question as to how the labour survived in such a situation of stagnant and low wages and high mortality needs to be addressed and explained. Most of the labour force, given their low level of earnings, lived on highly inadequate, low-calorie diets – for decades rice constituted the major item of food consumption in the labour households. This explains the high incidence of undernourishment among them. The planters paid part of the wage in kind through subsidized rice. Women and children constituted a significant percentage of the labour force and their combined earnings, though lower than men, helped the survival of the family.[12] Access to land for cultivation was at best supplementary to subsistence consumption of the labour family and not a source of extra cash earnings. The plots of land provided for private cultivation were not big enough to be commercially productive to provide extra cash earnings, besides being subject to payment of rent to the planters. Ironically, the incidence of debt, on account of advances from the employers and the purchase of everyday household subsistence needs from the Marwari[13] traders in the vicinity of plantations, was another source of survival, but also tied them to long-term servitude. Loss of working hands on account of a high rate of deaths, desertions and exodus was compensated for by continuous and uninterrupted sponsored recruitment and transportation of a fresh labour force throughout the period under study. The recruitment and transportation costs considerably declined and travel time reduced with improvement in the infrastructure like steamers and railways.

What role did the colonial state play in opening up the tea plantation enterprise in Assam, and what was its attitude towards the British planters vis-á-vis the labour force? Colonial authorities and imperial scientific establishments were the actual 'pioneers' who set up tea plantations in Assam in the 1830s. Private British capital was the beneficiary of the colonial state's benevolence when it bequeathed its successfully experimented tea plantations to Assam Company free of cost. This was followed by the grant of vast tracts of wastelands at very low prices and on easy terms to British capitalists for opening up new plantations. The state did not extend similar concessions of low revenue to native cultivators. For the development of the tea industry under the monopoly of European capital, the state utilized public revenues to construct the necessary infrastructure, like roads, railways, steamer services, etc., and promoted the marketing of tea and scientific research. Tea plantations were the exclusive beneficiaries of railway construction because it connected only the tea-producing areas with Calcutta and other ports, neglecting other important urban centres in the province.

State assistance was most crucial in the matter of mobilization of labour and regulating labour relations. During the early two decades the emphasis was on land policy suitable for the planters to acquire large tracts of wastelands cheaply. To then help the planters mobilize local labour, the government raised its land revenue demand on the Assamese peasantry, aiming to coerce them into wage employment in the plantations. Despite the imposition of increased revenue, however, the 'lazy' and 'indolent' Assamese peasants resisted their conversion into wage labour in the plantations. The incidence of abusive recruitment practices and the extremely high rates of mortality of migrant labourers during transit and on arrival in the plantations during the 'tea mania' speculative boom induced state intervention in the form of indenture labour legislations. The state justified this legislative intervention on two counts. First, the employer's investment on recruitment and maintenance of labour must be protected by making the labourer fulfil his contractual obligation, and he must not be 'allowed capriciously to withdraw himself from the service of the employer.' To ensure compliance by labour, penal provisions were introduced in the indenture law, and planters were given the extraordinary power of private arrest of 'absconding' labourers. Second, the labourer, on the other hand, being 'ignorant' and 'illiterate', needed state protection against abusive recruitment, proper facilities during transit, the statutory minimum wage, and other requisite comforts, medical attendance and other appliances for his well-being, which would be enforced by the law. For the colonial state such an arrangement appeared fair and equitable: 'A penal labour law and government protection to the labour are . . . correlative terms.'[14]

In the long history of labour relations in the Assam tea plantations, the colonial state, most of the time, did not act as a fair arbiter between capital and labour while regulating labour relations. Collusion between the planters and the bureaucrats, rendered possible by racial and cultural affinities, prevented any meaningful implementation of the welfare provisions of the labour laws. The official evidence shows excessive use of the penal sanction against the helpless labour in an extremely arbitrary fashion, while the labour protection clauses were rarely implemented. Blatant violation of the statutory minimum wage provision by the planters for over two decades was completely overlooked by the provincial bureaucracy. Despite the mounting evidence of a high rate of sickness, mortality and very low wages, the district officials continued to paint a rosy picture of harmonious labour relations, and comfortable and happy labour life. The planters constantly defied the provisions concerning labour welfare, but the state rarely took action against them. Deviation from this routine by any reporting officer was considered an affront and resented both by the industry and their supporters among the British community in Calcutta, and the higher bosses in the bureaucracy. Henry Cotton was to learn this at the cost of his career.

The colonial bureaucracy frequently overlooked the use of extra-legal coercion and the extremely harsh treatment of labour by the planters. The provincial judiciary acted as an arbitrary, oppressive and racially afflicted

arm of the colonial state. The labourers received extremely harsh imprisonment terms for the smallest display of confrontation against the employers,
often in self-defence, while the planters were let off or awarded extremely
lenient punishments like small fines for even serious offences against labour,
including murder. This was admitted by the highest echelon of the imperial
hierarchy: the private and official communications between Henry Cotton,
the Chief Commissioner of Assam, Lord Curzon, the Viceroy of India, and
George Hamilton, the Secretary of State for India, provide unambiguous
testimony of this.

The colonial bureaucracy, however, was not a monolith. While committed
to the maintenance of imperial authority and the monopoly of British capitalism in the tea industry, some among them were critical of the infringement
of law by the planters, and the use of coercive strategies both in the process
of recruitment and employment in the plantations. They were revolted by
the physical brutality unleashed by the planters on their labourers. They did
not hesitate from reporting the unpleasant realities of deceptive and abusive recruitment practices and the miseries of labour life in the plantations.
Without their critical reporting, the many tales of harsh servitude under the
authoritarian plantation regime may have remained untold. Henry Cotton
was lauded and felicitated in public by the nationalist intelligentsia and the
press for standing up to the planters and the Anglo-Indian press. Their efforts,
however, were extremely limited and could not restrain the colonial state from
its arbitrary and unfair attitude towards labour vis-á-vis capital. Cotton's fate
became a deterrent for display of empathy and support, however legitimate,
for the labour cause.

Apart from the sympathetic concern shown by some colonial bureaucrats,
the nationalist press, in Calcutta in particular, consistently championed the
cause of Assam Valley tea plantation labourers and critically debated issues
with the planters' vociferous supporters. Exposing the wretched working and
living labour conditions in the plantations, lending support for the proposed
higher wages by Henry Cotton and Indian members in the central legislative
council, and sympathetically reporting the labourers' collective resistance
were some of the important interventions of the nationalist press. However,
after an initial flurry of sympathetic activity, the nationalist leadership, both
in the province and outside, remained indifferent.[15] Only towards the late
1930s did some of the provincial nationalist leaders raise the issues of plantation labourers in the state legislative assembly, and the communist leadership
helped organize trade union activities in the 1940s.

How did the labourers respond to economic exploitation, physical and
sexual coercion, harsh working and living conditions, and state oppression?
Denied even a semblance of education and subjected to a life of total illiteracy,
the labourers left no written tales of their struggles against the authoritarian

plantation regime in Assam. A close reading of the colonial archival documents, however, helps us to construct the story of labour resistance challenging the servitude of a hundred years in their everyday lives, both individually and collectively.

Contrary to their depiction as 'ignorant' by the planters and the colonial bureaucracy, the labourers showed a clear awareness of their rights when they collectively approached the district officials demanding action against their employers for violation of the labour-protective provisions of the law. From the very inception of their incarceration as indentured labourers, they challenged the brutal violence of the planters supported by the oppressive arms of the colonial state, by combining strategies of individual forms of resistance in the Scottian sense and collective resistance.[16] Labour struggles were linked to the issues of low wages, harsh working and living conditions, extraction of excessive work, physical and sexual coercion, defending social and cultural rights, and preservation of human dignity. Individual acts of resistance were not confined to passive or accommodating strategies. Despite the risk of inviting extremely punitive action, there were numerous instances of labourers' defiance and retaliatory violence against the planters. The argument that the authoritarian nature of the indenture regime or the cultural and social diversity of the migrant labour communities constrained collective and organized labour resistance and the formation of labour organizations does not hold here. On the contrary, on several occasions they transcended ethnic diversities and stood in solidarity with their fellow labourers in retaliating against physical and sexual abuse by planters. In solidarity they faced the grave consequences of unfair convictions and long terms of imprisonment by the colonial judiciary.

The authoritarian nature of the labour regime may have delayed the formation of labour organizations till very late in its history. However, lack of organization did not mean the absence of collective resistance. Their increasing militancy and collective assertions worried Viceroy Curzon into action to seek details of conflicts in the plantations between labourers and employers, and finally paved the way to the withdrawal of penal provisions from labour law in 1908. Similarly, the large-scale labour revolts of 1921–22 across the Assam plantations hastened the demise of the indenture law in 1926. However the collective actions did not wait and were not confined to 'big moments' like the 1921–22 rebellion, or the strikes of the late 1930s and 1940s. Collective resistance assumed different forms which, in the official vocabulary, were variously and at different conjunctures described as 'assaults', 'unlawful assemblies', 'riots', 'desertions', ' *en masse* exodus' and strikes, depending on the nature of prevailing labour laws. Under indenture laws both individual and collective resistance were branded as criminal acts, and hence were not reported as such. Strike as a collective action was recognized only either before the imposition of indenture law or after the elimination of these provisions. One common and persistent feature of these acts of resistance was the resort to violence by workers in retaliation against extreme forms of physical and economic coercion, indignities, and sexual harassment of their women-folk by the planters. In the process of developing a collective consciousness, they maintained their diverse social and cultural identities. But these diversities were not a deterrent to their collective actions. These diverse labour communities kept the memories of their experiences alive, which helped them to cope with the everyday life of grief and wretchedness in the plantations. Through the preservation and celebration of their cultural and social traditions, the labourers resisted being transformed into 'tamed', 'docile' and 'disciplined' 'coolies'.

Their working and living conditions may have been akin to the slaves in the antebellam era plantations of Southern USA, but they were employed and worked under a capitalist wage contract system. They demonstrated the characteristic features of proletarians putting up a collective resistance against capital. The dependency relationship in the Assam plantations was an integral part of modern capitalist relations in the colonial context, and not 'semi-feudal' or 'pre-capitalist' in nature.[17] That was but natural because, as we have argued earlier in this work, the system of indentured labour in the Assam plantations was an integral part of capitalism in the colonial context, with some elements of the contractual relationship superficially resembling capitalist relations in form, but in substance, it was coercive exploitation for capitalist ends with the support of the colonial state.

Notes and References

[1] Moxham Roy, *Tea: Addiction, Exploitation and Empire*, New York: Carroll and Graph Publishers, 2004, chapter, 1.

[2] Sidney Mintz's analysis in his classic work on the sugar and dietary transforming impact of the western societies is equally appropriate in the context of growing tea consumption: 'The profound changes in dietary and consumption patterns in eighteenth- and nineteenth-century Europe were not random or fortuitous, but the direct consequences of the same momentum that created a world economy, shaping the asymmetrical relationships between the metropolitan centers and their colonies and satellites, and the tremendous productive and distributive apparatuses, both technical and human, of modern capitalism.' Sidney Mintz, *Sweetness and Power: The Place of Sugar in Modern History*, Harmondsworth: Penguin, 1985, p. 158.

[3] Papers Relating to Tea Cultivation in Bengal, *Selections from The Records of the Government of Bengal No. XXXVII*, Calcutta: Bengal Military Orphan Press, 1861, pp. 33–35; Papers Regarding the Tea, Calcutta, Parliamentary Papers, 1874, p. 11. In the Surma Valley district of Cachar, a staggering figure of over half a million acres of so-called wasteland was reported to have been acquired by the speculators for opening up tea plantations.

[4] Walter Rodney has argued that in post-emancipation Guyana in the Caribbean, the ex-slaves walked off *en masse* from sugar plantations because the British planters refused their demands for higher wages and better work conditions. Instead the planters opted to import

Indian labour under the indenture system. Walter Rodney, 'Plantation Society in Guyana', *Review* (Fernand Braudel Centre, Bighamton, NY), IV, 4, Spring 1981, pp. 643–66.

[5] This dependency relationship continues to be an important feature of Assam tea plantation employment even today, at the beginning of the twenty-first century. Part of the wage is still paid in kind, in the form of subsidized rice. The tea plantations, apart from the permanent labour force on its roles, employ a significant numbers of *basti/faltu* labour who are ex-tea garden labour on lesser terms.

[6] The increasing employment of ex-tea garden labourers on lower wages points to their dependency relationship even after leaving the plantations as no other avenues of earnings were available to them except subsistence cultivation on government-rented land.

[7] David W. Galenson, 'The Rise and Fall of Indentured Servitude in the Americas: An Economic Analysis', *The Journal of Economic History*, Vol. 44, No. 1, 1984, p. 24.

[8] P.C. Emmer, 'The meek Hindu: the recruitment of Indian indentured labourers for service overseas, 1870–1916', in P.C. Emmer (ed.), *Migration: Indentured Labour Before and After Slavery*, Dordrecht, 1986, pp. 187-207; P.C. Emmer, 'The Great Escape: The Migration of Female Indentured Servants from British India to Surinam 1873–1916', in Colin Clark, Ceri Peach and Steven Vertovec (eds), *South Asians Overseas*, Cambridge: Cambridge University Press, 1990, pp. 245–66.

[9] Their numbers grew to over 800,000 families by the end of the colonial rule.

[10] A similar observation in an insightful essay by Walter Rodney on labour in British sugar plantations in Guyana is worth quoting here: 'What is important in the post-slavery era is that in Guyana, as elsewhere, given the historical conditions of the time, women were discriminated against in terms of the rate of wages, and, of course, children were paid still less. Thus the ability to command family labor was at the same time the ability to incorporate cheap labour, because women and children were paid less.' Rodney, 'Plantation Society', p. 650.

[11] Official time-series here refers to the reported figures by the provincial Annual Emigration Reports.

[12] It was not a 'family-wage' earning in the sense used by Deshpande or the planters, which was supposed to provide 'comforts' and 'luxuries' to the labouring families.

[13] A trading community of Rajasthan who migrated to eastern India from the early nineteenth century.

[14] E. Gait, *A History of Assam*, Calcutta: Thacker, Spink & Co., 1906, p. 2.

[15] It was a different experience in Surma Valley during the Chargola revolt where senior congress leaders and C.F. Andrews were directly involved.

[16] For a new and nuanced understanding of the concept of collective actions of workers, see Marcel van der Linden, *Workers of the World: Essays towards a Global Labour History*, Leiden: Brill, 2008, chapter, 1.

[17] Walter Rodney put it succinctly when he argued that 'capitalism in its colonial variant operated with certain peculiarities. The plantation was par excellence a colonial form. It was perhaps the most effective of the colonial forms of exploitation that had been established.' Rodney, 'Plantation Society', p. 662.

Appendix Tables

Acreage and Tea Production in Kamrup District, 1853–59

Grant date	Name	Total acreage	Acreage under cultivation	Tea Production (lbs)
4.5.1853	Mr W Robinson	155	35	960
1.4.1857	– ditto –	460	5	None
July 1857	Mr Pink	222	30	1600
1.4.1857	Mr C.W. Delanouzerede	144	27	1040
2.11.1858	Mr Bruce	186	10	None
1.10.1857	Mr H Michel	253	30	480
4.4.1858	Mr J R D Cameron	136	5	None
5.3.1857	Mr J P Wise	1,204	125	480
– ditto –	Mr W Becher	121	30	1600
July 1859	– ditto –	9,326	...	None
Total		12,207	297	6160

Source: Papers Relating to Tea Cultivation in Bengal, 1861, p. 11.

APPENDIX TABLE 1.2.
Acreage and Tea Production in Lakhimpur, 1855–59

Year	Assam Company		Warren & Jenkins		Col Hannay		G.R. Barry		Higgs, Melany & Sevenoaks		Col Reid		A.C. Campbell	
	Acre	Lbs	Acre	Lbs	Acre	Lbs	Acre	Lbs	Acre	Lbs	Acre	Lbs	Acre	Lbs
1852	350	80000	120	12000	10	–	30	–	–	–	–	–	–	–
1853	–	85000	–	16000	5	160	–	–	–	–	–	–	–	–
1854	–	90000	–	20000	40	1000	40	3000	5	–	–	–	–	–
1855	–	90000	20	24000	30	3000	45	5000	5	–	5	–	5	–
1856	10	100000	10	28000	50	12000	50	16500	14	400	20	–	5	–
1857	40	110000	30	32000	35	24000	130	25500	6	2000	42	–	15	–
1858	–	120000	–	36000	30	36000	80	37000	75	4400	43	500	25	500
1859	–	120000	–	36000	30	40000	105	54000	45	12000	20	6000	30	3200
Total	400	795000	180	204000	220	116160	480	140500	150	18800	130	12000	80	5000

Source: Papers Relating to Tea Cultivation in Bengal, 1861, p. 14.

APPENDIX TABLE 2.1

Prices of Tea in Calcutta, 1880–1901 (per lb)

Year	January	July
	Rs	Rs
1880	1.23	1.31
1881	1.31	1.35
1882	1.38	1.23
1883	1.06	1.19
1884	1.12	0.94
1885	0.88	1
1886	0.88	0.64
1887	0.75	0.81
1888	0.81	0.94
1889	0.75	0.66
1890	0.62	0.63
1891	0.79	0.75
1892	0.69	0.88
1893	0.85	0.64
1894	0.5	1.25
1895	0.94	0.94
1896	0.81	
1897	0.63	0.56
1898	0.6	0.66
1899	0.56	0.63
1900		0.54
1901	0.44	

Source: Prices and Wages in India, Calcutta, 1901, Government of India.

APPENDIX TABLE 4.1

Comparison of Total Area under Tea Plantations and Operational Area under Tea Cultivation, Districts and Assam Valley, 1888–1947 *(000 acres)*

Year	Lakhimpur		Sibsagar		Darrang		Assam Valley	
	Total area (acres)	Operational area (acres)	Total area (acres)	Operational area (acres)	Total area (acres)	Operational area (acres)	Total area (acres)	Operational area (acres)
1888	129	32	221	47.4	104	20	536	117
1890	122	36	222	54.9	101	21	529	131
1895	188	45	230	63.3	93	29	579	154
1901	192	69	245	79.3	138	40	642	205
1905	219	71	234	78	101	42	620	207
1910	203	72	246	83	136	43	654	215
1915	246	81	284	92	167	48	765	238
1920	292	91	316	99	212	57	740	266
1925	322	96	324	98	222	57	939	271
1930	363	105	343	100	250	62	1039	285
1935	363	109	359	101	236	61		
1940	361	110	368	105	234	60	1037	292
1945	375	113	337	104	237	61	1030	299
1947	377	113	364	105	237	61	1056	300

Source: Revenue and Agriculture, Government of India, Emigration A, Nos. 6–14, 1891; Annual Reports on Tea Culture in Assam, 1888–1925; Indian Tea Statistics, 1930–47.

APPENDIX TABLE 4.2
**Number of Labourers Recruited and Sent to Assam Valley
Tea Plantations, 1934–47 (000)**

Year	Tea District Labour Association		Midland Bose & Co.	
	Assisted	Non-assisted	Assisted	Non-assisted
1934	46	8	1.4	0.2
1935	18	3.8	0.4	0.1
1936	22.2	3.9	0.8	
1937	24.7	4.7	1.2	2
1938	29.7	5.4	0.9	1
1939	27.6	4.8	0.7	
1940	22.6	4.2	0.7	1
1941	16.3	3.5	0.7	0.2
1942	12.8	2.4	0.5	1
1942	12.8	2.4	0.5	1
1943	55.3	5.6	1.2	0.2
1944	38.7	6	0.6	0.1
1945	42.5	7.5	1.2	0.2
1947	36.9	9.1	1.2	0.3

Source: Annual Reports on the Working of Tea Districts Emigrant Labour Act (XII of 1932) for 1934–47.

APPENDIX TABLE 5
**Total Number of Adult Labourers (on garden books) and Total Acreage of
Land Granted (for private cultivation) by Planters to Labourers, 1934–44**

Year	Lakhimpur		Sibsagar		Darrang	
	Adult labour (000)	Acreage granted (000)	Adult labour (000)	Acreage granted (000)	Adult labour (000)	Acreage granted (000)
1934	133.9	59.2	119.7	26	38.8	19
1935	132.5	39.8	123.7	35.1	37.3	19.5
1936	136.6	39	121.4	34.5	75.4	16.6
1937	135.2	38.7	117.3	35.4	72.8	18
1938	134.9	40.7	118	36.8	69.4	17.3
1939	136.4	38.9	121.6	38.4	70.8	19
1940	139.4	38.9	120	38.7	71.5	18.2
1941	133.9	42.4	108.1	41	57.3	21.6
1942	141.1	39.4	116	40.6	65	22
1943	131.3	45.4	117	41	69.2	21.7
1944	125	37.2	110	40.2	69.7	23.8

APPENDIX TABLE 5.1
Provincial Averages of Monthly Wages of Act Labourers
in Assam Tea Plantations, 1883–99

Year	Monthly Wages Collected during Inspections		Monthly Wages	
			Manufacturing season	Non-Manufacturing season
	Men	Women	Men	Women
	(Rs)	(Rs)	(Rs)	(Rs)
1883	4.32	3.44	–	–
1884	4.46	3.59	–	–
1885	4.54	3.52	–	–
1886	4.41	3.78	–	–
1887	4.54	3.61	–	–
1888	4.46	3.63	4.49	3.65
1889	4.4	3.51	4.41	3.46
1890	4.76	3.57	4.43	3.42
1891	4.28	3.45	4.26	3.88
1892	4.61	3.49	4.96	3.88
1893	4.7	3.6	4.78	3.71
1894	4.6	3.52	4.54	3.64
1895	4.76	3.76	4.75	3.72
1896	4.72	3.96	4.76	3.84
1897	4.77	3.76	4.75	3.72
1898	4.7	3.59	4.72	3.7
1899	4.7	3.71	4.73	3.71

Source: Proceedings of the Central Legislative Council, 1901, Vol. XL.

APPENDIX TABLE 5.2
*Yearly Averages of Monthly Wages of Act Labourers
in Assam Valley Tea Plantations, 1883 to 1918–19*

Year	Lakhimpur		Sibsagar		Darrang		Nowgong		Kamrup	
	Men	Women	Men	Women	Men	Women	Men	Women	Men	Women
	Rs	Rs	Rs	Rs	Rs	Rs	Rs	Rs	Rs	Rs
1883	4.88	3.63	4.44	3.63	4.5	3.88	4.62	3.78	4.2	3.76
1884	4.38	3.76	4.56	3.63	4.57	3.56	4.62	3.78	4.2	3.76
1885	5.38	4.59	4.61	3.48	4.48	3.38	4.91	3.88	4.07	3.58
1886	5.27	4.56	4.56	4.12	4.38	3.38	4.7	4.4	5.02	4.74
1887	6.57	4.56	4.31	4	4.5	3.25	5.38	4.69	3.58	3.31
1888	5.33	4.69	4.57	3.88	4.5	3.57	5.44	4.63	4.06	3.56
1889	5.33	3.89	4.32	3.49	4.6	3.4	4.81	3.63	3.82	2.76
1890	5.27	4.07	4.9	3.7	5.56	4.31	4.31	5	4.26	3.69
1891	5.06	4.06	4.97	3.95	4.98	4.63	4.8	3.92	3.7	3.31
1892	5	4.06	5.2	3.44	4.88	3.88	4.54	4.46	4.54	3.58
1893	5.25	4.12	4.63	3.63	5.75	4.46	5	4.4	4.5	3.53
1894	5.31	3.81	5.12	3.94	4.69	4.19	4.75	4.12	5.12	3.45
1895	5.15	4.94	4.94	3.69	5.12	4.56	5.12	4.19	4.57	3.81
1896	5.12	4.07	4.88	3.76	4.2	4.69	4.81	4.26	4.75	3.94
1897	5.75	3.89	5.39	4.19	4.81	4.38	4.88	3.88	4.77	3.52
1898	4.9	4	5.19	3.81	4.63	3.7	4.52	3.63	4.42	3.36
1900	4.09	3.33	5.12	3.83	4.75	3.38	4.51	3.69	4.75	3.63
1901	5.22	4.57	5.12	3.95	4.69	4.19	5.12	4.5	4.88	3.64
1902	5.56	4.38	5.12	3.95	4.69	4	4.89	4.06	4.69	3.63
1903	5.56	4.44	5.07	4	4.51	3.95	4.94	4.12	4.5	3.88
1904	5.5	4.25	5.13	4.12	4.45	3.9	4.63	4.07	3.69	2.58
1905	5.42	4.68	5.61	4.84	5.61	4.58	4.63	4.07	3.69	2.58
1906	5.42	4.66	5.4	4.58	5.63	4.88	5.57	4.81	4.56	3.76
1907	6.23	5.29	5.44	4.38	5.64	5.25	5.75	5.31	4.56	3
1908	5.56	4.81	5.45	4.63	5.56	5	5.63	5.08	5.28	4.43
1909	5.27	3.81	5.12	3.92	4.66	4.16	4.73	4.07	5.09	3.45
1910	5.41	4.14	6	5.02	5.82	6.11	5.33	5.08	4.65	3.7
1911	5.64	4.41	5.25	4.31	5.11	5.28	5.5	5.4	5.25	4.26
1912	5.35	4.47	5.28	4.58	4.71	5.3	5.05	5	5.15	3.71
1913	5.56	4.69	5	3.9	5.12	5.2	5.19	4.9	5.5	4.19
1914	5.28	4.54	5.17	4.61	4.8	5.36	6.05	6	–	–
1915	5.78	4.9	5.45	5.19	4.9	5.56	5.38	4.63	–	–
1916	5.57	5.08	5.33	4.94	5.12	6.02	5.07	5.31	–	–
1917	6.19	5.21	5.63	4.63	5.69	7.12	5.88	6	–	–
1918	5.81	5.02	5.69	4.63	5.45	6.69	5.56	5.81	–	–
1919	4.9	4.2	6	4.69	6.13	8.38	6.25	6.94	–	–

Source: Assam Labour Reports for respective years. These figures include the value of allowances paid under Sections (128(1) and 130(1), value of diet in lieu of such allowances and rations provided under Section 134(A), and also *ticca* earning and 'bonus' (calculated on the basis of number of labourers in the garden books).

APPENDIX TABLE 5.3

Yearly Averages of Monthly Wages of Non-Act Labourers in Assam Valley Tea Plantations, 1883–1932

Year	Lakhimpur			Sibsagar			Darrang			Nowgong			Kamrup		
	Men	Women	Children	Men	Women	Children	Men	Women	Children	Men	Women	Children	Men	Women	Children
	Rs	Rs	Rs	Rs	Rs	Rs	Rs	Rs	Rs	Rs	Rs	Rs	Rs	Rs	Rs
1883	5.56	4	2.75	4.88	4.25	2.31	5	3.75	2.19	5.52	4.55	2.56	4.65	3.95	2.44
1884	5.81	4.94	2.75	4.52	3.5	2.07	5.25	3.5	2.35	5.52	4.55	2.56	4.65	3.95	2.44
1885	6.75	5.75	3.08	4.94	3.08	2.34	3.24	3.12	2	5.2	4.5	2.75	4.62	3.64	1.8
1886	7.12	5.52	2.7	4.95	3.25	2.57	5.25	3.31	2.06	5.8	5.58	2.96	4.92	3.9	1.93
1887	6.77	5.56	3.46	4.12	3.08	2.07	6.14	3.81	2.33	5.88	5.13	2.75	3.25	2.76	1.63
1888	6.75	5.58	3.52	4.77	3.2	2.32	5.5	3.5	3.44	5.88	4.88	2.63	3.7	3.56	2
1889	6.33	4.7	2.72	4.56	3.15	3.24	5.2	3.4	2.75	5.03	4.07	2.56	4.42	3.38	2.76
1890	5.08	3.88	3	4.94	3.5	2.38	4.57	3.63	2.56	6.26	5	...	5.25	4.06	2.76
1891	6.98	5.48	2.8	5.05	4.75	2.41	4.6	4.45	3.71	5.3	4.75	2.92	4.3	3.78	2.44
1892	6.44	5.58	2.69	5.88	3.95	2.25	5.69	3.82	2.44	5.59	5.22	2.74	4.84	3.75	2.5
1893	6.46	4.82	2.71	5.51	3.57	2.31	4.94	3.25	2.51	6.06	5.04	2.72	4.6	3.77	2.3
1894	6.31	4.31	2.38	6.31	3.75	2.38	6.2	3.63	2.32	5.75	4.81	3	5.39	4.31	2.45
1895	6	4.06	2.02	6.02	3.82	2.63	5.19	4.12	3.56	5.31	4.75	2.7	4.81	3.81	2.51
1896	6.56	4.12	2.31	5.88	3.88	2.51	5.45	4.2	2.26	6.56	4.75	2.94	4.81	4	2.56
1897	4.9	3.82	2.31	5.56	3.82	2.32	5.56	4.19	2.56	6.07	4.81	2.88	5.08	4.07	2.64
1898	4.39	3.31	2.19	5.69	3.88	2.56	5	3.5	2.25	4.45	3.4	2.4	4.45	3.4	2.4
1900	4.24	3.22	1.94	5.56	3.88	2.44	5.31	3.44	2.07	5.19	3.75	2.45	4.63	3.64	2.68
1901	5.21	3.57	2.23	5.31	3.78	2.46	5.06	3.56	2.44	5.19	3.94	2.45	4.63	3.64	2.68
1902	4.65	3.46	2.31	5.02	3.69	2.5	4.64	3.56	2.44	5.19	3.94	1.81	4.25	3.12	2.07
1903	5.03	3.44	2.22	4.95	3.44	2.44	4.7	3.45	2.38	5.06	3.81	2.45	4.81	3.88	2.19
1904	6	4.33	2.94	4.95	3.63	2.32	5.12	3.63	1.95	4.89	3.69	2.4	4.8	3.64	2.76
1905	5.76	3.87	2.18	5.78	3.91	2.42	5.34	4.16	2.59	4.89	3.69	2.4	4.8	3.64	2.76

(continued on next page)

(continued from previous page)

Year															
1906	5.75	3.88	2.18	5.81	3.94	2.44	5.38	4.19	2.63	5.31	4.08	2.57	4.26	2.88	1.88
1907	5.58	5.72	2.26	5.69	4.13	2.56	5.25	4.06	2.57	5.81	4.38	2.75	4.44	3.31	2.12
1908	5.18	4.08	2.42	5.54	4.31	2.51	4.96	4.19	2.59	5.81	4.94	2.82	5.07	3.57	2.12
1909	6.28	4.28	2.32	6.27	3.72	2.36	6.2	4.19	2.33	5.73	4.78	2.97	5.57	4.29	2.45
1910	5.92	4.45	2.43	5.94	4.77	2.61	5.06	4.44	2.79	5.73	4.7	2.8	4.06	3.12	1.94
1911	5.46	4.59	2.4	5.79	4.57	2.78	5.38	4.76	2.63	5.81	4.76	2.82	3.94	3.81	2.13
1912	5.57	4.45	2.45	5.75	4.64	2.88	5.69	5.02	2.81	6.06	5.19	2.94	4.28	3.51	2.06
1913	5.63	4.64	2.56	6.06	4.75	2.82	5.83	4.88	2.76	5.75	5.06	2.45	4.19	3.51	1.88
1914	5.75	4.77	2.57	6	5	2.88	5.81	5	2.88	5.94	5	3.02	4.96	3.88	2.06
1915	5.64	5.12	2.56	6.25	5.07	2.94	5.96	5.38	3.01	5.69	4.94	2.95	5.63	3.82	2.83
1916	6.12	5.53	3	6.14	5.2	3	5.7	7.56	3.2	5.56	5	2.94	3.56	2.56	1.46
1917	6.44	5.58	3.7	6.08	5.33	2.84	6.25	4.83	2.31	5.77	5.44	3.12	5.77	5.44	3.12
1918	6.32	5.69	3.12	6.25	5.08	3.06	6.06	5.95	3.25	6.12	4.94	2.38	2.25	1.94	1.81
1919	6.45	5.95	3.3	6.19	5.32	3.19	5.88	5.71	3.25	6.07	5	3.12	7.19	7.69	2.27
1920	6.7	6	3.45	6.9	6.06	3.56	6.81	6.88	3.76	6.26	5.44	2.89	6.06	4.2	2.44
1921	6.5	5.26	3.38	7.06	5.94	3.76	7.32	6.81	3.88	6.45	5.56	3.13	5.75	3.5	
1922	7.31	6.31	3.82	7.63	6.44	4.06	7.25	6.32	3.82	6.96	5.81	3.75	6.13	3.69	1.94
1923	7.75	6.38	4	7.94	6.56	4.39	8	7.08	4	7.44	6.25	3.75	6.19	3.94	2.75
1924	7.75	6.5	4.12	8.12	7.07	4.63	7.69	6.81	4.31	6.82	6.25	3.44	6.25	3.95	2.75
1925	8.12	6.5	4.2	8.56	7.19	4.7	8.13	7.13	4.31	7.69	6.82	3.82	6.44	4.69	3.39
1926	8.83	6.89	Rupee	9.01	7.44	4.88	8.5	7.39	4.81	8.31	6.88	3.94	5.94	4.76	2.94
1928	8.72	7.46		9.12	7.5	5.07	9.12	8.18	5.36	8.9	6.64	4.1	8.33	6.22	4.22
1929	8.9	7.76	4.42	9.18	7.92	5.16	9.24	8.17	5.46	9.21	6.6	4.05	8.33	6.22	4.22
1930	9.18	7.9	4.75	8.9	7.68	5.1	9.18	7.73	5.38	8.98	6.74	4.12	8.24	6.38	5.28
1931	8.5	6.65	4.1	8.58	7.49	5.42	8.65	7.09	4.95	8.58	5.97	3.58	7.72	6.26	3.39
1932	7.82	6.16	4	8.55	6.68	5.28	7.84	6	4.55	7.77	5.6	3.68	5.7	4.31	2.46

Source: Assam Labour Reports for respective years. Total monthly cash earnings of non-Act labourers based on figures of total number of labourers on the books. The figures of cash wages include the value of *ticca*, diet, rations, subsistence allowance and bonus.

APPENDIX TABLE 5.4

Yearly Averages of Monthly Wages of Settled Labourers in Assam Valley Tea Plantations 1934–47

Year	Lakhimpur			Sibsagar			Darrang			Nowgong			Kamrup		
	Men	Women	Children	Men	Women	Children	Men	Women	Children	Men	Women	Children	Men	Women	Children
	Rs	Rs	Rs	Rs	Rs	Rs	Rs	Rs	Rs	Rs	Rs	Rs	Rs	Rs	Rs
1934	8.12	6.06	4.56	7.19	6.19	4.25	6.56	4.89	3.44	7.06	5.02	2.89	6.06	4.81	2.56
1935	8.31	6.31	4.12	6.44	5.06	3.56	6.25	4.56	1.5	6	4.56	2.56	5.7	3.64	1.94
1936	8.31	6.69	4.56	6.38	5.31	3.94	6.38	4.5	3.08	6.08	4.82	2.69	7.08	6.13	2.95
1937	8.31	6.75	4.88	6.75	5.63	4.06	6.69	4.94	3.32	6.25	5.04	5.69	6.56	5.14	2.69
1938	8.7	6.75	4.81	5.06	5.56	3.96	6.81	4.9	3.44	6.38	5.25	3.81	6.44	4.65	
1939	9.56	7.75	5.19	6.75	5.94	4.56	7.25	5.25	3.94	6.56	5.63	3.12	5.56	5.44	2.65
1940	9	7.12	5	6.82	6	4.38	7.75	5.75	3.94	6.64	4.9	2.94	6.64	4.9	2.94
1941	9.31	7.59	5.33	7.04	5.96	4.37	7.79	5.62	4.03						
1942	9.05	8.08	5.75	8.83	6.95	5.12	8.12	6.33	4.92						
1943	10.32	8.2	5.82	8.09	7.02	5.19	6.96	4.72	4.35						
1944	10.46	8.47	5.97	9.33	7.8	6.14	8.95	7.04	4.82						
1945	8.39	8.7	6.21	9.09	5.96	6.21	8.76	6.56	5.39						
1947	16.56	13.6	9.15	11.3	9.12	7.54	15.42	10.71	7.72						
1948	13.25	14.94	8.52	12.19	12.96	7.31	13.32	9.9	5.5	12.69	12.19	7.25	12.88	3.82	4.9

Source: Annual Reports of the Working of the Tea District Emigrant Labour Act (XXII of 1932) for respective years. Calculated on the basis of averages of two month – March and September. The figures include the value of diet, *ticca* work, rations and subsistance allowances.

APPENDIX TABLE 5.5
Number of 'Basti' or 'Faltu' Labourers employed in
Assam Valley Tea Plantations, 1934–47 (000)

Year	Lakhimpur	Sibsagar	Darrang
1934	18.5	22.8	4.7
1935	17.9	13.4	5.7
1936	17	15.1	9.3
1937	17.8	13.8	9.7
1938	19.7	14.3	3.99
1939	20.5	15.2	14.2
1940	19.6	13.5	7.8
1941	19.9	13.9	3.6
1942	18.2	14	9
1943	14.6	10.1	6.9
1944	9 .8	8.6	6.2
1945	3.7	10.3	5.7
1947	14.6	13.4	6.3

Source: Annual Reports on the Working of Tea District Emigrant Labour Act (XXII) of 1932 for respective years. The figures include men, women and children.

APPENDIX TABLE 5.6
Yearly Averages of Monthly Wages of 'Basti' or 'Faltu' Labourers
in Assam Valley Tea Plantations, 1934–47

Year	Lakhimpur			Sibsagar			Darrang		
	Men	Women	Children	Men	Women	Children	Men	Women	Children
	Rs	Rs	Rs	Rs	Rs	Rs	Rs	Rs	Rs
1934	5.28	4.86	2.91	3.73	4.32	2.47	4.05	3.73	2.54
1935	4.52	4.8	2.83	4.45	4.39	2.85	4.78	4.08	2.13
1936	4.8	4.91	2.96	4.44	4.39	2.74	4.9	4.24	2.99
1937	4.76	4.65	3.39	4.32	4.28	2.93	4.98	3.89	2.38
1938	4.88	4.92	3.42	4.55	4.58	4.05	5.09	3.86	2.52
1939	4.98	5.69	3.6	4.63	5.21	3.42	5.92	4.53	2.84
1940	4.84	5.33	3.59	4.83	5.15	3.53	5.74	4.86	3.08
1941	5.22	5.89	3.42	4.44	5.19	2.71	5.22	4.98	2.77
1942	6.59	6.61	3.6	5.51	5.06	3.85	5.9	5.27	3.31
1943	6.4	6.21	4.08	6.05	6.2	3.73	6.98	5.02	3.52
1944	7.27	6.71	3.97	7.1	6.43	4.6	8.01	5.8	4.05
1945	6.78	7.27	4.08	7.69	6.75	3.93	7.77	5.48	3.73
1947	10.19	10.39	6.47	9.48	9.41	5.76	13.35	9.23	5.39

APPENDIX TABLE 5.7
*Yearly Averages of Monthly Wages of Agricultural and
Plantation Labourers in Lakhimpur, 1900–10*

Year	Agricultural Labourers Rs	Act Labourers Rs	Non-Act Labourers Rs
1900	8 to 11	5.38	5.43
1901	9 to 12	5.57	5.21
1902	9 to 12	5.21	4.65
1903	9 to 12	5.29	5.03
1904	10 to 12	5.13	5.21
1905	8 to 10	5.42	5.76
1906	8 to 10	5.23	5.59
1907	8 to 10	5.57	5.18
1908	8 to 10	5.04	5.19
1909	8 to 10	5.4	5.93
1910	6 to 10	5.64	5.4

Source: Prices and Wages in India, 1900–10.

APPENDIX TABLE 5.8
Annual Expenses of a Labour Family of 5 Members (2 males, 1 female and 2 children) in Suntok Tea Garden, Sibsagar, 1921–22

Items of Expenditure	Cost (Rs)
Food	
Rice	216.00
Salt	3.00
Oil	3.00
Spices	1.50
Fish	3.00
Vegetables	1.50
Milk	1.13
Total	229.13
Other Household Expenses	
Betel Nut	1.50
Kerosine	1.50
Tobacco	1.50
Clothes	
Three 7 cubit dhotis	5.25
One 6 cubit dhoti	1.63
Two saris	5.25
Two blankets	5.00
One drill coat	4.13
Liquor and Ganja	21.00
Household Utensils: 1s	2.25
Two earthen jugs	0.38
One brass plate	1.88
Miscellaneous	6.00
Festivals and entertainment	3.00
Other expenses	3.00
Cigarettes	1.50
Grand Total	**293.90**

Source: Report of the Assam Labour Enquiry Committee, 1921–22, Appendix VIII (K), p. 128.

APPENDIX TABLE **5.9**
Prices of Foodgrain in Lakhimpur District and Assam Valley, 1900–20 (Rs per maund)

Year	Lakhimpur			Assam Valley		
	Rice	*Wheat*	*Gram*	*Rice*	*Wheat*	*Gram*
1900	3.50	6.19	4.58	2.88	4.59	4.26
1901	4.17	5.93	4.76	3.98	4.81	4.47
1902	3.71	4.97	3.83	3.73	4.21	3.99
1903	3.82	4.71	3.50	3.43	3.99	3.53
1904	3.16	4.32	3.18	2.82	3.46	3.20
1905	3.27	4.88	3.41	3.11	3.97	3.52
1906	4.68	5.59	4.36	4.87	4.74	4.31
1907	5.26	5.62	4.39	5.29	5.02	4.44
1908	4.73	6.57	5.36	4.88	6.50	5.62
1909	4.91	5.94	4.16	4.37	5.72	4.39
1910	3.84	6.37	4.01	3.84	5.02	3.79
1911	3.85	5.93	3.65	3.82	4.21	3.40
1912	4.07	5.72	4.02	3.86	4.48	3.79
1913	5.15	6.08	4.53	4.87	4.93	4.24
1914	5.29	6.71	5.28	5.37	5.74	5.29
1915	6.26	7.53	5.88	5.66	6.54	5.51
1916	5.70	7.62	5.00	5.23	6.25	4.82
1917	5.17	7.62	5.00	4.72	5.59	4.57
1918	4.49	7.38	5.14	4.16	5.78	4.99
1919	6.75	8.33	7.87	6.28	7.77	7.82
1920	7.97	10.00	7.22	7.74	7.45	7.59

Source: Prices and Wages in India, respective years.

APPENDIX TABLE **5.10**
Harvest Prices of Winter Rice and Raw Sugar ('Gur') in Assam, 1921–22 to 1929–30
(Index Base 1921–22 to 1925–26 = 100) (Rs per maund)

Year	Unhusked Rice	Index	Clear Rice	Index	Gur	Index
1921–22	2.61	84	5.31	98	9.25	102
1922–23	2.56	82	4.31	80	8.96	99
1923–24	2.88	92	4.81	89	8.75	96
1924–25	3.75	120	6.25	116	9.75	107
1925–26	3.81	122	6.38	118	8.75	96
1926–27	3.69	118	6.56	121	8.50	94
1927–28	4.00	128	7.06	130	7.56	83
1928–29	3.50	112	5.75	106	7.63	84
1929–30	3.13	100	5.00	92	7.81	86

Source: Agricultural Statistics of British India, respective years.

APPENDIX TABLE 5.11

Harvest Prices of Rice and Raw Sugar ('Gur') in Lakhimpur and Assam Province, 1931–32 to 1946–47 (Index base 1931–32 to 1934–35 = 100) (Rs per maund)

Year	Lakhimpur District						Assam Province					
	Winter rice	Index	Autumn rice	Index	Gur	Index	Winter rice	Index	Autumn rice	Index	Gur	Index
1931	3.81	157	4.13	117	7.75	116	2.94	106	3.63	123	4.88	116
1932	3.25	95	3.56	101	4.44	95	2.38	86	2.88	109	4.00	95
1933	3.19	132	3.13	89	4.44	91	2.69	97	2.63	89	3.81	91
1934	3.44	101	3.25	92	3.88	97	3.06	110	2.63	89	4.06	97
1937	3.69	108	3.19	91	4.25	95	2.81	101	2.94	100	4.00	95
1938	2.94	86	3.06	87	4.31	93	3.00	108	3.06	104	3.88	93
1939	3.25	95	3.19	91	3.5	111	3.19	115	3.31	113	4.63	111
1940	4.31	126	4.13	117	7.13	191	4.00	144	3.94	134	8.00	191
1941	4.88	143	4.81	137	6.19	133	4.44	160	4.38	149	5.56	133
1942	4.44	130	6.00	170			4.69	169	5.88	200		
1943	9.13	267	7.81	222	7.00	195	8.81	318	7.63	260	8.19	195
1944	16.63	486	22.75	646	22.88	476	13.13	474	18.75	638	19.94	476
1945	15.25	446	10.00	511	27.00	544	12.31	444	13.63	464	22.31	544
1946	13.38	391	13.75	391	10.25	325	10.25	370	12.00	408	13.63	325
1947	13.56	396	13.25	376	15.75	382	12.19	440	12.06	410	16.06	382

Source: Agricultural Statistics of India, Vol. 1, respective years.

APPENDIX TABLE 5.12

Mortality among Adult Labourers in Assam Valley Tea Gardens, 1882–99 (per mille)

Year	Lakhimpur	Sibsagar	Darrang
1882	42.6	36.5	62.7
1883	49.9	41.8	50.3
1886	49.1	42.7	46
1887	50.4	41.7	43.1
1888	53.4	57.7	43.1
1889	50.8		47.1
1891	41.4	35.4	42.5
1892	50	45.9	60
1893	43.3	34.9	47.3
1896	39.7	34.4	34.9
1897	47.9	45.3	39
1898	37.1	39.1	38.3

Source: Annual Rports on Labour Immigration into Assam, respective years.

APPENDIX TABLE 5.13

Mortality among Adult Labourers in Assam Valley Tea Gardens, 1900–32 (per mille)

Year	Lakhimpur		Sibsagar		Darrang	
	Act	Non-Act	Act	Non-Act	Act	Non-Act
1900	44.1	25.70	41.0	25.40	49.4	26.70
1901	34.8	25.90	34.7	25.80	45.2	27.00
1902–03	42.1	24.90	34.6	22.10	44.6	25.60
1903–04	41.9	23.00	31.8	20.30	39.0	27.20
1904–05	34.1	23.10	33.3	22.40	36.9	28.20
1905–06	34.9	25.20	29.0	23.90	39.5	28.60
1906–07	34.1	25.10	31.2	23.20	39.0	27.70
1907–08	43.5	29.70	49.0	30.80	55.4	37.60
1908–09	53.6	35.00	71.9	41.00	66.7	45.70
1909–10	53.1	35.10	58.4	31.80	53.7	36.40
1910–11	43.7	31.50	66.1	30.20	64.0	37.10
1911–12	54.2	33.10	76.9	25.90	59.3	34.00
1912–13	51.2	29.60	60.4	25.80	53.7	33.80
1913–14	56.7	25.60	71.7	25.30	48.3	32.30
1914–15	48.9	26.00	64.0	30.30	47.2	34.10
1915–16	54.6	31.20	48.2	31.20	48.7	37.50
1916–17	51.7	32.60	65.5	30.10	31.2	36.70
1917–18	28.6	28.10	21.4	27.30	40.8	27.60
1918–19	37.3	78.10	102.8	77.10	71.4	78.50
1919–20*		49.30		54.90		49.20
1920–21		32.90		29.50		37.70
1921–22		28.59		29.14		34.02
1922–23		25.48		26.63		27.64
1923–24		25.29		22.69		25.36
1924–25		26.52		23.19		26.87
1925–26		23.07		20.21		24.02
1926–27		22.04		19.31		24.60
1927–23		21.33		18.63		25.45
1928–29		22.30		22.22		22.32
1929–30		23.13		20.07		21.88
1930–31		23.82		20.59		24.62
1931–32		21.73				23.42

Note: * There was no Act labour after 1919 in Assam Valley.
Source: Annual Reports on Labour Immigration into Assam, respective years.

Appendix Table 5.14
Mortality among Tea Garden Labourers (Settled) in Assam Valley Tea Plantations, 1935–47 (per mille)

Year	Lakhimpur	Sibsagar	Darrang
1934	19.93	23.57	24.44
1935	20.93	21.71	21.57
1936	23.84	21.84	21.27
1937	22.24	23.36	20.88
1938	26.75	22.49	22.35
1939	23.71	21.29	20.72
1940	19.88	21.12	19.97
1941	16.86	19.93	20.85
1942	19.46	20.47	22.69
1943	27.29	25.08	29.35
1944	29.58	26.21	21.44
1945	23.76	25.81	26.00
1946			
1947	18.17	22.61	18.75

Source: Annual Reports on the Working of Tea District Emigrant Labour Act (XXII of 1932), respective years.

APPENDIX TABLE 5.15
Acreage under Tea Cultivation in Assam Valley Districts, 1872–1947 (000)

Year	Lakhimpur	Sibsagar	Darrang	Nowgong	Kamrup	Assam Valley
1872	7.9	17.5	3.4	2.3	2.1	33.2
1873	10.2	20.7	3.6	2.3	2.3	39.1
1874	11.7	22.6	3.9	2.9	2.6	43.7
1887	30.4	47.6	19.4	11.3	6.9	106.0
1888	32.1	47.4	20	11	6.2	117.1
1889	33.5	47.6	19.4	11.3	6.9	124.5
1890	36.4	47.4	20	11	6.2	130.8
1891	37.6	58.4	23.1	11.9	5.1	136.2
1892	40.2	57.9	24.6	12	4.8	139.6
1893	42.2	59.2	26.5	12.5	4.7	145.1
1894	44.5	59.9	33.1	11.8	4.6	153.9
1895	45.2	63.3	28.8	12.3	5	154.4
1896	48.2	66.4	31.9	12.6	5.3	164.3
1897	55.6	70.9	34	12.7	5.9	179
1898	59.7	75.9	38.8	12.9	4.2	191.5
1899	63.4	76.8	41.5	12.5	3.8	198
1901	68.7	79.3	40.4	12.9	3.7	204.7
1902	69	79.4	42.1	12.5	3.7	206.7
1903	69.3	78.5	40.5	13.9	3.5	207.3
1904	50.6	79.3	39.9	11.9	3.7	207
1905	71.1	78	42	12	3.4	207.3
1906	69.9	78.5	43.5	12.1	3.3	207
1907	70.7	79.8	42.1	12.2	3	208.6
1908	71.2	81.2	42.5	12	3.1	210.7
1909	71.2	82.4	42.9	12.2	3	212.5
1910	72.4	83	43.2	12.3	3	214.5
1911	73.9	84.5	43.4	12.4	3	218.2
1913	77.8	87.8	44.2	12.6	2.9	226
1914	79	90.7	45.5	12.7	3	231.9
1915	81.4	92	47.5	12.6	3.1	237.5
1916	83.8	92.9	49.2	12.7	3.1	242.5
1917	86.8	95.1	51	12.9	3.1	249.8
1918	88.3	96.6	52.3	13	3.7	255.8
1919	89.6	98.3	53.3	13	3.8	259.2
1920	91.3	99.2	56.7	12.6	3.9	266.2
1921	92.7	92.7	58.4	12.1	3.1	268
1922	93	98.6	59.3	12.1	2.6	265.8
1923	94.9	97.6	56.5	12.2	2.9	270.8
1924	95.6	97.6	57.3	12	3	274.2
1925	96.8	98.2	57.8	12	3	270.8

(continued on next page)

APPENDIX TABLE 5.15 *(continued from previous page)*

Year	Lakhimpur	Sibsagar	Darrang	Nowgong	Kamrup	Assam Valley
1926	98.3	98.4	58.8	12	3.4	274
1927	98.5	98.7	58.8			277
1928	100.4	99.1	59.6			280.1
1929	102.4	99.5	60.6			284.7
1930	104.1	99.5	61.7			285.8
1931	105.5	99.2	61.7			286.6
1932	106.5	98.6	61.4			286.9
1933	107.8	98.3	61.2			289.3
1934	108.8	102.3	61.4	12.2	4.4	293.2
1935	108.8	101.3	61.4			
1936	108.9	103.2	61.5			
1937	109.2	104.1	61.3			
1938	109.7	104.5	60.9			296.2
1939	109.9	104.5	60.6			296.2
1940	110.2	104.6	60.5			296.7
1941	110.6	104.9	60.7	12.3	3.4	292.2
1942	110	105.2	61	12.3	4.5	293
1943	111.2	107.9	61.3	12.2	4.5	299.6
1944	111.8	105.9	61.3	12.2	4.5	298.1
1945	112.4	104.2	61.3	12.2	4.5	298.7
1946	112.7	104.3	61.5	12.2	4.5	299.3
1947	112.8	105.2	61.3	12.2	4.5	300.2

Source: Report on Tea Operations in the Province of Assam, 1873–74; Annual Report on Tea Culture in Assam, 1887–1926; Supplement to the Indian Trade Journal, 1921–29; Indian Tea Statistics, 1930–47.

APPENDIX TABLE 5.16

Proportion of Labour Force (Daily Working Strength) to Total Numbers on the Books in Lakhimpur, Sibsagar and Darrang Tea Plantations, 1934–47

Year	Lakhimpur			Sibsagar			Darrang		
	Men %	Women %	Children %	Men %	Women %	Children %	Men %	Women %	Children %
1934	78	69	71	71	71	71	77	68	66
1935	82	72	69	69	69	69	79	69	-
1936	85	71	73	73	73	73	79	69	70
1937	78	70	76	76	76	76	80	67	68
1938	80	70	75	75	75	75	92	74	71
1939	86	73	76	76	76	76	69	71	76
1940	86	75	80	80	80	80	76	70	71
1941	79	77	76	76	76	76	83	71	71
1942	74	73	77	77	77	77	81	71	74
1943	86	76	76	76	76	76	85	76	87
1944	87	72	81	81	81	81	59	68	74
1945	73	67	72	72	72	72	84	72	76

Source: Calculated from figures of labour force published in the Annual Reports on the Working of Tea District Emigrant Labour Act (XXII of 1932), respective years.

APPENDIX TABLE 5.17

Labour Force (Act and non-Act, working and non-working)
including Children in Tea Gardens in Assam Valley, 1876–1948

Year	Sibsagar	Lakhimpur	Darrang	Nowgong	Kamrup	Assam Valley
1877	40.6	25.6	9.2	2.8	0.8	79.1
1879	49.7	34.1	14	5	1.3	104.1
1880	51	34.9	14.2	5.7	1.5	107.3
1881	47.3	33.8	14	6	1.5	102.7
1882	50	37.1	14.7	6.9	1.9	109.6
1883	56.6	40.7	20.4	9.7	2	129.4
1884	64.3	46.6	24.6	11.4	2.7	149.2
1885	66.5	49.4	26.5	12.1	2.9	157.2
1886	68.4	50.2	28.4	12.5	3	162.2
1887	73.5	54.3	31.8	12.4	2.8	174.7
1888	80	59.6	36.8	13.4	2.8	192.6
1889	80.1	59.6	36.8	13.4	2.8	192.6
1890	87.9	68.2	40.5	14	3.3	213.9
1891	96.4	80.6	47.3	16.4	3.6	244.3
1892	101.8	87.1	51.6	16.3	3.4	260.2
1893	109	91.2	51.5	16.4	3.2	271.3
1894	113.7	93.7	54.4	16.6	3.3	281.7
1895	120.3	101.2	59.7	17.6	3.6	302.3
1896	160.9	139.6	90.7	25.8	5.01	422
1897	129	108.3	65.5	19.2	3.7	325.7
1898	143	124.9	71.3	21.2	3.8	364.2
1899	145.4	127.9	72.2	19.4	3.4	368.4
1901	144.8	141.5	72.1	18.1	3.2	379.7
1902	147.4	144.2	73.9	18.1	3.2	385.8
1903	150	146.9	73.9	18.1	3.2	392
1904	149.9	155.7	74.7	17.1	3.5	396.8
1905	155	152.4	75.9	18	3.2	404.6
1906	156	159.2	77.9	18.1	2.3	414.2
1907	158.8	161.5	78.2	17.8	2.8	419.1
1908	172.6	180.2	88.6	20.7	3	465.1
1909	178.2	188.9	90.8	19.4	2.9	480.2
1910	184.5	191.5	91	19	3.2	489.2
1911	191.8	197.4	92.7	20.4	3.8	507.4
1912	202	206.8	96.7	20.7	4.2	530.7
1913	206.6	214.9	96.3	20.9	4	547.9
1914	217.2	223.2	104.3	22.1	4.3	571.1
1915	235.3	244.9	118	24.8	4.7	627.6
1916	237.8	240.2	119.8	23.7	5.3	626.8
1917	228.3	237.3	115.5	23.4	5.1	639.5

(continued on next page)

APPENDIX TABLE **5.17** *(continued from previous page)*

Year	Sibsagar	Lakhimpur	Darrang	Nowgong	Kamrup	Assam Valley
1918	265.7	269.5	156	28.8	5.6	725.7
1919	274.3	277.9	163.6	29	5.4	750.1
1920	259.6	265.7	142.7	26.3	4.5	698.8
1921	252.7	263.3	130.9	24.2	4.2	676.3
1922	247	263.2	130.5	23.8	4.1	665
1923	248.4	268.5	131.9	23.6	4.3	678.1
1924	246.1	266.8	130.1	24.1	4.6	674.2
1925	244.3	269.2	132.4	23.9	5.3	678
1926	247.4	275.9	135.5	23.7	5.3	690.7
1927	250.7	282.1	136.9	23	5.6	702
1928	261.3	293.4	146.4	23.7	6.5	735.1
1929	266.6	299.7	151.2	24.4	6.7	753.4
1930	264.3	294.6	148.4	24.3	6.9	743
1931	267.4	298.3	152.1	24.4	7.1	754.6
1932	283.2	307.2	152.2	24.3	7.2	778
1933	292.5	314.6	162.3	24.5	7.5	806.9
1934	298.8	311.3	161.8	24.3	7.7	809.5
1935	300.6	311	163	25.2	7	812.4
1936	297.8	304.4	160.1	24.4	7.5	800.5
1937	305.1	308.5	162.9	24.8	7.5	815.5
1938	309.4	312.2	166.2	25.7	7.5	827.8
1939	310.4	315	169.8	26.4	7.1	832.6
1940	306.7	310.9	160.6	24	7	820
1941	307	309	160.1	24.1	6.8	819.7
1942	311.4	313.7	166.2	24.3	7	821.5
1943	301.8	302.4	166.4	23.8	6.8	820
1944	299.9	302.6	166.5	24	6.7	822
1945	295.3	309.2	169.2	24.4	6.5	823
1946	297.4	313.8	175	25	6.4	825.9
1947	304.2	320.2	169	26.4	6.8	834.9

Source: Annual Reports on Labour Immigration into Assam, 1877–1932; Annual Reports on the Working of Tea Districts Emigrant Labour Act (XXII of 1932), 1935–47.

APPENDIX TABLE 5.18
Production of Tea in Assam Valley and Assam Province, 1872–1947 (million lbs)

Year	Lakhimpur	Sibsagar	Darrang	Nowgong	Kamrup	Assam Valley	Total in Assam
1872	1.5	3.8	1	0.3	0.3	6.9	7
1873	1.7	4.5	1	0.25	0.35	7.7	13.2
1874	1.8	5	1	0.38	0.37	7.4	15.2
1885						32.6	53.6
1886						37.5	61.7
1887	13	14.7	6.7	3.3	1	38.7	68.5
1888	14.5	16.1	8	3.4	1.1	43.6	72.7
1889	14.7	17.6	8.5	3.6	1.2	45.5	77
1890	15.6	19	8.5	3.8	1.1	48.1	82.1
1891	16	20.5	9.7	3.3	1	50.6	90.4
1892	15.6	18.1	11.3	3	0.75	49.1	84.2
1893	18.8	20.5	10.8	3.4	1	54.8	94.2
1894	17.14	21.8	12.5	3.8	0.75	56.5	94.8
1895	18.7	22.2	11.1	3.8	0.7	56.7	99.6
1896	19.5	24.1	11.4	5.5	0.7	61.4	109.7
1897	19	24	11.1	4	0.75	59.1	107.3
1898	27	24.4	12.5	3.9	0.7	63.9	109.3
1899	22.8	25.1	14.5	3.9	0.71	66.9	128.4
1900	23.6	29	15.3	4.3	0.77	75.3	141.1
1901	26.5	26.8	15.3	4.5	0.63	72.5	134.9
1902	26.9	26.3	15.7	4.2	0.54	73.9	132.1
1903	26.2	27.8	15.7	4.5	0.64	78.7	145.2
1904	30.7	29.6	15.7	4.6	0.64	81.7	152.2
1905	33.7	29.1	18.6	4.6	0.53	86.6	151.9
1906	38	30.6	21.5	4.9	1.2	95.9	162.5
1907	39	32.1	20.1	4.9	0.8	99.7	167.5
1908	37.6	33	19.7	5.3	0.62	96.7	166.6
1909	39.3	37.2	22	5.2	0.7	104.6	174.9
1910	37.8	38	22.4	5.8	0.69	105	175.1
1911	36.3	38.7	24.2	6	0.86	106.4	179
1913	43.9	46.7	26.4	6.5	0.93	124.8	199.7
1914	46.5	49.5	29	6.4	1.1	132.8	208.2
1915	59.5	59.2	35	7.7	1.2	162.8	245.4
1916	61.9	57.9	32.3	7.4	1.2	161.1	242.2
1917	60.1	59.7	31	7.4	1	159.5	243.6
1918	62.2	66.8	30.8	7.3	1.1	168.5	253.3
1919	64.8	58.8	31.1	7.3	0.6	163.9	239.1
1920	60	52.3	33.7	6.7	0.92	154.2	234.3
1921	49	48.5	27.6	5	0.54	131.2	181.5

(continued on next page)

APPENDIX TABLE **5.18** *(continued from previous page)*

Year	Lakhimpur	Sibsagar	Darrang	Nowgong	Kamrup	Assam Valley	Total in Assam
1923	63.9	55.6	25.9	6.4	0.72	160.3	237.6
1924	68	58.4	31.7	6.1	0.7	165.8	247.1
1925	61	53.2	30.7	5.9	0.71	152.4	225.2
1926	69.4	57.5	35.1	6.1	0.71	167.7	242
1927	70	60	34			163.3	235.8
1928	73	57.4	35.9			173.8	246
1929	73.1	57.2	35.6			185.2	258.9
1930	74	56.6	34.5			164	233.4
1931	72	56	32			172	243.2
1932	71	54	32.4			176.3	257.1
1933	70	52	33			155	219.3
1934	70.4	51.6	33.7	5.7	1.3	164.8	232.8
1935	71	52	33.4			159.9	226.4
1936	72	53	34.2			160.5	223.3
1937	74	54.8	37			174.2	241.5
1938	75.1	58.3	39			191.4	261
1939	76.2	60.8	40			183.1	252
1940	77.3	61.4	41.2	6.5	2.3	189	259.7
1941	89	66.7	44.5	7	2.3	209.8	288.7
1942	80	75	50.1	8	2.6	216.1	262.1
1943	85.6	68.5	46.4	7.2	2.4	210.2	250.6
1944	80.2	50.4	47.4	6.6	1.8	195.8	232
1945	85.8	68.9	46.9	6.8	1.8	204.3	246.6
1946	106.6	75.5	40.5	7.7	2	231.5	274.7
1947	109.5	77.8	55.8	8.1	2.7	253.5	297.4

Source: Report on Tea Operations in the Province of Assam, 1873–74; Annual Reports on Tea Culture in Assam, 1885–1926; Indian Tea Statistics, 1930–47.

APPENDIX TABLE 5.19
Average Prices of Indian Tea Sold at Calcutta Auctions, 1896–1943
(Index Variations 1901–02 to 1910–11 = 100)

Year	Price per lb (Rs)	Price Index
1896–97	0.44	117
1901–02	0.34	90
1905–06	0.34	90
1909–10	0.6	114
1913–14	0.5	129
1917–18	0.46	121
1921–22	0.63	168
1922–23	0.83	221
1923–24	0.94	250
1924–25	0.94	265
1925–26	0.84	224
1926–27	0.76	204
1927–28	0.88	247
1928–29	0.71	189
1929–30	0.57	165
1930–31	0.59	156
1931–32	0.41	107
1932–33	0.33	86
1933–34	0.61	160
1934–35	0.56	146
1935–36	59	157
1936–37	0.63	168
1937–38	0.71	189
1938–39	0.61	160
1939–40	0.72	190
1940–41	0.85	225
1941–42	1.06	279
1942–43	1	267
1946–47	1.62	
1947-48	1.5	

Source: Indian Tea Statistics, 1930, 1934, 1940–47.

APPENDIX TABLE 5.20
Quinquennial Averages of Per Acre Out-turn in Assam Valley, 1890–1947 (lbs)

Year	Lakhimpur	Sibsagar	Darrang	Assam Valley
1890–94	415	344	410	352
1900–04	405	353	373	367
1905–09	530	404	430	460
1910–14	561	516	602	526
1915–19	719	567	632	655
1920–24	676	563	580	558
1925–29	746	593	613	598
1930–34	706	577	574	578
1935–39	705	592	660	
1940–44	804	700	827	699
1945–47	951	771	845	767

Source: Calculated from production and acreage figures in Annual Reports on Tea Culture in Assam, 1890–1926; Supplement to Indian Trade Journal, 1921–29; Indian Tea Statistics, 1930–47.

APPENDIX TABLE 5.21
Quinquennial Averages of Per Labour Out-turn of Tea in Assam Valley, 1891–1947 (lbs)

Year	Lakhimpur	Sibsagar	Darrang	Assam Valley
1891–94	180	231	218	216
1895–99	186	257	235	251
1900–04	249	290	294	274
1905–09	353	324	382	357
1910–14	360	379	457	410
1915–19	427	458	471	429
1920–24	422	365	382	366
1925–29	497	382	459	
1930–34	481	363	439	
1935–39	498	380	574	601
1940–44	565	471	634	590
1945–47	662	524	616	620

Source: Calculated from figures of employmenr (daily average strength) and production in Annual Reports on Tea Culture in Assam, 1891–1926; Supplement to Indian Trade Journal, 1921–29; Indian Tea Statistics, 1930–47.

APPENDIX TABLE 5.22

Particulars of Tea Companies Registered in India, 1904–47: Aggregate Paid-up Capital and Percentage of Dividends on Total Aggregate Capital

Year	No of Cos. Registered in India	Total Paid-up Capital (Rs lakhs)	No. of Cos. declared Dividents	Dividend (%)	On Aggregate Capital (Rs lakhs)
1904	71	228	71	6	228
1905	71	228	71	6	228
1906	72	238	53	6.3	N.A.
1907	72	240	65	10.3	217
1908	75	244	62	9.3	199
1909	84	263	72	11.6	235
1910	86	270	75	13.36	247
1911	87	277	87	11.2	277
1912	N.A.	N.A	85	14.7	265
1913	98	301	88	17.4	274
1914	98	301	86	15.6	260
1915	N.A.	N.A.	97	26.5	305
1916	118	346	80	22.8	256
1917	117	349	81	20	N.A.
1918	125	397	86	21	269
1919	N.A.	N.A.	77	19.2	239
1922	132	447	88	33.2	319
1923	N.A.	N.A.	108	40.2	401
1924	138	496	113	46.5	412
1925	140	494	119	28.9	418
1926	141	506	113	27	422
1927	138	499	123	32	453
1928	139	500	98	23	392
1930	144	600	62	15.3	240
1931	144	500	38	11	127
1932	145	600	36	9.6	147
1933	148	600	84	17	351
1934	150	600	82	13.1	346
1935	151	600	93	12.9	388
1936	149	600	110	13	455
1937	147	600	120	17	488
1938	146	600	124	14	497
1939	147	600	128	15	531
1940	N.A.	N.A.	123	15	508
1941	155	620	142	18	584
1942	N.A.	N.A.	147	28	595
1944	140	N.A.	142	20	604
1946	149	878	145	34	834
1947	149	N.A.	139	25	855

Source: Annual Reports on the Production of Tea in Assam, 1904–20; Supplements to Indian Trade Journal, 1921–29; Indian Tea Statistics, 1930–46.

APPENDIX TABLE 6.1
Labour Import into Assam Valley Districts (including adults and children),
1873–1947 (000)

Year	Lakhimpur	Sibsagar	Darrang	Nowgong	Kamrup	Assam Valley
1873	7.2	15.2	2	2.2	0.3	26.9
1874	7.9	17.8	2.3	1.1	0.1	30.6
1877	7	8.9	2.6	0.6	0.3	19.2
1879	5.7	6.8	3.5	2.1	0.6	18.6
1880	4.9	4.9	1.2	1.1	0.2	11.8
1881	5.2	5.2	1.7	1.2	0.2	12.5
1882	6.9	6.9	2	1.5	0.3	15.1
1883	8.5	8.5	2.4	1.7	0.3	18.3
1884	9.3	9.3	4.6	2.7	0.4	27.4
1886	7.9	5.7	3.2	0.8	0.2	18.9
1887	10.4	8.4	5.3	1.4	0.2	26
1888	11.5	10.9	6.2	2	0.3	30.6
1889	14.7	12.5	6.2	2.7	0.5	36.6
1890	10	7.7	4.3	2.4	0.3	24.6
1891	13.1	9.4	7.1	2.2	0.7	32.4
1892	14.1	11.9	7.4	2.2	0.6	36.1
1893	14.1	11.3	5.9	2.1	0.3	33.8
1894	11.1	11.4	5.7	1.9	0.3	30.3
1895	13.2	11.1	7.9	2.5	0.2	35
1896	15	13.6	10.1	3.3	0.3	42.4
1897	27	21.7	12.5	5.3	0.4	67
1898	13.5	11.9	5.9	2	0.3	33.8
1900	18.4	12	11.4	2.5	0.3	44.5
1902	17.2	12	9.5	2.8	0.5	41.6
1903	16.2	7.8	9.2	1.7	0.2	35
1904	15.1	6.2	8.6	2.2	0.2	32.7
1905	12.3	7.8	4.5	1.2	0.5	25.9
1906	8.7	5	2.6	0.9	0.5	22.4
1907	10	5.6	4.8	0.8	0.9	23.5
1908	23.4	20.8	16.6	4.3	0.4	70.3
1909	19.8	16.7	9.9	2	0.5	49
1910	12.5	10.7	6.4	0.9	0.1	30.9
1911	13.5	12.2	7.5	1.2	0.7	34.4
1912	17.4	14.9	8.9	1.8	0.2	43.9
1913	18.6	16	9.1	2	2	45.8
1914	17.9	15	9.1	2.2	0.2	44.4
1915	21.4	19.7	14.6	2.9	0.3	61
1916	35.2	30.6	24.4	4.2	0.6	95
1917	14	26.3	10.3	0.9	0.3	37.5

(continued on next page)

APPENDIX TABLE **6.1** (continued from previous page)

Year	Lakhimpur	Sibsagar	Darrang	Nowgong	Kamrup	Assam Valley
1918	6	3.3	4.3	0.4	0.1	14.1
1919	55	56	52.6	6.5	0.7	173.4
1920	19.7	27.3	20.3	2.9	0.3	80.4
1921	9.9	6	4.5	0.7	0.1	21.2
1922	8.8	5.3	3.1	0.8	0.1	18.2
1923	9.6	3.8	3.5	0.7	0.1	17.8
1924	16.3	10.3	5.5	1.5	0.3	34
1925	12	9.2	4.9	1.1	0.1	27.4
1926	12.7	6.8	8	0.7	0.2	28.6
1927	20.3	7.7	11.3	0.9	0.3	40.6
1928	17.4	7.3	9.9	1.5	0.4	36.6
1929	22.5	12.8	17.8	3.1	0.2	56.5
1930	26.2	10.1	14.1	2.5	0.4	53.4
1931	25.3	10.5	13.7	1.6	0.5	51.5
1932	24.6	9.9	14.3	1	0.5	50.4
1935	7.7	5.6	5.2	1	0.1	19.6
1936	10.6	5.3	6.3	1	0.2	23.5
1937	11.9	6.5	8.1	0.7	0.3	27.5
1938	14.9	8	8.2	1.3	–	32.3
1939	13.2	6.5	8.7	1.3	0.1	29.6
1940	9.8	6	7.3	1		24.2
1941	7.2	4.4	5.5			17.4
1942	6.4	3.3	3.8			14.4
1943	23.2	13.3	15.7			38.7
1944	13.8	9.7	13.4			41.7
1945	18.4	9.6	11.9			41
1947	14.8	8.1	15.7			35.2

Source: Report on Tea Operations in the Province of Assam, 1873–74; Reports on Emigrant Labour in Assam, 1877–1932; Report on the Working of Tea Districts Emigrant Labour Act (XII of 1932), 1934–47.

Nationality and Sex of Adult Labour Force in Assam Valley Tea Plantations,
1878–1932 (000)

Year	Sex	Chotanagpur & Santhal Parganas	Bengal	North Western Provinces	Central Provinces	Bihar	Madras	Total
1878	Men	14.2	7.8	4.8			0.5	23.9
	Women	11	7.7	3.7			0.2	21.8
1879	Men	14.5	5	4.4			0.3	21.9
	Women	11.5	5.2	3.3			0.2	20.5
1880	Men	30	21.7	12.7			0.5	64.9
	Women	25.7	19.6	10.1			0.3	55.7
1881	Men	32	21	14.4			0.4	68.2
	Women	26	18.5	11.1			0.6	55.8
1882	Men	34.5	21.7	16.7			0.7	75
	Women	27	19.3	12.7			0.4	60
1883	Men	39.4	22.5	20			0.8	90.3
	Women	30.9	20.4	14.3			0.5	67.4
1886	Men	47.8	25.7	22.3			0.8	106.3
	Women	40.1	24.6	17.4			0.6	85.2
1887	Men	52	26.6	23.7			0.8	113
	Women	44	25.1	19.1			0.7	91.6
1888	Men	57.8	27.1	25.6			0.9	122.1
	Women	49.7	27	20.9			0.8	100
1889	Men	64.4	28.6	26.5			1.3	129.8
	Women	56.7	27.2	22			1.1	109.9
1891	Men	69	29.6	20.9	1	10.1	3.8	143.9
	Women	62.1	28.7	18.8	0.8	8.5	3.5	125.9
1892	Men	72.2	30.4	22.2	1.4	11.2	5	150.8
	Women	65.2	29.7	20.7	1.2	9.3	4.6	134.4
1894	Men	75	34	25.6	2.7	12.2	4.6	158.2
	Women	72.4	25.6	23.8	1.8	10.8	4.2	150.7
1895	Men	79.4	35.3	31.1	6.9	13.4	4.9	178
	Women	75.4	31.1	28.8	4.3	11.4	4.4	163.9
1896	Men	81.9	33.4	36.5	14.5	14.5	4.9	196.2
	Women	76.6	36.7	34.9	11.2	12.5	4.4	180.6
1897	Men	88.2	33.3	34.1	20.6	14.4	5.4	204.7
	Women	84.5	37.2	34.3	17.9	12.5	4.8	195.3
1898	Men	89.6	31.6	34.2	20.4	13.7	5.8	199
	Women	87	25	34.3	17.9	11.2	5	196.1
1900	Men	89.1	31.6	29.2	27.5	13.4	6.8	204.5
	Women	89.9	35.6	31.7	26.6	11.8	6.2	205.6
1901	Men	86.6	30.2	26.5	28	11.9	6.3	196
	Women	88.2	34.6	30	28.6	11	6	202.3

(continued on next page)

APPENDIX TABLE 6.2 *(continued from previous page)*

Year	Sex	Chotanagpur & Santhal Parganas	Bengal	North Western Provinces	Central Provinces	Bihar	Madras	Total
1902–03	Men	82.4	29.5	27.1	31.6	11.7	6.2	202
	Women	84.1	33.6	29.5	32.9	11	6.4	202.3
1903–04	Men	82.5	68.9	30.9			6.5	201.6
	Women	84.5	75	32			6.6	202.7
1904–05	Men	83	70.6	31.2			6.5	205.6
	Women	84.6	76.2	31.9			6.6	204.6
1906	Men	84.8	72.7	31.6			7.4	208.2
	Women	86.1	77.1	32.7			7.2	208.5
1907	Men	85.4	73	31.4			8.4	208.8
	Women	86.9	77.3	32.9			7.8	210.7
1908	Men	87.9	81.4	33.7			11.7	227
	Women	90	83.5	35.5			10.2	225.4
1909	Men	90	81.7	35.7			13	230.4
	Women	90.4	83.8	35.7			11.3	227.4
1910	Men	88	81.4	35.2			14.5	230.6
	Women	88.5	84	35.4			12.6	227
1910–11	Men	83.2	83.2	35			16.5	236
	Women	83.2	83.2	34.6			13.9	227.8
1911–12	Men	87.7	87.6	35.3			21.5	248
	Women	88.8	85	34.3			17.4	233.3
1912–13	Men	91	92.4	35.7			23.5	259.4
	Women	91	88	34.9			19.2	242.3
1913–14	Men	93.7	96.5	37.2			23.6	265.2
	Women	93.3	90.2	36.1			19.4	245.4
1914–15	Men	97.5	100.9	37.7			21.8	274.2
	Women	96.1	93.7	37			19	256
1915–16	Men	105.8	113	37.9			21.8	296
	Women	102.9	103.5	36.7			19.3	273.7
1916–17	Men	105.7	112.5	34.5			21	292.6
	Women	103.2	103.6	35.2			19	273.2
1917–18	Men	102	107.9	33.6			20.3	284
	Women	100.6	101.4	33.8			18.5	267.2
1918–19	Men	120.1	119.7	39.8			13.9	323.3
	Women	114.4	112.2	37.9			22.2	29.7
1919–20	Men	122.3	118	40.6			24.3	323.8
	Women	117.4	113.7	39			22.7	305.9
1920–21	Men	109	104.2	36.7			21	289
	Women	108.9	104	36.2			20.4	283

(continued on next page)

APPENDIX TABLE **6.2** *(continued from previous page)*

Year	Sex	Chotanagpur & Santhal Parganas	Bengal	North Western Provinces	Central Provinces	Bihar	Madras	Total
1922	Men	84.9	52.5	26.9			14.5	193.4
	Women	84.8	50.7	26.3			12.5	184.8
1923	Men	81	52.5	26.7			15.4	192
	Women	81.5	48.9	25.9			12.6	180.5
1924	Men	78.9	56.6	29.7			20.3	203.3
	Women	79.4	50.2	20.8			14.2	182.4
1925	Men	75.7	57.2	29			21.2	202.8
	Women	76.6	48.7	26			14.5	180
1926	Men	73.3	60.3	28			23.4	206.1
	Women	74	49.2	25.4			15	178.6
1927	Men	73.5	61	28.4			24	208
	Women	74.3	49	25.3			16	179
1928	Men	74.7	63.3	29.2			27	218.7
	Women	72.9	50	25.2			16.2	182.1
1929	Men	81.8	68.9	31.4			27.4	236.5
	Women	75.2	51.7	26.2			16.4	188.5
1930	Men	84	70.4	32			27.8	243.1
	Women	75.6	51.9	26.5			16.4	190.2
1931	Men	84.2	69.3	32			28.7	244.3
	Women	74.7	51	26.5			16.4	190.3
1932	Men	85	68	30.8			28.6	241.6
	Women	77	53	26.2			16.4	194.3

Source: Reports on Immigrant Labour in Assam, 1878–1932.

APPENDIX TABLE 6.3

Aboriginals and Tribals as Tea Garden Labourers in Assam Valley Tea Districts in 1911 and 1921 (000)

	1911				1921			
	Lakhim-pur	Sibsagar	Darrang	Assam Valley	Lakhim-pur	Sibsagar	Darrang	Assam Valley
Bhuiya	8.8	17.4	4.4	31.6	7.8	14.5	5.3	28.3
Bhumij	7.2	6.8	2.7	17.6	9.5	7.9	5.2	23.6
Gond	9.9	8.01	5.2	23.3	12.4	7.7	6.9	28.5
Kandh	1.2	0.7	0.7	4.3	Not	Enumerated		
Kharia	3.01	1.4	1.2	7.2	4.4	2.1	2.2	9.01
Kharwar	1.3	0.8	1.2	3.4	Not	Enumerated		
Mal Paharia	1.2	0.3	0.2	3	Not	Enumerated		
Munda	22.6	10.7	8.5	43.2	30.8	16.4	16.01	67.9
Oraon	4.3	2.2	1.6	8.6	7.1	3.1	3.5	14.4
Santhals	11.5	9.5	3.3	25.2	12.8	11.2	3.7	28.8
Total	72.7	58.4	30	167.3	86.9	62.9	40.9	200.5

Source: Census of India, 1911, Vol. III, Assam, Part II, pp. 236–50; Census of India, 1921, Vol. III, Assam, Part II, pp. 366–73.

APPENDIX TABLE 6.4

Lower Castes (other than Aboriginals and Tribals) as Tea Garden Labourers in Assam Valley Tea Districts in 1911 and 1921 (000)

	1911				1921			
	Lakhim-pur	Sibsagar	Darrang	Assam Valley	Lakhim-pur	Sibsagar	Darrang	Assam Valley
Bagdi	0.8	1.1	0.6	2.6	0.9	1.4	0.3	2.6
Bauri	4.2	7.5	1.9	15.9	3.3	8.3	1.4	13.6
Chik	1.1	0.7	0.6	2.6	Not	Enumerated		
Dosadh	398	1,139	175	1,714	255	909	69	1.2
Ghasi	3.2	3.5	1.07	8.2	4.9	5.9	1.8	13.3
Koiri	0.5	1.1	0.3	2.01	0.6	0.5	0.2	1.4
Kora	0.6	1.2	0.2	2	Not	Enumerated		
Mahli	1.7	1.7	0.7	4.01				
Mushar	0.3	1.4	0.2	2.1	0.2	0.8		1
Pan	3.5	3.8	1.7	10	4.6	6.8	3.4	15.9
Rajwar	1.01	1.7	0.4	3.3	Not	Enumerated		
Tanti	11.9	7.3	5.8	25.7	19.4	13.8	11.8	46.7
Turi	0.9	6.01	0.1	8.01	0.1	6.3	0.1	8.4
Kurmi	2.3	2.8	0.8	6.4	2.2	4.2	1.4	8
Total	32.2	41	15.3	94.6	37.8	51.01	21.7	112.3

Source: Census of India, 1911, Vol. III, Assam, Part II, pp. 236–50; Census of India, 1921, Vol. III, Assam, Part II, pp. 366–73.

APPENDIX TABLE 6.5
Other Castes (other than Aboriginals, Tribals and Low Castes) as Tea Garden
Labourers in Assam Valley Tea Districts in 1911 and 1921 (000)

	1911				1921			
	Lakhim-pur	*Sibsagar*	*Darrang*	*Assam Valley*	*La.khim-pur*	*Sibsagar*	*Darrang*	*Assam Valley*
Chasa	0.1	1	0.2	2.5	Not	Enumerated		
Chero	0.2	0.5	0.02	0.9	Not	Enumerated		
Kamar	6.7	6.7	2.8	16.8	9.7	10	3.3	23.6
Mal	0.9	1.4	0.3	2.7	Not	Enumerated		
Dom	1.7	3.7	1.6	9.3	6.7	5	1.9	13.9
Chamar	5.4	5.4	1.3	12.6	1	5.7	1.3	8.4
Total	18.8	18.8	6.4	44.9	17.3	20.7	6.5	45.9

Source: Census of India, 1911, Vol. III, Assam, Part II, pp. 236–50; Census of India, 1921, Vol. III, Assam, Part II, pp. 366–73.

APPENDIX TABLE 6.6

Total Number of Men, Women and Children as Labourers in Assam Valley Tea Plantations, 1934–1947 (000)

Year	Lakhimpur					Sibsagar					Darrang				
	Men	Women	Children	Total of Col. 3 & 4	Ratio of Col. 5 to 2	Men	Women	Children	Total of Col 8 & 9	Ratio of Col 10 to 7	Men	Women	Children	Total of Col 13 & 14	Ratio of Col 15 to 12
1	2	3	4	5	6	7	8	9	10	11	12	13	14	15	16
1934	74	60	21	81	1.09	67	53	19	72	1.09	21	17	5	22	1.05
1935	74	56	22	80	1.08	66	58	19	77	1.16	20	17	10	27	1.35
1936	75	61	21	82	1.09	64	57	19	76	1.18	41	34	9	43	1.05
1937	75	60	21	81	1.08	62	56	19	75	1.21	38	35	9	44	1.16
1938	74	61	22	83	1.12	62	56	19	75	1.21	38	32	9	41	1.08
1939	73	63	22	85	1.16	65	57	20	77	1.18	38	33	8	41	1.08
1940	76	64	23	87	1.14	65	57	21	78	1.2	39	33	9	42	1.08
1941	73	61	24	85	1.16	56	53	20	73	1.3	30	27	7	34	1.15
1942	79	62	25	87	1.1	60	56	23	79	1.32	34	31	10	41	1.2
1943	68	63	25	88	1.29	58	59	21	80	1.38	35	34	10	44	1.26
1944	65	60	23	83	1.28	55	55	19	74	1.35	35	34	10	44	1.26
1945	63	55	21	76	1.21	56	64	21	85	1.52	36	33	10	43	1.19
1947	69	55	22	77	1.12	62	53	20	73	1.18	36	31	11	42	1.17

Source: Annual Reports on the Working of Tea Districts Emingrant Labour Act (XXII) of 1932, respective years.

Glossary

anna	monetary unit equal to one-sixteenth of a rupee
arakati	private recruiter in the villages of tea labour districts
babu	clerk employed in the office of the plantation
badmash	a bad character
bari	garden
barkandaz	mercenary employed to track down deserting labourers
basti	area adjoining plantations occupied by ex-tea garden labourers
chowkidar	watchman
coolie	labourer
dal	lentil
faltu	temporary labour
haat	weekly market
hazira	payment for daily work
haziri	attendance at workplace
Kali Puja	worship of goddess Kali
kaya	Marwari (from Rajasthan) shopkeeper
Madrassee	labourer from Madras Presidency
maund	weighing unit equivalent to 36 kilograms
mohurrir	field supervisor in the plantation
nirikh	daily task set by the plantation manager
salaam	salute
sirdar	head labourer who worked both as recruiter and field supervisor for the planter
ticca	overtime work

Bibliography

Primary Sources

Unpublished

Government of Assam, Department of Revenue, Emigration Proceedings, Assam State Archives, Guwahati.

Government of Assam, Finance Department, Emigration Proceedings, Assam State Archives, Guwahati.

Government of Assam, General and Judicial Department, Emigration Proceedings, Assam State Archives, Guwahati

Government of Assam, Home Political Department, Fortnightly Reports. Government of India, Home Department Proceedings, November 1864, National Archives, New Delhi.

Government of Assam, Judicial Department, Emigration Proceedings, Assam State Archives, Guwahati.

Government of Bengal Proceedings, National Archives, New Delhi.

Government of Eastern Bengal and Assam, Department of Commerce and Industry, Emigration Proceedings, Assam State Archives, Guwahati.

Government of India, Department of Commerce and Industry, Emigration Proceedings, National Archives, New Delhi.

Government of India, Department of Revenue and Agriculture, Emigration Proceedings, National Archives, New Delhi.

Government of India, General Department, Emigration Proceedings, 1878, National Archives, New Delhi.

Settlement Rules, District Record Room, Tezpur, Darrang.

Published

The Agricultural Statistics of British India.

Annual Assam Administrative Reports.

Annual Reports on Labour Immigration into Assam, Shillong.

Annual Reports on Tea Culture in Assam, Shillong.

Annual Sanitary Reports of the Province of Assam, Shillong.

Arbhuthnott, J.C., *Report on Ceylon, Madras and Duars Plantation Conditions*, Shillong, 1904.

Assam Legislative Assembly Debates, 1938, Vol. II.

Assam Legislative Council Proceedings, 1923, 1927, Vol. VII.

The Bengal Inland Emigration Manual, 1912.

The Bengal Inland Emigration Manual, 1927.

Central Legislative Assembly Debates, Vol. III, 1932.

Census of India, 1911, Vol. III, Assam, Part I, Report and Part II.

Census of India, 1921, Vol. III, Assam, Part I, Report and Part II.

Coolie Trade, Parliamentary Papers, 1867.

Copy of Papers Received from India Related to the Measures Adopted for Introducing the Cultivation of the Tea Plant within the British Possessions in India, Parliamentary Papers, 1839.

Datta, K.L., *Report on the Enquiry into the Rise of Prices in India, 1914*, Vol. III.

Deshpande, Shantaram Ramakrishna, *Report on an Enquiry into the Cost and Standard of Living of Plantation Workers in Assam and Bengal*, 1948.

East India: Assam Coolies, Parliamentary Papers, 1889.

Evidence Recorded by the Assam Labour Enquiry Committee, 1921–22.

Government of Bengal, Report on Inland Emigration from Bengal, 1883, Calcutta.

Government of Bengal, Report of the Labour Enquiry Commission of Bengal, Calcutta, 1896.

History of Indian Railway, Constructed and Progress corrected up to 31st March, 1945, Government of India.

Papers Regarding the Tea, Calcutta, Parliamentary Papers, 1874.

Papers Relating to Tea Cultivation in Bengal, *Selections from The Records of the Government of Bengal*, No. XXXVII, Calcutta: Bengal Military Orphan Press, 1861.

Prices and Wages in India, 1910.

Proceedings of the Annual Meeting of General Committee of Assam Branch of India Tea Association, March 1920.

Proceedings of the Assam Labour Enquiry Committee in the Recruiting and Labouring Districts, 1906.

Proceedings of the Central Legislative Council, 1901, Vol. XL, Calcutta.

Rege, Dattaraya Varman, *Report on An Enquiry into Conditions of Labour in Plantations in India*, 1946.

Report of the Assam Labour Enquiry Committee, Calcutta, 1906.

Report of the Assam Labour Enquiry Committee, 1921–22.

Report of the Commissioners Appointed to Enquire into the State and Prospects of Tea Cultivation in Assam, Cachar and Sylhet, Calcutta, 1868.

Report of the Plantation Enquiry Commission, 1956.

Report of the Royal Commission on Labour in India, 1931.

Report of the Tea Districts Emigrant Labour Act (XXII of 1932).

Report on Tea Operations in Assam, Shillong, 1873–74.

Reports on the Administration of the Land Revenue in Assam.

Royal Commission on Labour in India, 1931, Written Evidence, Assam and Dooars, Vol. VI, Part I.

Tea Directory and Tea Areas Handbook, 1942.

Private Papers

All India Congress Committee (AICC) Papers, Nehru Memorial Museum and Library, New Delhi.

All India Trade Union Congress (AITUC) Papers, 1947–48, Nehru Memorial Museum and Library, New Delhi.

Annual Detailed Reports of the General Committee of the Indian Tea Association, Tocklai Tea Research Centre, Jorhat, Assam.

Assam Company Papers (ACP), Mss. No. 9924, Vol. 1, p. 1, London Minute Book, 12 February 1839, Guildhall Library, London.

Carnegie Papers, Mss. Eur/c/682, OIOC, British Library, London.

Curzon Papers, Microfilm, Acct. No. 1632, National Archives, India; original Mss Eur. F. 111/161, OIOC, British Library, London.

Indian Tea Association Papers, October 1929, Mss. Eur 174, OIOC, British Library, London.

James Finlay & Company Papers, UGD 91/139, Glasgow University Archives, Glasgow.

Private Papers of Sir Henry John Stedman Cotton, Mss. EUR D1202/2, OIOC, British Library, London.

R.C. Mahanta Family Papers, Jorhat, Assam.

R. Palmer Papers, Centre of South Asian Studies Archives, Cambridge University, Cambridge.

Tweedy Papers, Centre of South Asian Studies Archives, Cambridge University, Cambridge.

Newspapers and Journals

Amrita Bazar Patrika.

Assam Tribune.

The Bengalee.

Capital.

Chambers' Edinburg Journal.

Eastern Bengal and Assam Era.
Englishman.
Fraser's Magazine for Town and Country.
The Hindoo Patriot.
Penny Magazine of the Society for the Diffusion of Useful Knowledge.
Quarterly Journal, Scientific Department, India Tea Association, Tocklai Tea
    Research Centre, Jorhat, Assam.
The Times (London).

Secondary Sources

Books

Akhtar, S.M., *Emigrant Labour for Assam Tea Gardens*, Lahore, 1939.

Amrith, Sunil S., *Migration and Diaspora in Modern Asia*, Cambridge: Cambridge University Press, 1911.

Amrith, Sunil S., *Crossing the Bay of Bengal: The Furies of Nature and the Fortunes of Migrants*, Cambridge, Mass.: Harvard University Press, 2013.

Anonymous, *Assam: Sketch of its History, Soil, and Productions: with the Discovery of The Tea Plant, and of the Countries Adjoining Assam*, London: Smith, Elder and Co., 1839.

Antrobus, H.A., *A History of the Jorehaut Company Ltd, 1859–1946*, London: Tea and Rubber Mail, 1948.

Antrobus, H.A., *A History of the Assam Company*, Edinburgh: T. and A. Constable, 1957.

Baden-Powell, B.H., *The Land Systems of British India*, Vol. III, Oxford: Clarendon Press, 1892; reprint, Delhi, 1974.

Bagchi, Amiya Kumar, *Private Investment in India*, Cambridge: Cambridge University Press, 1972.

Bald, Claud, *Indian Tea*, Calcutta: Thacker, Spink & Co., 1922.

Baildon, Samuel, *The Tea Industry in India: A Review of Finance and Labour, and a Guide for Capitalist & Assistants*, London: W.H. Allen & Co., 1882.

Barker, George, *Tea Planter's Life in Assam*, Calcutta: Thacker, Spink & Co., 1884.

Barooah, N.K., *David Scott in North-East India 1801–31: A Study of British Paternalism*, New Delhi: Munshilal Manoharlal, 1972.

Barpuzari, H.K., *Assam in the Days of the Company 1826–58*, Shillong: United Publishers, 1963.

Beckford, G.L., *Persistent Poverty: Underdevelopment in the Plantation Economies of the Third World*, London, 1972.

Bhuyian, A.C. and S. De (eds), *Political History of Assam, 1920–39*, Vol. II, Gauhati, 1978.

Bhuyan, S.K., *Anglo-Assamese Relations 1771–1826*, Gauhati: Lawyer's Book Stall, 1949.

Bose, Manilal, *British Policy in North East Frontier Agency*, New Delhi: 1979.

Bose, Sanat Kumar, *Capital and Labour in the Indian Tea Industry*, Bombay: All India Trade Union Congress, 1954.

Bruce, Charles Alexander, *An Account of the black tea, as now practiced in Suddeya in Upper Assam by Chinamen sent thither for that purpose*, Calcutta: G.H. Huttmann, Bengal Military Orphan Press, 1838.

Buchanan, Daniel Houston, *The Development of Capitalistic Enterprise in India*, London: Macmillan Company, 1934; reprint, 1966.

Burnett, John, *Liquid Pleasures: Social History of Drinks in Modern Britain*, Florence: KY, USA: Routledge, 1999.

Chakravarty, Dipesh, *Rethinking Working-Class History: Bengal 1890–1940*, New Jersey: Princeton University Press, 1989.

Chandra, Bipan, *The Rise and Growth of Economic Nationalism in India*, New Delhi, 1966.

Chang, Hsin-pao, *Commissioner Lin and the Opium War*, Cambridge: Harvard University Press, 1964.

Chatterji, Basudev (ed.), *Towards Freedom, 1938*, New Delhi, 1998.

Chaudhury, K.N., *The Trading world of Asia and the English East India Company 1660–1760*, Cambridge: Cambridge University Press, 1978.

Cotton, Henry, *Indian and Home Memories*, London: T. Fisher Unwin, 1911.

Crole, David, *Tea: A Text Book of Tea Planting and Manufacture*, London: Crossby Lockwood and Son, 1897.

Das, Rajani Kanta, *Plantation Labour in India*, Calcutta: R. Chatterji, 1931.

Das, Rajani Kanta, *History of Indian Labour Legislation*, Calcutta: University of Calcutta Press, 1941.

Davis, Kingsley, *The Population of India and Pakistan*, New York: Russell and Russell, 1951.

Dunn, Richard, *The Rise of the Planter Class in the English West Indies, 1624–1713*, University of North Carolina Press, 1972.

Dowding, Charles, *Tea Garden Coolies in Assam*, Calcutta: Thacker, Spink & Company, 1894.

Forbes, Geraldine Hancock, *Positivism in Bengal:* A case study in the transmission and assimilation of an ideology, Calcutta: Minerva Associates, 1975.

Fraser, W.M., *The Recollections of a Tea Planter*, London: The Tea and Rubber Mail, 1935.

Fuller, Bempfydle, *Some Personal Experiences*, London: John Murray, 1930.

Ganguly, Dwarkanath, *Slavery in British Dominion*, edited by Siris Kumar Kunda, Calcutta: Jignasa, 1972: reprint of thirteen articles published in the newspaper *Bengalee* between September 1886 and April 1887.

Geertz, Clifford, *Agricultural Evolution: The Process of Ecological Change in Indonesia*, California: University of California Press, 1968.

Gladstone, John S., *History of Gillanders, Arbhuthnot and Company and Ogilvy, Gillanders and Company*, Gladstone Family Records, Clwyd Record Office, Howarden, UK, 1910.

Genovese, Eugene D., *Roll, Jordon, Roll: The World the Slaves Made*, New York: Pantheon Books, 1972.

Hanley, Maurice P., *Tales and Songs from An Assam Tea Garden*, Thacker, Spink & Co: Calcutta, 1928.

Harler, C.R., *The Culture and Marketing of Tea*, London: Oxford University Press, 1933.

Gait, E., *A History of Assam*, Calcutta: Thacker, Spink & Co., 1906.

Gardella, Robert, *Harvesting Mountains: Fujian and the China Tea Trade, 1757–1937*, Berkeley: University of California Press, 1994.

Greenberg, Michael, *British Trade and the Opening of China 1800–42*, Cambridge: Cambridge University Press, 1969.

Griffiths, Percival, *The History of the Indian Tea Industry*, London: Weidenfeld and Nicolson, 1967.

Guha, Amalendu, *Planter Raj to Swaraj: Freedom Struggle and Electoral Politics in Assam 1826–1947*, New Delhi: Indian Council of Historical Research, 1977.

Hetherington, F.A., *The Diary of a Tea Planter, 14 July 1907*, Sussex: The Book Guild Ltd., 1994.

Hsu, Immanuel C.Y., *The Rise of Modern China*, fifth edn, New York: Oxford University Press, 1995.

Janin, Hunt, *The India–China Opium Trade in the Nineteenth Century*, London: McFarland & Company Inc., 1999.

Jayawardena, Visakha Kumari, *The Rise of the Labor Movement in Ceylon*, North Carolina: Duke University Press, 1972.

Jones, Stephanie, *Merchants of the Raj: British Managing Agency Houses in Calcutta Yesterday and Today*, London: Macmillan, 1991.

Kinney, T., *Old Times in Assam*, Calcutta: Star Press, 1896.

Kling, B. Blair, *Partners in Empire: Dwarkanath Tagore and the Age of Enterprise in Eastern India*, California: University of California Press, 1976.

Kolsky, Elizabeth, *Colonial Justice in British India*, Cambridge: Cambridge University Press, 2010.

Kydd, J.C., *The Tea Industry*, London: Humphrey Milford, Oxford University Press, 1921.

Lahiri, Rebati Mohan, *The Annexation of Assam: 1824–54*, Calcutta: Firma K.L. Mukhopadhyay, 1975.

Lall, Diwan Chaman, *The Coolie: The Story of Labour and Capital in India*, Vol. II, Lahore: Oriental Publishing House, 1932.

Lees, William Nassau, *Tea Cultivation, Cotton and Other Agricultural Experiments in India, A Review*, Calcutta: Thacker, Spink & Co., 1863.

Macfarlen, Alan and Iris Macfarlen, *The Empire of Tea: The Remarkable History of the Plant that Took Over the World*, New York: The Overlook Press, 2004.

Mathrubuthan, R. and R. Srinivasan, *The Indian Factories and Labour Manual*, second edn, Madras, 1952.

Mann, Harold H., *The Early History of the Tea Industry in North-East History of India*, Calcutta: The Calcutta General Printing Co., 1918.

Mitchell, B.R. and Phyllis Deane, *Abstract of British Historical Statistics*, Cambridge: Cambridge University Press, 1962.

Money, Edward, *The Cultivation & Manufacture of Tea*, Calcutta: Thacker & Co., 1870.

Morris, D.M., *The Emergence of an Industrial Labour Force: A Study of Bombay Cotton Mills 1854–1947*, California: University of California Press, 1965.

Moulder, Frances, *Japan, China and the Modern World Economy*, Cambridge: Cambridge University Press, 1977.

Mukherjee, Radhakamal, *The Indian Working Class*, Bombay: Hind Kitab Limited Publishers, 1945.

Naquin, Susan and Evelyn Rawski, *Chinese Society in the Eighteenth Century*, New Haven: Yale University Press, 1987.

Pillai, P.P. (ed.), *Labour in South East Asia: A Symposium*, New Delhi: Indian Council of World Affairs, 1947.

Purcell, A. and J. Hallsworth, *Report on Labour Conditions in India*, London, 1928.

Rediker, Marcuse, *The Slave Ship: A Human Story*, New York: Penguin Books, 2008.

Roy, Himansu, *Tea Price Stabilization: The Indian Case*, Calcutta, 1965.

Rungta, Radhey Shyam, *The Rise of Business Corporations in India 1851–1900*, Cambridge: Cambridge University Press, 1970.

Sarkar, Sumit, *Swadeshi Movement in Bengal*, Calcutta, 1973.

Sen, Sukomal, *Working Class of India: History of Emergence and Movement, 1830–1970*, Calcutta: K.P. Bagchi & Co., 1977.

Sharma, Jayeeta, *Empire's Garden: Assam and Making of India*, New Delhi: Permanent Black, 2012.

Siddique, Mohammad Abu, *Evolution of Land Grants and Labour policy of Government: The Growth of the Tea Industry in Assam 1834–1940*, New Delhi: South Asian Publications, 1990.

Weatherstone, John, *The Pioneers 1825–1900: The Early British Tea and Coffee Planters and Their Way of Life*, London: Quiller Press, 1986.

Wickizier, V.D., *Tea under International Regulation*, California: Food Research Institute, Stanford, 1944.

Wood, Peter H., *Black Majority: Negroes in Colonial South Carolina from 1670 through the Stono Rebellion*, New York: W.W. Norton & Company, 1974.

Articles

Amrith, Sunil S., 'Indians Overseas? Governing Tamil Migration to Malaya 1870–1941', *Past and Present*, 208, (1), 2010, pp. 231–61.

Bhattacharya, Sabyasachi, 'Laissez-Faire in India', *Indian Economic and Social History Review*, Vol. II, No. 1, 1965.

Bhattacharya, Sabyasachi, 'Positivism in 19th Century Bengal', in Ram Saran Sharma (ed.), *Indian Society: Historical Probings*, New Delhi: Indian Council of Historical Research, 1974.

Behal, Rana P., 'Forms of Labour Protest in the Assam Valley Tea Plantations 1900–1947', *The Calcutta Historical Journal*, Vol. IX, No. 1, July–December 1984.

Behal, Rana P., 'Wage Structure and Labour: Assam Valley Tea Plantations, 1900–1947', NLI Research Studies Series, No. 043/2003, V.V. Giri National Labour Institute, NOIDA, 2003.

Behal, Rana P., 'Power Structure, Discipline and Labour in Assam Tea Plantations under Colonial Rule', in Rana P. Behal and Marcel van der Linden (eds), *India's Labouring Poor: Historical Studies c. 1600–2000*, Delhi: Foundation Books, Delhi, 2007, pp. 145–55.

Behal, Rana P., 'Coolie Drivers or Benevolent Paternalists? British Tea Planters in Assam and Indenture Labour System', *Modern Asian Studies*, 44, 1, 2010, pp. 29–51.

Behal, Rana P., 'Coolies, Recruiters and Planters: Migration of Indian Labour to the Southeast Asian and Assam Plantations during Colonial Rule' Crossroads Working Papers Series, No. 9, Bonn, July 2013.

Behal, Rana P., 'Communities: Indian Immigrant Labourers in South-East Asian and Assam Plantations under the British Imperial System', in Henryk Alff and Andreas Benz (eds), *Tracing Connections: Explorations of Spaces and Places in Asian Context*, Berlin: WVB, 2014.

Behal, Rana P. and Prabhu P. Mohapatra, '"Tea and Money versus Human Life": The Rise and Fall of the Indenture System in the Assam Tea Plantations 1840–1908', in E. Valentine Daniel, Henry Bernstein and Tom Brass (eds), *Plantations, Proletarians and Peasants in Colonial Asia*, London: Frank Cass, 1992, pp. 142–43.

Breman, Jan and E. Valentine Daniel, 'The Making of a Coolie', in E. Valentine Daniel, Henry Bernstein and Tom Brass (eds), *Plantations, Proletarians and Peasants in Colonial Asia*, London: Frank Cass, 1992, pp. 268–96.

Broakway, Lucile H., 'Science and Colonial Expansion: The Role of the Royal Botanical Gardens', *American Ethnologist*, Vol. 6, No. 3, 1979, pp. 449–65.

Chakravarty, Dipesh, 'Sasipada Banerjee: A Study in the Nature of the First Contact of the Bengali Bhadralok with the Working Class in Bengal', Occasional Paper No. 4, Centre for Studies in Social Sciences, Calcutta.

Deb, Keya, 'Impact of Plantations on the Agrarian Structure of the Brahmaputra Valley', Occasional Paper No. 24, Centre for Studies in Social Sciences, Calcutta, April 1979.

Duncan, James S., 'Embodying Colonialism? Domination and Resistance in Nineteenth-Century Ceylonese Coffee Plantations', *Journal of Historical Geography*, 28 (3), 2002, pp. 317–38.

Emmer, P.C., 'The meek Hindu; the recruitment of Indian indentured labourers for service overseas, 1870–1916', in P.C. Emmer (ed.), *Migration: Indentured Labour Before and After Slavery*, Dordrecht, 1986, pp. 187–207.

Emmer, P.C., 'The Great Escape: The Migration of Female Indentured Servants from British India to Surinam 1873–1916', in Colin Clark, Ceri Peach and Steven Vertovec (eds), *South Asians Overseas*, Cambridge: Cambridge University Press, 1990, pp. 245–66.

Frederickson, George H., 'Slavery and Race: The Southern Dilemma', in Allen Weinstein and Frank Otto Gatell (eds), *American Negro Slavery: A Modern Reader*, London: Oxford University Press, 1973.

Ghosh, Kaushik, 'A Market for Aboriginality: Primitivism and Race Classification in the Indentured Labour Market in Colonial India', in Gautam Bhadra, Gyan Prakash, Susie Tharu *et al.* (eds), *Subaltern Studies X: Writings on South Asian History and Society*, New Delhi: Oxford University Press, 1999, pp. 8–48.

Gordon, L.A., 'Social and Economic Conditions of Bombay Workers on the Eve of the 1908 Strike', in I.M. Reisner and N.M. Goldberg (eds), *Tilak and Struggle for Indian Freedom*, New Delhi, 1966.

Greeves, I., 'Plantations in World Economy', in *Plantation Systems of the New World*, Pan American Union, 1959.

Guha, Amalendu, 'Socio-Economic Changes in Agrarian Assam', in M.K. Chaudhury (ed.), *Trends in Socio-Economic Change in India 1871–1961*, Simla, 1967.

Guha, Amalendu, 'Colonization of Assam: Years of Transitional Crises, 1825–40', *Indian Economic and Social History Review*, No. 2, June 1968, pp. 125–40.

Gupta, Ranajit Das, 'Poverty and Protest: A Study of Calcutta's Industrial Workers and Labouring Poor, 1875–1899', in *Labour and Working Class in India: Studies in Colonial History*, Calcutta: K.P. Bagchi & Co., 1994, pp. 315–405.

Jones, Lloyd, *Standards of Medical Care for Tea Plantations in India*, 1946.

Mahato, Pashupati Prasad, 'World View of the Assam Tea Garden Labourers from Jharkhand', in Datta Ray and Sebastian Karotemprel (eds), *Tea Garden Labourers of North East India: A Multidimensional Study on the Adivasis of the Tea Gardens of North East India*, Shillong: Vendrame Institute, 1990, pp. 131–42.

Mann, Harold H., 'The Indian Tea Industry in its Scientific Aspects', in Daniel Thorner (ed.), *The Social Framework of Agriculture*, Bombay, 1967, pp. 437–55.

Mann, Harold H., 'Note on the Diet of Tea Garden Coolies in Upper Assam and its Nutritive Value', in Daniel Thorner (ed.), *The Social Framework of Agriculture*, Bombay, 1967.

Mohapatra, Prabhu P., 'Coolies and Colliers: A Study of the Agrarian Context of Labour Migration from Chotanagpur, 1880–1920', *Studies in History*, 1, 2, 1985, pp. 247–303.

Mui, Hoh-Cheung Mui and H. Lorna, 'The Commutation Act and the Tea Trade in Britain 1784–1793 *The Economic History Review*, New Series, Vol. 16, No. 2, 1963.

Samaraweera, Vijya, 'Masters and Servants in Sri Lankan Plantations: Labour Laws and Labour Control in an Emergent Export Economy', *Indian Economic and Social History Review*, Vol. XVIII, No. 2, April–June 1981, pp. 123–55.

Sengupta, Sarthak and Jagadeeshwar Lall Sharma, 'Jhumar: Folksongs and Dances of Tea Garden Labourers of Assam', in Datta Ray and Sebastian Karotemprel (eds), *Tea Garden Labourers of North East India: A Multidimensional Study on the Adivasis of the Tea Gardens of North East India*, Shillong: Vendrame Institute, 1990, pp. 214–26.

Sharma, Jayeeta, 'British science, Chinese skills and Assam tea: Making Empire's Garden', *Indian Economic and Social History Review*, Vol. 43, No. 4, 2006, pp. 429–55.

Shlomowitz, Ralph and Lance Brennan, 'Mortality and migrant labour in Assam 1865–1921', *Indian Economic and Social History Review*, Vol. 27, No. 1, 1990, pp. 85–110.

Varma, Nitin, 'For the Drink of the Nation: Drink, Labour and Plantation Capitalism in the Colonial Tea Gardens of Assam in the late nineteenth and early twentieth century', in Marcel van der Linden and Prabhu P. Mohapatra (eds), *Labour Matters: Towards Global Histories, Studies in Honour of Sabyasachi Bhattacharya*, New Delhi: Tulika Books, 2009), pp. 295–318.

Wilson (Dr) and Mitra (Dr), 'A Diet and Physique Survey in Assam Rural Bengal and Calcutta, a survey conducted for the All-India Institute of

Hygiene and Public Health, Calcutta', *Indian Journal of Medical Research*, Vol. XXVII, pp. 131–54.

Zurbrigg, Sheila, 'Hunger and Epidemic Malaria in Punjab, 1868–1940,' *Economic and Political Weekly*, Vol. 27, No. 4, 25 January 1992.

Unpublished Dissertations

Deb, Keya, 'Tea Plantations in Brahmaputra Valley 1859–1914: A Case Study in Colonial Set-up', unpublished Ph.D. dissertation, Centre for Studies in Regional Development, School of Social Sciences, Jawaharlal Nehru University, New Delhi, 1979.

Gupta, Bishnupriya, 'Stabilization of Prices in Plantation Economics: A Comparative Study of the Tea Industry in India and the Coffee Industry in Brazil', unpublished M.Phil. dissertation, Centre for Historical Studies, School of Social Sciences, Jawaharlal Nehru University, New Delhi, 1981.

Rana Pratap Behal, 'Some Aspects of the Growth of the Tea Plantation Labour Force and Labour Movements in Assam Valley Districts (Lakhimpur, Sibsagar and Darrang) 1900–1947', unpublished Ph.D. dissertation, Centre for Historical Studies, School of Social Sciences, Jawaharlal Nehru University, New Delhi, 1983.

Sarma, S.K., 'The Tea Industry in Assam: Being a History of the Industry Down to 1914 and of its Contributions to the Economic Development of Assam', unpublished dissertation, Department of Economics, University of Delhi, 1964.

Varma, Nitin, 'Coolie Exodus in Chargola: Mobilization, Control and Collective Action in the Colonial Tea Plantations in Assam', unpublished M.Phil. dissertation, Jawaharlal Nehru University, New Delhi, 2003.

Index